Women in American History

Series Editors

MARI JO BUHLE

NANCY A. HEWITT

ANNE FIROR SCOTT

The Working Class in
American History

Editorial Advisors

DAVID BRODY

ALICE KESSLER-HARRIS

DAVID MONTGOMERY

SEAN WILENTZ

A list of books in each series appears at the end of this book.

The Female Economy

Trade card of Madame Walsh, a Boston dressmaker and milliner, probably late 1850s or early 1860s. (Courtesy of the American Antiquarian Society)

Wendy Gamber

The Female Economy

THE MILLINERY AND DRESSMAKING
TRADES, 1860–1930

UNIVERSITY OF ILLINOIS PRESS * URBANA AND CHICAGO

This book is printed on acid-free paper.

Library of Congress Cataloging-in-Publication Data
Gamber, Wendy, 1958-
The female economy : the millinery and dressmaking trades, 1860-1930 /
Wendy Gamber.
p.   cm. — (Women in American history) (The working class in
American history)
Includes bibliographical references (p.   ) and index.
ISBN 0-252-02298-X (alk. paper). — ISBN 0-252-06601-4 (pbk. : alk.
paper)
1. Women in business—United States—History. 2. Women consumers—
United States—History. 3. Women's clothing industry—United States—
History. 4. Dressmakers—United States—History. 5. Millinery
workers—United States—History. I. Title. II. Series. III. Series: The
working class in American history.
HD6054.4.U6G355   1997
331.4'887'0973—dc20   96-25211
                                                                    CIP

For Tim

Contents

Acknowledgments

Writing a book is never a solitary endeavor, and I have accumulated many debts in the process. I owe the most to Morton Keller, who directed the dissertation on which this study is based and who has continued to provide criticism, guidance, and essential support. I have benefited enormously from his penetrating comments, encyclopedic knowledge, and appreciation for the nuances—and absurdities—of American history and culture. Joyce Antler's perceptive insights and useful suggestions were indispensable to the early stages of this project. Daniel H. Calhoun first suggested that a study of nineteenth-century women entrepreneurs might be a productive scholarly enterprise—one of many useful pieces of advice that he has given me over the years.

Three people greatly influenced this study's final shape and form. Alice Kessler-Harris and Susan Porter Benson each read the entire manuscript not once, but twice; their tough but supportive criticisms encouraged me to rethink earlier assumptions, clarify my arguments, and keep the big questions in mind. Thomas Dublin has been a mentor in every sense of the word, generously sharing ideas derived from his own study of New England workingwomen, offering encouragement at every turn, and even allowing me to use his own painstakingly assembled databases.

Several people read and commented on portions of this manuscript in its various incarnations. I thank Judith Allen, George Alter, Daniel H. Calhoun, Daniel A. Cohen, Patricia Cooper, Sarah Deutsch, Ileen De Vault, Virginia Drachman, Saul Engelbourg, Nancy Page Fernandez, Maurine Weiner Greenwald, Karen Halttunen, Erica Harth, John Ingham, Angel Kwolek-Folland, Margaret Levenstein, Glenna Matthews, Tamara Miller, Eva Moseley, June Namias, Elyce Rotella, Rob Schorman, Philip Scranton, David Sicilia, Carole Srole, Susan Strasser, and Carole Turbin for their keen insights and intellectual generosity. Thanks also to the members of the Boston area women's history writing group, especially Cynthia Brown, Janet Schulte, and

Jeanie Cooper Carson, for good food, lively conversation, and unstinting encouragement. Patricia Trautman introduced me to the mysteries of dressmakers' drafting systems and granted me unlimited access to her collection of instructional pamphlets. Finally, this book could not have been completed without the diligent research assistance of Shane Blackman, Nancy Godleski, Robert Slavin, and Deborah Zaccaro.

This book could never have been conceived—let alone written—without the assistance of able and resourceful librarians and archivists. I wish particularly to thank the staffs of the Interlibrary Loan Department at Brandeis University, the Historical Collections division of Baker Library at Harvard University, the Archives Center and the Division of Costume of the National Museum of American History at the Smithsonian Institution, the Massachusetts Historical Society, and the Arthur and Elizabeth Schlesinger Library. Anyone concerned with the history of American women knows the importance of the Schlesinger, and I am grateful for the assistance rendered me there by Anne Engelhart, Diane Hamer, and the late Patricia King. I owe a special thanks to Eva Moseley, Curator of Manuscripts, for suggesting research strategies and identifying sources, and for sharing her memories of her mother—"a little Viennese dressmaker"—with me.

Several institutions provided crucial financial assistance. An Irving and Rose Crown Fellowship in the History of American Civilization sustained me through my years as a graduate student at Brandeis University, and a Fellowship for Graduate Research on Women and Gender, awarded by the Women's Studies Program at Brandeis, supported my first forays into the history of dressmaking and millinery. Grants from the Smithsonian Institution, the Arthur and Elizabeth Schlesinger Library, and the Massachusetts Historical Society sponsored my research at those institutions. A summer Faculty Fellowship and a grant-in-aid from the Research and University Graduate School of Indiana University provided timely assistance in the later stages of my study.

I am grateful to Richard Wentworth, Director and Editor of the University of Illinois Press, for his early interest in this project and his unwavering commitment to its completion. Margie Towery's skillful copyediting saved me from numerous embarrassments and helped me to say what I wanted to say more clearly. Theresa Sears shepherded the manuscript with grace, efficiency, and humor, and James O'Brien lent his considerable expertise to the index.

Friends, colleagues, and family have nurtured this project in less tangible—but no less important—ways. The members of the Department of History at Indiana University, Bloomington, provided a stimulating and supportive environment for research and writing. Many of my former graduate school colleagues, especially Tamara Miller, June Namias, Thomas Pegram, and Susan Tananbaum, encouraged me from afar, their own work furnishing examples of scholarly excellence well worth imitating. My parents, Elinor David and Michael Gamber, continually affirmed their faith in my abilities and kept their doubts about the time it took me to finish my "paper" mostly to themselves. Without a doubt, Ian Byers-Gamber's arrival delayed the completion of this book. But he has more than made up for it. Of the many people mentioned here, Tim Byers has lived with this project the longest. The book's dedication is scant repayment for all that I owe him.

✳ ✳ ✳

Portions of this book appeared in slightly different form in "A Precarious Independence: Milliners and Dressmakers in Boston, 1860-1890," *Journal of Women's History* 4 (Spring 1992): 60-88; "Gendered Concerns: Thoughts on the History of Business and the History of Women," *Business and Economic History* 23 (Fall 1994): 129-40; and "'Reduced to Science': Gender, Technology, and Power in the American Dressmaking Trade, 1860-1910," *Technology and Culture* 36 (July 1995): 455-82. I am grateful to Dun & Bradstreet for granting me permission to cite the R. G. Dun & Co. records.

Introduction

In 1856, Dr. Harriot K. Hunt—feminist, abolitionist, and pioneer female physician—published her autobiography. In it she described the opposition to her attempts to enter a male-dominated profession and how she had come to resent the "contemptible insults which are heaped upon those who have independence enough to step out of the beaten track." Her experience encouraged her to formulate a critique of existing sexual divisions of labor. She opposed the contemporary custom of training women only for marriage; instead, she believed that all should be prepared for some useful vocation. Single herself, she was particularly incensed at "the wrong done to young women, who may never enter the marriage state, by giving them no trade, occupation, or profession, and thus leaving them to idleness, dependence, helplessness, and temptation."[1]

Hunt thought that there existed no better symbol of dependence and uselessness than the woman of fashion. In denouncing this phenomenon, she implicitly criticized an emerging consumer culture that diverted women from more serious pursuits and threatened to reduce them to mere ornaments. She failed to recognize the irony that "fashion," however oppressive to some women, created significant opportunities for others. In an era when women's ready-to-wear apparel had not yet triumphed—a period that lasted until the early twentieth century—the ever-increasing demand for feminine finery gave employment to a growing army of dressmakers and milliners.[2]

"Milliners engaged in custom work, like dressmakers," the labor historian Helen Sumner noted in 1910, "have always been aristocrats among the clothing makers." In large part this assertion was correct. Experienced workers commanded some of the highest wages in the female labor market; even Mathew Carey, best known for his vivid descriptions of the sufferings of needlewomen, included "milliners and mantua makers" among "certain classes of females, who are decently paid." Moreover, with the possible exception of prostitution, no trade contained larger numbers of female proprietors. "Mistress" dressmakers and milliners, many of whom had "never enter[ed] the marriage state," presided over most millinery and dressmaking shops. If the woman of fashion was a victim of oppression, the woman who made fashion appeared to enjoy an enviable independence.[3]

Hunt's assessment overlooked an even subtler irony. She believed that only by "step[ping] out of the beaten track"—by challenging a labor market rigidly divided into men's and women's jobs—could women gain true economic independence. And she was far from wrong; more often than not, sex segregation has worked to women's disadvantage, confining them to "unskilled," poorly paid jobs that offered few prospects for advancement and reinforced their dependence on marriage. In this respect, millinery and dressmaking contradicted conventional wisdom. The custom manufacture of feminine apparel held advantages that few "female" employments could match: highly skilled work, creative labor, relatively high wages, and the very real possibility of opening an establishment of one's own some day. Far from lessening women's chances, the sexual division of labor in the custom fashion trades created a "female economy" in which the principal actors—proprietors, workers, and consumers—were women.

This book is about the construction of sexual divisions of labor, how such arrangements change over time, and the consequences of those changes. Pronouncements to the contrary notwithstanding, labels such as "men's work" and "women's work" have little to do with biology and everything to do with cultural constructions of gender. (By "gender" I mean definitions of "masculinity" and "femininity."[4]) Indeed, as recent scholarship has revealed, sexual divisions of labor are neither fixed nor "natural" but are continually redefined. At various times and places and in various industries, diverse actors—employers and employees, women and men—have accepted, rejected, manipulated, and transformed the meanings of men's and women's work. Nowhere was this more true than in the fashion trades. Considered men's work in the sixteenth and seventeenth centuries, the production of feminine apparel became women's work in the eighteenth and nineteenth. Moreover, women did not meekly accept the portion accorded them; rather, they staunchly defended the femininity of their trades, treating "man milliners" with "derision."[5]

In the end, women were unable to maintain control over the sexual division of labor, an outcome that had tragic consequences for the erstwhile makers of feminine apparel. In many respects, the changes that revolutionized the making of women's clothing in the late nineteenth and early twentieth centuries—the triumph of mass production and large-scale retailing—repeated already familiar scenarios; during the course of the nineteenth century, factories and "bastard workshops"[6] had replaced countless artisan crafts, department stores sealed the fate of numerous small businesses. In the field of feminine fashion, these were gendered transformations. Once highly skilled crafts predominantly controlled by women, the manufacture of dresses and hats became relatively unskilled processes largely controlled—if not entirely executed—by men. By 1930 the female economy of fashion had been all but supplanted by the ladies' garment trade.

* * *

I began this study intending to examine the experiences of late nineteenth-century women entrepreneurs. I soon discovered that not only did milliners and dressmakers account for a sizeable portion of Gilded Age businesswomen but also that their endeavors exceeded the rather narrow boundaries of commercial enterprise. The fashion trades radiated both downward to embrace the wageworkers who labored for "Madame" and outward to incorporate the consumers who patronized her shop. Indeed, I found a female economy based on fragile, often tenuous relationships between women. Just as "cities of women" inhabited larger urban landscapes, so too did female economies exist apart from—but in integral relation to—the larger commercial and industrial economies of nineteenth- and early twentieth-century America.[7]

An entity that encompassed proprietors, workers, and consumers, the female economy defies conventional categories of historical analysis, for understanding it requires crossing the boundaries of several subdisciplines. I hope that this study suggests that the concept of gender has meaning not only for women's history but also for the histories of business, consumer culture, and labor.

Undoubtedly, the keepers of dressmaking and millinery shops have relevance for business history, which has only recently emerged from a "Chandlerian synthesis" that emphasized the structure and operations of large corporations.[8] Despite recent interest in the history of small-scale enterprise, the stories of female petty entrepreneurs for the most part remain untold. With few exceptions, existing accounts (most written by practitioners of women's—not business—history) are at best cursory, at worst celebratory, examples of what Gerda Lerner has called "compensatory history."[9] We need to know not only that women were "there, too," but also under what circumstances their businesses survived and flourished. My work suggests that hierarchies of gender, as well as of ethnicity and race, governed the nineteenth-century commercial world. Just as female wage earners confronted a sex-segregated labor market, so too did female entrepreneurs brave a commercial arena divided into "masculine" and "feminine" pursuits.[10] Notions of woman's proper place—often enthusiastically embraced by businesswomen themselves—determined "appropriate" venues of female entrepreneurial activity, even the disposition of credit. Similarly, the triumph of mass production and the rise of large-scale retailing created not only new business forms but also new configurations of gender, spaces in which women exercised less skill and less control. To be sure, new enterprises depended on men's access to greater capital and credit. But they also rested on powerful if faulty assumptions that masculine vitality and "male" skills were necessary components of a new commercial and industrial order.

This book also illuminates a hitherto unexplored facet of the history of consumption, a subject that has only recently begun to incorporate concerns of gender.[11] Most studies accept mass production as a given or, at best, seek to document seemingly clear-cut transitions from homemade goods to factory-produced commodities. But well into the twentieth century female shoppers inhabited two worlds, one based on the output of the factory, the other on the products of the custom workshop. For many a customer the attractions of the female economy lay, not in the impersonal if beguiling displays that characterized much large-scale retailing, but in the producer-consumer relationship itself. Tradeswomen and their clients created a peculiarly personal culture of consumption that thrived upon intimate—albeit frequently contentious—interactions, revealing relationships that were at once "sisterly" and ruthlessly exploitative. By placing dressmakers and milliners at the "service" of their customers, producer-consumer relations both confirmed existing class inequalities and created new ones. If, in E. P. Thompson's oft-quoted phrase, "class is a relationship," it was a relationship negotiated among women as well as men and in relations of consumption as well as production.[12] But interactions between tradeswomen and their clients also reveal common dependencies: the woman who ordered a gown for which her husband refused to pay was as powerless economically as the modiste engaged to make it.

The female economy included workers as well as proprietors and consumers, women whose stories raise intriguing questions for labor history. Just as many labor historians continue to suppose, despite abundant evidence to the contrary, that all workers were male, scholars have generally assumed that all artisans were men; indeed, a recent study concluded that "apprenticeship was a male institution."[13] Yet milliners and modistes practiced skilled crafts—deriving a good deal of satisfaction from the "artistic" aspects of their jobs, inheriting—if often defying—apprenticeship traditions, and believing themselves superior both to factory workers and lower orders of needlewomen. Women had no place in the male artisanal world so skillfully reconstructed by practitioners of the "new" labor history, for as females they were excluded from this political and cultural milieu. As far as we can tell, craftswomen failed to attend (nor, one suspects, were they invited to) the dramatic parades, political debates, and rowdy entertainments that helped to define that world, and their absence from these arenas has rendered them invisible to subsequent historians.[14]

Scholarly inattention to skilled needlewomen, I suspect, stems from additional misunderstandings about the nature and meaning of "women's work." On the one hand, historians are just beginning to realize, as Carole Turbin has noted, that "women's work was not uniformly unskilled, low paid, and temporary."[15] Women's occupations did not consist of an undifferentiated mass of unskilled jobs; neither did the term "needle trades" describe a homogeneous set of female employments. But historians have all too often adopted uncritically the viewpoint of contemporary reformers who perceived few differences between seamstresses, who stitched together precut versions of men's shirts and pants, and dressmakers and milliners, who designed and crafted individual garments for exacting customers. On the other hand, scholars—perhaps because they confused the ideology of separate spheres with reality—have generally assumed that professional needlework was merely an extension of women's household labor. Yet dressmakers and milliners did not simply transfer domestic skills to the marketplace; more often than not, they learned their trades in the workshop, not the home.

In recent years, women's labor history has emerged as a separate category of historical analysis. The result has been an extraordinarily rich, creative body of scholarship that reveals the significant presence of women in wage work, the hidden gender biases that lay beneath definitions of skilled and unskilled labor, and the myriad ways in which women wage earners resisted the demands of employers and, at times, those of their male coworkers.[16] As this description suggests, much of this literature focuses on formal or informal collective activism. But this "paradigm of protest" fails to capture the

complex and often contradictory nature of the fashion trades. Women—
employers and employees, skilled and less skilled workers—were both exploiters and exploited; nor did cleavages necessarily follow conventional
lines. Workers might side with proprietors against overbearing customers;
thus, experienced craftswomen might identify with the interests of their
employers, rejecting the overtures of often exploited "extra hands." Moreover, dressmakers and milliners by and large rejected labor activism, often
pursuing determinedly individualistic strategies for advancement. Yet their
relative lack of enthusiasm for collective endeavors did not necessarily imply acquiescence or "consent to oppression"[17] (although at times, indeed, it
did). Rather, their pursuit of economic independence had subversive, if not
radical, implications. Successful tradeswomen implicitly rejected both the
middle-class tenet of domesticity (in simplest terms, the idea that woman's
place was in the home) and the working-class ideal of the family wage (the
belief that male breadwinners should support female dependents).[18]

Just as existing approaches fail to accommodate these complexities, so too
did contemporaries find it difficult to describe people who in many respects
defied common expectations regarding woman's place. Most nineteenth-century (and even many twentieth-century) accounts depicted dressmakers and
milliners as one of two types: distressed gentlewomen or ambitious upstarts
of working-class origins. Pathetic victims who rarely entered the world of
business or wage work of their own volition, distressed gentlewomen remained "respectable" in the eyes of contemporaries precisely because they
failed to challenge cherished stereotypes of female dependency. Working-
class parvenues—vulgar, often disreputable, women—appeared in popular
culture not as victims but as villains. These "negative role models" demonstrated supposedly self-evident links between middle-class status and female
respectability; their vulgar demeanors, their bad taste in dress, even their
barely disguised ambition, numerous commentators implied, stemmed from
their lowly social origins. But this second, unfavorable stereotype also suggests that tradeswomen defied imperatives of gender as well as class, for their
very independence—usually reserved for men—excluded them from the
bounds of respectable womanhood.

The contrasts that commentators invoked recall familiar dualisms: good
and evil, victim and villain, angel and whore. But these categories were not
static. They constantly shifted to meet the ideological and economic needs
of various constituencies. Department store magnates might invoke the
image of the villainous milliner not to discourage consumption—as had an

earlier generation of moralists—but to demonstrate the supposed superiority of the "new kind of store." Faced with the unusual problem of dealing with an almost exclusively female clientele, wholesale millinery merchants fashioned an image of the "respectable businesswoman," a stereotype that acknowledged female retailers' entrepreneurial endeavors but evoked familiar "feminine" qualities.

The voices of dressmakers and milliners are more difficult to hear because they lacked meaningful forums. No newspaper recorded their collective opinions, and few of their diaries have been preserved. Nonetheless, evidence suggests that craftswomen did not necessarily accept the images that others constructed for them (although they might manipulate these images to their own advantage). Instead, they developed their own definitions of respectable womanhood, which often centered on the meaning of their work, not on marriage and motherhood—the supposed concerns of woman's sphere. The varying identities that craftswomen assumed had both conservative and radical implications; the respectable status that millinery and dressmaking conferred on their practitioners could fire craftswomen's ambitions, but it could also encourage them to view gentility as an end in itself. The identities that the trades offered—no less than the material opportunities they bestowed—comprised a variety of possibilities that included a good deal of misery and exploitation but also the prospect of female independence.

* * *

The women whose stories this book seeks to tell formed no small part of the nineteenth- and early twentieth-century female labor force. Together, they comprised the fourth most important occupational category for women in 1870; only domestic servants, agricultural laborers, and seamstresses were more numerous. Thirty years later, the U.S. census reported a total of 338,144 dressmakers and 82,936 milliners; at that time, dressmaking ranked third among female employments, and millinery fourteenth.[19] As these numbers imply, dressmakers and milliners were everywhere: "No town," an anonymous investigator noted in 1919, "is without its milliner."[20] But the geographical parameters of this study are more modest. Apart from occasional forays into the hinterlands, I focus on several cities in the Northeast and Midwest, where milliners and dressmakers tended to congregate. At times, my focus is local rather than regional. Parts of this book, especially chapters 2 and 3, rely heavily on Boston sources, not because New England's metropolis has any special significance for the history of fashion but because the available materials—credit records, city directories, and manuscript census schedules—have meaning only in a local context. To the historian interested in a detailed analysis of a particular occupational group, late nineteenth-century Boston—home to a not inconsiderable portion of the nation's dressmakers and milliners—provides a large city but one of manageable size for data collection purposes. When scholarly necessity demands venturing from the general to the particular, Boston is a good choice for another reason: organizations, such as the New England Women's Club and especially the Women's Educational and Industrial Union, furnish rarely surpassed documentation of the history of the city's wage-earning women. One additional point should be clarified: because this book addresses the experiences of dressmakers and milliners in the northern part of the United States, it is primarily a history of white working-class women, for entrance into the trades was often bounded by race. African American craftswomen gained a more secure foothold in the South; theirs is a story that is only beginning to be told.[21]

The book begins with a brief discussion of dressmakers and milliners in the early nineteenth-century city, tracing their origins to an antebellum consumer revolution and exploring the questions and concerns provoked by their presence. The remainder is divided into two chronologically overlapping parts—an organization that reflects the fact that the triumph of mass production was neither instantaneous nor absolute and that considerable continuities prevailed over relatively long periods of time. Part 1 details the successes and failures, hopes and disappointments, rebellions and accommodations of those who created the female economy of fashion—proprietors, workers, and consumers—an entity that flourished roughly between 1860 and 1910. Part 2, which spans the period 1860–1930, examines the changes wrought by technology, commerce, industry, and new sexual divisions of labor. In short, it shows how a nineteenth-century female economy gave way to a twentieth-century fashion industry that was predominantly controlled by men.

⟸➤*◂⟹ *One*

Fashion and Independence: Dressmakers and Milliners in the Antebellum City

Washington-street, on a sunshiny day, presents a most
magnificent spectacle. Silks, prints, embroidery, and
millinery, interspersed with sparkling plate and jewelry,
flash upon the beholder at every turn.
—*Boston Common: A Tale of Our Own Times*, by a Lady (1856)

*A*n eighteenth-century Bostonian scarcely would have recognized
the scene that the anonymous novelist described.[1] As late as 1805, Boston's
shopping district evidently remained a dull, dreary place that offered dim
prospects for the appearance of a "magnificent spectacle." The city directory of that year listed no dry or fancy goods merchants, no traffickers in silks
and lace, only several unspecified "merchants," "shopkeepers," and "retailers." Only forty years later New England's metropolis offered a dazzling
array of choices to prospective consumers; the *Boston Directory* of 1846 included dry goods dealers, jewelers, fancy goods merchants, and a number
of vendors who hawked highly specialized products: gent's furnishings,
corsets, hosiery, gloves, laces, silks, umbrellas, combs, looking glasses, hats
and caps, and boots and shoes. This changing urban landscape, evidence of
what Stuart M. Blumin has called "a newly affluent middle-class way of life,"
attested as well to a growing interest in fashion, especially women's fashion.[2]

As beneficiaries of rising standards of living and new methods of textile production, more Americans than ever before donned stylish garb. For men this was a simple matter; they could purchase ready-to-wear clothing as early as the 1840s, although many, especially those of the social elite, continued to patronize custom tailors and hatters. But the elaborate design, tight fit, and rapidly changing vogues that characterized much feminine apparel thwarted the ambitions of would-be manufacturers; ready-made dresses and mass-produced millinery would not be widely available until the twentieth century.[3] In the meantime, dressmakers and milliners performed a critical function: "making" fashion for women who could not or would not make their own clothes, transforming fabrics and flowers, ribbons and lace into "works of art." Central players in an emerging culture of fashion, they formed a female enclave in a largely male commercial world. But the terrain they inhabited was far from secure, for their very presence in the "public sphere" raised troubling questions in the minds of contemporaries.

Female Artisans and Feminine Pursuits

Nineteenth-century Americans believed that women had a "natural" affinity for the fashion trades. After all, were not ribbons and flowers, ruffles and lace, satins and silks intrinsically feminine? Had they looked into the not too distant European past, they would have discovered that what they regarded as a natural state of affairs was a relatively recent development. While women had long been responsible for the household manufacture of textiles and clothing, production for the market was traditionally men's work. Well into the seventeenth century, tailors—organized into guilds that excluded women—fashioned clothing for both sexes. The earliest milliners, who derived their name from fancy goods vendors in sixteenth- and seventeenth-century Milan, were also male. How dress- and hatmaking became women's work is far from clear. Evidently, both newfound concerns for sexual propriety and women's demand for trades of their own played a part. Not until the eighteenth century were millinery and dressmaking firmly established as female pursuits.[4]

The tradeswomen who kept shop in the cities and towns of colonial America—women such as Elizabeth Saunders Porter, who announced to the "Ladies" of Essex, Massachusetts, in 1770, that she would make "Gowns, Hats, Cloaks and Riding Habits in the best and neatest Manner"—were few in number, and they catered to a tiny elite. In the wake of independence,

Americans clung to republican simplicity; as late as 1805 there were only thirty-four milliners and "mantua makers" in all of Boston. Aided and abetted by an antebellum consumer revolution, the ranks of dressmakers and milliners increased fourfold during the next twenty-five years.[5]

We know little about the women who kept dressmaking and millinery shops or the women who worked for them during the first half of the nineteenth century (Figure 1). Evidence suggests that most proprietors, like the workingwomen they employed, were single. Attaining expertise in one's craft often required a commitment that precluded marriage; married women—"legally dead" for much of the period—faced weighty obstacles to doing business. Evidence also suggests that proprietors tended to be the daughters of relatively prosperous artisans or farmers, parents who could pay the not inconsiderable costs of apprenticeship. Clark Carter, a farmer

Figure 1. Interior of a millinery shop, 1836. Two milliners work at a table (right) while the proprietor helps a customer try on a hat. Note the sparse furnishings. As was typical of millinery shops throughout the nineteenth century, workroom and showroom are one and the same. (Courtesy of the Library of Congress)

in Shirley, Maine, and the father of the prospective milliner Sarah Carter, owned real estate worth two thousand dollars in 1850, a sum that placed him squarely in the "middling" ranks of rural society.[6]

Parental investment in craft training—a subject to which we will return—was often worth the price. Probably few tradeswomen attained the extraordinary success enjoyed by Eliza Dodds, a Washington, D.C., milliner whose creditworthiness allowed her to borrow more than $5,600 between 1813 and 1820; the capital reported by Boston dressmakers and milliners in 1850 ranged from $100 to $6,000, sums that bespoke more modest material achievements.[7] Nevertheless, in an era when commentators almost universally lamented the plight of women wage earners, these accomplishments should not be discounted. Nor were the rewards of dressmaking and millinery reserved solely for proprietors. Dressmaking and millinery workers stood at the top of the female needlework hierarchy in both prestige and pay. Unlike seamstresses who stitched but did not cut, modistes fashioned gowns to suit the sartorial and psychological needs of individual patrons. In an era when the "fit" of a dress—even more than the richness of its fabrics or the extravagance of its trimmings—distinguished the elite from "the puckered, gaping, baggy masses" (as Amy Simon puts it), theirs was an ability of no minor importance. Milliners, too, possessed skills that distinguished them from the ranks of plain sewers. They transformed a variety of raw materials—straw, buckram, wire, and silk—into an equally varied number of hat and bonnet shapes. Charged with the task of arranging numerous trimmings in pleasing and ever-changing combinations, they were designers as well as craftswomen, artists as well as artisans. More often than not, the possessors of such skills reaped both material and psychological rewards. Dressmakers and milliners typically earned twice as much as seamstresses. For example, one Massachusetts dressmaker received $6.86 for eleven and three-quarters days of work (about $3.50 per week) during her sojourn in a Lawrence shop in the early summer of 1847; in the same period, seamstresses might garner weekly earnings of as little as one dollar.[8]

Novices learned the "art and mystery of millinery and mantua-making" in much the same way as did preindustrial male artisans.[9] Bound to mistress craftswomen for periods as long as three years, young women in their teens labored without wages for the duration of their apprenticeships—a privilege for which their parents often paid a cash "premium." Such arrangements—which usually specified that novices board with their mistresses—left room for considerable exploitation; just as male apprentices often found themselves building fires, fetching water, and even performing the proverbial feminine task of making coffee, so too were female apprentices expected to play the role of errand girl and domestic servant. In the best of circumstances, however, aspiring modistes or hatmakers learned not only dressmaking or millinery (in this period many mistresses knew and practiced both), but the rudimentary reading, writing, and bookkeeping skills that would enable them one day to run their own businesses.[10]

As early as the 1840s and perhaps earlier, this system was beginning to break down. As was the case in a variety of "masculine" pursuits—in trades as diverse as printing, tailoring, and furniture and shoe making—milliners and dressmakers increasingly refused to board their apprentices, signaling a gradual erosion of relationships based on reciprocity in favor of those based on the market. During the 1820s, the Washington, D.C., milliner Eliza Dodds housed her apprentices, carefully recording the terms of their employment on the pages of her account book. By the late 1840s, when Sarah Carter decided to enter the millinery trade, the terrain had changed considerably. Responding to her request that she investigate prospects in Augusta, Maine, Carter's aunt, Esther Bodwell, obliged by describing the employment practices of two of the city's milliners. Miss Cromet took apprentices on the condition that they "get boarded out of the shop"; her competitor, the "amable" Mrs. Knoble, expected apprentices who lived with her to contribute a dollar a week, although she evidently allowed particularly apt pupils to stay without payment. Neither Cromet nor Knoble wished to "take girles who work for there bord," believing that the attendant labor would "unfit" their hands for the trade. Bodwell did not portray these women as especially exploitative—in fact, she encouraged Carter to accept Knoble's offer—but both exemplified a common tendency, apparent in both male and female trades, of shifting the financial burdens of apprenticeship from employers to parents—or to apprentices themselves.[11]

Esther Bodwell's letter to her niece reflects other, equally profound, changes. Neither Cromet nor Knoble seems to have adhered to any formal notion of apprenticeship: neither mentioned indentures nor specified any particular length of time required for learning the trade, eschewing specific terms in favor of a vague "few months." Although we have little reason to question Cromet and Knoble's sincerity, vagueness of this sort could have ominous implications for apprentices. While the labor historian Helen Sumner overstated the case when she charged that "apprenticeship in the sewing trades at least, has always been a farce," viewed from the vantage point of the 1840s, her accusation had merit. In 1845 the *New York Tribune* complained that aspiring milliners learned nothing "in regard to gracefulness of outline, harmony of colors, symmetry of form and general adaptation . . . to each peculiar style of face." They emerged "not much better milliners than when they began." New York dressmakers were equally duplicitous; three years later the same publication complained that they kept apprentices "sewing and learning nothing until the very day that their apprenticeship expired, when a few hours were spent in giving them some general directions about cutting a dress, and they were discharged."[12]

New work routines accompanied the gradual weakening of the apprenticeship system. Dodds merely distinguished between "apprentices" and "assistants" in her account book during the 1820s. Two decades later, new divisions of labor evidently had emerged in both the millinery and dressmaking trades. Dressmakers divided themselves into apprentices, finishers, and fitters, a scheme that separated cutting from sewing (apprentices and finishers stitched; fitters cut and fitted). Milliners, too, created new hierarchies; makers constructed the body of a hat; more prestigious and better-paid trimmers decorated it. Such transformations, as several studies of antebellum artisans make clear, were not unique to the fashion trades. But the changes that transformed custom dressmaking and millinery during the first half of the nineteenth century stopped far short of the minute subdivisions of labor, reduced prospects, and "bastard workshops" that marked occupations such as tailoring and shoe making. While they created new obstacles for aspiring tradeswomen, new divisions of labor did not eliminate prospects for advancement. Most nineteenth-century employers never entirely abandoned their commitment to apprenticeship (although they employed increasingly flexible definitions of the term). Into the twentieth century, workers continued to climb from finisher to fitter, maker to trimmer. A not insignificant proportion of these women, as we shall see, eventually became proprietors of their own concerns. Thus, the female economy, as it emerged in the decades after 1860, created a world of considerable exploitation but also one of significant opportunity.

Villains, Victims, and Disreputable Women: Literary Images

Although early nineteenth-century craftswomen left only scattered traces behind them, they made an enduring mark in the pages of popular literature. Antebellum writers imagined a very different world than that revealed by the limited "factual" sources that have survived; their works include no "amable" Mrs. Knobles, no resourceful Sarah Carters, only evil taskmistresses and innocent victims, predatory tradeswomen and hapless consumers. These portrayals contained elements of truth but masked a more complicated reality. They are best read not as accurate depictions of life and labor but as an index to anxieties concerning woman's place. Not insignificantly, the authors of advice books, short stories, and popular novels grappled with two of the issues that had plagued Dr. Harriot Hunt (whose concerns were discussed in the introduction): fashion and female independence.

First and foremost, milliners and modistes were ambassadors of fashion, a fact that rendered them controversial figures in the eyes of contemporaries. As Karen Halttunen persuasively argues, the pursuit of fashion was the cause of considerable anxiety. Even as middle-class Americans eagerly donned the latest vogues, they worried about the appropriateness of conspicuous display in a republican society. In a culture obsessed with sincerity, the stylish belle—rouged, corseted, and strategically padded—was the embodiment of artificiality and hypocrisy.[13]

Contemporaries had additional concerns. Some posited a link between feminine apparel and poor health: "So long as it is the fashion to admire . . . the wasp-like figures which are presented at the rooms of the mantua makers and milliner," Catharine Beecher lamented, "there will be hundreds of foolish women, who will risk their lives and health to secure some resemblance to these deformities of the human frame." Others thought that fashion symbolized women's social subordination and economic dependence. Hunt deplored the existence of a "fashionable class" who "fritter away their time in millinery shops and at mantua-makers." For these women, deprived of meaningful intellectual and vocational pursuits, "the choice of the color, stripe, and texture of fabrics . . . [was the] subject of *vast moment*."[14]

Acutely aware of the limited number of employments available to her sex, Hunt viewed with sympathy those who produced feminine attire.[15] Others, who shared her assessment of fashion but were less critical of current notions of "woman's place," believed that dressmakers and milliners foisted extravagant and outlandish attire on unsuspecting consumers. "When your dress-maker recommends you to have your skirt so long as nearly to touch the floor," Eliza Farrar appealed to the readers of the *Young Lady's Friend* in 1837:

> let common sense interfere. . . . And when, a few months afterwards, you are urged to let her make it so short, as not to reach the ankle-bone, let

good taste arrest her scissors, and plead for a few inches more, for the love of grace, if not of modesty.

When, at midsummer, your milliner shows you the last Paris fashion in a bonnet, and you see that what ought to shelter the face from the sun, is so formed as to leave it entirely exposed, do not lend your countenance to anything so irrational.[16]

In an era when the canon of domesticity was just beginning to crystallize, some Americans feared that devotees of fashion would abandon the home for the dressmaker's and milliner's shops. In Timothy Shay Arthur's "Blessings in Disguise," a young husband laments his wife's failure to discover "that in the quiet, healthful joys of home, there was a charm superior to all that could attract the affections abroad." Much to his dismay, she spent most of her time "abroad," shopping and gossiping with like-minded friends; she "never thought of busying herself in his absence in little arrangements for his comfort."[17]

That fashion presented a potent threat to home and hearth was illustrated even more strikingly in Eliza Leslie's *Mr. and Mrs. Woodbridge; or, A Lesson for Young Wives* (1847). The newly married Charlotte Woodbridge, taught by her mother to seek extravagant pursuits, spends her time making "costly visits to . . . fashionable shops, and to . . . fashionable milliners and mantuamakers." These recreations exhaust the greater portion of the family budget. As a result, dinner at the Woodbridge home is "always a paltry and uninviting repast," and poor Mr. Woodbridge's modest requests for books and bookshelves are denied. After refusing several times to entertain her husband's friends, Mrs. Woodbridge relents but serves "a pig that looked as if he had been killed just in time to save him from dying . . . which . . . she got at half price." Upon discovering that her father is a drunkard—driven to intemperance by his wife's indifference to domestic affairs—and hearing of her mother's sudden demise "while a mantuamaker was fitting her for a new dress," Mrs. Woodbridge reforms. She hires a carpenter to install bookshelves and resolves to abandon the glittering world of commerce for "the quiet, healthful joys of home." In this traditional happy ending, a renunciation of fashion literally confines the heroine to the domestic sphere.[18]

Significantly, Leslie—the author of numerous housekeeping manuals as well as a prolific writer of domestic fiction—did not condemn all forms of consumption. Books and bookshelves, intended to enhance the attractions of the home, were acceptable purchases; personal adornments, intended for public display, were not.[19] In Leslie's all-too-transparent morality tale, the dressmaker is a shadowy figure, albeit one who plays an important role. In company with dry goods merchants, fancy goods dealers, and other vendors of feminine finery, she tempts Mrs. Woodbridge from the domestic circle, encouraging her to exchange selflessness for selfishness. She is a fomenter of marital discord, even an angel of death.

Most fictional businesswomen fared no better; they ranged from the ridiculous to the villainous but rarely appeared in a favorable light. The dressmaker's or milliner's shop, novelists and short story writers made clear, was the domain of the parvenue, an elaborately garbed woman seeking unsuccessfully to disguise her humble—and sometimes disreputable—origins. "Madame Millefleurs, the celebrated Parisian artiste," was none other than "Miss Flower, the driving New York milliner, originally of Division Street." The proprietor of a "splendid establishment" on Broadway "had formerly been an actress in an inferior theatre in France."[20]

Two depictions are particularly intriguing. The first appeared in a short story by the pulp writer Joseph Holt Ingraham. "The Milliner's Apprentice; or, The False Teeth" was introduced to the readers of *Godey's Lady's Book* in 1841. The villain of the tale is a Philadelphia milliner named Mrs. Carvil, "a little lady, with a very little foot, a very little waist, a very little beauty, a very little sense, a very little pug nose, and a very great deal of temper." Even worse, her "ghastly smile" displays "two ill-shapen rows of yellow teeth, with an intermixture of glaring, ghastly white ones."[21] The anonymous author of *Caroline Tracy* (1849) created an equally unsympathetic character. In the first few pages we meet Mrs. Randall, who presides over a New York millinery. She is "on the shady side of forty, showily, if not vulgarly dressed." Her "large ears" are accentuated by "larger ornaments" and she wears "numerous gew gaws strung about her." Her appearance "betrayed the woman whose notions of elegance were singularly at variance with those of an educated and refined taste."[22]

How should such portraits be interpreted? Both the unappealing Carvil and the "overdressed" Randall represent the excesses of fashion; they violate the precepts of republican simplicity and good taste. Indeed, by none too subtly equating class and taste, the creators of such characters underscored their lowly social origins. Carvil and Randall are also products of literary convention. Victorian fiction required a set of stock characters, some of whom were recognizably good, others demonstrably evil. The two milliners were "bad" women. While Carvil contented herself with the merciless exploitation of her employees, Randall was involved in a host of "nefarious" activities—intemperance, illicit sex, and prostitution.[23]

Randall's sinister undertakings suggest another common literary theme: the milliner as prostitute. In *Tom, Dick, and Harry; or, The Boys and Girls of Boston* (1849), the pulp writer Justin Jones describes the establishment of Madame P_____ as a place "where virtue was . . . lightly prized." A paternalistic benefactor advises the novel's innocent heroine not to return to her job as a milliner's apprentice because he has "heard intimated some dark things concerning" her employer. Tempted by the prospect of wealth and luxury, a second fictional bonnet maker deceitfully arranges for a millionaire to seduce her own daughter.[24] These portraits had a basis in fact: milliners' and dressmakers' shops served occasionally as fronts for brothels. But such portrayals also had more complex ramifications. Certainly, they reflected prevailing hostilities toward fashion. A reporter for the *New York Tribune*, for example, claimed to be unable to distinguish between the fashionably attired woman and the prostitute. Describing a madam as "highly rouged . . . and overdressed to decided vulgarity," he added that "we have seen quite as stylish a turnout in the front seats of the Astor-place Opera."[25]

Portrayals that linked tradeswomen with prostitution also disparaged women who crossed the supposedly impregnable boundaries between home and work, public and private. By depicting them as madams or procurers, novelists, journalists, and short story writers transformed female entrepreneurs—inhabitants of a public, if gender-segregated commercial world—literally into "public women," that is, prostitutes.[26] Women's business, these portraits implied, was illegitimate business.

The illegitimacy of women's concerns reflected more than their public nature, for the fashion trades also offered their practitioners the prospect of female economic independence. Randall's indiscretions aside, many readers might have envied her situation. Apparently, she had amassed a sizeable fortune, for she possessed "elegant parlors" and "superb sofas." She was also relatively free from male control; her status was not derived from marriage or family. For all her faults, she had achieved an enviable independence. Despite her vulgar appearance, she evinced "the most perfect self-satisfaction and self-possession." In the eyes of her creator, she presented a frightening specter of female autonomy.[27]

Literary incarnations of "good" tradeswomen reinforce this conclusion. Unlike their evil counterparts, they are pathetic figures, thrust unexpectedly into the commercial marketplace. In contrast to "driving milliners," they are decidedly unambitious. Mrs. Anson, a minor character in Ingraham's *Grace Weldon*, is a dressmaker who finds herself in unfortunate circumstances. "An interesting woman, about thirty-five," she retains only "traces of former loveliness." A reluctant breadwinner and the wife of a drunkard, she is a sympathetic figure precisely because she is a victim. Meek and self-effacing, she exhibits none of Randall's "self-satisfaction" or "self-possession."[28] Similarly, in a short story entitled "Grace Ellerslie," we learn how the beautiful protagonist became the proprietor of a small millinery and fancy goods store. Because her father had lost his fortune through "a series of unfortunate and aggravating events," poor Grace had no choice but to go into business. The lesson was clear: respectable middle-class women did not enter the commercial world of their own volition.[29]

Not coincidentally, most "good" milliners were *workers*, not proprietors. Uniformly exploited and consistently unambitious, they are pathetic victims of "pecuniary tornados." Caroline Archer, Carvil's "beautiful . . . apprentice," is the daughter of a "highly respectable merchant" who died insolvent. Marriage to a wealthy "gentleman" rescues her from a life of toil. The hardships of Alice Leary, Millefleurs's "patient-looking shop-girl" who labors to support her "invalid mother" and "delicate little sister," are assuaged only by the prospect that a certain "*somebody*" is coming to walk her home.[30]

These portrayals undoubtedly had more to do with middle-class fears of downward mobility—fears made palpable by the depression that followed the panic of 1837—than the actual circumstances of dressmakers' and milliners' lives. As Amy Gilman has suggested, plot formulas that transformed female wage earners into distressed gentlewomen bespoke Americans' reluctance to accept the reality of class divisions in a supposedly egalitarian society. Indeed, "class" was a matter of character.[31] "Good" women deserved to be rescued; "bad" women deserved to remain in the tawdry commercial world. By equating dependence with gentility and independence with vulgarity, literary depictions of custom clothiers conveyed an obvious message: woman's place was in the home, not in the dressmaking or millinery shop. Nonetheless, as the nineteenth century wore on, this was a precept that producers as well as consumers increasingly violated.[32]

* * *

The chapters in part 1, which focus on the period 1860–1910, reveal a very different landscape from the one created by antebellum moralists and novelists. Unlike the fictional Mrs. Woodbridge, customers were seldom the passive victims of unscrupulous tradeswomen. The interpretation of fashion was a responsibility that producers and consumers shared. Workers were considerably more resourceful—and often more successful—than the pathetic apprentices who toiled in imaginary millinery shops. While a few distressed gentlewomen undoubtedly found their way into the commercial marketplace, merchants' daughters—common among consumers—surface only rarely in the ranks of workers and proprietors. In status if not demeanor, the typical dressmaker or milliner more closely resembled the "nefarious" Randall than the genteel Archer.

Despite these inaccuracies, the categories that early nineteenth-century writers constructed proved remarkably resilient. Throughout the nineteenth and into the twentieth century, a variety of commentators—dress reformers, social investigators, credit reporters, and labor advocates—classified dressmakers and milliners as one of two types: hapless—and therefore genteel—victims, or vulgar, often disreputable, villains. By emphasizing the victims' dependence, they incorporated female artisans and entrepreneurs into the ranks of "respectable," if downtrodden, women; by emphasizing the villains' independence, they condemned their failure to conform to middle-class ideals of domesticity. By exaggerating both their failures and their successes, nineteenth- and early twentieth-century observers ignored the contradictions and complexities that characterized tradeswomen's careers. Neither fully dependent nor fully independent, ambitious workingwomen and enterprising entrepreneurs challenged "woman's place," but they did so within the confines of a "feminine pursuit."[33]

This is not to say that the insights offered by advice books, didactic short stories, and popular novels were insignificant. Their writers raised issues that were relevant to many tradeswomen's lives. Interactions between producers and consumers, relationships between employers and employees, economic conflicts between husbands and wives, and tensions between marriage and independence figured prominently in millinery and dressmaking careers. But these issues were neither so simple nor so easily resolved as the typical Victorian melodrama implied.

Real dressmakers and milliners were neither victims nor villains but women who sought to make the most of what the nineteenth-century commercial world had to offer. They profited from a unique conjunction of circumstances. The long-standing dominion of custom production conferred highly skilled, creative labor on its practitioners. The cultural identification of fashion as a feminine pursuit reserved for women all rungs on the occupational ladder—from lowly apprentice to haughty proprietor. Whether or not she was respectable, Randall's real-life counterpart was the embodiment of an authentic—if precarious—entrepreneurial independence.

Nevertheless, the story is not so simple. As wage earners, proprietors, and consumers, women usually found themselves on the short end of the economic stick. Hampered by insufficient capital, limited credit, and customers who habitually refused to pay their bills, many dressmakers and milliners found entrepreneurship a perilous undertaking that lasted a few years at most. The pecuniary circumstances of proprietors often had dire consequences for those in their employ. As women who lacked control over material resources, even middle- and upper-class consumers confronted the reality of their dependent status. Thus, the female economy of fashion was a fragile entity, built on often tenuous relationships between tradeswomen and customers, employers and employees. For all its faults, the nineteenth-century system of custom production provided women with an outlet for ambition, a pathway to independence. It is to the nature of that independence that we now turn.

Part One

The Female Economy:
Proprietors, Workers, and
Consumers, ca. 1860–1910

⟵⟶ *Two*

A Precarious Independence: Female Proprietors in Gilded Age Boston

*H*elen Harkness, the protagonist of William Dean Howells's *Woman's Reason* (1883), was probably the most famous literary milliner of her day. Like many a fictional heroine, Helen did not begin life in such humble circumstances. Instead, unforeseen calamity propelled her from the domestic circle: her father, a proper Bostonian and formerly prosperous merchant, died unexpectedly—and insolvent.

Unlike her predecessors, Helen does not passively accept her fate. Indeed, she exhibits considerable resourcefulness. Refusing the financial assistance of well-to-do family friends, she tries several ill-fated schemes: painting ceramics, tinting photographs, and writing literary reviews. When such pursuits fail, she turns to "aesthetic millinery." Engaging a veteran of "a well-known" establishment as her assistant, she sets up shop in her landlady's parlor, hoping to attract a fashionable clientele. This experiment meets with modest success; her bonnets, though scorned by the Beacon Street ladies, suit the tastes of immigrant and working-class women across the river in Cambridgeport. But Helen's foray into the business world is a temporary interlude in her life's career; the return of her long-lost fiancé cuts short her stint as a third-rate milliner. At the end of the novel, she joins the ranks of genteel heroines who are rescued by marriage.[1]

As Howells no doubt was aware, his portrait of a naive young woman's quest to support herself reflected a wider popular discourse on the subject of women and business. During the last quarter of the nineteenth century, variations of Helen's story appeared again and again in the pages of popular literature. While female reformers such as Virginia Penny and Caroline Dall—removed from the mainstream of popular debate—decried the narrow range of remunerative occupations open to women, staid publications such as *Harper's* offered "moneymaking" suggestions to entrepreneurially inclined "ladies." Even *Demorest's Monthly Magazine,* best known for its review of fashions, published articles entitled "What to Do with a Thousand Dollars," "Business Education for Girls," and What Can I Do?"[2]

If the small business was—in the words of one early twentieth-century commentator—"a school of manhood," its meanings for womanhood were far less clear. While entrepreneurship supposedly taught men the virtues of self-reliance and rugged individualism, most observers assumed that women—"naturally" lacking these traits—would enter the commercial world only out of sheer desperation, that is, if established channels of male support failed to materialize.[3] Few seem to have contemplated that women might choose entrepreneurial livelihoods instead of waiting until calamity struck; even Howells, as his text's ending indicates, failed to take seriously his heroine's aspirations. Moreover, as titles such as "What to Do with a Thousand Dollars" suggest, most commentators did not look beyond the "respectable" middle class, a perspective also evident in the nature and content of the occupations they proposed. Business pursuits theoretically shielded their adherents from the economic disabilities and supposed moral contagions of working-class life; "genteel" employments, such as keeping crockery stores, marketing one's own fancy work, or knitting, and—Harkness's final avocation—running millinery shops, promised to preserve both the respectability and womanly nature of ladies forced to fend for themselves. Female entrepreneurship, as most commentators saw it, should be "middle-class" and "feminine."

The voices of Harkness's real-life counterparts—the keepers of Boston's millinery and dressmaking shops—were absent from this discussion, but their existence challenged its very premises. Apart from their allegiance to "feminine pursuits," they bore little resemblance to the images presented in novels and Gilded Age magazines. Rarely pathetic victims unexpectedly thrust into the commercial marketplace, most dressmakers and milliners seem to have been upwardly mobile daughters of the working class, women whose ambitions and social origins defied the assumptions of genteel social commentary. If fictional milliners like Harkness yearned for marriage, actual tradeswomen distinguished themselves by their widespread rejection of it. Propelled by "unwomanly" ambition, conceived outside the bounds of female dependence and domestic life, most millinery and dressmaking careers were far more subversive than implied by the image of the distressed gentlewoman.

They were also far more precarious. For if the comforting advice conveyed in popular magazines promised effortless—if modest—success, most dressmakers and milliners presided over marginal, short-lived concerns, a fact that reflected both the hazardous nature of business enterprise in general and women's unique disabilities in that realm in particular. Nor did the favorite plot resolution of sympathetic fiction writers—eventual marriage—work quite the same way in real life. Matrimony represented less a refuge than a gamble to tradeswomen who pondered it; those who married risked both their psychological autonomy and their economic security. Prescriptive literature and fiction aside, businesswomen, like businessmen, sought "independence." But women played for higher stakes.

Understanding Women's Businesses

Late nineteenth-century Boston was home to hundreds, perhaps thousands, of female entrepreneurs whose presence silently disputes scholarship that assumes—implicitly or explicitly—that business was necessarily a masculine concern. Yet gender did matter, for women who contemplated commercial enterprise found the scope of their activities severely circumscribed. Although female proprietors surface even in such patently "unfeminine" pursuits as blacksmithing and silversmithing, these nonconformists, a small minority, usually fell into one of two categories: widows who assumed the places of departed husbands and wives who were proprietors in name only.[4] Exceptional circumstances notwithstanding, the nineteenth-century business world was as rigidly sex-segregated as the larger labor force. Hampered by limited capital and constrained by social convention, most female entrepreneurs clustered in occupations that mirrored traditional conceptions of women's work. More than four-fifths of the women who advertised their services in the *Boston Directory* of 1876 were purveyors of food, clothing, or lodging; well over half catered to members of their own sex (see Table 1). Those who sold trimmings, ladies' furnishings, ribbons, false hair, and hoop skirts created a "women's sphere" within a largely male commercial arena.[5]

Table 1. Female Proprietors in Boston, 1876

Apparel and adornments

Boots and shoes (retail)	4
Boys' clothing	2
Cap makers	1
Clothing (retail)	2
Clothing (secondhand)	7
Corsets	5
Costumers	4
Dressmakers	191
Dry goods (retail)	20
Embroidery stampers	1
Fancy goods (importers and wholesalers)	1
Fancy goods (retail)	47
Feather trimmings	1
Hair	3
Hair work	10
Hairdressers' supplies	1
Hoop skirts	3
Kid gloves	1
Laces	1
Ladies' furnishings	2
Ladies' and childrens' underwear	1
Machine sewing	2
Milliners	80
Patterns [garment]	2
Ribbons	1
Supporters	2
Vest makers	5
Wig makers	1
Worsted and [garment] patterns	2
	403 (62.0%)

Food and lodging

Bakers	5
Boarding houses	33
Bread stores	20
Confectionery	9
Fish	1
Fruit	1
Grocers (retail)	46

Hotels	1
Lager beer saloons	4
Liquor (retail)	2
Provisions dealers	1
Restaurants	18
Tea dealers	1
	142 (21.8%)

Household furnishings

Birds and cages	1
Carpet makers	4
Crockery	4
Flowers	2
Furniture dealers	1
House furnishings	1
Pictures, frames, etc.	1
Wax flower materials	2
Wax flowers	6
	22 (3.4%)

Personal service

Copyists	1
Hairdressers	13
Employment offices	18
Laundries	4
	36 (5.5%)

Other

Apothecaries	3
Booksellers	1
Cigar and snuff stores	2
Coal and wood dealers	1
Periodical dealers	12
Variety stores	28
	47 (7.2%)
Grand total	650 (99.9%)

Note: This table underestimates the total number of female proprietors because it includes only those who could be identified as women, those who used the titles "Miss" or "Mrs.," and those who listed their first names.

Source: Boston Directory (1876).

While dressmaking and millinery certainly fit this model, they occupied a special niche in the commercial world. First, they were distinguished not only by the number of women they employed but also by the near exclusion of men from their domain. Milliners and dressmakers constituted 42 percent of *all* female retailers in Boston in 1876; women accounted for about 95 percent of the city's dressmaking and millinery proprietors in both 1860 and 1890. Even dry goods dealers and fancy goods vendors, merchants who catered primarily to "shopping ladies," were male for the most part. But "man milliners" and "man dressmakers," as the very construction of those terms suggests, trespassed on female terrain.[6]

Unlike women who kept fancy goods shops and crockery stores, milliners and dressmakers laid claim to a much older craft tradition, a fact that helped to ensure that their entrepreneurial endeavors reflected not sudden calamity—the death of a male provider or an unexpected change in family fortunes—but calculated strategy. Women without prior experience might become retailers of prefabricated merchandise, but inexperienced modistes could not simply start a business; those who tried usually failed. In the fashion trades, keeping shop required craft expertise as well as business acumen. Dressmakers and milliners were makers as well as sellers; in contrast to prevailing commercial trends, the typical establishment evinced little separation between production and retailing.[7]

Women owed their monopoly on millinery and dressmaking not only to their carefully cultivated skills but to social and sexual mores that defined the prevailing division of labor in the trades as suitable and natural. The demands of Victorian propriety banished men from fitting rooms; powerful ideological imperatives reinforced women's dominion over these "essentially feminine" pursuits.[8] To be sure, some men (at least 10 of 222 in 1860 and 18 of 325 in 1890) risked public humiliation to reap profits from the sale of feminine finery; others, as we shall see, intervened behind the scenes.[9] Wholesale millinery firms, relatively large-scale enterprises that supplied raw materials to retailers, were almost always operated by men. But the rewards of dressmaking and custom millinery were reserved primarily for women. As late as 1913 the editors of the *Milliner* could proclaim of their trade, "It offers women an independence."[10]

Boston's Milliners and Dressmakers: Who Were They?

In 1867, Miss M. E. Downey left her position with a Boston milliner to open her own shop. Downey was the beneficiary of a distinctly feminine mode of upward mobility that owed its existence to the vagaries of fashion—and she was not alone. In an era renowned for gaudy display, the demand for skilled craftswomen proceeded apace. One hundred and fifty-nine milliners and dressmakers kept shop in the city in 1850; three decades later the *Boston Directory* listed nearly four times as many (see Table A-2 in the appendix).[11]

Who were the proprietors of Boston's dressmaking and millinery shops? From 15–25 percent of all dressmakers and milliners in the city, they were a select, albeit heterogeneous, group.[12] Consider, for example, the contrast between Mrs. M. A. Boswell and Madame Santin. Boswell specialized "in a cheap class" of merchandise; Santin, a "prominent lady milliner," imported Parisian goods—and attempted to increase her profits by eluding local customs inspectors.[13] The more exclusive tradeswomen presided over elegant establishments in the heart of the downtown shopping district, on Washington and Winter Streets and—the most fashionable location of all—Temple Place. (Santin's shop was on Otis Street, not far from the most desirable section of Washington Street.) The bargain hunter could patronize the cheap shops of Hanover Street in the city's north end; here Boswell hawked her wares. Several locations welcomed milliners of intermediate status. The "best" modistes situated themselves beside their bonnet-making counterparts, while second-rate dressmakers, more likely than milliners to work at home, were dispersed throughout the city. These distinctions were part and parcel of a recurrent urban geography of fashion. In New York, the denizens of Broadway and, later, Fifth Avenue scorned Division Street; in Philadelphia, the clientele of Chestnut Street sneered at Frankfort Avenue.[14]

Both Hanover Street and Temple Place accommodated a variety of business practices. Some women kept shop, others—especially dressmakers—went "out by the day." Some combined dress- and hatmaking; others, especially milliners, carried "side lines" of fabric and trimmings. Still others, probably the majority, contented themselves with producing a single commodity. Individual proprietors—assisted by a small corps of employees—ran most establishments, but alternate arrangements surfaced as well. Sisters or, less commonly, unrelated women might join forces against an often hostile commercial world. These female partnerships competed with an even smaller number of husband-wife teams (Table 2).

But common circumstances lurked beneath this surface diversity; by and large, Boston's dressmakers and milliners represented a distinctive female status and social experience. Despite considerable variations, it is possible to paint a portrait of the typical tradeswoman (or at least of the most common type): she was a white, native-born spinster of working-class origins who

Table 2. Business Practices of Female Proprietors, Boston, 1853–87

	Number	Percentage
Individual proprietor	170	75.9
Female partnership	31	13.8
Husband-wife team	23	10.3
	224	100.0

Source: MA 67–91, RGD.

had reached what nineteenth-century Americans called a "certain age." Her entrepreneurial efforts seldom paved the way to riches; more often than not, she presided over a marginal, ephemeral concern.

In sharp contrast to the larger female entrepreneurial universe that seems to have been the province of widows, "maiden ladies" dominated the fashion trades; widows made up a substantial, but only the second largest, contingent. Married women, not unknown among dressmakers and milliners, constituted a distinct minority. Depending on the source one consults, they accounted for as little as 7 percent or as much as 21 percent of the city's custom clothiers (Table 3).[15] Far from serendipitous, this unique marital configuration revealed tradeswomen's subtle but significant challenges to women's dependent status.

Exclusive or humble, married or single, Boston's "Madames" shared a common characteristic: age—an attribute that indicated both the extent of their training and the depth of their commitment to their trades. Most had reached their thirties or forties; on average they were about ten years older than the workers they employed (Table 4). In most cases, age reflected expertise. Both trades—especially dressmaking—were vulnerable to amateurism, a problem that would grow more severe as the nineteenth century drew to a close. But the dilettantish Harkness, a woman in her early twenties, bore little resemblance to her real-life counterparts, many of whom had spent years perfecting their crafts. Julia Butler "was formerly a seamstress" who had "worked for other parties." The Misses Kelly and Hallahan had previously labored for Madame Pierrot. Ellen Hartnett had risen to the position of "foreman" of the workroom before embarking on a venture of her own.[16]

As these career patterns suggest, entrepreneurship was an experience

Table 3. Boston Milliners and Dressmakers: Marital Status of Female Proprietors, 1853–87[a]

| | 1860 Census | | 1870 Census[b] | | Dun & Co. (1853–87) | |
	N	%	N	%	N	%
Never married	43	38.4	50	46.3	104	46.4
Widowed, divorced, or separated	23	20.5	27	25.0	72	32.1
Unknown	38	33.9	19	17.6	0	0.0
Married (living with husband)	8	7.1	12	11.1	48	21.4
Total	112	99.9	108	100.0	224	99.9

a. The 1860 and 1870 censuses do not designate an individual's marital status. Marital status, therefore, has to be inferred from either household structure or titles listed in city directories. I designated tradeswomen listed in the census as living with a man of similar age and the same surname as married. I considered those who lived alone or with apparently unrelated individuals (people with different surnames) *and* who listed themselves as "Mrs." in the city directory as widowed, divorced, or separated; I applied the same label to female heads of household who lived with children who had the same last name. I assigned those residing with people who appeared to be their parent(s) or adult sibling(s) (adults with the same surname) and all tradeswomen who identified themselves as "Miss" in the city directory to the never married category.

b. Results based on 25 percent sample.

Sources: 1860 FMPC, Boston, M653, reels 520–25; 1870 FMPC, Boston, M593, reels 640–49; MA 67–91, RGD; *Boston Directory* (1860, 1861, 1870, 1871).

grounded in class as well as gender; Hartnett and her colleagues generally hailed from middle- or working-class backgrounds. Merchants' daughters fallen on hard times figured prominently in the pages of fiction, and Boston's millinery and dressmaking population probably included a sprinkling of distressed gentlewomen, but evidence culled from the manuscript censuses of 1860 and 1870 indicates that they were few and far between. The Irish-born Hartnett is a case in point. In 1860, a decade before she went into business for herself, a census taker found her in a two-family house in Boston's Tenth Ward. The seventeen-year-old millinery worker lived with two sis-

Table 4. Boston Milliners and Dressmakers: Age
of Female Proprietors, 1860–70

	1860 Census		1870 Census[a]	
	N	%	*N*	%
20–29 years	32	28.6	23	21.3
30–39 years	48	42.9	46	42.6
40+ years	32	28.6	39	36.1
Total	112	100.1	108	100.0
Average age (years)				
proprietors	34.4		37.1	
nonproprietors	25.4		27.0	

a. Results based on 25 percent sample.

Sources: 1860 FMPC, Boston, M653, reels 520–25; 1870 FMPC,
Boston, M593, reels 640–49.

ters, both of whom evidently "kept house," and a brother who worked as a
mason. None of them owned property. Hartnett's ascension from wagework-
er to proprietor clearly exemplified upward, not downward mobility.[17]

However humble their origins, the keepers of Boston's dressmaking and
millinery shops represented a relatively privileged segment of the female
working class, for they were overwhelmingly native born (nearly 80 percent
in 1870) and almost uniformly white (no African American proprietors
turned up in either census sample, although two merited a listing in credit
ledgers). Despite their predilection for exotic titles, very few "Parisian modistes" had in fact emigrated from France; with few exceptions, immigrants—22–29 percent of all Madames—hailed from Ireland, Great Brit-
ain, or Canada (Table 5).[18]

Native birth was an attribute that a majority of employers and employees
shared, but proprietors were even more likely to have been born in the United
States than those who toiled in their workrooms (Table 5). Yankee women
doubtless had greater resources at their disposal; concerns of "gentility" may
also have played a part. We can easily imagine proper Bostonians flocking to
the millinery shop run by Maria and Catherine Roeth, representatives of a tiny
French minority, but disdaining to enter the establishment of M. T. McManus.

Table 5. Origins of Boston Milliners and Dressmakers, 1860–70

| | Female Proprietors | | | | All Milliners and Dressmakers | |
| | 1860 | | 1870[a] | | 1870[b] | |
	N	%	N	%	N	%
United States						
Massachusetts	37	33.0	42	38.9		
Maine	24	21.4	23	21.3		
New Hampshire	15	13.4	10	9.3		
Other	4	3.6	9	8.3		
	80	71.4	84	77.8	1,196	68.9
Foreign origins						
Great Britain	6	5.4	4	3.7	55	3.2
Ireland	15	13.4	8	7.4	227	13.1
Canada	11	9.8	11	10.2	242	13.9
Other	0	0.0	1	0.9	17	1.0
	32	28.6	24	22.2	541	31.2
Grand total	112	100.0	108	100.0	1,737	100.1

a. Results based on 25 percent sample.
b. Results based on published census materials.
Sources: 1860 FMPC, Boston, M653, reels 520–25; 1870 FMPC, Boston, M593, reels 640–49; USBC, *Statistics of the Population . . . Ninth Census,* 1:778.

While McManus, who enjoyed "a fair Irish trade," made little effort to attract the patronage of the city's most elite families, some tradeswomen—like Catherine Bradley, an Irish dressmaker and milliner who had "a good class of customers"—evidently transcended their origins. Josephine McCluskey's transformation into "Miss Delavenue" suggests that immigrant proprietors were pressed to assume the trappings of respectability. Indeed, although millinery and dressmaking promised upward mobility, they did so to a select group. Invisible but not entirely impermeable racial and ethnic barriers surrounded the trades, largely preserving them for members of the upper strata of a far from homogeneous female working class.[19]

What sorts of livelihoods did the Miss Delavenues of the trade enjoy? The entrepreneurs of fashion included both the affluent and the impoverished, a division that corresponded roughly but by no means absolutely to the distinction between "cheap" and "exclusive" establishments.[20] While some achieved extraordinary success, others, clearly the majority, did not. Mrs. E. M. Wilson, a Boston dressmaker who traveled to Europe each year to view the latest fashions, fell into the first category, as did Hartnett, the Irish milliner. Unlike her illustrious counterpart, Hartnett apparently never visited Paris. Nevertheless, her achievements were impressive. A penniless wage earner in 1860, she had amassed $10,000 by 1886.[21] But most of her competitors lived in far humbler circumstances. Few women in either trade had any property the census taker thought worth recording (Table 6). Even a majority (62 percent) of those who merited the interest of R. G. Dun & Co., the nation's leading credit reporting firm, possessed "no means" or "small means."[22]

More often than not, entrepreneurship offered only a temporary respite from wage labor. The average tradeswoman stayed in business for about six years, but that figure masks at least as much as it reveals. About a quarter, clearly the elite, kept shop for a decade or longer. Hartnett's career spanned

Table 6. Boston Milliners and Dressmakers: Combined Real and Personal Property of Proprietors, 1860–70

	1860				1870[a]			
	Female		Male		Female		Male	
	N	%	N	%	N	%	N	%
$0	77	68.8	0	0.0	97	89.8	1	33.3
$1–499	21	18.8	0	0.0	4	3.7	0	0.0
$500+	14	12.5	13	100.0	7	6.5	2	66.7
	112	100.1	13	100.0	108	100.0	3	100.0

a. Results based on 25 percent sample. Property estimates based on the census of 1870 may have been affected by a new regulation that instructed enumerators to record only personal property worth more than $100. See U.S. Census Office, *Instructions to Marshals, Instructions to Assistants* (Washington, D.C.: George W. Bowman, 1860), 15, and *Instructions to Assistants* (Washington, D.C.: Government Printing Office, 1870), 10.

Sources: 1860 FMPC, Boston, M653, reels 520–25; 1870 FMPC, Boston, M593, reels 640–49.

twenty-nine years. Few followed in her footsteps. A third of all milliners and modistes closed their doors before their second anniversaries; 60 percent remained in business for five years or less.[23]

A glance at the fortunes of businessmen underlines the precarious nature of female enterprise and suggests that, even within the volatile world of small-scale retailing, women confronted greater challenges. To be sure, male shop-keepers faced uncertain futures; then as now, small businesses failed at astro-nomical rates.[24] But the trials of small businessmen pale in comparison to the hardships that plagued businesswomen. Milliners and dressmakers typically made do with less, indeed, far less than their male counterparts. Almost two-thirds of the Boston tradeswomen evaluated in the credit ledgers of Dun & Co. possessed assets of $1,000 or less, a predicament shared by only 35 percent of the grocers and fancy goods dealers in Poughkeepsie, New York.[25] If mas-culine and feminine ventures persisted at similar rates,[26] the credit reporter's stock phrase "out of business" had greater meaning for women than it did for men. Failed businessmen might reenter the marketplace—sometimes many times—but most women had neither the resources nor perhaps the resolve to begin anew. Once they left the business world they rarely returned.[27]

If we confine our analysis to the millinery and dressmaking trades, the gulf between businesswomen and businessmen widens. Virtually all man milliners, in contrast to their women counterparts, owned property (Table 6). Indeed, their average holdings amounted to over $6,000, compared to $284 for female proprietors! Men's businesses, on average, lasted two and a half times as long. Men, like Jonathan Stevens, who presided over "a large dressmaking establishment" tended to control the more substantial business-es.[28] As the nineteenth century wore on, small businesswomen faced com-petition from the dressmaking and millinery departments of dry goods hous-es and department stores, large-scale enterprises managed almost entirely by men. Hampered by lack of capital and a corresponding shortage of credit, women remained on the margin of the commercial world.

"Milliners make lots of money," the fictional Harkness believed.[29] On the contrary, most met with as little success as Howells's fictional heroine. Still, we should not exaggerate their failures. Although the line dividing them was sometimes thin, these women were proprietors, not wageworkers; most were both entrepreneurs and employers. Given women's unequal access to eco-nomic resources and a culture that defined them as dependents, the millinery and dressmaking shops that lined the streets of Boston represented no small achievement.

"I . . . Will Admire Your Independence": The Business of Singlehood

At first glance, the proprietors of dressmaking and millinery concerns have little to offer historians in search of "usable pasts." Their implicit acceptance of prevailing sexual divisions of labor, their association with the accoutrements of conventional femininity, and their apparently individualistic aspirations inspire none of the drama evoked by the collective struggles of workingwomen in the shoe making, collar, and textile industries or the demands articulated by participants in the Gilded Age woman's movement.[30] But the circumstances of tradeswomen's lives reveal a more complex story than this simple assessment suggests. Indeed, female proprietors occupied an ambiguous position in the nineteenth-century social structure. On the one hand, they confirmed accepted definitions of women's work. On the other, their very existence challenged conventional gender roles. As entrepreneurs, not wage earners, they assumed a status usually reserved for men; as permanent workers, not temporary toilers, they bore little resemblance to the stereotypical working girl. Women like Eunice Lord, a forty-year-old dressmaker who lived alone and claimed assets worth $900, violated both the middle-class standard of domesticity and the working-class ideal of the family wage. Yards of ruffles, trimmings, flounces, and lace concealed an alternative to female dependence and (at times) abject poverty, an alternative that at least some tradeswomen consciously embraced.

If female entrepreneurship presented a rebellion of sorts, few modistes saw themselves as crusaders against the restrictions of "woman's sphere." Inspired perhaps by the reform-minded atmosphere of nineteenth-century Boston, a small number of proprietors took up the cause of woman's rights. Olivia P. G. Flynt, the wife of a wealthy furniture and window shade manufacturer and a dressmaker renowned for her "artistic" creations, was active in feminist and dress reform circles. Maria Theresa Hollander, the proprietor of a children's clothing store in the 1850s and 1860s, later became an ardent advocate of woman suffrage. (In 1884 Lucy Stone asked her, "Can you not[,] having your business knowledge and experience . . . help us to find out how to increase the circulation of the *Woman's Journal* [?]") Unfortunately, Hollander, an enthusiastic proponent of abolitionism and a dabbler in spiritualism, failed to record her reasons for entering the commercial world. Although she may not have perceived her business aspirations as a frontal assault on women's wrongs (unlike Flynt, she was motivated at least somewhat by economic necessity), her "business knowledge and experience" may have given her the confidence to embrace unpopular causes. Perhaps, too, her economic independence encouraged her to claim political rights, long denied to women on the grounds of their supposedly dependent status.[31]

Other tradeswomen undoubtedly campaigned for suffrage or joined voluntary organizations, but they left no mark on the historical record. Yet there is reason to suspect that their numbers were not large. As makers of fashion—widely believed to be a source of women's oppression—dressmakers and milliners often incurred the hostilities of woman's rights advocates; as women of working-class origins they were unlikely members of newly established women's clubs. If dressmakers and milliners only infrequently recorded their reasons for entering the public, commercial world, one suspects that they were less interested in abstract notions of woman's rights than in concrete matters of pecuniary survival; their efforts first and foremost were driven by economic necessity. If they were not nascent feminists, neither were they pathetic victims of the nineteenth-century marketplace. For while necessity loomed large, ambition was hardly absent from their careers. Although direct evidence of their motivations is rare, surviving documents attest to women's desires for "independence."

To be sure, young women entered the trades for any number of reasons; the prospect of proprietorship was only one of several attractions. The custom production of feminine apparel offered advantages that few female occupations could match: skilled work, relatively high wages, "respectable" social status within the working class (subjects that will be discussed more thoroughly in the next chapter). But many found dressmaking and millinery appealing precisely because they offered a rare outlet for female ambition, a possible pathway to economic independence. Indeed, the very structure of the trades, which reflected a declining but still viable system of apprenticeship, revealed their potential to overcome women's dependent status and to provide female aspirants with the sort of independence sought by male craftworkers. A report issued by the New England Women's Club in 1869 recognized as much. While its authors revealed their ignorance of craft nomenclature (no references to apprentices, makers, or trimmers embellish their description), they described the progress of a milliner succinctly and matter-of-factly:

> When a girl enters a Milliner's Establishment, she must give three or four month's time to learning the business. After that, she receives five dollars

a week; and, in some instances, as she improves, her wages are increased to fifteen. When she has saved enough to set up business for herself, she hires a room, and buys materials as they are needed, until experience and practice have made her sure enough of success to warrant buying stock for herself. This she can do on thirty day's credit; and, if tasty and thrifty, she will not only make a living, but be able to save a good deal every year.[32]

Though accurate in its outlines, this assessment erred on the side of optimism. Not every worker reached these heights, and not every proprietor achieved success. The club's Algeresque enthusiasm notwithstanding, the difficult journey up the occupational ladder was not necessarily a solitary enterprise. Just as "self-made" businessmen often had help, tradeswomen might act not as isolated individuals but as participants in wide-ranging family economies. Credit records reveal that fathers, and sometimes mothers and brothers, occasionally furnished the capital for women's businesses. Jennie Boston, one of the city's more successful milliners, began business with $1,000. A Dun & Co. reporter noted that she received "assistance from some party unknown"; more than likely, that party was her father, a relatively prosperous provisions dealer who reported property worth $3,600 in 1860. Misses C. and M. McCaffrey's mother, who owned "a little real estate . . . assisted them to start." Patrick Donnelly, a stabler, supplied his sisters with $1,000 so they could open a hat shop—a sum he expected them to repay: Donnelly could "scarcely be supposed to have made them a present of that amount." Although some relatives benevolently shared their resources, others expected returns on their investments.[33]

Yet it would be misleading to view businesswomen solely within the context of a family economy; indeed, such a perspective—because it views the family as a male-dominated but indivisible unit—obscures the potentially subversive nature of their enterprises.[34] Few relatives had the means with which to finance entrepreneurial ventures; even the Dun & Co. records—which chronicle the careers of the dressmaking and millinery elite—only occasionally mention family support. Equally significant, tradeswomen rarely inhabited "traditional" households. A clear majority of unmarried proprietors (58 percent in 1860, 53 percent in 1870) lived alone, in boardinghouses, or with female companions. Roughly a quarter resided with adult sisters or with their own children. Only about 16 percent lived with fathers or mothers, and 4–6 percent with brothers who might have served as surrogate fathers (see Table 7). Demography does much to explain these arrangements. Many craftswomen were orphans by the time they reached their thirties and

Table 7. Living Arrangements of Unmarried (Widowed and Never Married) Female Proprietors[a]

	1860	1870[b]
Not in family	60 (57.7%)	51 (53.1%)
Family, lives with:		
Father	5 (4.8%)	4 (4.2%)
Mother only	10 (9.6%)	7 (7.3%)
Adult brother(s)	4 (3.8%)	6 (6.3%)
Adult sister(s) only	11 (10.6%)	14 (14.6%)
Own children	14 (13.5%)	14 (14.6%)
	104 (100.0%)	96 (100.1%)

a. Relationships between household members have to be inferred because the 1860 and 1870 censuses did not designate them. See Table 3, note a.

b. Results based on 25 percent sample.

Sources: 1860 FMPC, Boston, M653, reels 520–25; 1870 FMPC, Boston, M593, reels 640–49.

forties, the ages at which the fortunate among them went into business for themselves. Moreover, the evidence, while limited, suggests that nearly half of Boston's tradeswomen—many of them natives of rural and small towns in New England—were living on their own well before they became proprietors of their own concerns. Distance did not preclude relationships based on love or money,[35] but migration may well have loosened the economic ties that bound women to their families. However much parental intervention aided their early careers (an issue that the next chapter explores), most dressmakers and milliners pursued their vocations outside the confines of familial authority.

Largely bereft of paternal beneficence and male support, such women needed gainful employment, but they did not necessarily "need" to open their own businesses. Indeed, the decision to do so indicated a willingness to *risk* economic security, for it meant leaving a job that paid well—by female standards—for the uncertain rewards of petty entrepreneurship. Neither economic necessity nor familial duty entirely explain the extraordinary determination that drove many millinery and dressmaking careers. Boston practiced her trade for at least thirteen years before opening her own concern at the age of thirty-seven. Apparently her training paid off; a Dun & Co. correspondent described her as "a very good milliner." Boston's dedication was surpassed by M. E. Ford, who brought nearly two decades of experience as a head trimmer to her own entrepreneurial venture.[36]

Finally, Ford and her sisters may well have viewed their careers as alternatives to marriage. For if the typical female wage earner was young and unmarried, the typical female proprietor was middle-aged by the standards of her day *and* single. Perhaps female entrepreneurship was nothing more than the product of pecuniary desperation on the part of widows and spinsters, women unable to depend upon men in a era when marriage presented the most viable economic option. Male migration and the ravages of the Civil War left the sex ratio in nineteenth-century New England severely imbalanced; eligible bachelors were in short supply. Though the keepers of millinery and dressmaking shops usually earned modest profits at best, they generally enjoyed a higher standard of living than did most female wage earners. Unmarried women, especially those who hailed from the middle or working classes, may have needed to work, but successful proprietors—women like Julietta Reed who claimed $2,000 in personal property—were able to support *themselves*.[37] If rewards of this sort often failed to materialize and if Reed represented more an exception than a rule, the prospect of entrepreneurial success—however elusive—proved attractive to independent-minded women. In other words, proprietorship had the *potential* (albeit one that was not always realized) to free women from economic dependence on men, a means of preventing what one commentator called "the crime, and I might say *necessary crime* of marrying for a home."[38] An alternative hypothesis emerges: perhaps some businesswomen consciously rejected marriage.

There was precedent for such a decision, as Lee Chambers-Schiller's recent study of nineteenth-century spinsters ably demonstrates. Inspired by an ethos of republican individualism and armed with ample knowledge of the deficiencies of matrimony, small but significant numbers of women who came of age in the antebellum Northeast chose not to marry. Despite economic insecurities and only qualified social support, these pioneers self-consciously embraced singlehood, believing marriage to be incompatible with their desires for autonomy, self-development, and meaningful work. At first glance, the keepers of millinery and dressmaking shops appear to have little in common with the predominantly middle- and upper-class women who declared their independence in the pages of diaries, letters, and autobiographies. Although the former expressed a decidedly self-interested ambition, the latter were less concerned with achieving economic independence than in pursuing "vocations" that nurtured their intellectual, artistic, and philanthropic aspirations.[39] But women who took up dressmaking or millinery—especially the native-born daughters of New England who accounted for most of Boston's Madames—may have absorbed many of the same messages as their wealthier counterparts.[40] If middle-class women rejected marriage, might not their humbler sisters have done the same?

Few milliners and dressmakers recorded their impressions of matrimony for posterity. But at least some modistes deliberately opted for singlehood, viewing entrepreneurial status as a feasible alternative to wifely dependence. The author of "Talks with Women," a regular feature of *Demorest's Monthly Magazine,* described the attitude of one successful dressmaker: "The fact is, when women have once tasted the charm of an honorable independence achieved by themselves it is very difficult to persuade them to marry." Caroline Woods would have agreed. Her fictionalized autobiography, *Diary of a Milliner,* begins: "I am left a widow with the necessity upon me of getting my own living." She did not stop there. Addressing her departed husband, she writes, "I did love you dearly, Will; but I will own to one decided objection to married life. I was often obliged to go one way when I wished to go another." Declaring that "business will be independence," Woods explicitly links marriage to dependence: "Plodding women may sit down to the restraints of married life in order to obtain the remuneration of a living, and a poor one at that, without the power of making it better; but as for me, instead of marrying again I choose business."[41]

Equally intriguing is the story of Sarah Carter, introduced briefly in chapter 1. Born in 1827, the daughter of a "middling" farmer, she left her home in Shirley, Maine, in the 1840s to learn the millinery trade in the relative metropolis of Augusta. Geographic mobility and occupational instability marked her early career. Abandoning hatmaking for teaching, she moved from one Maine town to another, frequently returning to Shirley for extended visits. By the next decade, she stood on a firmer vocational footing; in 1854 she secured a position in a Foxcroft dry goods store (here she evidently practiced millinery as well as clerking, a not unlikely scenario in the less specialized world of small-town retailing), a job she would hold for the next twenty years.[42]

Carter left behind clearer indications of her motives than did many of her peers. Much to the dismay of several spurned suitors, she declared repeatedly her intention of remaining an "old maid." Fearing for her health, a childhood friend beseeched her to abandon the stale atmosphere of the store, "where the sun is never permitted to shine," for the security and comforts of the domestic sphere. "You never have taken the least care of yourself and 'tis a wonder that you are alive now. I wish you would get married if you would *take* a husband who would *take* care of you." This entreaty, like several others, ended on a note of resignation: "I will not quarrel with you, but will admire your independence."[43]

Carter's independence was admirable indeed. By 1860 she had saved $1,200, a sum that single women rarely possessed. But financial autonomy had its liabilities. Despite her solvency—or perhaps because of it—she acquired the "immoral" reputation that often clung to wage-earning women, especially dressmakers and milliners. Her "associates," it was rumored, were "nearly all of an exceptionable kind," and Carter herself was "no better than she ought to be." Even worse, she was seen "walk[ing] the streets . . . at night" with Dr. Gordon, a man "not considered . . . respectable" and a reputed adulterer. These reports reached Carter's hometown and fueled an estrangement from family and friends.[44]

Carter may have eventually reentered respectable society; she appears in the 1870 census as the wife of Benjamin Vaughan, the dry goods merchant for whom she had labored for so many years. Unlike the shadowy Gordon, Vaughan was "a gentleman" who possessed real and personal property valued at $15,000. But forty-three-year-old Sarah Carter Vaughan did not merit the usual census designation for married women—"keeping house"; rather, she was "in charge of [the] store." (Her husband, seventeen years her senior, had by this time retired.) What is more, she claimed property worth $12,500 in her own right.[45]

Carter failed to keep her vow of singlehood, but she married on extremely advantageous terms. Certainly, she paid a price for her transgressions against woman's place, an emotional cost that surviving documents do not allow us to measure.[46] But her experience reveals the multiple meanings of independence for those women who sought it: economic security, psychological autonomy, control over their own sexuality, and the right to choose freely whether or not to marry.

We will probably never know whether Boston's milliners and dressmakers were either enthusiastic proponents of "single blessedness" or reluctant spinsters.[47] While some wholeheartedly embraced maiden status, others no doubt viewed their situations with a good deal of ambivalence. But craftswomen who labored for years at their callings, hoping one day to open shops of their own, bear little resemblance to stereotypical apathetic wage earners waiting to be "rescued" by marriage. Those who reached the highest rungs on the millinery and dressmaking ladders had made a decision of sorts, a choice that required considerable ambition and at least an inchoate conception of a "career"—and one that very well may have precluded matrimony. Whatever its source, autonomy had a price. Single businesswomen were uniquely free from male control. They were also the most economically vulnerable, for they generally had access to less capital than their married sisters.

The small numbers who could count on aid from their families were especially fortunate. But most were forced to rely on a less predictable method: saving money from their salaries, a strategy that handicapped their enterprises from the outset, because it relied on "women's wages." A. M. and S. M. Ebbett, dressmakers who began their entrepreneurial careers with "some \$300 to \$400," followed this pathway as did Ford, eighteen years a head trimmer. As these examples demonstrate, saving was by no means impossible; experienced dressmakers and milliners commanded some of the highest wages in the female labor market. But in an era when a skilled craftswoman earned about as much as an unskilled male laborer, the capital amassed by women such as the Ebbett sisters entailed considerable sacrifice.[48] Casually dismissed by credit reporters, these tiny nest eggs offer poignant testimony to the ambition that drove much female enterprise.

To be sure, there were happy endings. Catherine M. Kelleher, who began business with "very little means," nevertheless had "done very well." Indeed, there was no clear relationship between access to credit and business longevity. Clara Adams, whom a Dun & Co. reporter pronounced "thoroughly good for nothing," remained in business for sixteen years; Miss D. L. Capen, whose "means . . . [were] probably in book accounts and not large," had an extraordinary forty-seven-year career.[49] But nineteenth-century businesswomen discovered—as have many women before and since—that independence often meant economic vulnerability.

In economic terms, widows—women suddenly bereft of male support—often fared worse than their never-married sisters. Some successfully utilized inherited capital. But widows with substantial amounts of property were scarce among milliners and dressmakers. Mrs. C. P. Smith, who presided over a thriving millinery business, was the heir to an impressive legacy: a house worth \$13,000. Mrs. L. A. Doherty was probably more typical. Doherty derived "a small income" from an invention patented by her late husband. These additional funds helped little; her tenure as a milliner lasted less than a year. Perhaps more than any other group, widowed proprietors resembled the stereotypical victims of Victorian melodramas. But their circumstances, however pathetic, only rarely elicited sympathy. Indeed, they were more likely to be refused credit than were married or single women.[50]

Credit investigators based their judgments on more than malice, for evidence suggests that widows, rather than young unmarried women like Howells's Harkness, swelled the ranks of amateurs. Mrs. H. B. Remick, remarked a reporter for Dun & Co., "is not a practical milliner [that is, not a trained craftswoman] and probably has hard work to live." Mrs. C. J. Hall, a dressmaker, possessed "no business experience." Regretfully, the correspondent rendered his verdict: "A likely woman, but no basis for credit." Mrs. M. A. McCarty naively paid a high price for outdated goods; not surprisingly, an investigator expressed little confidence in her venture. "She is regarded as [an] honest well meaning woman," he wrote, "but the competition in this locality is thought to be too sharp for her." Unfortunately, his prediction proved correct; a year later McCarty was out of business.[51]

"Not Much of a Help": The Business of Marriage

Given the financial circumstances in which unmarried businesswomen often found themselves, marriage—or remarriage—made good economic sense. Mrs. L. N. Mason might have agreed. "Her husband is said to support her," noted a credit investigator, "but she is in business because she likes it." Others, like Mrs. L. P. Clark, who was "unfortunate in having a Sick Husband, Son and Daughter to support," benefited little from wedded bliss.[52]

Mason and Clark occupied opposite poles on a relatively narrow economic spectrum; most married milliners and dressmakers were neither heroic breadwinners nor dilettantes but women whose endeavors stemmed from more subtle marital negotiations. An inventory of husbands' occupations reveals employments whose remuneration was modest at best, unpredictable at worst: piano tuner, glasscutter, salesman, roofer, artist. Linked to spouses with less than certain prospects, these women were not in business merely because they "liked it"; at the same time, their circumstances suggest that they were driven less by economic desperation than by the desire for more comfortable subsistences, for cushions against hard times. In these goals, Mrs. and Mr. J. P. Davis appear to have succeeded. Davis, the husband of a Chelsea milliner, was a carpenter who eventually found a job "as canvasser for a book entitled *The World*." As a result of his good fortune, Mrs. Davis gained a credit line of $25.[53] This arrangement, undoubtedly a common one, worked to the Davises' mutual benefit. Her profits provided a welcome addition to family income; his earnings boosted his wife's credit rating. Indeed, while marriage seldom meant riches, it substantially enhanced women's prospects. Married women had access to far greater resources than their single counterparts and their businesses, on average, lasted twice as long.[54]

Nonetheless, to many dressmakers and milliners, marriage proved a mixed blessing. Matrimony usually meant some loss of independence. Despite the protections offered by married women's property laws, wives exercised less control over their enterprises than did *femes soles*. Marriage to the wrong man could spell financial disaster, a danger of which contemporary businesswomen were well aware. In 1900, the *Illustrated Milliner*, a trade journal dedicated to the interests of retailers, asked its subscribers a series of questions: "Should a successful milliner marry? If so, should she continue in business after marriage? If her husband is a man without means, should she associate him with her business?" Eight replies appeared. Only two readers believed marriage and millinery were compatible; the most exuberant proponent of matrimony was a man. Two readers invoked traditional gender ideology and, while they wrote at a time when singlehood increasingly provoked attack, their responses offer a rare glimpse of the tensions and anxieties that earlier businesswomen must have experienced. Mrs. C. B. Hunt, of Ronceverte, West Virginia, declared that "a wife's place is in the home." "An Engaged Modiste" proclaimed, "Isn't a happy home better than a successful millinery shop any day? If either has to go, then good-bye shop. An old maid milliner, even if she if rich, is a failure." Mary A. Strittmatter harbored no such romantic illusions: "A successful milliner should not marry unless she can find a husband that can support her. I do not believe that a married lady should associate her husband with her own business. Married or single, a lady should always keep her business in her own name." Mrs. H. S. Kidwell was even blunter. A milliner, she maintained, "had better invest her money in wax figures than in a man without means."[55]

The Dun & Co. records suggest that Strittmatter and Kidwell had reason for concern. Maria Forgeot, née Maria Caffrey, almost certainly was the victim of a fortune hunter. Born in Ireland, she had already "been some years in business" before she married John Forgeot in 1868 at the age of 33. A Dun & Co. correspondent described her husband uncharitably but accurately as a "dead weight." Two years later she had two children in addition to a ne'er-do-well husband to support. Her business faltered after this, perhaps as a result of John's inept attempts to manage the concern. In 1876 she was forced to file for bankruptcy. She resumed business after settling with her creditors but thereafter was never able to meet her payments promptly and could get only limited credit. When Maria died in 1886, John vowed to "continue the business for the present." Not surprisingly, the firm survived only a year under his stewardship.[56]

Maria Forgeot's experience confirmed the opinion of one respondent to the *Illustrated Milliner*'s survey: "Marriage is truly a leap in the dark."[57] Equally conspicuous was John Forgeot's insistent meddling in his wife's commercial affairs. Despite his lack of business ability, he seems to have assumed that his position as male head of household gave him the right—perhaps even the responsibility—to oversee the workings of Maria's concern. Female entrepreneurs who married gained capital and—sometimes—economic security, but they often lost a significant degree of control over their enterprises. At times, this meant not merely diminished personal autonomy but economic calamity.[58]

At best, married women continued to do business without their spouses' intervention. At worst, male intervention dissolved women's hard won gains. Alternatively, wives might serve as mere figureheads, "fronts," for male-owned and male-operated concerns. Mrs. M. M. Rogers, listed in business directories as the proprietor of a hat shop, was not an independent businesswoman at all; she was "the wife of W. Hosken Rogers who does business in her name." When Leonard P. Marvin's millinery business failed, he placed his two stores in his wife's name, thereby protecting his property from creditors. Several man milliners followed his example.[59] Their wives were hardly ladies of leisure; all worked in the shops that bore their names. But control ultimately rested in the hands of their husbands. Dun & Co. correspondents acknowledged Nancy Beals's skill as a milliner but recognized that Levi Beals dealt with creditors, often dispensing payments in the form of "solid silver turned out of a stocking leg."[60]

Other arrangements, such as the one devised by James and Margaret Grace, granted women greater autonomy, suggesting that marriage and millinery need not necessarily work at cross-purposes. Margaret Costello was the proprietor of a hat shop for four years (first with a female partner, later on her own) before she married James J. Grace at the age of twenty-eight. As an unmarried woman in business she enjoyed unusual success. Assistance

from family members contributed to her prosperity; in 1868, two years before her marriage, a Dun & Co. investigator estimated her worth at $2,000.

Costello's prospective husband was a salesman for a dry goods firm; perhaps a business relationship preceded the romantic one. Business, in any case,
was an integral part of their marriage. James immediately assumed control
of Margaret's shop; as a credit reporter put it, he "married Miss M. A. Costello and has taken her business." Fortunately, James was not a "dead
weight." He was "a close buyer and a good business man" who brought
$8,000–10,000 to his marriage. Moreover, the Graces appear to have fash-
ioned a strikingly egalitarian relationship in matters of money, and perhaps
in matters of love. Six years after their marriage the couple owned two stores,
one run by Margaret and one by James. Both prospered; together the Graces represented "probably the most lucrative in their line in the city." Each
was a good credit risk; indeed, Margaret paid her bills more promptly than
her husband. Apparently, she enjoyed considerable independence, for a Dun
& Co. correspondent remarked that she "keeps her business entirely separate from her husband's and owns and manages by herself."[61]

For Margaret Costello, matrimony proved economically advantageous,
to say the least. In 1878, the couple's combined assets were estimated at
$50,000. They were the proud owners of a fashionable estate, and their
household included a domestic servant, a convenience few milliners could
afford. Margaret could never have attained such wealth on her own. In fact,
millinery was only partially responsible for the Graces' affluence; James had
probably made "most of his money" in "outside transactions."[62]

The case of Mrs. W. B. Crocker strikes a balance between the disastrous
experience of Maria Forgeot and the enviable career of Margaret Costello
Grace. Unlike James Grace, W. B. Crocker was a stranger to the millinery
trade. Nevertheless, he was intimately involved in the affairs of his wife's
bonnet-making concern. Variously identified as bookkeeper, manager, and
secretary of the Globe Nail Company, he furnished the capital for her business, amounting to something between $1,000 and $2,000. That sum was
crucial to Mrs. Crocker's success. It allowed her to keep shop at the expensive Temple Place, a location bound to excite the envy of her competitors.
Unlike many of them, she always paid her bills on time and her credit was
"in excellent standing." Her business lasted for nineteen years.[63]

While marriage gave her access to greater resources than she could have
amassed on her own, Crocker apparently exercised only limited power over
her business affairs. Although two credit investigators agreed that she pos-

sessed "a good practical knowledge of the business," her husband doubted her abilities. On February 1, 1883, a Dun & Co. correspondent reported: "Mr. Crocker calls and says his wife has not filed a certificate to do business in her own name . . . and he will manage the finances." Three years later the situation had changed. "Mr. Crocker states that his wife has now filed a certificate to do business in her own name and that he has no interest in the business, except to advise in matters of finance." What provoked this shift? Did Mrs. Crocker demand greater independence? Was Mr. Crocker embarrassed to be a man milliner? Did he place the business in his wife's name to elude potential creditors? We do not know; the Crockers left no other record. But there is good reason to place greater emphasis on the third alternative. Under Massachusetts law, if a married woman failed to file a certificate to do business in her own name, her husband was responsible for her debts.[64] For Mr. Crocker, pecuniary motives may very well have triumphed over abstract notions of "manliness."

Mrs. W. B. Crocker and Margaret Costello Grace had much in common, but subtle differences marked their careers. Both represented the millinery elite; few of their competitors, married or unmarried, equaled their achievements. Marriage was a necessary prerequisite to success for both women. Yet their experiences diverged in a crucial respect: Grace evidently exercised complete control over the affairs of her store, while Crocker did not.

According to the law books, Grace's experience should have been typical; neither the debilitating interventions suffered by Maria Forgeot nor the more subtle tyranny endured by Mrs. Crocker should have been allowed. But married women's property laws presented little if any challenge to the business arrangements devised by husbands and wives. In legal terms, Massachusetts women were particularly fortunate. A comprehensive statute passed in 1855 granted married women the right to engage in business independently of their husbands and guaranteed them complete control over their earnings.[65] But as several historians have noted, such innovations often worked to men's advantage.[66] The most common example, documented many times in the Dun & Co. records, was the husband who placed his property or business in his wife's name, not as a demonstration of his commitment to gender equality but as a means of shielding his investments from creditors. In theory, married women's statutes offered significant protection. But a woman's ability to make the most of her lawful rights depended on her capacity to decipher complex legal codes (or the financial means to hire an able lawyer) and her willingness to challenge her husband's authority if necessary.[67]

Indeed, contrary to legal maxims, evidence suggests that Grace represented the exception, Crocker the rule. Certainly, the advice offered by Mrs. C. H. Buell, a Wisconsin businesswoman who responded to the *Illustrated Milliner*'s questionnaire, indicates that the Crockers' relationship was far from unique: "I find that if I do the buying, selling and managing of the workroom, I have my hands more than full. My husband keeps the stock in shape, attends to the correspondence and manages the financial part of the business."[68] Several Boston couples embraced comparable divisions of labor, or—in the case of millinery—forged relationships in which husbands (either as merchants or as clerks) operated as wholesalers, wives as retailers.[69]

However beneficial the arrangement or happy the marriage, such alliances assigned women to subordinate social, economic, and commercial positions. Whenever millinery marriages linked wholesaling with retailing, husbands represented the former, wives the latter. Sexual divisions of labor within individual firms, while invariably distinct, were scarcely equal. As Stuart M. Blumin has demonstrated, nonmanual labor—work performed by bookkeepers, clerks, and retail merchants—gained increasing respectability during the course of the nineteenth century, further discrediting the already lowly status of manual work.[70] Acting effectively as managers, husbands administered "the financial part of the business," relegating wives—who *made* dresses and hats or supervised the workingwomen who did—to the status of forewomen or employees. Not only did husbands hold the economic upper hand, they performed work accorded a higher social value. Denied both the formal education and the informal training that male clerks took for granted, women might have been grateful for male assistance. Nevertheless, the typical husband/wife partnership was a microcosm of the larger commercial world, where inequalities of gender meshed neatly with unequal relationships between wholesaler and retailer, white-collar worker and manual laborer.

Even when husbands refrained from meddling in their wives' business affairs, their very existence affected, for better or worse, their spouses' access to both capital and credit. In 1856, Mrs. T. M. Bailey, a widowed milliner, married Mr. Johnson. Matrimony clearly worked in Mrs. Johnson's favor, for a short time later she had "taken a new and elegant store." That move in turn "brought her an increased and better class of trade," and "her credit somewhat improved." Rosa Downing represented the other side of the coin. One of a tiny number of African American businesswomen in the city, she did a small but sound millinery business until her marriage dissolved. A Dun &

Co. credit reporter noted that "her husband has left her and she has not been so prompt this season." "Not a very desirable risk," he concluded.[71]

As these examples suggest, Dun & Co. correspondents seldom failed to investigate the characters, occupations, and assets of husbands, reflecting some of the subtle ways in which concerns of gender affected seemingly mundane matters of credit and commerce. While experts expressed their general preference for married businessmen—crediting them with "a greater degree of stability" than their single counterparts—investigators cast a suspicious eye on married businesswomen. Reporters' judgments of tradewomen's spouses no doubt reflected their notions of proper gender roles; very likely, as Sarah Deutsch suggests, they believed that women should not "support" men.[72] At the same time, "worthless" husbands often justified the appellations applied to them. In any case, these assessments were clearly significant, for wholesalers who consulted the ledgers of R. G. Dun & Co. were privy to the same information. In an era when character and credit were closely intertwined, such disclosures had consequences above and beyond any particular recommendations. Regardless of a correspondent's final pronouncement, a dealer in dry goods or millinery supplies might look kindly upon the wife of a "worthy man." Conversely, he might be reluctant to extend credit to the spouse of a "poor tool" or of one who was "not much of a help."[73]

Although some tradeswomen quite justifiably viewed matrimony with suspicion, we know little about the day-to-day experiences of those who chose to marry. One thing is certain: whatever the role played by romance, these unions were economic relationships. In some instances, businesswomen's marriages were clearly more equal than others; the lives of women like Sarah Carter Vaughan and Margaret Costello Grace indicate that women's economic endeavors had the potential to alter the domestic balance of power. But the evidence suggests that the seemingly unconventional combination of business and matrimony rarely transformed gender roles, although at times it may have granted women extra leverage. If proprietorship allowed single tradeswomen to step outside the boundaries of the family economy, custom and law (in practice, not theory) often reaffirmed married businesswomen's place within it. Despite the possibilities they offered, the fashion trades all too often presented their adherents with an unenviable dilemma: a precarious independence or marriage—as risky a business as business itself.

* * *

The small businessman, long a symbol of independence and autonomy, holds an important place in American culture. The small business*woman* has not similarly captured the national imagination. That disparity is hardly surprising, given the near universal equation of women with dependence on the one hand and the popular association of entrepreneurial ambition with masculine vigor on the other.[74] But in a tiny corner of an intensely gendered commercial world, women held sway. If their individual businesses were often ephemeral, their collective importance was by no means marginal to nineteenth-century urban economies.

Of course, images bear a complicated relation to reality. Historians aware of the extraordinarily high failure rate of small businesses are puzzled by the continuing appeal of becoming one's own boss. But if men seldom attained the independence and economic security promised by self-employment, the benefits of entrepreneurship proved even more elusive for women. Even when they congregated in "feminine" pursuits, they were uniquely handicapped—victims of limited capital and limited credit. These drawbacks notwithstanding, dressmaking and millinery attracted the entrepreneurial energies of thousands of American women in the late nineteenth and early twentieth centuries. How should this fact be interpreted? Let us return briefly to Helen Harkness, the heroine of Howells's *Woman's Reason*. Harkness suggests one pattern: she consciously defies social convention when she *chooses* to support herself.

Few of her real-life counterparts could afford the luxury of such a decision. The vast majority were not crusaders bent on righting women's wrongs. Neither did they have much in common with the contemporaneous "new woman," a model derived from the educational gains, organizational activities, and career achievements of some upper-middle-class women; most Madames worked out of economic necessity.[75] At the same time, new women held no monopoly on ambition. However important the part played by financial need, wage earners who aspired to proprietary status were ambitious by definition. However inchoate their motivations, their very existence presented a challenge to contemporary definitions of "woman's place," for they refused to be defined by assumptions of female dependency.

In nineteenth-century America, as before and since, women's lives were in large part defined by economic dependence on men. Seen in this light, the proprietors of successful millinery and dressmaking businesses (albeit a small and select group) attained an enviable degree of independence, for their profits freed them, however unwillingly, from reliance on male support.

Whether or not they consciously recognized it—and some clearly did—
marriage had a special significance for these women. As the editors of the
Illustrated Milliner implied, matrimony meant different things to businessmen
and businesswomen: "Most men look upon marriage not as an escape from
work, but rather as a stimulus to still greater endeavor. What does the successful business woman think about this same matter?"[76] The female operators of marginal and unsuccessful concerns may have been eager to "escape
from work," and certainly men have been known to marry for money. But
while marriage offered pecuniary benefits to men and women alike, businesswomen (unlike businessmen) almost invariably lost control over their enterprises as a result of matrimony. More often than not, women's entrepreneurial
undertakings failed to overcome the unequal gender relations culturally
embedded in most nineteenth-century marriages.

Most of the proprietors of Boston's millinery and dressmaking shops were
single and therefore independent women. Their endeavors offered a solution
to the problem of female economic dependence and provided examples that
middle-class commentators—wisely or not—encouraged their readers to
emulate.[77] All too often, tradeswomen found such solutions wanting. The
typical shop was a temporary, precarious venture. It was also an enterprise
that rested on a base of exploitation.

Three

The Female Aristocracy of Labor: Workers in the Trades, 1860–1917

On August 27, 1837, Mary Ann Laughton of Boston, Massachusetts, recorded in her diary: "Went to see a lady about learning my trade." This is hardly the sort of statement we expect from nineteenth-century women workers, often portrayed as unskilled, poorly paid toilers for whom wage labor represented nothing more than a way station on the road to marriage. But Laughton's assertion—"learning *my* trade"—suggests purposeful dedication to her chosen pursuit.[1]

Recent scholarship has begun to shatter the traditional historiographical mold. While recognizing the considerable disadvantages under which women labored, historians are constructing a more complex—and ultimately less pessimistic—account that allows for ambition, dedication to vocation, and the possibility of life outside the confines of the working-class family. Scholars such as Susan Porter Benson, Carole Turbin, and Mary Blewett have demonstrated that women workers might derive a good deal of satisfaction from their jobs and that work was neither unskilled nor temporary for some female wage earners.[2]

Laughton no doubt would have agreed. As a dressmaker, a custom producer of women's clothing, she had reason to devote herself to her calling. Whether Laughton realized her hopes is unknown; two years after voicing her ambitions, she disappeared from Boston records. But the fashion trades continued to offer significant attractions into the twentieth century. For Laughton and her successors benefited from a peculiar contradiction in the nineteenth-century sexual divisions of labor. More often than not, sex segregation has been the bane of working women's existence, confining them to poorly paid jobs with few prospects for advancement. But the firmly entrenched belief that the making of feminine fashion was an "essentially feminine" pursuit defined dress- and hatmaking, crafts that required considerable skill and training, as largely female terrain. The near-absence of men left women in charge: the lowly apprentice who worked for nothing, the experienced veteran who commanded good wages, even the shop's proprietor were likely to be female. One observer noted: "Workers work with women, for women, and do not have to face the competition of men."[3]

This chapter examines the experiences of those women who worked for women, the wage laborers who formed the backbone of the millinery and dressmaking trades. While the chapter focuses on the period 1860–1900, it also makes use of a rich body of studies undertaken in the 1910s. The labor economists May Allinson, Lorinda Perry, Edna Bryner, and Mary Van Kleeck completed their investigations at a moment of transition, when ready-made dresses and factory hats threatened to eclipse earlier methods of production. But continuity as well as change characterized the trades, and twentieth-century investigators encountered practices and conditions that had changed little over the course of sixty years.[4]

Taken together, these sources tell a complex story that includes failures and successes, obstacles and opportunities. For millinery and dressmaking exemplified both the possibilities *and* the constraints that shaped working-class women's lives in nineteenth- and early twentieth-century America. The custom manufacture of feminine apparel offered advantages that few women's occupations could match: relatively high wages, chances for advancement, and privileged status within the female working class (a status, to be sure, that was reinforced by race and ethnicity as well as by occupational identity). These benefits were not available to all. Dressmaking and millinery were predominantly the domain of two overlapping groups: white women of native birth, and women whose families could afford to support them while they labored as unpaid or barely compensated apprentices. Like most female wage earners, custom clothiers encountered conditions that left much to be desired. Even in this female territory, making one's way from the lowest to the highest echelons was never easy. Success usually came at considerable cost.

Indeed, aspiring craftswomen confronted a division of labor that simultaneously promised economic independence and reinforced dependence; although they occupied some of the most privileged positions within a sex-segregated labor market, they toiled in crafts that were also hierarchically segmented. Obscured by the pronouncements of nineteenth-century reformers—who were more interested in arousing public sentiment than in accurately portraying workroom life—the workings of this dual labor system are not always easy to discern. Nonetheless, it is clear that each shop, no matter how small, relied on two labor forces: one highly skilled, amply compensated, and relatively permanent; the other less skilled, poorly paid, and temporary. While it was by no means impossible for ambitious women to climb from the bottom tier to the top—indeed, millinery and dressmaking were distinctive for the upward mobility they offered—the organizational structure of the trades created divisions that employers easily exploited.

The situation of the dressmaker or milliner was far from ideal. But in a world that offered working-class women few alternatives, May Allinson's enthusiastic recommendation was not unwarranted: "Custom dressmaking and millinery . . . show opportunities for self-development and financial advancement discovered in few other industries open to the woman of limited education."[5] Millinery and dressmaking did not "liberate" women, but they provided a space in which their ambitions might flourish.

Age and Ethnicity

In 1870, an uncommonly meticulous Boston census taker recorded 35-year-old Sophrania Johnson's occupation as "works for dressmaker" (much to historians' chagrin, enumerators usually failed to distinguish between proprietors and employees, regardless of trade). Yet according to conventional wisdom, the typical female wage earner was a woman in her late teens or early twenties. Trapped in a low-paying, dead-end job, she left the labor force at the earliest opportunity. Wage earning was a disheartening, demoralizing experience that made marriage look all the more attractive.[6]

At first glance, dressmakers and milliners conform to this standard account. Most were young: women between the ages of sixteen and twenty-four made up the single largest category in 1900 (Table 8). But while Sophrania Johnson may not have been typical, neither was she an anomaly. A quarter of all dressmaking and millinery workers in Boston in 1860, and a third in 1870, were over age thirty. Forty-six years later in 1916, the social investigator Edna Bryner noted matter-of-factly that more than a fifth of Cleveland dressmakers were over age forty-five.[7]

In this respect custom clothiers were not unique. As historians are beginning to recognize, the term "working girl" reflected not an accurate assessment of biological age but a cultural convention that—in a society that equated marriage with maturity—condemned unmarried women to "perpetual girlhood."[8] Contrary to popular terminology, nearly a third of all female wage earners in 1900 were thirty-five or older (Table 8). These women, when they are observed at all, are portrayed as pitiful figures. Wage work, it seems, was the last resort for destitute widows, impoverished spinsters, and aban-

Table 8. Percentage of Women Wage Earners by Age Groupings in Selected Occupations, 1900

	16–24	25–34	35–44	45+
Cigar makers	63.8	20.6	9.8	5.7
Stenographers and typists	63.2	30.5	5.1	1.0
Saleswomen	62.3	26.6	7.7	3.2
Confectioners	61.7	16.6	10.6	11.0
Cotton mill operatives	61.7	22.4	10.3	5.4
Printers	60.3	28.3	7.6	3.7
Clerks and copyists	59.3	26.8	8.7	4.9
Woolen mill operatives	59.0	25.0	10.4	5.4
Hat and cap makers	55.6	26.0	11.3	7.0
Shoe workers	54.3	27.1	12.5	6.0
Servants and waitresses	53.4	24.0	11.0	11.2
Tailoresses	52.6	23.0	13.2	11.0
Milliners	49.4	27.8	13.0	9.6
Teachers	46.4	34.8	11.7	6.7
Seamstresses	42.7	25.4	15.6	16.0
Dressmakers	32.6	30.6	20.9	15.8
All occupations recorded in 1900 census	44.2	24.2	14.0	17.3

Note: This table includes proprietors as well as employees (census reports did not distinguish between the two).

Source: USBC, *Statistics of Women at Work*, 36.

doned wives. For some groups, such as seamstresses, this interpretation makes a good deal of sense. But recent scholarship has demonstrated that significant minorities of wage-earning women—shoe workers, collar workers, and saleswomen, for example—labored in occupations in which age, experience, and dedication were rewarded.[9]

Nowhere was this more true than in dressmaking and millinery. Each trade had its own hierarchy. After completing their apprenticeships, aspiring milliners advanced from makers, the workers who fashioned hat shapes or "foundations," to trimmers, the "artists" who adorned unfinished shapes with varying combinations of feathers, flowers, ribbons, and lace. Dressmakers, too, began their careers as apprentices, usually assigned such menial tasks as sewing long, straight seams and running errands. Accomplished modistes became finishers, mistresses of fine needlework, then fitters (sometimes called cutters), workers who cut garment pieces from the cloth. Once they had mastered their trades, successful workingwomen often embarked on businesses of their own.

Seen in this light, women like Sophrania Johnson, the 35-year old dressmaker, and Annette Chamberlain, a 42-year-old milliner, were not necessarily downtrodden toilers forced to reenter the labor market at an advanced age. On the contrary, they had probably labored many years at their callings; very likely they possessed considerable skill, commanded substantial authority, and earned relatively high wages—at least by female standards.

Of course, the meticulous census taker who noted that Johnson worked for a dressmaker and that Chamberlain worked for a milliner could have been more meticulous, for he failed to record craftswomen's precise occupational standings. His shortcomings reveal a common deficiency in nineteenth-century sources. Like many of his contemporaries—committed to a vision that saw all wage-earning women as members of a uniformly downtrodden group—he probably saw little reason to investigate his subjects further. Yet labels such as "milliner" or even "works for milliner" mask distinctions that mattered a good deal to workers themselves. We do not know, for example, whether Chamberlain was a trimmer, a maker, or an aging apprentice. But we have good reason to reject the third possibility in favor of the first. While few descriptions of nineteenth-century workplaces have survived, early twentieth-century observers found that older workers monopolized the most desirable positions and reaped the highest rewards. Lorinda Perry noted "a striking difference" between the ages of makers and trimmers: at least half of the makers, but less than a tenth of the trimmers, were under age twenty-one (Table 9). Unlike the stereotypical female wage earner, the custom cloth-ier had reason to stay at her job.[10]

Milliners tended to be younger than their dressmaking sisters because millinery careers required greater investments of capital (custom dictated that hatmakers, unlike dressmakers, keep stock)—however insignificant to modern eyes—and because seasonal unemployment wreaked greater hav-oc on their trade. Their relative youth suggests that they were more likely to leave millinery for alternative employments or marriage. Nevertheless, both trades—even the relatively youthful domain of bonnet making—com-manded the loyalty of significant numbers of "older" women (Tables 8–10). More than a third of the dressmakers and about a sixth of the milliners in Gilded Age Boston were age thirty or older. In 1913, 9 percent of Boston milliners and 8 percent of those in Philadelphia were at least age thirty-five. Success was neither instantaneous nor assured, but age and persistence were often rewarded.[11]

This is not to say that initiative and tenacity were sufficient in themselves. Race and ethnicity did much to determine craft membership. "Milliners en-gaged in custom work, like dressmakers," one analyst noted, "have always been aristocrats among the clothing makers."[12] But "aristocracy" was not

Table 9. Custom Millinery Workers under Age Twenty-one, 1913

	Percentage of Total	Total Surveyed
Boston		
All milliners	47.4	114
Apprentices	100.0	6
Makers	56.1	82
Trimmers	7.7	26
Philadelphia		
All milliners	41.6	120
Apprentices	100.0	9
Makers	50.0	80
Trimmers	3.2	31

Source: Perry, *Millinery Trade,* 96.

Table 10. Average Age of Women Wage Earners in Selected Occupations, Boston, 1880

	Average Age (Years)	Number Surveyed
Boot and shoe workers	20.08	26
Paper box makers	21.50	32
Textile operatives	21.85	12
Tobacco workers	22.36	11
Saleswomen	22.56	17
Printers	23.43	28
Bookbinders	24.13	29
Milliners	24.73	15
Tailoresses	26.19	72
Dressmakers, employees	26.48	62
Seamstresses	28.04	36
Dressmakers, self-employed	30.59	38
Carpet sewers	39.50	12
All occupations surveyed	24.81	1,032

Source: Wright, *Working Girls,* 39–40.

available to all. Throughout the nineteenth and into the twentieth century, dressmaking and millinery were occupations in which native-born white women (at least outside the South) were the overwhelming majority (Tables 11–14). Much scholarly literature has depicted women as victims of segmented labor markets, and certainly women's occupational choices were limited at best. Yet women themselves helped to shape the sexual division of labor by barring men from their workrooms and by actively seeking to preserve the fashion trades as female terrain.[13] As employers, workers, and consumers, they also maintained racial and ethnic boundaries, by refusing to hire, stitch beside, or patronize those who failed to qualify as "genteel" working-women.

Of course, "native born" meant different things in 1860 and 1900. As opportunities for advancement within the trades declined and as the attractions of clerical work (even more likely than the skilled needle trades to be dominated by women of native birth) increased, the daughters of immigrants

Table 11. Percentage of Milliners, Dressmakers, and Mantua Makers Born in the
United States, 1870

	Percentage of Total	Total Surveyed[a]
United States	78.7	90,480
New York City	52.6	9,747
Boston	68.9	1,737
Worcester, Mass.	89.2	445
Philadelphia	76.7	5,556
Cleveland	61.2	393
Chicago	52.7	1,924

a. Includes men as well as women and proprietors
as well as nonproprietors (published census figures do
not distinguish between the two).
Source: USBC, *Statistics of the Population . . . Ninth
Census*, 712–13, 778, 782, 793–94, 804.

made up an ever-growing portion of dressmakers and milliners (Table 12).
As early as 1860, at least a quarter of Boston craftswomen were second-generation immigrants, most of them Irish. Forty years later, more than a third
of all milliners and dressmakers had foreign-born parents; in urban areas they
outnumbered "American" women within the trades (Table 13). Yet in this
respect the trades had become only slightly more accommodating, for custom dressmaking and millinery rarely welcomed women from "new immigrant" families (Table 14).[14]

There was one exception to the rule of Yankee (and in later years, Irish)
dominance: no group possessed greater advantages than immigrants from
the fountainhead of fashion. Women from France constituted only a tiny
segment of America's milliners and dressmakers, but they exerted an influence far out of proportion to their numbers. "We were told that the French
are born with a knowledge of millinery and that an American can never equal
them," Mary Van Kleeck noted in 1917. Amelia Des Moulins, herself a dressmaker from France, made essentially the same point: "All the world knows
that we French have the true artistic taste, and we show it most in our
dress. . . . Those other people do not understand, they cannot comprehend,

Table 12. Race and Ethnicity of Women Wage Earners in Selected Occupations, by Percentage, 1900

	Native White, Native Parents	Native White, Foreign-born Parents	Foreign-born, White	African American, Asian, Native American
Teachers	63.5	27.0	5.3	4.2
Printers	55.1	37.1	7.2	0.6
Milliners	54.5	34.7	10.6	0.2
Stenographers and typists	53.3	39.6	6.9	0.2
Clerks and copyists	50.6	39.6	9.1	0.7
Dressmakers	45.2	34.7	16.4	3.7
Seamstresses	43.4	30.2	18.1	8.3
Saleswomen	42.3	45.6	11.9	0.3
Shoe workers	40.3	45.2	· 14.3	0.2
Cotton mill operatives	36.1	20.9	42.7	0.3
Hat and cap makers	35.3	42.4	22.3	0.0
Cigar makers	34.3	27.0	26.1	12.5
Confectioners	29.7	45.2	24.3	0.9
Servants and waitresses	26.2	19.2	27.6	27.0
Woolen mill operatives	25.0	41.9	32.8	0.3
Tailoresses	22.9	38.4	38.1	0.7
Laundresses	12.7	8.7	13.0	65.6
All occupations recorded in 1900 census	36.7	22.6	17.4	23.4

Source: USBC, *Statistics of Women at Work*, 34.

it is impossible to convey to them the conception of true harmony. It is like trying to teach the blind about light."[15] Des Moulins's skill was in fact as much the result of training as "instinct"; she had several years' experience in a Parisian dressmaking shop before coming to America. Her expertise was amply rewarded. In 1904, after several years in New York, she was earning

Table 13. Race and Ethnicity of Dressmakers and Milliners, Urban versus Rural, by Percentage, 1900

	Native White, Native Parents	Foreign-born Parents	Foreign-born, White	African American, Asian, Native American
Dressmakers				
Cities 50,000+	28.6	41.0	25.6	4.8
< 50,000	58.3	29.7	9.2	2.8
Milliners				
Cities 50,000+	35.3	47.0	17.3	0.3
< 50,000+	66.2	27.1	6.5	0.2

Source: USBC, *Statistics of Women at Work,* 71, 76.

nearly forty dollars a week, seven or eight times what the average working-woman could expect.[16]

Des Moulins's experience, while hardly typical, demonstrates that the potential benefits of skilled needlework were considerable. Of course, the contest was far from fair; women of "American" and French descent stood a better chance than recent—non-French—immigrants or women of color. Ethnicity and race were not the only factors that separated dressmakers and milliners from their sister toilers. Custom clothiers often depended on the support and encouragement of their families.[17]

Motives: Family and Independence

Why did women enter the trades? The first answer is simple: they needed the money. Few dressmakers and milliners could afford the luxury of leisure; the Boston manuscript censuses of 1860 and 1870 reveal self-supporting boarders, mechanics' and laborers' daughters, and an occasional widow or tradesman's wife. By every indication, children and spouses of the well-to-do contributed relatively few women to the female aristocracy of labor. Women like Mary Murphy, a grocer's daughter, were rare; women like Jennie Boston, the daughter of a prosperous provisions dealer, rarer still.[18]

Even so, the need to work encompassed a wide variety of circumstances.

Table 14. Ethnic Origins of Women Wage Earners, by Percentage, 1900

	Dressmakers	Milliners	All Women Wage Earners
Native parents (total)	48.3	53.9	61.1
White	44.8	53.7	36.2
African American, Asian, and Native American	3.5	0.2	24.8
First- and second-generation immigrants (total)	51.7	46.1	38.9
Total	100.0	100.0	100.0
First- and second-generation immigrants			
Canada	7.9	9.2	8.7
Great Britain	10.5	12.3	9.9
Ireland	30.6	25.0	30.6
Germany	27.8	30.8	25.9
France	1.5	1.4	1.0
Scandinavia	6.5	4.9	7.0
Italy	1.4	0.5	1.3
Poland	1.0	0.9	1.9
Russia	1.7	2.7	2.0
Other countries	4.7	4.5	6.2
Mixed foreign parentage	6.4	7.7	5.4
Total	100.0	100.0	100.0

Source: USBC, *Statistics of Women at Work*, 71, 76–77.

As Carole Turbin has so skillfully demonstrated, women's wages carried very different meanings in different types of families.[19] Mary Gallagher, a nineteen-year-old milliner, lived with her widowed mother, an immigrant from Ireland. The family owned no property. The twenty-six-year-old Rebecca F. Jackson, a dressmaker, found herself in much the same predicament, even though both she and her mother, a servant, had been born in Massachusetts. The thirty-year-old Charlotte Chase lived in a boarding house; it appears that apart from her earnings she was penniless. Others were more fortunate. Margaret Lee had emigrated from Ireland with her family. Her father, a blacksmith, was worth $200. Catherine Fitzgerald's father, although a mere laborer, was even wealthier; he reported real estate worth $2,000 and personal property valued at $100. The nineteen-year-old Lavinia Titus, daughter of a Vermont-born mason who owned property valued at $17,000, must have inspired the envy of her coworkers.[20]

The motivations of these women ranged from earning "pin money" to maintaining a bare level of subsistence. The scales tilted toward subsistence needs more often than the former; few could afford to eschew wage work entirely, and family fortunes depended in part on sons' and daughters' earnings. Fitzgerald and even Titus may very well have contributed to their fathers' prosperity.

Twentieth-century social investigators noted a similar degree of diversity. New York milliners, Van Kleeck remarked in 1917, were hardly "a homogeneous group." She found a self-supporting craftswoman "with earnings large enough to be subject to the income tax," another who labored to support "her sick mother and herself," "a married woman whose husband owned two houses and a saloon," who worked "because she was lonely at home," and "two or three instances of 'pin-money workers.'" Van Kleeck described the circumstances of one family as "far more typical": "The father was a mechanic and the three daughters, one a dressmaker, one a milliner, and one in a novelty factory, were all at work. . . . They are all alert and ambitious, and it is in no dilettante spirit but in down-right earnestness that the girls are doing their share to maintain the family standard."[21] Another family, "equally typical," was "much less cheerful." The father, a tailor, was "old and cannot work much." The earnings of the milliner and her brother, who worked in a clothing store, furnished necessities instead of luxuries. Allinson painted a similar portrait of Massachusetts dressmakers. Fathers' occupations ranged "from the laborer to the professional man," she wrote, "but the family income in the majority of cases is not large."[22]

While milliners and dressmakers were firmly rooted in the working classes, they did not necessarily represent the most impoverished segments of the population. Instead, their origins reveal subtle but important differences within a heterogeneous working class. More than 40 percent of the fathers of Boston tradeswomen in 1860 and 1870 were skilled workers, compared to only 36 percent in the general population; another 9–12 percent were petty proprietors and clerks; 3 percent were merchants and professionals. Daughters of unskilled laborers accounted for a substantial portion (38–40 percent), but they were not the majority (Table 15). Twentieth-century tradeswom-

Table 15. Social Origins of Boston Dressmaking and
Millinery Workers, 1860–70

Father's Occupation	1860		1870[a]	
	N	%	N	%
High white collar	10	2.6	4	2.8
Low white collar	46	11.9	12	8.5
Skilled	156	40.5	61	43.0
Unskilled	153	39.7	54	38.0
Unemployed	20	5.2	11	7.7
	385	99.9	142	100.0

Note: These figures are only for women who lived in two-parent families; 385 of 1,477 fell into this category in 1860; 142 of 790 in 1870. I classified substantial proprietors (merchants and wholesale dealers) and professionals such as physicians and attorneys as high white collar; clerical occupations (such as clerk, bookkeeper, and salesman) and petty proprietors (such as grocers and saloon keepers) as low white collar. I defined manual occupations that required some training (such as carpenter, mason, printer, and shoemaker) as skilled; manual jobs that required little training (such as day laborer, gardener, and teamster) as unskilled. See Hershberg et al., "Occupation and Ethnicity," 175–87, for a useful classification scheme.

a. Results based on 45 percent sample.

Sources: 1860 FMPC, M653, reels 520–25; 1870, M593, reels 640–49.

en, more likely to be daughters of immigrants, were probably poorer than their predecessors. But they too constituted a wage-earning elite. The dressmakers of Worcester, Massachusetts, Allinson noted, were "from distinctively a higher social stratum" than factory workers.[23]

Given the predominance of native-born women, it is not surprising that dressmakers and milliners were a "cut above" factory workers. At the same time, the peculiar requirements of the trades created often insurmountable barriers for the truly destitute. Nineteenth-century apprentices spent three months to two years (six months seems to have been the usual term by the 1850s) learning their trades, often without pay. Sometimes they even paid for the privilege; in rare instances the age-old practice of requiring apprentices to post a "premium" survived into the late nineteenth century. Whether or not they forfeited a premium, the parents of apprentices had to be willing to do without the immediate income their daughters could earn in a variety of less prestigious occupations. This was a strategy that only the reasonably well-off could afford.[24]

While it is possible to generalize about workers who lived with their families, assessing the hopes and fears of boarders is a more hazardous task. As Mary Blewett has noted, historians—committed to viewing wage-earning women as "appendages of their families"—have ignored or overlooked significant numbers of self-supporting female lodgers.[25] During the nineteenth century, "women adrift" formed no small part of the millinery and dressmaking population. In 1860, for example, nearly half (49 percent) of Boston's tradeswomen lived in lodging houses or boarded with local families. Nearly 80 percent of these women were native born; the others were immigrants, many of them Irish. While we can easily surmise that Irish newcomers who found themselves "adrift" were among the very poorest dressmakers and milliners, the social origins of native-born lodgers are more difficult to determine. Many who fell into the latter category (25 percent at the very least) had come from Maine, New Hampshire, Vermont, and western Massachusetts, part of a wider stream of female migrants who abandoned the farms and small towns of New England for the workrooms and factories of Boston, Worcester, Lawrence, and Lowell.[26]

We do not know what situations these women left behind. Historians argue over whether migration stemmed from economic desperation or "purposeful choice," and it may be that the terms of the debate pose too stark a distinction between motives that were less than mutually exclusive. Whether they left propertied households—confident that they could return to their rural homes in times of need—or desperately poor parents eager to be rid of an extra mouth to feed, one thing is certain: in an era of declining household production, female migrants left rural areas and small towns that offered few opportunities, if not families who could ill afford to support them. Both "push" and "pull" factors were undoubtedly at work. To young women like New Hampshire–born Lucinda Nash, Boston must have promised opportunity and adventure.[27]

How Nash and her sister migrants managed to subsist once they arrived in the city is equally uncertain, and here, perhaps, the workings of the trades' two-tiered labor system can be discerned. Boarders tended to be older than home dwellers; they may have been experienced workers—trimmers or fitters—who had learned their trades elsewhere and who commanded relatively high wages.[28] Some, like forty-year-old Hattie Jellison, a dressmaker from Maine, accumulated property worth a few hundred dollars. But according to the census takers' notations, more than 90 percent were penniless. To be sure, blank entries masked a variety of standards; propertyless tradeswomen were not necessarily destitute, for enumerators failed to record miniscule amounts of real or personal estate. At best, boarders enjoyed a comfortable subsistence and a degree of social and economic independence; at worst, they barely kept body and soul together.[29]

Some employers served the needs of migratory apprentices (and perhaps those from the poorest local families) by providing room and board. By the mid-nineteenth century, this practice—if it had ever been widespread—was declining. About a fifth of proprietors in Gilded Age Boston housed unrelated workers, but the latter account for a mere 3 percent of boarding dressmakers and milliners. If age is any indication of occupational status, those who resided with Madame were not apprentices but experienced workers, who on average were no younger than the overall boarding population. While evidence suggests that the custom of housing apprentices survived longest in smaller cities, mistress dressmakers, much like master craftsmen, increasingly lived apart from those they employed.[30]

By the turn of the century, novices as well as veterans were much more likely to reside with their families, a circumstance that in all likelihood reduced women's ability to make their "own" occupational decisions. In 1900 only about a sixth of urban dressmakers and a seventh of urban milliners lived on their own, compared to almost half forty years earlier. As Thomas Dublin has demonstrated, this development—not unique to custom clothiers—was closely tied to demographic changes. At mid-century, rural migrants and recent immigrants constituted the majority of female wage earners; by 1900 this distinction belonged to second-generation immigrants. Earlier generations were likely to be boarders because migration entailed separation from their families; American-born daughters of immigrants, because their parents settled in urban areas, did not have to leave home to seek work.[31]

Employers apparently acquiesced in—perhaps even fostered—changing residential patterns. By the early twentieth century the offer of board—already relatively rare in the 1860s—had been replaced by the requirement that apprentices and even relatively experienced workers live at home. One proprietor aptly summarized the situation: "A girl needs the help of her family." And no wonder! While beginners as a rule received wages, their earnings were nominal at best. Workers at one Boston dressmaking shop started at fifty cents a week; millinery apprentices in early twentieth-century Cleveland received weekly wages of one dollar—to be used for carfare—and free hats. Theoretically, by boarding with her employer until she could afford to support herself, the would-be dressmaker or milliner of the nineteenth century could pursue her calling without her parents' consent. This option was not available to her twentieth-century counterpart.[32]

Why were families, few of whom were wealthy, willing to sacrifice immediate income for future earnings? Twentieth-century social investigators offer some insight into their motivations. Working-class parents evidently believed that dressmaking and millinery, like clerical work, represented what Ileen DeVault has termed "conspicuous employment." As Allinson observed, the trades conveyed "a certain prestige. Parents . . . frequently determine for the girl that she shall be a dressmaker just as those of a higher social level decide the daughter shall become a teacher, because it is the 'genteel' thing to do."[33]

Although some parents undoubtedly hoped that dressmaking and millinery would enhance their daughters' prestige and, perhaps implicitly, improve their marriage prospects, others had different purposes in mind. These, Allinson acknowledged, were less interested in gentility than in making sure their daughters learned a "good trade." Van Kleeck noted that "the hope of having one's own business some day . . . is something for which we have found the family also willing to make sacrifices."[34] These comments are intriguing in light of prevailing stereotypes about working-class families. According to the standard interpretation, parents—firmly committed to "family wage economies"—saw their daughters' wages as temporary and supplemental though necessary; they saw no reason to waste time and money on training girls who would soon marry anyway. Some mothers and fathers must have thought otherwise. To be sure, parental decisions were influenced, if not driven, by economic considerations. Families must have eagerly anticipated the income that "craftsmanship" and entrepreneurship would yield, concerns that probably gained urgency as male workers found their skills—and their wages—increasingly undermined in the late nineteenth and early twentieth centuries. Like the parents of skilled collar workers described by Carole Turbin, some may have persuaded their daughters to delay, even forgo, marriage in order to reach the highest rungs on the millinery and dressmaking ladders.[35]

Others may have been motivated less by self-interest than by concern for their children's futures; a spinster with a "good trade" was less vulnerable than one with few marketable skills. Skilled needlewomen would be better able than unskilled operatives to provide for widowed mothers. Such considerations were not theoretical. In 1860, 14 percent (184 of 1,348) of Boston milliners and dressmakers lived with widowed mothers; 9 percent of the workers Allinson interviewed were the sole support of their families.[36]

In sum, parents appear to have been surprisingly supportive of female ambition when it complemented family economic strategies. Working-class parents were hardly proto-feminists, bent on promoting their daughters' careers at every available opportunity. Still, the family wage economy may have been more flexible than previously thought; interpretations that stress the conservatism of working-class families may overstate the extent to which parents propelled their daughters toward traditional pathways of marriage and motherhood.[37] Under certain circumstances, parents were willing to do for daughters what they routinely did for sons.

Finally, the fact that many dressmakers and milliners came from artisan families may have reflected fathers' desires to imbue daughters as well as sons with a sense of craft, to provide them with work that had psychological meaning as well as monetary value. For a small number of Boston millinery and dressmaking workers, skilled needlework—not just skilled work—was a family tradition. In 1860, 3 percent of Boston's craftswomen were the daughters of tailors. The dressmakers among them were particularly fortunate; their fathers may very well have taught them skills that their employers, normally denied the privilege of learning tailoring, could not. Female craft traditions played an equally important role. Four percent (20 of 548) of Boston's tradeswomen lived with mothers who were tailoresses, dressmakers, or milliners; if we count only widowed mothers (whose occupations were more likely to be recorded than those of married women), the proportion increases substantially, to 10 percent (19 of 184).[38] To be sure, widows who recruited their daughters into the trades may have been less interested in transmitting craft knowledge than in sheer economic survival. Almedia Blake provided her mother, Ann, with a crucial (and one suspects unremunerated) source of labor. In return Almedia gained both a skill and a legacy; she would eventually take over her mother's business.[39]

This is not to say that parents and children always agreed. Daughters' inclinations toward dressmaking or millinery probably caused many family quarrels. Some parents may have been unwilling to make the necessary economic sacrifices. As fewer and fewer daughters lived away from home, their occupational decisions depended increasingly on parental cooperation. Although women were not entirely free to choose their callings, neither should they be viewed as passive members of indivisible family units.[40] Young women had their own reasons for entering the trades. As Van Kleeck observed, "the hope of having one's own business some day" inspired workers as well as their families.[41]

Indeed, the decision to take up dressmaking or millinery was rarely an act of caprice; on the contrary, it was often the result of careful consideration informed by experience. Many craftswomen had previously been servants, factory operatives, and saleswomen and found these employments wanting; their experiences suggest that women wage earners perceived choices where Victorian observers and subsequent scholars—blinded by the assumption that all women's work was uniformly unrewarding—did not. The reminiscences of an anonymous dressmaker, recorded in the early 1890s, are particularly revealing. At age seventeen she became a clerk in a dry goods store, joining "the great army of shop-girls in New York." Despite her "positively ardent" attitude toward her work, she reached "the end of the financial ladder"—ten dollars a week—in three years. Frustrated with what social scientists would later call "blocked mobility," she left clerking for domestic service, despite misgivings about the social status of her new occupation. When an opportunity to learn dressmaking presented itself, she seized it eagerly, eventually becoming the "partner of the modiste with whom I learned." Six years later, she proudly pronounced herself "independent" and in possession of an "enviable bank account."[42]

Not every story had such a happy ending. Success, as we shall see, was not easily achieved; for many aspiring dressmakers and milliners the obstacles proved overwhelming. The shopgirl-turned-dressmaker made her choice within the very limited universe of female occupations; whatever the benefits of particular types of jobs, women rarely received the same rewards as men. Nonetheless, the trades provided an outlet for female ambition and held out the possibility of economic independence.

Work and Gentility

While the fashion trades offered significant pecuniary advantages to those who pursued them, they also promised less tangible benefits of equal if not greater importance. Not the least was the promise of genteel status. If dressmakers and milliners expected more satisfying future prospects than did

many of their sister wage earners, they also reaped larger psychological rewards. Much to the dismay of the Reverend James Porter, author of *The
Operative's Friend and Defence* (1850), milliners and dressmakers considered
themselves the social superiors of factory workers. "Why she who *works* the
fine fabric should be considered a lady, and she who *makes* . . . *it*, a despica-
ble drudge, is inconceivable," the exasperated clergyman sputtered. We can
easily imagine that this complaint fell upon deaf ears—at least in dressmakers' circles. By every indication, the "aristocrats among the clothing makers" were a proud and haughty lot.

Porter's lament no doubt masks many subtleties and complexities—we do
not know how craftswomen's perceptions of their status varied (for example,
if fitters and trimmers considered themselves to be more "genteel" than their
coworkers) or how these ideas changed over time. Available evidence suggests
considerable agreement and striking continuity; professions of gentility, perhaps not surprising among American-born daughters of relatively prosperous
working-class families, seem to have emanated from apprentices as well as their
"betters" and failed to diminish as the nineteenth century drew to a close. "The
dressmaker's assistant," the reformer Helen Campbell noted in 1900, "look[s]
down upon the factory hand or even the seamstress as of an inferior order."
Throughout the nineteenth century and into the twentieth, dressmakers and
milliners gave three main reasons for their self-proclaimed superiority: they
did not labor in factories, they worked with "fine things," and (since most shops
drew little distinction between "workers" and "saleswomen"), they interact-
ed with "ladies" of the middle and upper classes.[43]

By asserting their genteel status, craftswomen did more than reveal their
snobbery; they also challenged unfavorable assessments of their collective
character and worth. While middle-class moralists cast doubt on the respectability of all female wage earners—women who stood outside the domestic
sphere—they singled out dressmakers and milliners for particular censure,
often linking them to prostitution. This belief was not entirely without foundation; millinery and dressmaking shops, as we have seen, occasionally
served as fronts for brothels. But the identification of the two trades with vice
was more symbolic than real. Dressmakers and milliners manufactured feminine apparel, a commodity that itself was sexually charged. As Valerie Steele
has argued, scholarly characterizations of Victorian clothing as "repressive"
are less than accurate; to the contrary, it "revolved around an ideal of feminine beauty in which eroticism played an important part."[44] This fact ensured
that fashion would remain a controversial subject in nineteenth-century

America. Guilty by association, dressmakers and milliners acquired the ambiguous reputation of their product.

Perhaps more realistically, some observers worried that constant exposure to "fine things" and high society would lead young women to ruin. This conviction had a corollary: any working-class woman who wore fine things must be a prostitute. As the statistician Carroll Wright acknowledged in 1884, "the idea that well dressed girls receiving low wages must live disreputable lives is a very common one." To be sure, few female wage earners rivaled the fashionable attire of millinery and dressmaking workers—except prostitutes. But for modistes, as for prostitutes, dressing well was a requirement of the job; ragged, unkempt workers were unfit to wait upon clients. Moreover, dressmakers and milliners made the most of their skills, transforming remnants donated by their employers—or "extra" fabric unwittingly donated by customers—into stylish garb for themselves. In any case, available evidence fails to confirm reformers' suspicions; women in the fashion trades contributed a relatively small share to the ranks of prostitutes. Finally, middle-class commentators who feared the detrimental effects of fine things may have been less concerned with protecting workingwomen's morality than with preserving precariously established social distinctions.[45]

What middle-class observers saw as evidence of depravity, craftswomen interpreted as badges of honor, symbols of their privileged position as workers and of their respectable status as women. Proud of their skills, their ability to manipulate expensive materials, and their association with the latest in feminine fashion, they regarded themselves and their work not only as quintessentially feminine but as genteel and respectable. The pursuit of gentility was a double-edged sword. It bolstered women's self-esteem and encouraged them to forge an identity based on work rather than home and family, indeed to formulate a notion of respectable womanhood that rejected domesticity. Craftswomen considered themselves "ladies," even if "ladies" disagreed. It also fanned the flames of ambition. This positive self-image no doubt played a crucial role in cementing the aspirations of women who devoted many years to learning their crafts.

Dressmakers' and milliners' snobbery could also work against their own best interests, creating circumstances in which they "consented to oppression." While New England shoe workers successfully parlayed an image of the "lady stitcher" into a basis for labor protest, genteel modistes by and large rejected collective activity, maintaining that unions were for factory operatives. Some craftswomen—especially those who occupied the lower eche-

lons of the trades—endured low beginning wages, overtime, and seasonal
unemployment in exchange for status, a weakness that employers consciously
exploited. As Perry shrewdly noted, "They are willing to accept such social
position as the trade gives them in part payment for services."[46]

While parents and children might agree on the desirability of genteel
occupations, issues of status also created divisions within families by estrang-
ing craftswomen from working-class values and traditions. Allinson's visits
to the homes of Boston dressmakers reveal this aspect: "A ring at the door-
bell of a tumble-down frame house in one of the poorest sections of the city
might be answered by a well-dressed girl with the unquestionable 'air' of one
who comes in contact with people of refinement. She was a fine lady to her
sister who worked in a factory and to the rest of the family, who had not had
her opportunities to see, to imitate, and to develop ease of manner, and good
taste in dress." Allinson failed to recognize the poignancy of this scene, displaying instead her own class-bound assumptions. "The girl from the poor
uncultured home" could only benefit by interacting with "a class of workers superior to that in manufacturing industries" and by "handling beautiful materials." The dressmaking shop furnished more than work: it was a
school that imparted middle-class mores and consumerist values to its willing pupils. In the eyes of the middle-class social investigator, neither "benefit" was open to question.[47]

Of course, this scenario lends itself to several interpretations. Dressmakers and milliners may not necessarily have agreed with Allinson's assessment.
Like a later generation of salesclerks confronted with the bourgeois world
of the department store, some may have accepted and others rejected the
"refining" influences of the custom shop.[48] Some may have seen themselves
not as students but as teachers who both displayed stylish apparel to their own
working-class communities and introduced "ladies" to the latest in feminine
finery. Alternatively, proximity to a world of wealth and luxury—a world
to which most craftswomen had only limited access—may have nurtured a
sense of what Carolyn Steedman has called "the unfairness of things."[49] As
Allinson's impression—perhaps not entirely misguided—suggests, for some
craftswomen becoming a "fine lady" was an end in itself. If gentility enabled
working-class women to fashion an alternative basis for female identity, it
could also encourage them simply to emulate the "ladies" they served.

Within the narrow confines of dressmaking and millinery shops, women
developed myriad and sometimes contradictory conceptions of women's
work and woman's place. Some of these might be labeled as conservative,

others were perhaps every bit as radical as the remedies proposed by nine-teenth- and early twentieth-century feminists, for they implicitly challenged women's dependent status. To be sure, the custom production of feminine fashion appealed to several constituencies; dutiful daughters, ambitious boarders, proud craftswomen, and snobbish social climbers all found reason to enter the trades. But at their best, millinery and dressmaking provided working-class daughters with an avenue to economic independence and a means of fashioning an identity that was—to paraphrase Gerda Lerner— somewhere between the "lady" and the "mill girl."[50] To ascertain whether craftswomen's dreams were realized or whether status was worth the price, we must move out of the home and into the workshop.

Work and Wages

Did parents and children forfeit time, money, and labor in vain? Contradic-tory answers surface as early as the 1830s. The social reformer Mathew Carey included milliners and mantua makers among "certain classes of females, who are decently paid"; the English visitor Harriet Martineau pronounced "the lot of the needlewoman . . . almost equally dreadful, from the fashion-able milliner down to the humble stocking-darner." "Most proprietors of millinery establishments make a handsome profit on their goods," Penny declared in 1863, "but some of the girls employed receive but a scanty pit-tance." A year later, a commission convened by the state of Massachusetts announced that "milliners, dressmakers, and tailoresses were well paid" but that "women engaged . . . [in] coarse sewing received very low wages."[51]

Placed within the context of the trades themselves, these seeming contra-dictions disappear. The poorly paid apprentice labored alongside the amply compensated trimmer or fitter, a fact that observers' blanket pronouncements often obscured. Regional differences also help to explain conflicting percep-tions. Wright's 1880 survey of the "working girls of Boston" revealed that dressmakers and milliners in the smaller cities and towns of Massachusetts— places where skilled workers were likely to be scarce—earned higher sala-ries than those who labored in the metropolis. Finally, the social standing of a particular shop mattered a good deal. Martineau's claims aside, the needle-woman employed in a "fashionable" concern usually earned more than one who tended the bargain counter. Milliners who worked in "general" estab-lishments, the Massachusetts Bureau of Labor noted in 1871, netted $2.50– 8.00 a week, but those in "first-class" shops might make as much as $20.[52]

Indeed, the "fashionable milliner" and "the humble stocking-darner" were far from identical. Nineteenth-century observers and subsequent historians incorrectly assumed that the trials of seamstresses, those downtrodden toilers who sewed men's shirts and pants, represented the experience of all needlewomen. Just as women's wage work encompassed a variety of occupations rather than a mass of indistinguishable, unskilled jobs, the clothing trades boasted innumerable distinctions that merited differing rewards. The "aristocrats among the clothing makers," milliners and dressmakers (especially the trimmers and fitters among them) hovered near the top of the needlework wage hierarchy; seamstresses congregated near the bottom. The earnings presented in tables 16 and 17, based on observations that often were hasty or impressionistic, should be interpreted with caution. Nonetheless, dressmakers and milliners clearly chose their callings well; their wages were consistently as high as or higher than those earned by most gainfully employed women.

To be sure, some jobs paid better. The earnings of cigar makers, some boot and shoe workers, and certain members of the men's clothing trades

Table 16. Average Wages of Women Workers in Selected Occupations, 1880

	Boston	Elsewhere in Massachusetts	Other States
Dressmakers	$7.42	$10.22	$7.60
Milliners	7.97	12.50	10.00
Domestic service	4.96	5.12	4.53
Saleswomen	5.75	8.00	7.00
Boot and shoe shops			
Best rates	7.25	7.38	8.50
Lower rates	4.23	4.00	—
Seamstresses	6.18	5.50	4.00
Cotton mill operatives	3.94	6.02	8.00
Candy makers and packers	4.04	—	—
Cigar makers	7.83	—	—
All occupations surveyed	$6.03	$6.68	$6.69

Source: Wright, *Working Girls*, 76–81.

Table 17. Weekly Wages of Women Workers, 1859–1916

Wage-earning women, 1859
New York
  Dressmakers

Apprentices and finishers	$1.50–4.50
Fitters and forewomen	4.00–7.00
Out by day	3.50–7.50 + meals
Milliners	3.00–12.00
Seamstresses	2.25
Confectioners	1.25–6.00

Boston

Dressmakers	7.50
Milliners	3.00–15.00
Cotton mill operatives	1.00–5.00

Boston garment workers, 1870
Dressmakers

Apprentices and finishers	4.00–8.00
Fitters and forewomen	9.00–12.00

Milliners

General establishments	2.50–8.00
First-class establishments	8.00–10.00
First-class establishments,	
trimmers and forewomen	up to $20.00

Cap and hatmakers (men's)

Custom	9.00–15.00
Manufacturing	2.50–8.00

Wage-earning women, 1913
United States, milliners
  Apprentices

1st season	4.50
2d season	6.00–7.50
Expert makers	10.00–12.00
Trimmers	15.00–25.00
Designers	40.00–75.00

Boston milliners

Makers	less than 4.00–15.00
Trimmers	less than 10.00–50.00

Philadelphia milliners

Makers	less than 3.00–13.00
Trimmers	less than 10.00–45.00

New York (median wages)

Milliners	9.69
Department stores	8.07
Paper box factories	6.83
Candy factories	5.79

New York milliners, 1914 (median wages)

All milliners	9.91
Apprentices	2.47
Improvers	5.07
Preparers	6.27
Makers	10.22
Trimmers	11.18
Forewomen	18.33
Designers	30.95

Dressmakers and milliners, 1915–16

Cleveland, 1915

Dressmakers

Apprentices	0.50–4.00
Helpers	6.00–9.00
Finishers	10.00–12.00
Drapers	18.00–20.00

Milliners

Makers	3.00–16.00
Trimmers	10.00–40.00

Boston, 1916

Dressmakers

Apprentices and finishers	1.00–15.00
Cutters, fitters, drapers, and forewomen	5.00–35.00

Sources: Penny, *Employments of Women,* 151–52, 172–73, 310, 317–18, 325–26; MBSL, *Report,* 215–17; *M* 24 (Dec. 1913): 50; Perry, *Millinery Trade,* 71, 73, 85; Bryner, *Dressmaking and Millinery,* 39, 62; Van Kleeck, *Wages,* 51, 111; Allinson, *Dressmaking,* 134.

rivaled those of modistes and bonnet makers. Clerical occupations, available only to the reasonably well-educated, probably offered more secure livelihoods by the turn of the century. Nevertheless, the potential rewards of millinery and dressmaking were considerable. Allinson found that nearly half of custom dressmakers earned a "living wage" (a sum on which self-supporting women could reasonably subsist) of nine dollars a week or more; according to Van Kleeck's calculations, almost 60 percent of custom milliners met this standard. By contrast, only a third of boot and shoe workers, a fifth of ladies' garment workers, 13 percent of pant, shirt, and cap makers, 18 percent of printers, 11 percent of bookbinders, and 9 percent of paper box makers enjoyed a "living wage." "Although the wages of adult women workers in the dressmaking trade may seem discouraging," Allinson concluded, "comparison with other industries shows that relatively they are high."[53]

As this comment suggests, any final assessment depends on the standards selected. Using women's earnings as a measure, dressmakers and milliners fared quite well. Compared with men's earnings, the results are sobering. Although dressmakers and milliners commanded some of the highest wages in the *female* labor market, their earnings rarely approached those garnered by male craft workers.[54] Even if we rely solely on statistics for women, several caveats are in order. Seasonal unemployment, we shall see, substantially reduced craftswomen's earnings. Moreover, as Alice Kessler-Harris has noted, Progressive Era experts who calculated living wages for women workers assumed budgets that "included almost nothing beyond the barest sustenance"; if dressmakers and milliners reaped better rewards than many of their sisters, they did not necessarily live lives of luxury or even comfort.[55]

Once again, viewing craftswomen simply as "dressmakers" or "milliners"—as did many who calculated their wages—obscures important distinctions. The highest salaries within the trades were reserved for trimmers, fitters, and forewomen—workers who netted $7–15 a week at mid-century, $15–25 by 1900. Depending on the source consulted, they constituted 12–33 percent of the millinery and dressmaking labor force. Beginning wages, on the other hand, were low, far lower than in other occupations. In 1914, New York millinery apprentices might earn $2 or less a week; in the same city twelve years earlier, many learners—makers of paper boxes, artificial flowers, and jewel cases, laundry workers—garnered weekly wages of $3–4.[56] The journey from the lowest to the highest echelons was often long and arduous. Early twentieth-century dressmakers had to work about five years before they commanded weekly earnings of $9, ten years before they mer-

ited $15. Few hat trimmers reached the $15-range before their fifth year—
and bear in mind that the typical maker advanced to trimmer only after several seasons of toil.[57]

Did female employers consciously accept the notion of a "woman's wage"
(in simple terms, the idea that women should earn less than men)? Surviving testimony suggests that economic realities, not gender ideology, guided
their decisions. As proprietors of woman's concerns, they received less for
their services than did their counterparts in the predominantly male tailoring trade. Bound by the deficiencies of a relatively impoverished female economy, they could ill afford to pay more. At the same time, the compensations
that they offered reinforced larger social perceptions of "woman's worth."[58]

Additional factors further compromised dressmakers' and milliners'
worth. Few could expect year-round employment; "the seasons" were the
bane of proprietors and workers alike. Fashion was the leading culprit. By
long-standing tradition, new styles appeared in the spring and fall. From
March to June and from September to December, custom shops were del-
uged with orders for dresses and hats, to be "manufactured" according to the
latest vogues. Once the excitement died down, so did the work; in winter and
summer, many tradeswomen found themselves idle.[59]

The seasons were a matter of no minor significance. Many milliners, Penny observed, had no work for the months of July, August, January, and February. Eight years later, in 1871, the Massachusetts Bureau of Labor sounded
a gloomier note: women in both trades, its report maintained, were busy for
only sixteen weeks of the year. The length of the season varied from year to
year, city to city, and even shop to shop. A cold spring could literally dampen
the demand for new dresses and hats. More so than other modistes, urban needlewomen who served the very wealthy faced certain unemployment in the
summer when elites abandoned the city for the countryside. For all these variations, periodic idleness was a curse that few craftswomen could avoid.[60]

Contemporaries disagreed as to dressmaking's relative place. Some declared that modistes lost as much time as milliners; others argued—probably correctly—that, all things considered, dressmaking was one of the steadi-
er employments available for women. But few disputed the assertion that
millinery was "the most seasonal of trades." The seasons could have a devastating impact on annual earnings, especially for milliners, who might have
work for as little as four out of twelve months. As one worker explained in
1917, "I think maybe $8.00 is a large enough wage for a girl to live on if she
gets it every week, but for a milliner it must be $12."[61]

Irregular employment was not unique to dress- and hatmakers; cloak makers, shoe workers, bookbinders, and box makers, among others, endured "dull" times as well. Explanations regarding the wider prevalence of seasonal unemployment rested on often faulty assumptions about working women's lives. As Alexander Keyssar has noted, neither women nor men in the working class could expect year-round work, but women tended to be concentrated in those occupations plagued by the shortest working seasons. Employers and middle-class observers justified this state of affairs by arguing that women were supplementary, not primary wage earners; safely ensconced in working-class families, they neither "needed" nor "wanted" to work full-time. Such rationalization became self-fulfilling prophecy; periodic idleness and low wages exacerbated the hardships of the diminishing but still significant proportion of women "adrift" and made it difficult for women to live apart from their families.[62] Whether the proprietors of millinery and dressmaking shops—women whose careers boldly contradicted such sentiments—subscribed to similar notions is unclear. Most seem to have viewed the seasons as unfortunate but unavoidable facts of their working life. Yet the madame who insisted on hiring only workers from "good home[s]" because "it worries me to turn . . . [them] off in the dull season," unwittingly or not, reinforced workers' dependence.[63]

Coming from a "good home" did not necessarily solve the problem of seasonal unemployment (and, at any rate, not until the turn of the twentieth century did a decisive majority of craftswomen live at home). Not all workers could afford to remain idle; many a dressmaker or milliner embarked on a biannual search for temporary employment. "When work is dull," Wright explained, "the girls work at anything they can do, sometimes in retail stores for a few weeks." How the "girls" fared depended on the available alternatives and their own resourcefulness. From the late nineteenth century on, dress and bonnet makers, like many of their fellow toilers, found work at summer resorts. Others, like one milliner interviewed by Van Kleeck, became mistresses of all trades:

> One girl, who had been at work six years, gave us a list of the occupations in which she had worked in dull season. They included the making of handkerchiefs, paper boxes, ladies' waists, babies' hats, and buttonholes in sweaters, stock work in a leather goods factory, canvassing for a music school, taking charge of her brothers' cleaning and dyeing store, selling hats in a millinery shop on the lower East side, saleswork in a dry-goods store, and the manufacture of embroidery.[64]

Faced with such prospects, many would-be milliners abandoned the trade altogether, exchanging a "well-paid seasonal job" for "an all-year-round low-paid job." Indeed, some observers attributed the relative youth of milliners to exasperation with the seasons. Many women understandably were reluctant to dedicate themselves to a calling that left them idle for months at a time.[65]

This pattern did not affect all workers equally; it weighed most heavily on those who could least afford it. Just as wages varied considerably according to one's position within the craft hierarchy, the seasons reinforced distinctions between different types of workers in the trades. Apprentices, makers, finishers, and "extra hands" bore the brunt of seasonal unemployment; fitters and trimmers, better paid from the start, suffered far less.[66] Perry's analysis of the payrolls of Boston millinery shops showed the consequences of such distinctions. Almost all trimmers, she found, received nine dollars a week or more, regardless of the season. But once lost time was taken into account, the number of makers who earned a "living wage" fell from nearly a tenth to none at all.[67]

Every shop contained two sets of workers. Apprentices, makers, and finishers, relatively poorly paid and constituting a reserve army of female labor, were almost certain to be laid off in dull seasons. Trimmers, fitters, and forewomen not only enjoyed a modicum of security but commanded higher wages than most working women. Between an eighth and a third of the labor force, they were the true "aristocrats among the clothing makers." To be sure, it was by no means impossible to climb from the lower into the higher tier; indeed, dressmaking and millinery offered better opportunities for advancement than most female occupations. But more often than not, upward mobility entailed considerable sacrifice. Constrained by low beginning wages and buffeted by seasonal unemployment, many workers—especially milliners—gave up the fight. Meanwhile, the very different experiences of novices and veterans created divisions that proprietors easily exploited.

Madame, the Employer

"The cruelty exercised by some milliners and dress makers toward those in their employ . . . is very great," Penny observed in 1863. Five years later, the Working-Women's Protective Union, a New York organization headed by middle-class reformers, echoed her view. The organization's fifth annual report featured a description, pirated from *Putnam's Magazine*, of a wealthy and fashionable dressmaker who "holds her court" in "a handsome building." Beneath the glowing facade lurked evil and despair.

> Let us slip down these stairs into the basement. This is the work-room. Faugh, how it smells! There is no attempt at ventilation. The room is crowded with girls and women, most of whom are pale and attenuated, and are being robbed of life slowly and surely. The roses which should bloom on their cheeks have vanished long ago. The sparkle has gone out of their eyes. They bend over their work with aching backs and throbbing brows; sharp pains dart through their eyeballs; they breathe an atmosphere of death.[68]

Examples of "good" employers could also be found. The milliner Caroline Woods paid her workers "the highest wages that any can command." Believing herself responsible for their spiritual development as well, she readily dispensed moral and religious advice, embracing standards of conduct that historians have attributed to preindustrial (male) artisans. The dressmaker Olivia Flynt, according to the Massachusetts Bureau of Labor's report for 1871, provided her employees with numerous benefits, including "large and airy" workrooms and "a dining-room . . . for the exclusive use of those girls who carry their dinners." More important, she decreed an eight-hour day for those in her employ.[69]

Nevertheless, given the overwhelming evidence of exploitation, any notion of a "maternal" style of labor relations must be discarded. Female employers could be just as ruthless—or as kind—as their male counterparts. Many nineteenth-century dressmakers and milliners toiled in cramped, ill-lit quarters without adequate ventilation, conditions that left them vulnerable to "diseases of the spine and eyes." Unsafe and unsanitary conditions were as ubiquitous in the twentieth century as in the nineteenth; small shops easily evaded inspectors charged with enforcing a growing body of labor legislation.[70]

Overtime, too, was a significant problem, especially during rush seasons and on Saturday evenings, when the retail trade was at its busiest. In the 1860s and 1870s, milliners might be kept working until midnight, adding five or six hours to their customary ten-hour day. Dressmakers fared no better. The modiste who went out by the day, although nominally self-employed, was particularly vulnerable to the whims of her patrons. As Penny explained, "the length of the day depends on the mercy of the employer."[71] By the early twentieth century, the standard work day had been reduced to nine hours, but violations were rampant. Hat shops stayed open until 10:00 P.M. on Saturdays, requiring that employees "stay late to catch every possible bit of custom." One dressmaker admitted that she had worked "every night until 12 o'clock" for three months. Her employer, a "Miss B.," quieted potential dissent by announcing that "'no girl need expect to stay who wouldn't work overtime.'"[72]

For many craftswomen the problem of seasonal unemployment offset the evils of overtime. Indeed, some employers justified the practice by arguing that workers could "rest" during the dull season. Others sought to make the additional hours as pleasant as possible. One dressmaker's custom of providing tea and sandwiches elicited the admiration of her employees: "She's an angel. You won't find anyone like Madame." Of course, Madame's motives were ambivalent at best. Tea and sandwiches, a relatively inexpensive means of quelling protest, seldom matched the value of workers' time and labor. Such rituals were enacted only in larger shops; in many instances, proprietors worked alongside their employees. According to the typical reformer's account, Madame left the shop precisely at 5 P.M., leaving her workers to toil long into the night. More often than not, overtime was a shared burden; indeed, employers who scrupulously observed labor laws might find themselves working longer than those they hired.[73]

Long hours were not the only problem. Formal indentures had disappeared by the mid-nineteenth century, and by the turn of the twentieth, proprietors had acquired a well-deserved reputation for discharging apprentices without teaching them anything about their trades—ruses in which more experienced workers must have participated. By the 1910s, many smaller shops—threatened by larger, male-operated concerns on the one hand and ready-made clothing on the other—had abandoned the concept of apprenticeship altogether, either refusing to hire inexperienced workers or employing them explicitly as "errand girls" who stood little chance of ascending the trade hierarchy.[74]

Even worse, promised wages often failed to materialize, as the dressmaker Mary Elizabeth Bradlee's diary entries for November 1875 reveal: "Mrs. S. owes me $1.00," "Mrs. S. owes me $3.00," "Mrs. S. . . . owes me $6.00." Bradlee's complaints were far from unique; modistes who failed to pay their workers frequently figured in the records of the Protective Committee (active between 1878 and 1904) of the Boston branch of the Women's Educational and Industrial Union (WEIU), a "class-bridging organization" committed, as Sarah Deutsch describes it, "to assist[ing] all women in gaining more economic and intellectual self-reliance." Naive workingwomen, a turn-of-the-century report explained, might labor "on in hope till $10.00, 20.00, 40.00 are due them, months of work at $1.00 a day." Like wage rates and seasonal unemployment, employers' refusal to pay their employees seems to have hit less experienced workers particularly hard; Protective Committee minutes contain references to apprentices and seamstresses but never to fitters.[75]

Middle-class reformers, like those who joined the Protective Committee, were quick to place the blame on evil and exploitative taskmistresses, women who suffered from "a want of moral integrity." Of course, many "bad" bosses probably deserved the label. The fictional "Madame Fripperie," a fashionable dressmaker who "pays her girls four dollars a week" but "lives in as fine a style as the richest lady she serves" was the very embodiment of acquisitive individualism. But simply distinguishing between good and bad employers—the WEIU kept lists of both—was insufficient. Proprietors' precarious economic circumstances, not their inherent immorality, were at the root of abusive labor practices. Fripperie was an exception; most millinery and dressmaking shops were marginal, short-lived concerns.[76]

Exploitation was bound to flourish in such circumstances. Some historians have held that female employers created a benevolent "women's culture" in the workplace; indeed, contemporaries seem to have assumed that women would behave differently than their male counterparts and condemned them harshly when they failed to meet such expectations.[77] But the significance of gender may lie less in any presumed maternal propensities than in harsh economic realities. Perennially short of capital, few dressmakers and milliners could afford to become model employers. Seen in this light, even the refusal of promised instruction had a source other than pure maliciousness. The limited range of employments available to women was at least partly to blame. If the fashion trades offered rarely equaled opportunities to young women of the working classes, the lack of available alternatives encouraged ambitious wage earners to flood already overcrowded dressmaking and millinery labor markets. Training an apprentice to perform routine tasks was cheaper and less time-consuming than teaching her the tricks of the trade. In the absence of any means of regulating the number of workers allowed into the ranks, it was also a method, albeit a deceitful one, of curtailing future competition.[78]

This is not to say that proprietors had no interest in profits or that they emerged untarnished from a mythic artisanal past. However pressed by economic necessity, their willingness to overlook apprenticeship traditions, adopt exploitative labor policies, and postpone payment of wages reveal women who were poised uneasily between an artisanal and an entrepreneurial orientation. In this respect they had much in common with other nineteenth-century employers who presided over crafts that were undergoing profound transformations. "Learning"—the hiring of apprentices under false pretenses—was an accepted practice in many lines of work, especially the production of men's clothing. In the years before the Civil War, artisans and mechanics of all stripes lamented the fact that market considerations, not mutual obligation, increasingly governed relations between masters and workmen.[79]

Nevertheless, mistress craftswomen failed to adopt the kinds of innovations that dramatically altered such crafts as shoe and furniture making and tailoring. Piecework and outwork—two potent vehicles of exploitation—were relatively rare in dressmaking and millinery; subcontracting or "sweating"—the bane of seamstresses and tailoresses—was nonexistent. At a time when once proud craftsmen found their work "subdivided . . . into its minute details," hat- and dressmaking retained the customary division of labor between apprentice (although in certain circumstances she might not learn much more than the "mechanical" aspects of her trade),[80] maker or finisher, and trimmer or fitter. To be sure, these prohibitions had more to do with practicality than benevolence. Payment by the piece meshed poorly with the rhythms and variety of custom production. Understandably, employers were reluctant to let workers leave the shop with expensive materials that might be lost or soiled. Sweating and minute subdivisions of labor better suited the mass production of identical products than the custom manufacture of one-of-a-kind dresses and hats. If nothing else, the persistence of custom work spared dressmakers and milliners the worst abuses of what Sean Wilentz has called "metropolitan industrialization."[81]

Yet if custom production provided its adherents with a measure of protection, it also gave rise to other forms of exploitation, practices that disproportionately affected the lower reaches of the trades. Reformers' complaints notwithstanding, the employer was seldom the only guilty party. Campbell complained that Madame told her penniless employees "a pitiful tale of unpaid bills and conscienceless customers, who could not be forced." More often than not, the story was true. Dressmakers' and milliners' patrons were notorious for failing to pay their bills on time. Workers—especially apprentices, extra hands, and other relative newcomers—were the ultimate victims of this custom. One dressmaker asked her employees, "How can I pay you until my customers pay me?"[82]

While the reality of exploitation is apparent, it is important to place milliners' and dressmakers' experiences into perspective. The conditions under which they worked were probably no worse than those in which many wage-earning women labored, and in many respects they were better. Given that employers generally did business with few financial resources, it is surprising that overall wages were so high. Once again, expediency triumphed over beneficence; the enviable earnings of trimmers and fitters reflected the skill that custom production required. Without question, these benefits were achieved at others' expense; only by ruthlessly exploiting lesser skilled workers could Madames afford to pay higher wages than many employers (such as mill owners and department store magnates) who commanded larger amounts of capital. Shaped by powerful though not impermeable distinctions between apprentices, makers, and finishers, on the one hand, and trimmers and fitters, on the other, the dressmaking and millinery trades incorporated opportunity as well as exploitation, progress as well as poverty.

Accommodation and Resistance: Workers' Responses

While ample evidence documents proprietors' deficiencies, assessing workers' attitudes toward their jobs—and their bosses—is a more hazardous enterprise. Militant activists they were not; by any standard, dressmakers' and milliners' contributions to the history of organized labor was less than impressive. This is not to say that activism was nonexistent. Women from both trades were among the members of a short-lived labor federation, the Female Improvement Society of Philadelphia, organized in 1835, which demanded—and won—wage increases for workers in the sewing trades. A decade later, they participated in a somewhat less successful effort, the Ladies' Industrial Association of New York. In 1863, New York modistes once again joined with other needlewomen to form "a combination of the working girls for general protection." Evidently, the proposed association—if it ever materialized—was an ephemeral phenomenon, for it immediately disappeared from the historical record. Little is known about custom clothiers' role in these struggles, nor do we have figures to show just how many dressmakers and milliners joined the fray. Existing evidence suggests that they were minor actors in organizations dominated by seamstresses and tailoresses, women with whom they shared little apart from a common allegiance to the needle. (The 1863 meeting concluded with a reading of Thomas Hood's "Song of the Shirt.")[83]

Dressmakers and milliners appear to have been no more interested in unions during and after the Civil War than before. Troy, New York, boasted a Milliners' and Dressmakers' Union (an organization about which little is known), demonstrating that a city with a strong labor movement might induce craftswomen to join the ranks of trade unionists. Small numbers—again, we have no reliable statistics—joined the Knights of Labor in the late 1880s, most of them congregating in "mixed assemblies" that encompassed workers in a variety of occupations. Only two exceptions countered this general pattern: New York boasted one local made up entirely of dressmakers and Toledo one composed of cloak and dressmakers.[84] Apart from their existence, we know next to nothing about those dress- and hatmakers who became "Lady Knights" as members of either mixed assemblies or separate locals: their age, ethnicity, or marital status, their motives for joining the organization, even whether they were proprietors attracted by a "producer ideology" that welcomed small businesspeople as well as wage laborers, or workers resisting oppression. More to the point, they accounted for only a tiny proportion of the nation's custom dressmakers and milliners. To be sure, these collective efforts, like previous attempts, should not be discounted. Indeed, as we shall see, given the obstacles that confronted potential organizers, the fact that any custom clothiers joined unions is surprising. Nevertheless, no tradition of labor protest, such as that evinced by New England shoe workers or Troy collar workers, marked the millinery and dressmaking trades. By the early twentieth century, there was little reason to dispute one labor leader's exasperated assertion: "You might as well try to direct the wind as to organize milliners."[85]

At first glance, this apparent disdain for organized resistance is puzzling. Millinery and dressmaking included significant numbers of highly skilled, highly paid workers, who saw themselves as permanent wage earners, not temporary toilers; recent scholarship suggests that these are just the sort of workingwomen who should have vigorously supported labor protest.[86] Of course, dressmakers' and milliners' relative lack of interest in trade unions implied neither greater commitment to family and marriage—an interpretation often invoked to explain women's quiescence—nor passive acceptance of less than desirable conditions.[87] Rather, their perceptions of their place within the larger hierarchy of female occupations, their assessments of their prospects for advancement, the positions they occupied within their respective crafts, and the peculiarities of their trades shaped their responses.

We have already seen that some craftswomen saw union membership as incompatible with their notions of respectable womanhood. If gentility gave them pride in their work, it played no small part in discouraging forms of activism that they identified—however misguidedly—with factory workers. Like other female wage earners, milliners and dressmakers received scant assistance from their male counterparts, who might have provided them with an alternative basis for resistance; indeed, the very absence of men from their trades further distanced craftswomen from the male-dominated labor movement. As several historians have demonstrated, the political and social world of nineteenth-century urban craftsmen was a determinedly masculine universe that held no place for female wage earners, no matter how skilled or steeped in artisanal traditions. Indeed, labor newspapers employed the same stereotypes as did middle-class reformers, indiscriminately lumping all needlewomen into one homogeneous group. While *Fincher's Trades' Review* exhorted workingwomen to "learn wisdom from the action of the opposite sex, and rely solely upon united efforts," its contributors described dressmakers and milliners in familiar terms: ruthless proprietors and passive victims, models hardly designed to inspire prospective activists. Cast adrift from a male artisanal culture, women made their own paths—often in highly individualistic ways.[88]

By any criterion, the fashion trades amounted to an organizer's nightmare. Most craftswomen labored in tiny concerns employing very few women— as late as 1890 Boston's millinery and dressmaking shops *averaged* three to four workers per establishment—circumstances that made it difficult for them to forge connections with their sisters in other shops or to assert their independence from their employers, who ordinarily cut and stitched beside them. While single-industry towns nurtured female activism in such places as Lowell, Lynn, Haverhill, and Lawrence, Massachusetts, and Troy, New York, dressmakers and milliners confined themselves to no single city or geographical locale, and workers who congregated in downtown shops might live in different neighborhoods. To make matters worse, craftswomen's penchant for classifying themselves according to the "quality" of customers they served had dire consequences for citywide—or even neighborhood-wide— solidarity. While coworkers might form close personal bonds, the seasonal nature of the trades, especially millinery, undermined potential alliances. Moreover, the workforce of a particular shop might vary from season to season. As Van Kleeck noted, "It is exceedingly difficult to organize a trade in which the majority of the workers are together but half the year."[89]

Rather than lament their quiescence or condemn them for subscribing to "false consciousness," it is important to try to understand the attitudes of dressmakers and milliners themselves. The experience of the successful dressmaker, detailed earlier, provides one key. The anonymous modiste approached her first job on the selling floor of a New York dry goods firm "loaded with faith in my future usefulness and pecuniary independence." Much to her disappointment and confusion, her "fidelity to detail and conscientious devotion" earned her the "contempt of . . . [her] co-workers," some of whom "went so far as to rebuke . . . [her] for . . . [her] zeal." More than likely, what she interpreted as "apathy" and "listless spirit" reflected what Benson has described as "saleswomen's work culture," a set of values and practices with which clerks collectively enforced selling quotas and standards of conduct toward customers, supervisors, and coworkers. But this was a culture that held few attractions for the ambitious clerk who had "almost unlimited views on the subject of women's independence."[90] That she found independence in dressmaking suggests not only that the fashion trades offered unique opportunities but that women who entered them entertained very different expectations than did their counterparts in other pursuits.

To be sure, the promise of upward mobility did not necessarily preclude labor activism, but it may have encouraged dressmakers and milliners to choose individual advancement over collective efforts. Fitters and trimmers—those who possessed the greatest economic and psychological resources—were especially predisposed toward this attitude. Women who remained in the trades past their thirties stood a far greater chance of eventually opening shops of their own (see Table 18). Theoretically the most likely activists, they were also most likely to set their sights elsewhere.[91]

As this scenario suggests, workers were divided among themselves, a fact that may well have precluded, or at least diminished, solidarity in the workroom. Trimmers and fitters, better paid and more likely to be retained during dull seasons, had greater reason for contentment than did apprentices, makers, and finishers. Closer in age to proprietors, they were more likely to identify with—and even to live with—Madame. Indeed, they might be trusted to oversee the business in their employers' absence or (as in the case of the shopgirl turned dressmaker described above) be admitted as business partners. Occasionally, favored employees even inherited the shop when Madame died or retired. Divisions between the highly skilled and the relatively unskilled were reinforced by the structure of authority. Even in the smallest concerns, fitters and trimmers often assumed supervisory functions; one fictional head trimmer "bossed the other girls around to beat the band."[92]

Table 18. The Relationship between Age (in Years) in 1860 and Eventual Proprietorship

	Under 30	Over 30
Becomes proprietor	95 (9.0%)	56 (13.4%)
Does not become proprietor	960 (91.0%)	362 (86.6%)
	1,055	418

Note: Eventual proprietors are women who appeared in business directories sometime within the next forty years. Results significant at .01 level.

Sources: 1860 FMPC, Boston, M653, reels 520–25; *Boston Directory* (1861–1900).

The peculiar distribution of power within the shop was further complicated by the omnipresent patrons. Custom clothiers responded not to abstract laws of supply and demand but to the whims and desires of individual consumers. Unlike her successor who perused the department store rack, the customer who decreed on Thursday that her hat or gown be ready on Saturday exerted an immediate influence on workroom life (Figure 2). Conventional trade union tactics, which pitted employer against employee, were ill suited to the realities of dressmaking and millinery shops. Customers' often unreasonable demands and cost-cutting proclivities imposed hardships on proprietors and workers alike. Little wonder that workers sometimes "sided" with their employers against customers![93] Under these conditions, identifying the oppressor was no easy task. Who was responsible for overtime and low wages: the trimmer or fitter (who often set the pace of labor and judged the quality of work), the proprietor, or the patron?

Similar queries prompted early twentieth-century social investigators, less inclined to moralistic condemnation than their predecessors, to propose creative solutions that acknowledged the social and economic complexities of the fashion trades. "The customer of the small dressmaker . . . has a serious obligation which she often does not recognize," wrote Allinson in 1916, "because she does not realize the far-reaching effects of her negligence or failure to pay her bills promptly." In the same year, Perry called for "a campaign of education among customers as a means of eliminating overtime in the millinery trade." Neither of these insights yielded any discernible results; extra hours and uncertain compensation were endemic to dressmaking and millinery as long as the trades survived.[94]

Figure 2. "Milliners." From a series of illustrations depicting "women and their work in the metropolis." A millinery worker finishes a hat while a customer waits. From *Harper's Bazar*, Apr. 18, 1868, p. 393. (Courtesy of the Indiana University, Bloomington, Library)

Finally, whether they deserved it or not, some employers inspired devotion. David Brody has noted that small businessmen had one advantage over their counterparts in larger concerns: they more easily commanded the loyalty of their employees. The same can be said of small businesswomen. Affectionate ties between employer and employee, based on a shared female identity, coexisted with the most ruthless exploitation, a state of affairs hardly surprising in a trade where proprietors typically labored alongside their workingwomen, sharing the burden of long hours and enduring collectively the slights of arrogant patrons. Indeed, in some circumstances, maternalism might compensate for exploitation. The relative youth of apprentices, makers, and finishers rendered them especially vulnerable to motherly overtures. Des Moulins cried when she left Madame's to take another position. A second young dressmaker "worshipped" her employer, even though the latter failed to reimburse her for weeks at a time.[95]

Not all workers were fooled by Madame's professed concern for "her girls." The absence of trade unions should not blind us to other forms of resistance, for available evidence hints at the existence of a vibrant work culture, albeit one that emphasized individual ingenuity rather than collective resistance.[96] Victorian sentimentalists might speak of "delicate girls, with consumptive looks"—women who evidently lacked the slightest degree of initiative or resourcefulness—but most craftswomen were neither pitiful victims nor naive dupes. If they eschewed union activism, they had other, less formal, means of registering their protest. Again and again they voted with their feet; if conditions in one shop proved unsatisfactory, they moved to another. Employers complained of workers who resigned suddenly for "no reason," but changing jobs signified more than "restlessness." It was often a "reasoned practice," a calculated attempt to increase wages. Dressmakers liked to "'tell a good story.'" "'If I was getting $7 a week at my last place,' one modiste explained, 'I tell the next employer I was getting $8.'" Des Moulins and her friend and coworker, Annette, told a prospective employer that they were currently earning eighteen dollars a week. "That was true, too," she revealed, "because each of us got $9." The ruse worked; Amelia and Annette were soon making twenty dollars a week *each*. Indeed, workers' mobility resulted in many a "promotion"; erstwhile apprentices often transformed themselves into experienced craftswomen when they moved to another shop.[97]

While employers and employees were ill-matched contestants, certain workers were far from powerless. Contemporaries agreed that while inexperienced toilers abounded, skilled craftswomen were in short supply. Talented trimmers and fitters were highly valued—and they wielded considerable leverage. An early twentieth-century trade journal told of a trimmer who "walked out at six" while customers were present, informing her horrified employer, "It's quitting time, and I am not going to stay longer." According to the editors, the story had a happy ending: "The trimmer . . . was not fired—she was talked to kindly and made to feel so ashamed of herself that there is nothing now she will not do to atone for her disinterestedness."[98]

However reassuring to employers, this was an unlikely scenario. Firing a trimmer at the height of a busy season was suicidal; "talking" to her was equally hazardous, since chances were that others were eager to acquire her services. "Is there a trimmer in a rival shop whose hats are your special admiration?" the *Illustrated Milliner* asked in 1900. "If so, can you add . . . [her] to your force in a legitimate way?" Much like craftsmen, trimmers who "walked out at six" could afford to enforce their own notions of a fair day's work—whether or not such actions suited their employers.[99]

Proprietors who risked the wrath of trimmers and fitters did so at their own peril, for experienced workers might leave to open their own shops.

Lizzie G. Lang, "a smart, ambitious girl" who started a millinery business in the fall of 1880, is a case in point. Before embarking on her entrepreneurial career, Lang had labored for several years in a shop where she had become "popular with the customers." In losing Lang, her employer lost not only a valued worker but patrons as well.[100]

* * *

Lang had reached the pinnacle of her profession. Nevertheless, her future, based on "no capital of consequence," was uncertain. As it turned out, she was relatively successful by millinery standards: her venture lasted six years, possibly longer.

Workers' livelihoods were even more precarious. Privileged though they were, milliners and dressmakers did not escape the consequences of a sex-segregated labor market: lower wages than their male counterparts, less than desirable working conditions, and seasonal unemployment. Since they worked for women, most of whom possessed "no capital of consequence," custom clothiers—at least the apprentices, makers, and finishers among them—often left the shop empty-handed at the end of the work week. Only trimmers and fitters and the occasional maker or finisher could expect to be treated differently; they were the beneficiaries of a dual labor system that pitted novice against veteran, extra hand against "loyal" employee. Although dressmaking and millinery promised women the benefits of artisanal livelihoods, they also bore no small resemblance to modern service occupations that rely on women's (and increasingly men's) part-time, temporary labor.

Thus, in the face of substantial obstacles, workers demonstrated considerable resourcefulness. While few turned to conventional labor activism (a tactic many of their wage-earning sisters—and brothers—likewise eschewed), they did not necessarily acquiesce to proprietors' demands. Highly skilled veterans, hardly the pitiful victims of reformers' accounts, wielded a substantial degree of authority at the workplace.

Any final assessment must consider the perspective of workers themselves. By every indication, they were well aware of the available alternatives. Many chose dressmaking and millinery precisely because they offered avenues of upward mobility that other female employments lacked. To rise from apprentice to fitter or trimmer, to become the proprietor of a tiny concern—these were distinct possibilities as late as the 1910s. However modest these goals, this was a world in which "smart, ambitious girls" could expect little more.

═══*═══ *Four*

The Social Relations of Consumption: Producers and Consumers in the Era of Custom Production

Had a most turbulent morning seeing the washerwoman, dressmaker & milliner . . .
—Diary of Emily Marshall Eliot, June 9, 1864

On that June day, 32–year-old Emily Marshall Eliot, a Boston Brahmin by birth and marriage, was in Paris.[1] Despite the turbulence of her morning, she could be grateful that her wealth and social position allowed her to patronize French modistes, renowned for their artistry and creativity. Whatever their shortcomings, the millinery and dressmaking trades flourished in the United States as well. Until the triumph of ready-made clothing and mass-produced hats in the early twentieth century, American women either made their own clothes or engaged the services of dressmakers and milliners. In cities and towns across the nation, Eliot's "turbulent morning" was replicated countless times.

Her experience exemplifies an earlier form of consumption that has been eclipsed by mass production and large-scale retailing. Custom manufacture was the rule in Eliot's day; in close collaboration with her dressmaker or milliner, the consumer ordered a product that had yet to be conceived. In contrast to the relatively anonymous exchanges that characterize modern commerce, the older system thrived on direct and highly personal transactions between producers and consumers.

Analysts who celebrate the "democratic" features of ready-made clothing find little of value in this earlier regime. After all, custom manufacture was time-consuming and expensive; ready-to-wear clothing was convenient and economical.[2] In reality, the story is not quite so simple. For women who could afford the services of dressmakers and milliners (and they were by no means confined to the elite), the made-to-order system had distinct advantages. In contrast to modern "shopping," it gave customers the chance to exercise both originality and control. Unlike the purchaser of a ready-to-wear dress, the patron of an earlier time participated actively in designing her garment. The finished product differed, no matter how slightly, from everything else the tradeswoman "manufactured." One observer succinctly summarized consumer demand: "No woman wants a hat like any other hat that has ever been made." Custom manufacture fulfilled this mandate; mass production could not.[3]

Still, we should not romanticize the lost world of custom production. Moreover, a close examination of the relationship between producers and consumers strengthens the case against a sentimental portrait. At best, tradeswomen and their clients mingled business with friendship, transporting sisterhood into the business world. But interactions between buyers and sellers, while intensely personal, were frequently contentious and exploitative. Middle- and upper-class consumers bent upon affirming their social superiority reaped psychological benefits at dressmakers' and milliners' expense; indeed, producer/consumer relationships not only reflected class differences but helped to define them. Tradeswomen charged with the task of creating beauty braved the wrath of unhappy clients. All too often, personal ties broke down under the weight of pecuniary concerns. The fragility of the female economy of fashion underscored women's tenuous economic position as producers *and* consumers, exemplifying both the "bonds" that united women of different social classes and the forces that divided them.[4] Albeit in different ways, producers and consumers alike confronted the reality of women's economic dependence.

A Different Kind of Consumerism

While a great deal of scholarly attention has been devoted to the "culture of consumption" that emerged around the turn of the twentieth century, historians are just beginning to examine its nineteenth-century antecedents.[5] In many respects, the consumer culture that appeared in the antebellum years pales in comparison to its better-known successor; nineteenth-century shoppers had yet to encounter national markets, brand names, and advertisements that conveyed the "therapeutic promise of a richer, fuller life."[6] Even so, they lived through a period of momentous social and economic change. As factories proliferated and markets expanded, Americans abandoned production for consumption, homemade products for ready-made purchases. As definitions of "needs" multiplied, goods increasingly served purposes that were less than utilitarian; individual identity and personal worth increasingly depended on the ability to buy and display fashionable merchandise. Perhaps most significant, conspicuous consumption became a means by which members of a new, white-collar middle class distinguished themselves from their working-class counterparts, a process in which female consumers played a vital role. No longer weavers of homespun or churners of butter, women of the urban bourgeoisie purchased the commodities that symbolized middle-class status.[7]

Although it overstates the demise of household production, this story is accurate in its outlines.[8] But it neglects an important dimension of nineteenth-century consumption, for it assumes a mass market for factory-produced goods. "By the Civil War," writes one historian, "many ordinary Americans entered the commercial marketplace to purchase mass-produced clothing, furniture, and items for preparing and consuming food." Those "ordinary Americans" who wore "mass-produced clothing" were predominantly male. To be sure, factories produced both the accompaniments and the "foundations" of nineteenth-century women's fashion—cloaks, shawls, corsets, hoop skirts, and bustles. But well into the twentieth century, women's dresses and hats were made either at home by amateurs or to order by professionals.[9]

This anachronism resulted from a fortuitous marriage between fashion and technology. By the mid-nineteenth century, men—who had abandoned tightly fitting coats and trousers for simple, loosely fitting "sack suits"— could buy their clothes ready-made. As Claudia B. Kidwell has pointed out, the tight fit and elaborate styles of women's garments rendered a comparable revolution in the production of feminine apparel technologically impossible. As women's dress became ever more intricate, it strained the abilities of home manufacturers and strengthened the demand for professionals. Indeed, the Gilded Age was the golden age for dressmakers. Similarly, all but the plainest hats—in an era renowned for elaborate concoctions of flowers, feathers, and ribbons—had to be made by hand.[10]

Custom production, in turn, demanded a degree of intimacy that the sale of ready-to-wear clothing did not. Both trades, especially dressmaking, required numerous consultations and fittings. These imperatives gave rise to a peculiarly feminine culture of consumption that thrived on intensely personal relationships between producers and consumers.

Just as woman's sphere—seemingly divorced from the rough-and-tumble world of industry and commerce—owed its existence to industrial capitalism,[11] so, too, did the female economy of fashion depend on factory products. Most dressmakers and milliners were indebted to the technological innovations engineered at Waltham, Lowell, and Lawrence. Their colonial counterparts had catered to a tiny elite. But factory production of textiles made stylish attire—and the services of milliners and modistes—available to middle-class, even working-class consumers. Like it or not, tradeswomen (and their customers) were part of a bustling nineteenth-century industrial and commercial world.

The making of a dress or hat, ostensibly a matter between a tradeswoman and her client, actually involved several parties, exposing the vital connections between the female economy and a larger, male-operated commercial universe. First, the purchaser of a dress made a trip to the dry goods store for fabric, then she visited the fancy goods shop for trimmings. The dressmaker's shop was her final destination on an often exasperating commercial journey. (Only the larger establishments, which tended to be run by men, could afford to "keep stock.") Like their dressmaking sisters, "private milliners" expected their patrons to provide—or at least pay for—the necessary raw materials. But most hatmakers "kept stock"—fabric, artificial flowers, ribbons, lace, feathers—that they purchased from wholesale dealers. Thus, the nineteenth-century milliner found herself immersed in a network of often perilous credit transactions, her dealings monitored by "mercantile agencies." Try as she might, she could not escape the trappings of modern commerce.[12]

If tradeswomen were inseparably linked to an urban industrial economy, they nonetheless occupied a separate place within it. Indeed, the contrast between the world of the dressmaker and milliner and the larger "consumer society" was striking. By the mid-nineteenth century, sellers of a variety of products—jewelry, dry goods, boots and shoes, crockery, and carpets—hawked their wares in elegant establishments, far from the factory or workroom where their merchandise was actually produced.[13] But for tradeswomen and their customers, settings were relatively unimportant; face-to-face relations took precedence over display. Of course, wealthier businesswomen did not hesitate to adopt retailing innovations. Gilded Age credit investigators bestowed their approval on "elegant rooms" and "nicely fitted up stores." The most fashionable milliners and modistes presided over establishments that rivaled in ornateness if not in size the most elegantly appointed dry goods firms and department stores. Although the larger part of their trade consisted of custom work, milliners also displayed ready-to-wear hats (most of them handcrafted and produced on the premises) that served as inducements and as models.[14]

As a rule, though, millinery and dressmaking businesses were humble affairs. Dressmakers who "went out by the day" did not keep shops at all; many proprietors in both trades worked out of their homes. Miss Esther, a fictional turn-of-the-century tradeswoman recalling the 1860s, mused, "In those days . . . the milliners' shops wasn't the big, elegant affairs they are now. Instead, they was usually just one room in a little cottage that was home to the milliner, too." But the home shop survived well into the twentieth century. In 1916, the "best" establishment in Somerville, Massachusetts, closely resembled Esther's recollection; in it "the making and selling of hats . . . [were] carried on in the milliner's own home."[15]

Most nonresidential shops were by no means palatial. Many of the more "exclusive" tradeswomen of late nineteenth-century Boston sequestered themselves in tiny rooms on the upper floors of commercial buildings in the downtown retail district. Little had changed by the early twentieth century. "The majority [of millinery parlors] occupy but one room with but one corner shut off by curtains for a workroom." Not all went to such trouble. Visiting a small-town hat shop in the spring of 1912, the author of the *Milliner*'s "Just among Ourselves" column was horrified to discover "a workroom that was not screened from the show room."[16] Such omissions very likely resulted from limited capital, not conscious anticommercialism; still, they suggest that a considerable psychological distance lay between the physical intimacy of small dressmaking and millinery shops and the ostentatious display of dry goods houses and department stores.

Consumers evidently believed that the custom shop offered considerable advantages, even as ready-made apparel became increasingly available. Indeed, milliners and dressmakers demonstrated remarkable longevity in the face of commercial innovation and technological change (see Table A-2 in appendix).[17] What accounted for this tenacity? Consumers valued originality, a requirement that mass production by definition could not fulfill. While the dictates of fashion circumscribed the creative potential of custom production, within the limits set by prevailing vogues, tradeswomen and their clients devised endless combinations of colors, styles, fabrics, and trimmings. When Sarah Ellen Browne visited a millinery shop in downtown Boston in 1857, she tried on a bonnet "with blue ribbon and white lace" that did not fit. All was not lost; her chaperone merely asked the milliner to make up a similar headdress but with white ribbon, the color she preferred.[18]

This flexibility continued to attract consumers long after ready-to-wear clothing presented a practical alternative. "Woman's insistence on individuality of style . . . [has] hindered and delayed large-scale production," the social investigator May Allinson wrote of the dressmaking trade in 1916. Lorinda Perry, who published her study of Boston and Philadelphia milliners in the same year, noted that while department stores offered "large variety, convenience, and dispatch . . . for many patrons . . . these advantages are more than offset by lack of individuality."[19] Perhaps the *Illustrated Milliner* said it best. A February 1915 editorial compared those who predicted the demise of the "exclusive milliner" to "the kind of people who believe weather forecasts, fish stories, and fairy tales":

> It isn't every woman who wants to buy a hat for $3.48 or for $4.98, but there are millions that do and that will; there are also vast numbers of women who will buy their hats in a shop. They want something different; they want that special attention and advice that an experienced and up-to-date Madame can give them. . . . For this special service they are willing to pay (and they generally do) for the polite Madame who can create and deliver a work of art.[20]

Although this prediction proved overly optimistic, the journal touched upon a crucial point. As its reference to "special attention" made clear, some consumers preferred "my little French milliner who makes hats just to suit me" to the relative anonymity of a department store.[21]

The relationship between tradeswomen and their customers has received only cursory attention from historians. In *American Beauty*, Lois Banner portrayed nineteenth-century dressmakers and milliners as representatives of a "commercial beauty culture" who were "intent on selling products for which the demand was largely artificial." According to Banner, successful dressmakers "had . . . mastered the relationship between salesperson and client and were effectively able to manipulate their patrons by a subtle mix-

ture of flattery and imperiousness."[22] This analysis undoubtedly contains
elements of truth; as arbiters of fashion and potential creators of beauty,
modistes were far from powerless. But it is too simple, for it sees consumers
solely as victims, an assumption unsupported by the evidence.

In sharp contrast to Banner's assessment, genuine intimacy could develop between producer and consumer. Elizabeth Keckley, dressmaker to Mary
Todd Lincoln, became Mrs. Lincoln's closest friend and confidante during
her years in the White House. Catherine Broughton's anonymously published *Suggestions for Dressmakers,* a manual published in 1896, described
what must have been a long-standing tradition: a dressmaker "is supposed
to have a brain large enough to remember all the foibles and fads of all her
customers, and a heart sensitive and loving enough to bathe each one in sympathy for all the troubles and trials to the unbosoming of which the fitting
of a dress somehow leads." As late as the 1950s, Isabella Zetlin Steiner lis-
tened sympathetically as her customers divulged their sorrows. "I remember one who married the same man twice and divorced him twice, and my
mother heard all about it," her daughter recalled. Milliners, too, enjoyed—
or endured—close personal relationships with their patrons. Caroline
Woods's fictionalized version of her stint as a proprietor of a Boston millinery shop in the 1860s suggests that she was closely acquainted with many
of her customers. Some thirty years later the *Illustrated Milliner* argued that
it was the retailer's duty to "curb [the] extravagance" of young women who
could not afford expensive hats, and thus help their customers to avoid "paths
that have led many girls to ruin." Such advice tacitly assumed that the milliner was familiar with the financial circumstances of her clients.[23]

Perhaps, then, producer/consumer relations are merely another example
of women's culture, a concept that—while hardly limited by time and
space—has particular relevance for nineteenth-century America. Historians
of the period have uncovered distinctive female subcultures characterized by
cooperation, empathy, and emotional intensity, intimate bonds between
women that stood in sharp contrast to the relative formality that governed
interactions between women and men. Should we replace Banner's portrait,
which pitted predatory tradeswomen against hapless consumers, with a "female world of love and ritual"?[24] It would be equally incorrect to assert that
relationships between producers and consumers were characterized by intimacy alone. The highly personal nature of these interactions did not preclude conflict; indeed, familiarity may have bred contempt.

More often than not, ritual triumphed over love. Many "service" occupations—teaching, nursing, and hairdressing among them—exploit women's "nurturing" qualities. Dressmaking and millinery were no exception: tradeswomen were expected to perform the nineteenth-century equivalent of what sociologist Arlie Russell Hochschild has called "emotional labor," work that "requires one to induce or suppress feeling in order to sustain the outward countenance that produces the proper state of mind in others." Listening sympathetically to customers' problems was part of the job—a part that at least some tradeswomen privately resented. "Oh, the folly of such women in thinking for a single moment that their dressmakers have the slightest interest in their relations with their husbands!" complained one modiste, treated to a "frank statement" of a spouse's "deficiencies and delinquencies." As this outburst suggests, such relationships were rarely reciprocal; few dressmakers or milliners told *their* troubles to patrons.[25] This is not to say that all "friendships" between producers and consumers were facades or all emotions insincere. But no simple invocation of women's culture adequately describes their interactions. Inequality, not sisterhood, was the hallmark of producer/consumer relations, a fact that was often grounded in the realities of social class.

The Ambiguities of Class

"The popularization of fashion, and the increasing variety of styles," *Demorest's Monthly Magazine* proclaimed in July 1879, "render it essential that a higher and more educated class of workers should take hold of this department than are ordinarily to be found in its workers, who will know something about the principles of art, and who will not butcher rich material." These strictures involved something more than a simple assessment of dressmakers' skill and taste; in the editors' opinion, both were inexorably linked to social class. That they equated artistry and expertise with the "better" sort was evident in their proposed solution: college graduates should take up dressmaking.[26]

It is not at all clear that *Demorest's* did justice to the abilities of the average modiste, but its editors accurately described her social origins, even as they denigrated her skills. As *Demorest's* implied, milliners and dressmakers—even those who presided over the most fashionable establishments—were usually from the working or lower-middle classes. Customers, on the other hand, tended to represent the middle and upper classes. Moreover, the meaning of class in the nineteenth and early twentieth centuries cannot be understood apart from gender. In the eyes of many Americans, business-women—however wealthy or successful—shared the ambiguous social position accorded to all women who left the private sphere of the home for the public world of commerce. Neither the distressed gentlewoman nor the ambitious parvenue presented a challenge to the middle-class "lady"; indeed, both stereotypes reinforced the "lady's" superiority. In an era when domesticity defined middle-class status, interactions between producers and consumers were seldom between social equals. Thus, class differences posed a powerful barrier to intimacy between tradeswomen and their clients.

This model, it should be emphasized, best describes producer/consumer relations in the urban Northeast. Much as the distinction between "help" and "domestics" was partly a rural/urban one, relationships between producers and consumers varied according to geography. In rural areas and small towns, the social distance that separated them was slim. Mary and Bessie Huntting of Sag Harbor, New York, spoke warmly of "Miss Hetty," the family dressmaker; Bessie and Miss Hetty even worked together on a dress (albeit only because a second dressmaker was unavailable). As late as 1900, a letter to the *Illustrated Milliner* explained, "women in villages consider the millinery store strictly a woman's public property where they can meet, exchange views, try on hats, and stay as long as they please. In fact, it is a kind of home place down town."[27]

Even in eastern cities, producers and consumers alike eschewed sharply drawn class lines in favor of minute social distinctions. The precise meanings of categories employed by correspondents for the credit reporting firm R. G. Dun & Co. are elusive. Some terms were evidently synonymous, others denoted subtle differences in status. One dressmaker enjoyed "a good class of customers," another a "select class of customers," still another, "the first class of customers." One modiste worked for the "first families of New York and Boston," while another received clients who were "not the Bon-ton but . . . a responsible class."[28] Milliners and dressmakers themselves were well aware of such distinctions, and they bestowed the highest status upon those within their ranks who attracted the most exclusive clientele.[29]

To be sure, the products of custom work were not the monopoly of the rich; indeed, those who were "not the Bon-ton" extended nearly to the bottom of the social scale. As early as the 1840s, New York City had a group of dressmakers who catered to domestic servants. Nineteenth-century credit records refer to milliners who served a predominantly Irish clientele, and a 1916 study noted that Italian tradeswomen in Boston's north end made hats for their countrywomen. "I'm quality with that hat on," an African American woman in the turn-of-the-century South told her milliner. By 1900, "fashion," though in varying quantities and qualities, was within the reach of all but the most destitute.[30]

More often than not, the production and sale of feminine apparel brought together women from different social milieus. While working-class—and even middle-class—women relied on dressmakers and milliners for their "best" gowns and "Easter bonnets," the wealthy were more likely to patronize tradeswomen on a regular basis. As a result, class differences often determined the tenor of interactions between producers and consumers. In *The American Woman's Home* (1869), Catharine Beecher and Harriet Beecher Stowe elucidated correct behavior for tradeswoman and client: "Your carpenter or plumber does not feel hurt that you do not ask him to dine with you, nor your milliner and mantua-maker that you do not exchange ceremonious calls and invite them to your parties. It is well understood that your relations with them are of a mere business character. They never take it as an assumption of superiority on your part that you do not admit them to relations of private intimacy."[31] But Beecher and Stowe's insistence that such relationships did not involve "superiority" rang hollow. The tone of Sarah Preston Everett Hale's diary entry for July 11, 1859, certainly suggests that she viewed her milliner as her social inferior: "I went in [to town] to give the woman directions about my bonnet." Some fifty years later, the customers of a peripatetic dressmaker allowed her to sit at the family table (a privilege that had yet to become universal) but put her in her place by confining the conversation to "perfunctory" topics, "the point of which would be clear to one who sewed."[32]

At times, interactions between producers and consumers were further complicated by ethnicity and race. In June 1908, Helen Jackson Cabot Almy, best known as the director of a Cambridge settlement house, sent for "my little Irish dressmaker." A study undertaken by the Women's Educational and Industrial Union reported that French and Portuguese dressmakers in New Bedford "work for the better class of American people in the city, not for those of their own race." Race in the modern sense of the term affected Keckley's relationship with her most famous patron, Mary Lincoln. Keckley was a former slave who had purchased her freedom with the funds she earned by dressmaking. Despite her close personal relationship with the First Lady and despite Lincoln's relatively progressive attitudes toward race relations, Keckley's autobiography makes it clear that she was the inferior partner. For her, the primacy of race and the legacy of slavery determined the nature of her interactions with her patrons; as she put it, "I cannot forget the associations of my early life."[33] Similar, if less intense, notions of service shaped relations between white tradeswomen and their customers as well.

Thus, intimacy did not preclude inequality; rather, one reinforced the other. Interpretations that stress intraclass bonds between women notwithstanding, evidence suggests that customers could confide in their dressmakers precisely *because* the latter were social inferiors; "ladies" could divulge secrets that pride and propriety forbade them from telling their peers.[34] Indeed, ladies who wondered how to treat "their" dressmakers and milliners had a convenient model; relationships between producers and consumers evinced considerable similarity to those between domestic servants and their mistresses. Surely the notion of service—helping patrons to dress and undress and attending to their psychological and emotional needs—was integral to the production of women's clothing.

Some tradeswomen apparently accepted the servile role foisted upon them, believing deference a small price to pay for the privilege of serving wealthy clients. Others, members of a tiny elite who wielded considerable authority over the sartorial lives of their customers, resembled the imperious modistes of popular folklore. Still others, like the dressmaker whose patrons never guessed "that I might be intelligent," reacted with resentment.[35] For producer/consumer relations presented dressmakers and milliners with a painful irony. While many garnered considerable respect within their own racial, ethnic, or working-class communities (Keckley, Lincoln's dressmaker, was a member of Washington's African American elite), the etiquette of consumption required them to strike a subservient pose. Thus, while the fashion trades offered their practitioners the prospect of economic independence, they also exacted a psychological toll. Proud, often intensely ambitious women, modistes were expected to remain deferential when faced with overbearing consumers.

To be sure, dressmakers and milliners were not domestics; working-class girls who eschewed domestic service viewed the two trades as highly desirable occupations. As arbiters of fashion and makers of beauty, modistes and bonnet makers possessed a psychological authority that servants lacked. Finally, few tradeswomen were beholden to their customers "seven days a week." Nevertheless, women often employed dressmakers or milliners for many of the same reasons that they engaged domestics. Just as "ladies" did not do their own housework, the truly genteel did not make their own clothes.

In reality, this was an ideal to which only the very wealthy could conform. Ideology aside, most middle-class women *did* do housework and make clothing.[36] Nevertheless, the ability to hire "help" distinguished the lady from her social inferior. Indeed, as several historians have noted, servants conferred psychological as well as practical benefits on their employers. The servant did more than clean house; she affirmed her mistress's status. Similarly, the very act of patronizing a dressmaker or milliner often represented an assertion of class identity. Almy's reference to her "little Irish dressmaker" is a case in point. Her attitude was at once proprietary and affectionate. Even in this slight remark she carefully noted the social distance that separated her from her dressmaker, taking pains to mention the modiste's ethnicity—but not her name—and to describe her as literally beneath her in stature.[37]

Milliners and dressmakers did not passively accept this servile role. Their own yearnings for respectability, bolstered by the knowledge that customers equated taste with middle-class status, encouraged strenuous efforts to disguise their social origins. Antebellum fiction, as we have seen, ridiculed these pretensions; story after story exposes the humble beginnings of "the celebrated Parisian artiste."[38] While writers reduced milliners and dressmakers to caricatures, literary portrayals had some basis in reality. The near-universal adoption of the sobriquet "Madame," regardless of nativity, was a staple of both fact and fiction.

While asserting their claims to respectability, some dressmakers and milliners sought to recreate themselves in their clients' image. An advertisement for J. S. Cook's millinery and dressmaking establishment, published in the 1849 edition of *The Stranger's Guide in the City of Boston,* made a point of noting the proprietor's "lady-like" demeanor. A year later Philadelphian Bessie Huntting wrote to her mother of her decision to buy a new bonnet: "Mrs. Jones was telling me of a very good miliner [*sic*] where she goes, in Pine St. A lady who was once in excellent circumstances—she always goes to such persons she says."[39] Perhaps the milliner in question really had fallen from "excellent circumstances." The distressed gentlewoman, like the ridiculous parvenue, was a popular fictional motif. Equally plausible is the assumption that the Pine Street milliner's story was the product of invention, a calculated attempt to attract customers. After all, distressed gentlewomen—bona fide members of the "deserving" poor—met requirements for respectability that ambitious, upwardly mobile working-class women did not.[40] At the same time, the "lady who was once in excellent circumstances" did not challenge the status of the "lady" who could afford to patronize her.

Susan Porter Benson notes that twentieth-century department store managers attempted to train saleswomen to act more "middle-class."[41] A similar if less coercive process was at work much earlier among the proprietors of dressmaking and millinery shops. In this case, however, the trappings of gentility were often self-imposed. When the salesperson could be as important as the product, this strategy promised to boost both profits and morale. The more genteel a tradeswoman's bearing, the more prestigious her potential clientele and the higher her prices. But milliners' and dressmakers' attempts at self-creation, whatever their pecuniary benefits, were also efforts to assert their dignity and worth.

Tradeswomen's responses to their clients ranged from gender solidarity to class antagonism. Abigail Scott Duniway opened a millinery shop in Albany, Oregon, in the late 1860s, after her husband met with a permanently disabling accident. Albany was a small frontier town where social distinctions were relatively unimportant. Duniway served as her customers' confidante; they related tales of the indifference, cruelty, and abuse suffered at the hands of their husbands. Her newfound awareness of the widespread oppression of women had a lasting impact. Convinced that injustice could be remedied only through political means, she became a leader of the woman suffrage movement on the West Coast.[42]

At first glance, Mary Harris had much in common with Duniway. The Irish-born Harris entered the dressmaking business in Chicago in 1860 after a brief stint as a schoolteacher. A few months later, she moved to Memphis and resumed teaching; the following year she married George Jones, a miner. In 1867, after a yellow fever epidemic claimed the lives of her husband and four children, she returned to Chicago, formed a partnership, and opened a dressmaking shop where she served the city's "aristocrats." She remained in business until her shop was destroyed by Chicago's Great Fire of 1871. Harris, too, learned lessons from her experience. The contrast between "the luxury and extravagance" of her patrons and "the poor, shivering wretches, jobless and hungry" she observed from her window fueled her developing class consciousness. "My employers," she explained, "seemed neither to notice nor to care." Like Duniway, Harris would earn her place in history. But for Duniway, who met her customers on more or less equal terms, gender was the crucial source of oppression; for Harris, later to achieve notoriety as Mother Jones, the relevant category was class. That one of the most famous figures in the annals of American labor radicalism got her start as a dressmaker attests to the bitterness that wealthy patrons could inspire.[43]

Fashion and Beauty: Contested Terrain

As nineteenth- and early twentieth-century consumers saw it, dressmakers and milliners performed the necessary function of clothing them according to prevailing vogues. This task was not a simple one; the Victorian wardrobe—requiring multitudinous yards of fabric and infinite quantities of ribbons, ruffles, and lace—was (at least by late twentieth-century standards) complicated and cumbersome. Victorian fashion, of course, is shorthand for nearly a century of varying modes; indeed, the very term "fashion"—as opposed to "costume"—presumes a system of rapidly changing styles.[44] Leg-of-mutton sleeves reigned in the 1830s, voluminous skirts in the 1850s and 1860s, bustles in the 1870s and 1880s—vogues that contemporaries hardly considered interchangeable. One diarist, writing in 1853, was quick to note the "ludicrous appearance" of a neighbor who donned "a bonnet which was worn in 1830." But as Valerie Steele has pointed out, the fashions that prevailed between 1820 and 1910 shared a common characteristic: a "female silhouette . . . formed by two cones—the long full, structured skirt and the tailored, boned bodice—intersecting at a narrow and constricted waist." Signaling an abandonment of earlier, relatively androgynous styles, Victorian garments emphasized and in some cases literally constructed the "feminine" attributes of their wearers, physical embodiments of the doctrine of separate spheres.[45]

Such clothing incited considerable controversy. Beginning in the 1850s, amorphous coalitions of feminists, physicians, utopians, and health reformers demanded and sometimes initiated alternative apparel; the bloomer costume is one of the most famous examples. Representing a much broader spectrum of public opinion, newspaper reporters and magazine writers frequently ridiculed the extravagance and absurdity of feminine fashion. While they eschewed the radicalism of Bloomerites and their successors (if anything they denounced reform dress even more vociferously than they did fashionable dress), members of the "respectable" media ensured that women's fashion remained a widely discussed topic.[46]

There was much to criticize. As numerous observers made clear, clothes designed to accentuate the "natural" qualities of the feminine figure depended on highly artificial devices. Corsets constricted waists; heavy petticoats and cumbersome crinolines lent support to flaring skirts. As some woman's rights advocates saw it, not only was Victorian costume uncomfortable, unhealthy, and impractical, it symbolized women's social and economic dependence; by emphasizing women's "difference" it reinforced the existing sexual division of labor. Woman's "manner of dress," one analyst remarked, "would make it rather inconvenient for her to go to the mast-head in a gale, or handle goods in a wholesale grocery establishment." Some went so far as to proclaim that "rational dress" was the key to women's liberation. "The want of the *ballot* is but a *toy* in comparison!" declared a particularly dedicated advocate of dress reform.[47]

While dress reformers offered perceptive insights, half-truths and unrealistic expectations marred their critiques. Though corsets were less than comfortable and probably less than healthful, tales of severed livers and crushed ribs had little basis in fact; contrary to popular belief, only a few women appear to have indulged in the much condemned practice of "tight-lacing." Stories of fiery deaths sparked by flammable hoop skirts—while not entirely fictional—appeared with suspicious frequency in reformers' accounts. And all too often, proponents of rational dress pursued an antifeminist agenda, evincing less interest in liberating women than in keeping them in their place. Proposals advocating the substitution of "modest" dresses for "immoral" garments betrayed a (conscious or unconscious) desire to control female sexuality. Male physicians (who also decried the impact of female education on maternity) jumped on the dress reform bandwagon in the 1880s because they believed that "sensibly" attired, uncorseted women would make better mothers. Even those who explicitly connected dress reform to women's rights were naive at best; as subsequent generations would discover, changing fashions did not in themselves transform women's status.[48]

If denunciations of feminine apparel masked more complex meanings, the role that popular discourse assigned to dressmakers and milliners was equally misleading. Portrayed as pitiful figures in discussions of women and work, they quickly became omnipotent despots when the subject changed to fashion. No longer pathetic victims, dressmakers and milliners unscrupulously imposed ridiculous and extravagant attire on hapless consumers.

This argument conveniently exempted "respectable" women from blame; just as the lady who appeared in unflattering, outmoded, or even ultra-fashionable attire could easily point to her dressmaker, vulgar modistes, whose social origins belied refinement, bore collective responsibility for elaborate, expensive, and unhealthy styles. Evelyn Smith Tobey, instructor of millinery at Columbia Teachers' College (and herself the representative of a burgeoning home economics movement that benefited mainly middle-class women), argued in 1910 that the trade desperately needed "the influence of the cultured woman." Despairing of the "absurdly inappropriate" appearance of the typical milliner, she lamented, "This type of American business woman is the dictator of millinery fashion for us." Not surprisingly, these dictators sold "extreme, ridiculous, and extravagant hats."[49] Whether she realized it or not, Tobey's complaint was far from new; portrayals of villainous tradeswomen who forced naive customers to don outlandish vogues appear at least as early as the antebellum period. Neither was her insistence that taste "naturally" reflected social class, although she voiced her convictions in particularly explicit terms. Tobey's comments and others like them suggest that tradeswomen's position as arbiters of fashion fueled resentments; keeping up with the latest trends meant deferring to the advice of social inferiors. Put another way, dressmakers' and milliners' authority represented an inversion of the proper social order.

These complaints notwithstanding, milliners and dressmakers did not bear the entire responsibility for the making of fashion. The vast majority held to widely accepted standards. While American tradeswomen offered their customers advice on styles and fabrics, few were actually originators; most adapted Paris styles to individual tastes. Nor did they glean their information directly from France. To keep abreast of the latest vogues, rural dressmakers traveled to urban areas; New York was the domestic mecca for those who could afford the trip. Only the wealthiest and most exclusive modistes and milliners made yearly journeys abroad.[50] Magazines and trade journals, perhaps the closest approximation to a fashion "industry" in nineteenth-century America, also apprised tradeswomen of new developments. Milliners and mantua makers possessed no monopoly over such information. While trade publications catered to retailers, *Godey's, Demorest's,* and *Peterson's* were read by producers and consumers alike.

If tradeswomen exerted control over their clients, their authority was never absolute. Customers in fact seldom played the role of passive victim. "I am to comply with what the taste of my customers requires," a Boston milliner declared, "I cannot regulate their tastes." Abba Woolson, a staunch advocate of dress reform, caustically dubbed a dressmaker the "divinity" but unwittingly described a scenario in which the consumer enjoyed a great deal of choice. Not only did the patron select the fabric, she decided—in Woolson's words—"with" the modiste on the precise style, relying on fashion plates in addition to the dressmaker's advice.[51]

By every indication, consumers played an active part in designing their apparel. The selection of a new bonnet was a momentous decision for sixteen-year-old Sarah Ellen Browne, a student at the Cambridge school run by Louis and Elizabeth Agassiz. She consulted first her classmates, then her mother:

> Last evening Sallie Howe was here. We were all talking about bonnets. They all wish me to have some kind of a bright flower inside my bonnet. Sarah and Lizzie wish me to have a Geranium scarlet, white strings with a scarlet edge, not to have purple by any means, they say. . . . I wish to know what you like. I do not think pink is becoming. . . .
>
> They say I must not have white or purple—I will leave it for you to decide.

When Browne finally purchased the bonnet, Miss Mary, her chaperone, made the decision (white ribbon and white lace). The milliner apparently played no part in the choice. If Browne was unhappy with her purchase, she had only herself and Mary to blame.[52]

Dissatisfied customers did not necessarily suffer in silence. In December 1864, Lincoln informed Ruth Harris, her New York milliner, "I can neither wear, or settle with you, for my bonnet without different inside flowers. . . . I cannot retain or wear the bonnet, as it is—I am certainly taught a lesson by your acting thus." Lincoln's reaction revealed much about the nature of the relationship between tradeswoman and client. She did not interpret Harris's choice of trimmings as a matter subject to differences of opinion. To the contrary, she implied that Harris, by selecting the "wrong" flowers, had deliberately offended her. At the same time, Lincoln (a woman who privately expressed a good deal of anxiety about her social status) none too subtly asserted her class position, proclaiming her taste to be superior to that of the errant milliner. Tradeswomen did not always meekly accept such criticism; Bostonian Sarah Appleton Lawrence worried that her dressmaker would refuse an order because she was "hurt at a note I sent her." In the end, the aggrieved modiste relented, perhaps because she possessed a forgiving nature—more likely because she could not afford to lose Lawrence's custom.[53]

No issue caused greater discord than the "fit" of a dress. Fashioning a garment in the correct shape and proportions was no easy matter, and the results were evaluated by highly selective criteria. A perceptive observer acknowledged that "any woman knows how difficult it is to decide upon what is satisfactory where the fitting of a waist is concerned."[54] But as this assessment implied, more was at stake than whether or not the dress fit.

Indeed, the very nature of the fashion trades conferred a special vulnerability upon their practitioners, a problem that continues to plague today's hairdressers. Clothing meant many things to many women: a badge of social status, an assertion of gender identity, a presentation of self. Whatever their conscious or unconscious motivations, most wished to be attractive. Long before the emergence of what T. J. Jackson Lears has called "therapeutic advertising," patrons expected to be transformed by the dressmaker's and milliner's arts. Sometimes the process succeeded. "When I put my bonnet on and looked into the glass I hardly knew myself it made me look so handsome," one satisfied customer exclaimed. Disaster could just as easily have been the result, as one dressmaker's bitter complaint reveals: "They expect us to remake them in spite of nature."[55]

These disappointments notwithstanding, custom manufacture had advantages that at least some consumers must have recognized. However exasperating the details of garment making, the dressmaker's or milliner's patron exerted a degree of control over production that her late twentieth-century counterpart does not. However unsatisfactory the result, the made-to-order system granted her the authority to specify the style of *her* dress or hat, its color and embellishments. The Gilded Age devotee of fashion, swathed in an elaborately trimmed gown that required as many as sixteen yards of fabric, was the very symbol of conspicuous consumption. Scholars troubled by the "passivity" of modern consumers might do well to examine this earlier sort of consumerism in which customers played an active role.[56]

Time and Money

Additional tensions beset interactions between tradeswomen and their clients, which had less to do with individuals' anxieties regarding status and appearance than with the inherent limitations of the made-to-order system. Custom production took time and was expensive. For many consumers, factors of convenience and cost at least partially offset the attractions of originality and the therapeutic benefits of patronizing personal clothiers.

Dressmakers and milliners offered their customers considerably more variety and individuality than did the manufacturers and sellers of readymade clothing. But their products were not immediately available. Complaints that dresses and hats were never ready when promised were legion. Even here the personal nature of the producer/consumer relationship intervened; patrons often attributed delays to tradeswomen's ill-will rather than to "busy" seasons or painstaking craftsmanship. These accusations contained a grain of truth; evidence suggests that tradeswomen and their employees collectively punished troublesome customers with habitual tardiness, rewarding their "favorites" with prompt service. But more often than not, impatient customers merely increased the potential for exploitation; rush orders meant long hours for proprietors and workers alike.[57]

While patronizing a dressmaker or milliner was a less cumbersome process than making her own clothes, it nevertheless required a considerable investment of the client's time. By every indication, dressmaking was a particularly troublesome affair: "'Trying on.' Dinner. After dinner went out with a list from the dressmaker & shopped till six," reads Almy's diary for December 16, 1880. On December 17, she noted: "Went down town early to do some errands for the dressmaker. . . . After dinner, trying-on, & more errands till dark. Trying-on & accounts before tea." On December 18, she had a "final trying on."[58]

Class tensions, competing conceptions of fashion and beauty, and the cumbersome nature and snail-like pace of custom production undoubtedly strained relations between producers and consumers. But the most common source of conflict was economic. Put simply, dresses and hats cost money. And no wonder: in theory at least, nineteenth-century ladies required a bewildering variety of garments—distinctive costumes for morning, afternoon, and evening and specific ensembles for walking, traveling, shopping, and various stages of mourning.[59] Available evidence indicates that few women followed religiously the advice dispensed by fashion magazines and etiquette manuals. Diarists occasionally wrote of "traveling bonnets," "walking dresses," and "boating suits," but most merely distinguished between summer and winter apparel, everyday and best wear. While her wealthy counterpart might possess a large and varied wardrobe, the typical middle-class woman owned a washable calico "wrapper" in which to perform the considerable work of housekeeping, one or two dresses of silk or better quality cotton for making and receiving calls, and a silk gown for special occasions. Similarly, most women found that an everyday hat and a dress bonnet sufficiently satisfied the social convention that required their heads to be covered whenever they left their homes.[60]

Thus, real-life shoppers failed to confirm popular images of female extravagance. To the contrary, most obtained one or two new dresses or bonnets—worn until hems frayed and feathers drooped—each season. (Indeed, this state of affairs may have intensified conflict between tradeswomen and their clients; consumers who pinned their hopes on the transformative powers of a single garment were apt to be disappointed.) Nevertheless, these relatively paltry (by today's standards) wardrobes represented a significant expense to those who wore them, a matter of no small consequence to the makers and sellers of feminine apparel.

In this, dressmakers and milliners were not alone; dry goods merchants, fancy goods dealers, lace vendors, and ribbon sellers likewise braved the fury of bargain-hunting consumers. But modistes and bonnet makers faced a unique form of competition: women often made their own clothes in order to save money. In 1870, a young woman who identified herself as "Nellie" complained to the "Ladies' Club," a regular feature of *Demorest's Monthly Magazine:* "I have forty dollars a month to dress with. It takes it all, and I don't have anything very nice either." The editors replied, "Forty dollars per month ought to dress you very nicely, with management. But you should do a good deal of your own sewing." In an era when unskilled laborers earned between 75 cents and $1.50 per day, Nellie, who had $40 a month to devote to clothing alone, was very wealthy indeed.[61] Even so, she could not afford to rely entirely on milliners and dressmakers.

Augusta Sewall, a teacher in Trenton, New Jersey, confronted a similar dilemma, albeit with considerable resourcefulness. Relying on acquaintances to secure fabric and trimmings at wholesale prices ("real cheap," as she put it), she produced a bonnet with $3.43 worth of materials, triumphantly proclaiming it "(in my modest opinion) prettier than any silk bonnet I saw in the city for seven or eight dollars." Sewall's self-congratulatory statements aside, homemade hats and dresses were often inferior in quality to those fashioned by professionals, as one tradeswoman's self-serving but probably accurate denunciation of "quack millinery" pointed out. The do-it-yourself approach took time, too, as even the thrifty Sewall recognized. "Last spring I sewed a good deal," she remarked, "but I don't mean to this year." Nevertheless, Sewall found the decision to sacrifice money for time a difficult one. In the end, only the dressmaker's assurances that she had indeed gotten her fabric "cheap" assuaged her misgivings.[62]

As a second consequence of their attempts to economize, consumers routinely engaged both milliners and dressmakers to "make over" dresses and hats, work that was far less remunerative than the production of new garments.[63] Alternatively, tradeswomen might be employed to perform only part of the process. Mrs. George Hodges sewed the skirts for her daughter Kate's new dresses but instructed Kate to hire a dressmaker for the more difficult task of making the bodices. Beecher and Stowe advised their readers "to get a dress fitted (not sewed) at the best mantua-maker's." Some tradeswomen evidently resisted such procedures. Keckley "never cut and fitted work to be made up outside of my work-room." But as numerous diarists, who described visits to the dressmaker to have garments cut but not sewn, make clear, Keckley's was a prerogative that only the most exclusive modistes could enforce.[64]

As might be expected, the quest for economy dominated the fashioning of new clothes as well. When a patron announced that "the price was of no consequence," Woods wondered whether she was "the subject of an illusion." At the age of sixteen, the schoolgirl Browne (the purchaser of the white-ribboned bonnet described earlier) had already learned to dispute the notion that money was no object. In a letter to her mother she described her visit to a Boston milliner in June 1857. Mary, her adviser and chaperone, had haggled with the shopkeeper, ultimately reducing the price of a "simple, and yet a stylish looking bonnet" from eight to seven dollars. Even so, she expressed misgivings. "Do you think I have done wrong to get such an expensive bonnet? We tried, but could not get one for less."[65]

Thrift motivated women in all walks of life, a fact bound to endanger in particular the health of marginal business concerns. "My dear Madame Harris," Lincoln wrote to her milliner in 1861, "I want you to make up a purple *silk* velvet headdress . . . trimmed exquisitely. . . . I want it very beautiful, exercise your taste, to the utmost. . . . You must not ask me over $5.00 for it," she concluded.[66] Both Sewall and Browne indicated that seven to eight dollars was the going price for a dress bonnet in this period; Lincoln was thrifty indeed. Moreover, her position as First Lady granted her a greater degree of coercive power than most.

The pursuit of economy was not one-sided. Dressmakers and milliners, like most businesspeople, sought the highest possible prices for their goods and services. Some developed ingenious means of enriching themselves at their customers' expense; modistes who followed the "dressmakers' rule" deliberately overestimated the amount of fabric necessary to clothe their customers, keeping the remaining pieces for themselves.[67]

Nonetheless, the milliner or dressmaker was usually at a disadvantage; she was economically the less powerful member of the producer/consumer relationship. Before department stores instituted the practice of fixed prices and cash transactions, all merchants—large and small, male and female, wholesale and retail—granted their customers credit, often for a period as long as six months. While the relatively lenient lending practices that governed nineteenth-century retailing created considerable uncertainty for businesspeople, they proved particularly troublesome for dressmakers and milliners. A variety of sources indicate that their customers were especially tardy in settling their bills, suggesting that patrons recognized and exploited businesswomen's pecuniary vulnerability. As one dressmaker complained, "They will settle the heavy bills of florist and caterer and jeweler, but I, who am poorer and more dependent on their good will, must wait." Moreover, etiquette prevented the tradeswoman from pressing her claims. The importance of word-of-mouth advertising placed a premium on retaining the allegiance of one's clientele; the modiste or milliner who demanded payment risked losing both actual and potential customers. The wealthier the client, the greater the degree of delicacy required.[68]

The customer's reluctance to pay was more than merely inconvenient; it had a particularly deleterious effect on businesses that relied on small amounts of capital. "The greatest cause for failure in the retail millinery business," one analyst noted, "is the fact that . . . the milliner does business on too much of a credit system." A second observer declared that delinquent accounts resulted in bankruptcy and even death; a New York dressmaker, she wrote, committed suicide, leaving behind "large assets in uncollectible bills against fashionable people."[69] Such tragedies were not entirely gender specific; custom tailors who served an affluent male clientele faced similar pressures. But while many tailors qualified as small businessmen by the standards of their day, their assets on average outstripped those possessed by their female counterparts. If small businessmen faced uncertain futures—a situation exacerbated by irresponsible customers—small businesswomen shouldered an even heavier burden. This was especially true of dressmakers, who kept no stock and rarely had cash to spare.[70]

The records of the Protective Committee of the Women's Educational and Industrial Union (WEIU) of Boston, mentioned in the previous chapter, document the far-reaching consequences of customers' tardiness and reveal the fragility of the economic links that bound together the female economy. Founded in 1878, the committee provided legal assistance to working women; dressmakers and their customers figured prominently in its reports. Members helped tradeswomen to recover their earnings, threatening and sometimes instituting legal action against reluctant debtors. A typical case involved a dressmaker "who had made rich dresses for two sisters who deferred payment for two years, until our lawyer dealt with them and compelled restitution."[71]

Employers who neglected to pay their workers made far more frequent appearances in the Protective Committee's minutes. As noted in the previous chapter, tardy customers were often to blame, a fact that the committee's members did not always recognize. Indeed, it could hardly have been otherwise. The strength of popular stereotypes that portrayed dressmakers and milliners as ruthless exploiters of female labor and unprincipled purveyors of useless fashions clearly affected the Protective Committee members' responses; tradeswomen's unsavory—if often undeserved—reputations gained them little sympathy even from their most likely supporters. After all, committee members must have reasoned, Madames did business by victimizing other women, both workers and consumers. Influenced by an increasingly "professional" ethos, the committee began to investigate the sources of labor exploitation during the second half of its twenty-seven-year career. Later reports acknowledged that the proprietors of smaller firms were particularly hard-pressed and that customers who deferred or delayed payment adversely affected dressmakers' ability to reimburse their employees. But in its heyday in the 1880s, the committee's analyses did not usually extend beyond condemnations of unscrupulous employers.[72]

To be sure, the Protective Committee provided valuable assistance to wage-earning women who had few means with which to remedy their plights. But this help often came at the expense of female proprietors. Consciously or not, committee members—part of a larger organization that actively promoted women's independence—opted for a solution that reinforced women's dependence, frequently aiding starving seamstresses but rarely assisting struggling entrepreneurs.

Equally significant, the method employed by the committee inevitably exacerbated tensions between producers and consumers. The committee relied on a highly successful tactic: the trustee process. Its attorneys legally attached—or garnisheed—employers' property until the latter compensated their workers. Since most modistes possessed little property, the committee seized on the idea of attaching the partially completed garments that lay in the dressmakers' workrooms. Technically, most modistes "owned" only their labor (and that of their employees), since customers generally provided the necessary raw materials. Nevertheless, "trusteeing" a dress proved effective, for it prevented dressmakers from collecting their fees. This strategy required the cooperation of customers; to gain it, WEIU members used and perhaps abused class privilege. As representatives of Boston's elite, they relied on social acquaintances to assist their proceedings. The minutes of a meeting in March 1880 illuminate their methods: "Mrs. Sewall said she heard that Mrs. Lunt and Mrs. Louise Chandler Moulton were having dresses made by Miss Adams, and thought perhaps we might trustee them."[73]

The trustee process often penalized the most vulnerable denizens of the commercial world. "Adams" was probably Clara Adams, fifty-six years old in 1880, who enjoyed a "very good class of trade" but whom credit investigators had pronounced "thoroughly good for nothing." Committee members professed their willingness to take action against "women whom we knew in society," but class loyalties often prevailed over gender solidarity. Thus, while the committee compiled lists of "bad" employers and even contemplated publishing their names, it never launched a campaign against customers who failed to fulfill their obligations.[74] A strategy that might have revealed the true sources of exploitation foundered on the shoals of class.

The Sexual Politics of Fashion

Some customers certainly deserved censure. The litany of excuses recorded by Allinson reveals women who were thoughtless at best, callous at worst: "'I am going to Europe this summer and must be economical.'" "'John is going to college this winter and there are so many expenses.'" "'Why I never realized that it made any great difference.'"[75]

But if some patrons deliberately exploited their dressmakers and others justified their actions as a rational response to the indignities they endured in the hands of supposedly omnipotent "divinities," still others were in fact powerless to settle their accounts. For men were the behind-the-scenes actors in a drama that seemingly concerned only women. Female extravagance, real or imagined, was a potential source of friction between husbands and wives, fathers and daughters. This tension had significant consequences for those whose livelihoods depended upon the manufacture and sale of feminine apparel. Because their customers by and large were economically dependent on men, dressmakers and milliners relied at least indirectly on male economic support. In one sense, this was not at all a female world.

Economic conflicts between husbands and wives (or less frequently, fathers and daughters) have long been the stuff of comedies. But the question of who controlled the purse strings was a serious issue that often determined the balance of power within a marriage. By the mid-nineteenth century, women's responsibility for household consumption was widely acknowledged. Yet as Elaine S. Abelson has argued persuasively, the ability to consume did not necessarily imply control over family finances; women spent what their husbands frequently regarded as "*their*" money." As workers who—according to popular perception—did not "work" (even paid labor performed by middle-class wives remained for the most part invisible), they had at best limited claims to the wages men earned.[76] Just as proprietors and workers walked a fine line between economic autonomy and financial dependence, so too did consumers confront the reality of their own dependent status. Patronizing a dressmaker or milliner was a very different matter from purchasing food, clothing for others, or home furnishings, because it meant spending money on oneself. "Millinery takes the place in many families of books and pictures and father's new overcoat," one satirist half humorously complained.[77] All too often, female extravagance—especially when unleashed on personal adornment—embodied more than a hint of wifely insubordination.

Contemporaries recognized as much. The novelist William Dean Howells wryly observed that the crowds of women who packed Boston's downtown shopping district were "intent upon spending the money of their natural protectors." The British author of *The Habits of Good Society*, an advice manual reprinted in the United States, made much the same point. "A love of dress," he wrote, not only benefited unjustly "the extortionate class of persons in the shape of milliners and dressmakers" but elicited "remonstrances and often reproaches from the person most likely to suffer from his wife's indulgences—her husband."[78]

Of course, few husbands expected their wives to garb themselves in homespun; as Thorstein Veblen argued nearly a century ago, a woman's clothing was an important indicator of her spouse's status.[79] But men hoped that feminine "indulgences" could be purchased at minimal cost. Indeed, the reformer Virginia Penny argued that women's reputation for extravagance was often unfounded and that they were just as likely to err in the opposite direction. She attributed the unfortunate effects of female stinginess not to women themselves but to the constraints that men placed upon them. Penny observed that "the spirit that prompts a married woman to beat down the prices, and contend for a bargain . . . arises mostly from the consciousness that her husband, in whose hands the purse is very likely to be, will expect the ultimatum of the money's worth." While husbands might display a "mean parsimony" when allocating funds to their wives, they placed few restraints on their own purchases. "What a man gets easily he spends freely," Penny concluded; "what a woman earns dearly she parts with sparingly."[80]

As Penny's analysis implies, the economic war between the sexes was not confined to the pages of prescriptive literature and fiction. One mother, responding to her daughter's frequent demands for "presents," warned, "Your father . . . was quite angry at your request . . . and told me to ask if you thought money grew on trees." Lincoln greatly feared that her husband would be defeated in the 1864 election—because then he would find out that she owed thousands of dollars to A. T. Stewart's New York dry goods store. After Abraham Lincoln won reelection, Mary used her position as First Lady to best advantage. She devised a partially successful scheme whereby prominent Republicans paid her debts in exchange for her "influence" with her husband. Apparently, the president never learned of this arrangement.[81]

An anonymous patron of the Boston dressmaker Olivia Flynt was not so lucky. In December 1869, Flynt charged her customer $2,000 for making four dresses, a price she believed her "artistic skill" justified. Unfortunately for Flynt, the woman's husband did not agree. He refused to pay for the garments, leaving Flynt no recourse but to sue (available records fail to record the outcome).[82] Fourteen years later, the WEIU's Protective Committee recorded an equally revealing incident. Mrs. Waterman refused to pay her dressmaker, and the latter took her complaint to the committee. On November 19, 1883, Waterman explained her predicament to committee member Kate Gannett Wells. Wells revealed the true cause of Waterman's tardiness: "Her husband pays her her allowance on the 20th. She dares not ask for it sooner, and promises I shall have it on the 20th. I told her that the Committee at my request had stopped any legal proceedings till they heard from me. She was very grateful."[83] (It is worth noting that Wells's sympathy for Waterman's plight contrasted sharply with the committee's derisive comments about employers.)

Just as tradeswomen were not entirely powerless in their negotiations with customers, neither were wives entirely powerless when dealing with their husbands. Indeed, consumers might manipulate the sexual politics of fashion to their own advantage—at tradeswomen's expense. Husbands who "did not like" new garments served as convenient excuses for dissatisfied customers who would rather keep their money; so did spouses who "refused" to pay. While ample evidence suggests that men exercised considerable control over women's purchases, consumers might falsely invoke masculine tyranny to gain feminine sympathy and pecuniary advantage—or so many modistes and milliners believed.[84]

Dilatory and delinquent customers affected the fortunes of many types of retailers, not just milliners and dressmakers; Mary Lincoln's bill at Stewart's is one example. But women's reluctance or inability to settle their accounts— and the paternal or marital tensions behind such practices—did not affect all retailers in the same way. As early as the 1860s, A. T. Stewart's "marble palace" was a vast establishment, although Lincoln's $27,000 bill caused considerable consternation. Exceptional circumstances like this aside, a customer who ran "long accounts" simply did not have the same impact on a large dry goods firm, whose owners were likely to hold sizeable cash reserves, as on a small dressmaking or millinery shop. Women's businesses, handicapped from the outset by scant capital and limited access to credit, suffered disproportionately from the sexual politics of a supposedly "private" sphere.[85]

These themes found expression in a sample advertisement that the *Illustrated Milliner*, a trade journal, presented to its subscribers in August 1900. The title indicated the ad's purpose: "Only an Advertisement. But a Business Story so Enticingly Told that It Must Have Brought a Lot of Trade to the Boston Store." As its promoters explained, "The best thing about this cleverly designed advertisement is that it is good, easy reading, so bright and breezy that one keeps on to the very end without skipping a word."

The "story" concerned the source of annual "trouble in the Mortimer Jones family." As the text of the advertisement explained, "It is not the first time the Easter bonnet question has disrupted a household and brought husbands and wives into the divorce court." It seems that the exorbitant prices charged by Mrs. Jones's milliner, "Miss Jezebel Hanks," had a devastating impact on the family's finances. To pay for his wife's Easter bonnet, poor Mr. Jones had to forgo a summer suit, skip "the lawyer's clambake," and evade the "coal man's collector." But all was not lost. As Mrs. Jones explained, "I'm not going to Miss Jezebel Hanks this Spring, dear. She simply cheated me out of my eye teeth last Spring. I'm going to the Boston Store this time. Their hats are the sweetest things in town and you can get two of them for the price of one from Miss Hanks."[86]

"Only an Advertisement" was not a true story and perhaps not even a real advertisement (whether or not the Boston Store actually used the ad is unclear), but its text is intriguing in several respects. It presented variations on two age-old themes: the disreputable milliner who preyed upon hapless consumers and the marital conflict created by female extravagance. The story impugned Hanks's commercial and personal reputation; not only was she a "Jezebel," but her surname was probably derived from "hanky-panky," a term that connoted both shady business dealings and sexual impropriety. In the end, the ad promised to put both women in their places, transforming Mrs. Jones into a model wife and "sensible" consumer and consigning the villainous Hanks to richly deserved commercial disaster. "Only an Advertisement" foreshadowed the future. It pitted a small female-run business, Hanks's millinery shop, against a Chicago department store, a large-scale enterprise run by men. By emphasizing quantity over quality, its creators strongly implied that the hats available at the Boston Store were ready-made, factory-produced affairs, not custom creations. For all its exaggeration, the text reflected economic realities. Hanks's high prices were the cost of business survival; small female-operated concerns could not enjoy the same economies of scale as larger firms. By the same token, factory-produced hats were cheaper than their custom-made counterparts, allowing consumers to purchase many more hats than the two or three a year to which they were accustomed.[87]

By presenting the department store as a benign, "legitimate" alternative to dressmakers' and milliners' shops (a questionable assumption at best[88]), "Only an Advertisement" offered the consumer a way out—but at the expense of women entrepreneurs. Indeed, substituting the name of a female retailer for the Boston Store would have spoiled the ad's effect. Mary Brown (the name of a milliner listed in the Boston city directory of 1900) versus Jezebel Hanks fails to muster the drama inspired by the Boston Store's challenge.

* * *

In the end, consumers voted with their feet—and their money. The Boston Stores triumphed over the Jezebel Hankses. Who won and who lost in the course of this development? Clearly, milliners and dressmakers lost. Certainly, they labored in circumstances that were far from ideal; as both proprietors and workers discovered, the women's world of custom production was often an exploitative one. Nonetheless, millinery and dressmaking offered women—many of them daughters of the working classes—rare opportunities to exercise skill and creativity and avenues, however precarious, to economic independence. Whatever else she may have represented, Jezebel Hanks, an unmarried woman of business, was a symbol of female autonomy, an image that evidently disturbed the advertising men who penned "Only an Advertisement." The triumph of the Boston Store signaled the victory not only of large-scale retailing over smaller concerns but of businesses operated by men over businesses controlled by women.

The victory of mass production and large-scale retailing, as we shall see in the following chapters, was neither instantaneous nor absolute. Some customers eagerly embraced the ready-made fashions displayed on department store racks, others only reluctantly abandoned their dressmakers' and milliners' shops. Those who valued time and money—clearly the majority—chose the first option; those who preferred intimacy to anonymity, originality to uniformity, and quality to quantity selected the second. As the twentieth century wore on, members of the latter group would constitute an ever tinier minority. Custom clothiers were hard pressed to equal the achievements of the factory; not only did ready-made dresses and prefabricated hats offer unprecedented convenience, they made fashionable attire available to more women than ever before. Nonetheless, these gains were realized at producers' expense; new methods of manufacture would spell the end of a female entrepreneurial and artisanal tradition. To be sure, the success of ready-to-wear fashions ultimately depended on women's willingness to purchase and wear them. But technological change made mass production feasible. Thus, the twentieth-century ready-made revolution had its roots in nineteenth-century innovations.

Part Two

Gendered Transformations: Toward Mass Production, 1860-1930

Among the artifacts of a bygone era is the catalog of J. R. Libby's Portland, Maine, department store, "the Biggest, Lightest Store in North Eastern America." Libby's catalog, probably published around the turn of the twentieth century, resembled a folksy almanac. Interspersed between descriptions of dry goods and cookstoves was a list of "novel suggestions for bazaar booths." Acknowledging that "many old ideas . . . are hard to improve on . . . but [that] a few new suggestions . . . will be worth following," Libby proposed "a man milliner show." "The promoters," he explained, "should induce as many as possible of their gentlemen friends to compete for a prize given for 'The best lady's hat trimmed by a gentleman.'"[1]

Clearly, the "man milliner show" entailed a reversal of ordinary circumstances, a comic example of men performing women's work. By none too subtly equating millinery with femininity (and by extension with "effeminate" men), it marked a seemingly impassable boundary, to be crossed only in fancy, never in fact. But the man milliner show lent a false permanency to the sexual division of labor in the fashion trades. By the time Libby's suggestion appeared, a series of complex transformations had already begun to challenge women's control of both millinery and dressmaking.

The nature of these changes reveals both similarities and differences between the two trades. Women's dominion over dressmaking came under attack as early as the 1870s and 1880s, with the introduction of new, "scientific" methods of garment cutting, explicitly intended to replace the means by which modistes traditionally learned and practiced their craft. This seemingly innocuous ascendency of "science" over "art" had gendered consequences: most drafting systems and paper patterns were made and marketed by men, not women. By promoting "masculine" technologies at the expense of "feminine" skills, the inventors of new techniques challenged female authority and laid the technological groundwork for ready-made clothing (a possibility yet to realized).

Changes of a different sort—more commercial than technological—confronted milliners after 1900. Male wholesalers increasingly abandoned paternalistic behavior for more "businesslike" conduct, altering the rules that governed the sale of millinery merchandise and the disposition of credit. At the same time, these millinery merchants—who had once confined themselves to the sale of raw materials—began to offer their customers prefabricated frames and shapes, tendencies that culminated in the appearance of ready-made hats. Rather than transforming the process of production—as was the case in dressmaking—these innovations eventually eliminated "manufacturing" from the millinery shop; once makers of handcrafted headwear, milliners became sellers of factory-made products. Both the shift to businesslike behavior and the increasing distance that separated production from retailing represented not merely the inexorable march of commercial and industrial progress but also gendered transformations; both processes, however inadvertently, favored larger male-owned shops and department stores at the expense of women's concerns.

The eventual triumph of ready-made hats and ready-to-wear garments—increasingly evident among the merchandise artfully displayed in opulent department stores—severed milliners from their artisanal moorings and rendered custom dressmakers superfluous. While women accounted for large numbers of the workers in the newly reconstituted fashion trades, they labored in arenas controlled by men and in settings that offered them only marginal compensations. As the "ready-made miracle" triumphed over custom production, mixed workrooms replaced single-sex shops, creating circumstances in which men and women reaped highly unequal rewards.[2] The forces of change invaded even the custom shop. Desperately attempting to compete with mass production on the one hand and elegant "consumer palaces" on the other, both dressmakers and milliners—at least those who commanded the necessary resources—tried to imbue their establishments with the pace of the factory and the ambience of the department store. Ultimately, their efforts failed, as female economies slowly gave way to male-controlled fashion industries.

Five

A Feminine Skill: Work, Technology, and the Sexual Division of Labor in the Dressmaking Trade, 1860–1920

*I*n Germany," the writer-reformer Virginia Penny mused in 1863, "many dress makers are men, and there is one on Broadway, New York." Penny's observation—one of many such comments sprinkled throughout her massive *Employments of Women: A Cyclopedia of Woman's Work*—reveals much about cultural distinctions between men's and women's work in nineteenth-century America. The very incongruity of a "man dressmaker" affirmed a rigidly decreed sexual division of labor that assigned the making of feminine apparel to women; indeed, "man milliner" was an epithet leveled not only at men who made women's dresses and hats but at all who deviated from established norms of "masculine" behavior.[1] On the surface, at least, there was little conflict between ideology and reality. In 1870, women constituted 98 percent of the nation's milliners, dress, and mantua makers, a proportion that remained largely unchanged as the century drew to a close.[2]

Contemporaries attributed this state of affairs to the "natural" consequence of biological factors—after all, was not sewing woman's "natural" vocation? Yet sexual divisions of labor are neither fixed nor natural but continually redefined.[3] Dressmaking proved no exception; women's continuing dominion over the trade masked profound if subtle changes in the nature and meaning of their work. For craftswomen were victims of the same cultural assumptions that upheld their right to labor; unlike men's work, women's work had a dual meaning: paid labor in the workplace and unpaid labor in the home. For dressmakers, as for all who plied the needle, the two definitions were easily confused. Indeed, the very flexibility of gender ideology provided male innovators with a means of challenging craftswomen's monopoly over dressmaking skills during the last quarter of the nineteenth century. Shrewdly manipulating the popular notion that garment making was an ability that *all* women naturally possessed, the proponents of new dress-cutting techniques sought to replace female craft traditions with "scientific" methods made and marketed by men.

Inventions such as pattern drafting systems and proportional patterns have been viewed as part and parcel of the "democratization of fashion," a process, culminating in the appearance of mass-produced, ready-made clothing, that placed stylish apparel in the hands of ever-increasing numbers of eager consumers.[4] While this interpretation can be faulted for its uncritical acceptance of consumer culture, it also fails to acknowledge that "progress" did not benefit equally all parties. For if patterns and drafting systems served the interests of middle-class home sewers, they undermined the foundations of the dressmaking trade.

Equally significant, the democratization of fashion approach obscures the role of gender in the manufacturing and merchandising of dressmaking innovations. By marketing their creations to "ladies" and dressmakers alike, the proponents of new techniques employed a particular definition of women's work that ignored the very real distinctions between the dressmaker's workshop and the middle-class home. This blurring of boundaries had unhappy consequences for professional clothiers. Tradeswomen not only lost work to would-be customers who instead fashioned their own clothes, but they also became increasingly vulnerable to amateurs who believed that their domestic skills qualified them for the marketplace. Scientific methods also represented a potent challenge to female authority. The designers and promoters of patterns and drafting systems firmly believed that dressmaking was women's work. But most of them also assumed that men—uniquely endowed with "scientific knowledge" and tailoring skills—were the best-qualified teachers of the dressmakers' art. Thus, late nineteenth-century craftswomen faced a unique form of deskilling based not on the prerogatives of "management" but on distant inventors' conceptions of the meaning of women's work.[5] What contemporaries saw as a feminine skill was increasingly defined by men.

A "Feminine" Skill

As late as 1911, an investigator for the Women's Educational and Industrial Union (WEIU) pronounced dressmaking one of "the two most highly skilled trades for women" (the other was millinery). Recent scholarship has cast doubt on such assertions; feminist historians have noted that all too often work done by men has been labeled as "skilled" and work done by women as "unskilled." If the anonymous social worker inadvertently maligned a large proportion of the female workforce, her assessment was probably correct. For dressmaking required mental as well as manual labor, "designing" as well as making. The vagaries of feminine fashion and the endless variety of work precluded the manufacture of a standardized product; each dress was an original creation, a "work of art." Even the basics were not easily grasped, a fact reflected in the time it took—five years at the very least—to ascend from apprentice to proprietor. Dressmaking was indeed a "highly skilled trade," and women had much to lose from its decline.[6]

The most difficult part of "achiev[ing] any good result" was cutting, that is, fashioning a shape that would fit the wearer—a skill that distinguished dressmakers from seamstresses, tailoresses, and other needlewomen who typically stitched together garments that had been cut from the cloth by male tailors. In the late nineteenth century, an era when women's clothing tended toward the elaborate, cutting was no easy matter. The tightly fitting bodice (also called a basque or waist), a staple of Gilded Age fashion, posed a particularly vexing problem. According to one expert, it should fit "like wall paper" (Figure 3).[7]

Cutting a garment that fit "like wall paper" or "like the skin"—already made difficult by the variability of female forms—was further compounded by a host of seemingly mundane problems. A dress that lay smoothly across the shoulders when the wearer was standing was apt to wrinkle when she sat down. Similarly, the customer who stood ramrod-straight during fittings was surprised that her dress hung differently when she assumed her "natural" posture.[8] Perhaps no item caused greater aggravation than the corset. More often than not, this frequently maligned undergarment created a shape quite different from the wearer's natural form. A dress that fit perfectly over one corset might collapse into unsightly folds over a different one; a garment cut for a tightly laced client no longer fit when the corset strings were loosened.[9]

Nonetheless, the dressmaker's first priority was to cut a garment that fit

Figure 3. From "Every-Day Dresses," *Peterson's Magazine* 81 (May 1882): 404. Cutting tight-ly fitting garments such as these required considerable expertise. (Courtesy of the Indiana University, Bloomington, Library)

her patron. By the early nineteenth century, tailors had developed theories of bodily proportions, enabling them to create general patterns that could be altered to suit individual clients. But they were loath to share their knowl-edge. "We do not see why the plan used by tailors, of fitting by measure, is not more generally applied to dress fitting," complained Penny, ordinarily a perceptive observer. The answer was simple: tailors kept their secrets to themselves. Denied access to "male" skills, dressmakers made do with a different method, one that costume historian Claudia B. Kidwell has called the "pin-to-the-form" technique. The modiste draped and pinned paper or inexpensive fabric (such as cambric or muslin) about the "form" of her client (Figure 4).[10] From the resulting "pattern," she cut the inside lining of the dress; if she used fabric instead of paper, the cloth itself became the lining. As a precautionary measure, she basted the lining together and asked her customer to try it on—often several times—before touching her shears to the more costly materials that comprised the outer part of the garment. Despite numerous innovations, many tradeswomen clung to the pin-to-the-form method because it remained the most accurate—albeit the most time-consuming—means of obtaining a good fit.[11]

Compared to the mysterious art of cutting, the process of stitching together the pieces of a garment represented a matter of minor importance. But sewing, too, was a task that involved considerable talent, for ineptitude or inexperience easily ruined the "lines" of a dress. A skillful craftswoman knew that bodices required tiny, interlocking stitches, whereas skirts needed longer and looser ones, for seams that were pulled too tightly caused dresses—intended to fall gracefully to the floor—to hang awkwardly. "Skirt seams," one observer explained, "do not bear the strain of bodice seams, and sit better if the long stitch is employed." And in an era when bodices fit "like wall paper," it was in the dressmaker's best interest to make her "sewing last while the garment does."[12]

The distinction between cutting and sewing furnished the organizing principle of the dressmaking shop. Workers who cut garments from the cloth stood at the top of the trade hierarchy; in most establishments this was Madame's prerogative. Those who cut often bore responsibility for the final fitting as well; hence "cutters" and "fitters" were usually synonymous terms, designating workers who performed the same function. Workers who sewed dresses together called themselves finishers; as this nomenclature implied, they also added the final decorative touches. When they were not running errands or making deliveries, apprentices performed the less critical functions of basting, overcasting, making (that is, stitching together) linings, attaching hooks and eyes, and sewing skirt seams—"straight-away work."[13]

Because of the difficulties involved in cutting, observers placed a good deal of emphasis on the "mechanical" aspects of dressmaking. Still, many believed that dressmaking, like millinery, was an art. Catherine Broughton's

Figure 4. Pin-to-the-form technique, from *The Book of English Trades* (London: C. and J. Rivington, 1827), which states: "The plate represents the Dress-maker taking the pattern off from a lady by means of a piece of paper or cloth" (illustration, p. 187; quotation, p. 189). (Courtesy of Old Sturbridge Village, Sturbridge, Mass.; photograph by Amanda Richardson)

Suggestions for Dressmakers clearly distinguished between the artist who possessed "a clear comprehension of the laws of beauty in dress" and the artisan who "knows only the technical part of her trade." Broughton implied that artistic dressmaking was something that had to be learned, but others attributed this skill only to the naturally gifted. "You must have a natural taste for decorating the female form artistically; and thousands of girls have it," explained William Drysdale in *Helps for Ambitious Girls.* "Some girls are so expert at this that they produce better effects without any special training, than most of the dressmakers can produce."[14]

Thus, some argued that dressmaking was a natural skill, others that it was an acquired talent. This seemingly trivial debate had not so trivial consequences. As Drysdale suggested, women with natural taste—but no training—might be tempted to enter the professional arena, lowering trade standards and exposing craftswomen to competition from amateurs. Natural taste was apparently not restricted to the few: "Thousands of girls have it." Enterprising inventors carried this idea to its logical extreme by arguing that dressmaking was the natural employment of all women, an idea that found ready acceptance in a culture that equated women's labor with domesticity. And they sought to turn ideology into reality by making and marketing products that were intended to endow amateurs with the same skills as professionals.

Much was at stake. Dressmakers, as we have seen, enjoyed advantages that many of their wage-earning sisters did not: skilled work, high wages by female standards, and the chance, perhaps, to open shops of their own. But as discussions of the trade's artistic aspects make clear, it bestowed a less tangible benefit on its practitioners: creative labor. A turn-of-the-century craftswoman declared "love of the work" a necessary prerequisite for trade success. Nearly two decades later, a Boston dressmaker seconded her opinion, confidently expressing her joy at "'work[ing] with beautiful materials.'"[15] Benefits of this sort—prized by *all* workers—had particular meaning for women who were more likely than men to be assigned repetitive, monotonous tasks in the industrial workplace. In light of Sarah Eisenstein's suggestion that the experience of wage work routinely crushed women's ambition, "reinforcing" their commitment to marriage, dressmaking presented a compelling alternative to domesticity.[16]

Craftswomen's comments suggest that they particularly valued the "mental" attributes of their calling, the fact that their trade "made them think."[17] But even as they spoke, their work had already become more mechanical. In this respect, dressmakers were far from unique; as labor historians have shown, industrial employers increasingly sought to separate mental from manual labor, to eliminate "thought" from the time-honored routines of male craftworkers.[18] After about 1900, modistes would experience "masculine" forms of deskilling (although change occurred slowly and unevenly): minutely subdivided tasks, reduced prospects for advancement, and alienation from the products of their labor. But during the late nineteenth century, the greatest threat to their skills came not from managers intent on exerting control over production but from inventors of new technologies who perceived that the ambiguous meaning of women's needlework might yield them tidy profits. Far removed for the most part from daily life in the dressmaking shop, these mostly male innovators marketed their wares with a particular definition of "women's work" that drew little distinction between labor performed by professionals and labor performed in the home. As a result, dressmakers faced increasing competition from an unlikely source: home sewers who fashioned their own clothing. Armed with drafting systems and paper patterns—both intended to make dressmaking "easy"—amateurs were free to leave the domestic circle for the marketplace. It became increasingly difficult to distinguish between the workshop and the home.

Home and Workshop: The Double Meaning of Women's Work

Most craftswomen learned their trades through a more or less traditional system of apprenticeship; long after new ways of learning had appeared, the workshop remained the best teacher. This fact did not deter an untold number of amateurs. "There is probably no occupation in which there are so many incompetent persons as that of dressmaking," Penny had complained in 1863. "Many persons take it up without having learned that trade at all, and many who become reduced in circumstances immediately resort to it without any preparation, and are destitute not only of experience, but of skill, ingenuity and taste."[19]

Why did "incompetent persons" assume that they could easily transfer their domestic skills to the marketplace? They, too, believed that women were naturally endowed with garment-making skills. This belief was not without foundation: in an era when ready-to-wear garments were unavailable, many women—perhaps the majority—fashioned their own clothing. "I worked on Lucie's Basque and my own dress very steadily all day," Sarah Preston Everett Hale recorded in her diary on March 22, 1859. Hale's accomplishments should not be minimized. Home sewing, like all housework, was no more natural to women than blacksmithing was to men; on the contrary, it required considerable expertise.[20] And well before the introduction of techniques that promised to simplify their endeavors, housewives might transgress the always artificial boundaries between home and marketplace by making garments for friends and neighbors, sometimes for cash, sometimes for payment in kind.[21]

Still, a considerable gulf separated amateur from professional. The typical tradeswoman, a single woman of working-class origins, had spent years perfecting her craft—in the workshop, not in the home. The typical home sewer, engaged in performing domestic labor in the middle-class household, was a generalist, not a specialist; as Nancy Page Fernandez has ably demonstrated, the home sewer "made" her dress, not by designing a pattern anew, but by laboriously picking apart an older garment and using its pieces as her guide.[22] Historical and contemporary impressions notwithstanding, different life courses, different priorities, and above all, different levels of expertise distinguished professional clothiers from their domestic counterparts.

Nevertheless, aspiring amateurs found support in the pages of advice manuals such as *The Ladies' Hand-Book of Millinery and Dressmaking* and *Beadle's Dime Guide to Dress-Making and Millinery.* "Hints to Dressmakers and Those Who Make Their Own Dresses" was a regular feature of *Godey's Lady's Book;* established three decades later, *Demorest's* offered "Hints in Regard to Dress-Cutting and Fitting" (both periodicals also offered advice to home milliners).[23] Tips of this sort provided valuable aids to women who could not afford the services of professionals; no doubt such hints contributed to what Margaret Walsh has called the "democratization of fashion." At the same time, such columns also betrayed a profound disrespect for craftswomen's skills. Adding insult to injury, fashion periodicals deprived tradeswomen of actual and prospective customers. "I take [your magazine] . . . as a matter of economy," a dedicated subscriber wrote to *Demorest's,* "for its suggestions, hints, and good advice are worth more than its price, and save more than that in a dressmaker's bill." "Your Magazine has emancipated me from dependence upon milliners and dressmakers," wrote another, "and there is a delightful satisfaction, to say nothing of the immense saving to one's purse, in being able to serve myself."[24]

The next step was predictable: advice writers and fashion editors argued increasingly that by following their hints, any woman could turn her natural talents to profit. To be sure, early manuals addressed themselves primarily to home sewers; antebellum how-to writers seldom implied that the knowledge they imparted constituted sufficient preparation for professionals.[25] But a change was evident as early as 1860. In that year, Marion M. Pullan recommended her "dime guide" both to dressmakers "who would be glad of an opportunity to learn the principles of their art" and to "private individuals who . . . can not afford to employ a dress-maker." By the turn of the twentieth century, how-to manuals presented themselves as effective substitutes for apprenticeship. Simply by mastering the "twenty complete lessons" that comprised her *Dressmaking Self Taught*, Madam[e] Edith Marie Carens explained, "ambitious girls and women" could become professional dressmakers: "The author has aimed to make this work a school in itself—taking the place of . . . actually coming in contact with a sewing establishment." "Lesson 20" even offered advice on selecting shop locations, designing business cards, and hiring assistants.[26]

Fashion magazines took up the refrain. "Will you tell me if there is any . . . trade that can be acquired quietly at home, without a teacher?" "M. C." asked *Demorest's* in February 1887. The answer was predictable: "Dressmaking is often pursued quietly at home." To be sure, advice of this sort often reflected genuine sympathy for women unexpectedly forced to earn their own livings; indeed, it may have held particular appeal for middle-class women who found the prospect of apprenticeship distasteful. But advice writers and fashion editors challenged craftswomen's authority by substituting the written page for workshop traditions, "book learning" for apprenticeship.[27]

Advocates of book learning participated in a wider cultural transformation, evident as early as the late eighteenth century, that eroded the authority of master craftsmen in a variety of trades. But the hints they proffered differed in an important respect from those conveyed to would-be printers, weavers, and engineers. Those who penned such treatises as *The Young Mill-Wright and Miller's Guide* expected their readers to use them for profitable employment, not domestic pursuits (a probable exception, *The Family Dyer and Scourer*, evidently addressed itself to housewives as well as future tradesmen). Fashion experts, on the other hand, predicated their advice on a flexible definition of women's labor, appealing not only to aspiring professionals but to unpaid home sewers as well.[28] Equally significant, the technological innovations that bolstered fashion editors' assurances had profoundly gendered implications. Those who argued that anyone could learn dressmaking and millinery had a point: new inventions *were* making it easier for the untrained to fashion stylish apparel. But by and large these "improvements" were designed not by women but by men.

Two innovations, drafting systems and proportional patterns, wreaked considerable havoc on the dressmaking trade. Manufactured and marketed in a milieu that contrasted sharply with craft traditions, their presence in the dressmaking shop signaled nothing less than a corporate invasion. While women dominated fashion editing (although not necessarily publishing), the makers and sellers of the new technologies were predominantly men.

"Reduced to Science": The Transformation of Dressmaking

"Scarcely any dress-maker is now without a Wheeler & Wilson, however small her establishment," an observer noted in 1860. This statement, an exaggeration in its day, was an undisputed fact ten years later. In 1860, no Boston dressmaking establishments used sewing machines; in 1870, 95 percent used them.[29] Much has been written of the devastation that sewing machines wreaked upon seamstresses, that is, outworkers who sewed men's shirts, vests, and pants for a mass market. "If the sewing machine accomplished the work quicker," a perceptive analyst noted, "the amount [of work], for a given amount of pay, was increased in precisely the same ratio." The vagaries of feminine fashion prevented a similar upheaval in the world of dressmaking.[30] As Fernandez has noted, sewing machines neither reduced the time and skill involved in cutting nor eliminated the need for hand sewing. While admirably suited to stitching the long, straight lines of the skirt, machines were ill adapted to the curved seams of the bodice. Long after the sewing machine had become a fixture of the dressmaking shop, "finishing"—overcasting seams, attaching trimmings—continued in the traditional manner. As late as the 1920s, stitches rendered by hand distinguished high-quality custom creations from their humbler ready-made counterparts. In some instances, knowledgeable modistes eschewed mechanization entirely, for machines easily ruined fragile fabrics.[31]

To be sure, the sewing machine wrought subtle changes in the workplace. Dressmakers had always been harried during rush seasons; labor-saving devices no doubt only increased the pressure. By the 1910s and possibly earlier, larger shops boasted a permanent class of "machine operators," workers who remained outside the traditional channels of advancement. Moreover, the widespread use of sewing machines in the home gave rise to a new breed of apprentice who was less prepared than ever before. Hand sewing, late nineteenth-century employers complained, was becoming a lost art.[32]

If the impact of the sewing machine was less than revolutionary, a second development had more ominous implications. In the last quarter of the nineteenth century, hundreds of systems for drafting patterns challenged the dressmaker's most precious skill: her monopoly over cutting. Armed with a belief in progress and a desire for profits, the authors of treatises such as *The Scientific Lady Tailor System*, *The Science and Art of Cutting and Making Ladies' Garments*, and *Scientific Dress Cutting* sought to replace trade secrets with scientific principles, feminine skills with masculine technologies.[33]

Much of this furious invention took place outside of the dressmaking shop. The majority of innovators fell into two categories: tailors and men with little practical experience in the clothing trades. Charles Hecklinger, a tailor, denounced those in the second category as charlatans who combined already discredited methods "with a few superficial ideas learned from their wives." As Hecklinger's criticism (itself an interesting indication of male attitudes) implied, women were not entirely absent from the ranks of systematizers. The "Buddington dress cutting machine," invented by Mr. and Mrs. F. E. Buddington, was a joint venture (although Mr. Buddington held the copyright); so was the "Excelsior Square," brainchild of Mr. and Mrs. B. T. Phelps of Bellows Falls, Vermont. And women, some of whom were dressmakers, accounted for more than a fourth of the creators of drafting systems.[34]

Nonetheless, men, who also manufactured and marketed the most financially successful inventions, dominated system making. Condescending at best, deprecating at worst, they sought to reduce the feminine art of dressmaking to a science. Hecklinger, "himself a practical tailor of a large and varied practice, . . . endeavored . . . to bring the art of dress cutting to the standard of an exact science, and to make this science a common benefit to the whole mass of dress makers."[35] The instructions to the 1896 edition of *S. T. Taylor's System of Dress Cutting* included a heartfelt dedication to "the inventor of our system . . . Mr. S. T. Taylor." The venerable founder was aptly named: "His profession was that of a men's tailor, with a thorough knowledge of cutting as it is done for men by the best artists." Taylor, his proponents insisted, was motivated by benevolence alone: "He saw the difficulties under which the dressmakers labored, and applied a life's study to elaborate a way of dress-cutting which would be on a par with cutting done by tailors."[36]

These humble pretensions aside, many systematizers presided over vast corporate enterprises, and the contrast between inventor-entrepreneurs like

Samuel T. Taylor and the typical dressmaker highlights the gendered nature of commercial and industrial power. Taylor and his corporate heirs not only marketed at least sixteen versions of his dress-cutting system between 1850 and 1915, they also sold patterns and published the fashion magazines *Le Bon Ton, La France Elegante,* and *Die Modenwelt.* The McDowell Garment Drafting Machine Company created *The French Dressmaker;* in the early twentieth century, the J. J. Mitchell Company, manufacturer of garment-cutting systems and "correct and perfect fitting" patterns, countered with *The American Dressmaker.*[37]

Equally significant, even the lowliest inventors did not purport to teach women the secrets of tailoring, to endow them with truly "masculine" skills. Rather, they used their expertise to devise various methods of cutting women's garments that could be learned without training, a process that displayed little respect for the abilities of dressmakers *or* home sewers. The McDowell Company claimed that its invention was "so simple . . . that a child can use it." The creators of Taylor's dress-cutting system believed that they had found no better demonstration of the ease with which their system could be mastered: "Pupils have learned the system well, and use it successfully[,] who are both deaf and dumb, and foreigners who did not know a word of English, but had to be taught by sign."[38]

Bolstering their authority with repeated references to the at least implicitly masculine arena of science, systematizers rarely missed an opportunity to assert the superiority of masculine (tailoring) over feminine (dressmaking) skills. "We frequently meet cutters," Hecklinger wrote, "who have practiced the greater part of their lives, and yet, who . . . work by such a crude system, compared to that sanctioned by experts in the art, that they can scarcely be mentioned beside them." "Among the many thousands of professional dressmakers in this country the number who excel in their profession are comparatively few," Caleb H. Griffin and David Knox, inventors of the "Great American Drafting Machine," regretfully acknowledged.[39]

What did "dress cutting . . . reduced to science" entail? Most systems—characterized by odd assortments of "tools," "charts," "scales," and "machines"—were designed with the difficult task of cutting bodices in mind; they attained their greatest popularity in the 1880s and 1890s when basques were at their tightest. There was no shortage of ideas; between 1841 and 1920, the U.S. Patent Office bestowed its blessing on more than 366 systems. Kidwell, the author of the most extensive study of the subject, maintains that this number was deceptive; each system, she argues, was actually a variation on one of three basic themes: "proportional," "hybrid," and "direct measure."[40] Whatever the particular scheme they endorsed, drafting systems differed from the pin-to-the-form dressmaking technique in a crucial respect, for they relied not on acquired skill and the ability to envision mentally the shape of a garment (what one dressmaker called "good eyes for measures")[41] but on numeric measurements and "scientific" theories of bodily proportions.

As Kidwell's nomenclature implies, proportional systems reflected inventors' conceptions of the relative dimensions of the female form. A single measurement—usually the breast or bust but occasionally the waist—determined the remaining proportions. Accuracy was crucial, as Aaron Tentler, the inventor of an early system (1842), explained. The bust "measure is to be taken very exactly, being the main measure, on which the whole calculus of cutting a dress is based."[42]

Tentler's system consisted of a tool or chart, a sheet of cardboard through which a series of holes—numbered eight through twenty-four—had been punched. These numbers corresponded to half the bust measurement, the figure that determined the remaining dimensions of the pattern piece—or more accurately, half the pattern piece. Thus, if the prospective wearer measured thirty-eight inches, the all-important number was nineteen. The sewer placed the chart over a folded piece of paper or lining fabric and made a mark through each of the perforations numbered nineteen. To draft the pattern, she merely connected the dots. After the shape had been cut, she unfolded the paper or cloth to reveal a whole front or back bodice (each, for obvious reasons, was drafted separately).[43]

Tentler's creation was remarkably easy to use. The dressmaker needed to make no calculations; she needed no measuring tape. Instead, she measured the wearer with an unmarked strip of paper. To obtain the essential number—that is, half of the breast measurement—she folded the paper in half and compared it to an inch scale printed across the bottom of the chart.[44]

More complicated versions substituted scales—sets of numbered strips— for charts. *Powell and Kohler's Practical System* (1868) came equipped with twenty-seven scales, each corresponding to a particular bust measurement. Using an L-shaped tailor's square as a guide, the student of their "practical system" drew two perpendicular baselines on the paper or lining cloth. After measuring the wearer, she selected the appropriate strip, placed it beside the vertical line and made a series of dots at specified points along the scale. Next, she drew a horizontal line through each dot (using a square ensured that each line was parallel to its predecessor), laid the scale along each one, and made a mark where directed. Once again, drafting the pattern was merely a matter of connecting the dots.[45]

As Powell and Kohler's instructions suggest, drafting systems were not always easily mastered. Even connecting the dots, seemingly a straightforward matter, was more difficult than it looked. The inventors of early systems provided illustrations of pattern pieces but no guides, leaving the dressmaker to determine the "slopes" of particular lines. Curves, especially the "arm's eye" (the opening for a sleeve, that is, the armhole), were difficult to draw freehand, and instructions such as "Follow the diagram by making curves and swells where needed, in conforming with the human figure" offered little practical assistance. Late nineteenth-century inventors offered a partial solution: by the 1880s many systems included "French curves," "curvilinear pattern instruments," and "circular attachments."[46]

The problem of drawing lines and curves was endemic to all "scientific" methods, but two difficulties plagued proportional systems in particular. Because the drafting points—the dots—were fixed, the proportional method could be used to cut only one style of garment; changes in fashion rendered charts and scales obsolete. But the most common complaint was that they served the few rather than the many; in other words, the fit depended on how well the wearer conformed to the inventor's conception of bodily proportions. One critic summarized the problem: "Charts cut the same shape for every figure measuring the same size breast! The fallacy of this idea is apparent when you consider that persons measuring the same size breast are rarely, if ever, shaped alike."[47]

Predictably, advocates of rival methods heaped insults on proportional systems. "Most of them," the S. T. Taylor Company complained, "are charts of very little value but of high-sounding names, generally *invented* by a so-called '*professor*' and warranted to fit anything from the Venus of Milo to a baboon monkey."[48] Despite these accusations, inventors continued to flood the market with proportional methods. As late as 1887, Mrs. M. V. Coleman based her *Science of Gynametry* on the supposition "that one part of the body is in proportion to the other throughout the entire structure." By this time, more adventurous tinkerers had developed an alternative: the "hybrid" system, in which some drafting points were determined by proportional means, others by direct measurement.[49]

Taylor's *System for Cutting Ladies' Garments* exemplifies scientific methods in their second incarnation. Taylor's system, patented in 1871, required ten measurements for a basque. Eight were used in the actual drafting of the

8

DIRECTIONS FOR MAKING THE HOLDER.

In preparing the scales for use, you must cut off the margin at the sides and ends. By referring to the illustration given, you will find it very easy to make the scale-holder. Every one cutting by the system should have it. In this way you keep the scales clean, smooth, and nice, and can more easily find them when required for use. Lines A and B are 24 inches long ; lines C and D must be sufficiently wide to support the scales, or if you have a set of scales not cut apart, you can get the length and width by them. The holder is made by sewing two pieces of linen or muslin together, leaving space for each scale as represented by the black lines. Let the front part extend up near the end of the scales.

Back, No. 1.

The breast measure gives the number of the scale used on the long arm of the square ; and the waist measure the number for the short arm.

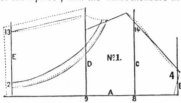

Line A is the base line or starting-point in all drafting. Place the long arm of the square on the fold of the cloth, with the short arm near the top. Before moving the square, draw line B ; dot for the length of waist ; then dot at 8 of the breast scale for line C, which gives the height of neck. Then move the corner of the square to 8, and draw line C; observing to have the long arm of the square precisely parallel with line A or fold of the cloth. Then dot at 9 numbers of the breast scale ; move the square as for line C, and draw line D. Line E is drawn from the length of waist, by observing the same rule. Dot at 2 numbers of the waist scale for the side-body before moving the square.

The width of back on line B, is 4 numbers of the breast scale from line A, and 14 numbers of the same scale on line C. The width of back on line D is obtained by actual measurement, and should be very carefully taken.

The length of shoulder is obtained by actual measurement, and drawn from 4 on line B, through 14 on line C. This measure is a very important one, and should never be taken too long.

The line drawn from the length of shoulder to line D is about 1½ inches from the side-seam. A small cord about once and a half the width of back on line D, will give the necessary curve for the side-body. The sweep is made by taking the crayon and one end of the cord in your right hand, between the finger and thumb, and with the left hand at a point where the pencil or crayon will touch at 2 on line E, and the centre between lines C and D, as represented on the diagram. Then add a small seam to the back ; dot for the neck and shoulder as represented, cutting by the dotted lines.

The side-body is drafted by simply placing the back straight with the cloth, and extending lines D and E ; obtain the width of back on line D as before, and 13 on line E of the waist scale, including the back. The side seam can be cut straight or curved a little at pleasure. Prove the length of side-seam before cutting it out.

Figure 5. S. T. Taylor's illustrated instructions for drafting the front and back of a bodice exemplify a hybrid system that combined proportional techniques with a series of direct measurements. One of the most prolific and successful inventors of drafting systems, Tay-

9

EXPLANATORY REMARKS.

In all garment-cutting it is necessary that the practical cutter should understand the why and the wherefore of each thing taught.

Line A, for a close-fitting back, is the fold of the cloth ; for an open back, you must allow the width necessary for the lap, commencing with the selvage toward you. The 8 numbers to find line C, regulates the height of neck. Should you find the dress too high in the neck for any customer, then use 7½ or 7, or even less than this, if necessary. Four numbers on line B, and 14 on line C, places the shoulder-seam in the best place for a well-proportioned figure. If the lady be round-shouldered, then use 4½ on line B, and 13 on line C. In making this change you do not affect the size of the dress, but simply place the shoulder-seam so as to improve the form for such a figure.

If desired, you can cut the back and side-body narrower on line E, by adding the amount taken off to line B of the forepart, though I think this in bad taste. All backs should be cut separate from the side-body, and be rounded more on the shoulder above the 14 on line C, for ladies with high shoulders ; and if much so, a little round may be given at the same place on the forepart. If this be neglected, the dress will bind, and fit badly. To test this, rip the seam just there, and the dress will at once drop to where it belongs.

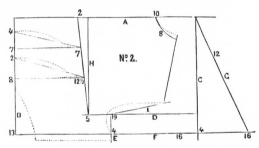

FORE PART, No. 2.

To get line A, you must place the long arm of the square parallel with the edge of the cloth, allowing width for making up ; and the short arm near the end of the cloth. Before moving the square, dot for line C, by going up on line A, four inches more than the length of the natural waist; that is to say, if the length of waist be sixteen inches, you will dot at 20 ; then turn the square, and place the short arm perfectly parallel with line A, and draw line C by the long arm, as represented on the diagram.

The width of chest from line A on line C is actual measurement. (See measure taken.) Now place the short arm of the square parallel on line C, and draw line D by the long arm. From line C to line E is 19 numbers of the breast scale. You get this by going down 16 and 3, then 5 more for the height of darts. Then turn the square with the short arm on line D, and draw line E, dotting at 4 numbers of the breast scale for line F, and 4 more as represented on line C. This is to enable you to draw line F precisely parallel with line D.

lor emphasized mechanical step-by-step instructions that contrasted sharply with the spirit and rationale of the pin-to-the-form method. From *A System for Cutting Ladies' Garments* (New York: T. Holman, 1871), pp. 8–9. (Courtesy of the Library of Congress) garment, two—the circumference of the arm at the shoulder, the distance between the waist and the bottom of the arm hole—served as "proofs" by which to judge the finished pattern. A "breast scale" predicted the height of the neck, the width of the front and back at some points (but not others), the "arm's eye," and the length of the side seam. As Taylor's instructions for drafting the back of a bodice indicate, his method was considerably more complicated than its predecessors (Figure 5):

> The width of back on line B, is 4 numbers of the breast scale from line A, and 14 numbers of the same scale on line C. The width of the back on line D is obtained by actual measurement, and should be very carefully taken.
>
> The length of shoulder is obtained by actual measurement, and drawn from 4 on line B, through 14 on line C. This measure is a very important one, and should never be taken too long.[50]

More often than not, even hybrid methods proved no match for the tightly fitting bodices of the 1880s and 1890s. Inventors rose to the challenge by patenting "direct-measure" systems, that is, those that relied on measurements alone. But these innovations presented dressmakers with a painful dilemma: although they were more accurate than other techniques, they were far more difficult to learn.[51]

Elizabeth Gartland's *Original American Lady Tailor System* was deceptively simple; it required no tools except an inch tape, a tailor's square, and perhaps a "circular attachment." But this minimal equipment masked a more complex reality. After taking thirteen measurements, the user was ready to draft a "plain basque." She then confronted a bewildering list of instructions (Figure 6):

1. Draw line 1, ten inches above the bottom of paper, the entire length of square, for *waist line.*
2. Draw line 2 from centre of line 1, according to *length of back.*
3. On line 2 make a dot above the waist line, for the *under-arm measure,* and draw a line parallel to line 1, for line 3.
4. Place centre of circle on line 2, resting on line 3, and *draw a circle* according to *arm's-eye measure.*
5. Draw line 4 though the centre of circle, the same length as line 3. Also line 5 parallel to line 4, so it will touch the top of circle on line 2.
6. Draw line 6 touching right of circle from line 5 to line 1.

When she had reached step number forty, the pattern was complete. Whether systems such as Gartland's represented an improvement over older methods of garment cutting is doubtful.[52]

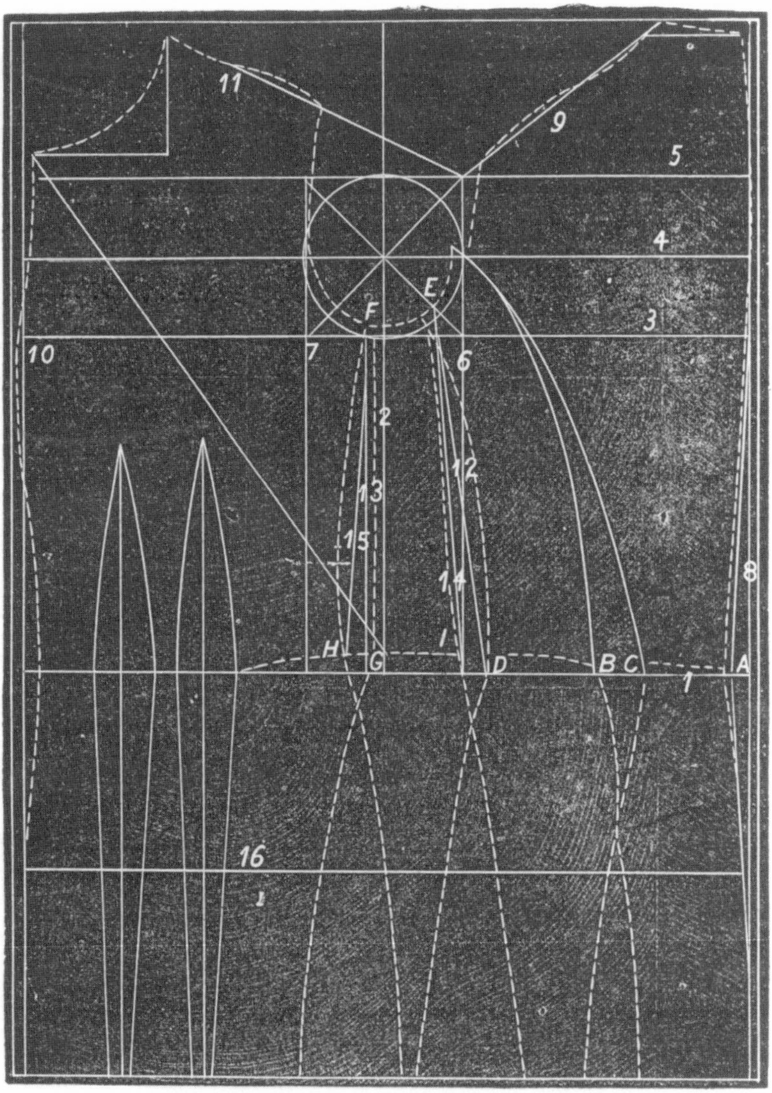

PLAIN BASQUE.

Figure 6. Elizabeth Gartland's diagram for drafting a "plain basque" illustrates the complexity of direct measure systems for drafting patterns. From *The Original American Lady Tailor System* (Philadelphia, n.p., 1884), p. 16. (Courtesy of the Library of Congress)

Help for those unwilling or unable to use the Original Lady Tailor System or one of its many variants appeared in the form of bizarre contraptions known as "machines." The makers of the McDowell Drafting Machine, probably the single most popular drafting device of its day, acknowledged that systems such as Gartland's "could only be used by parties of excellent judgment and sense, who had a talent for figures and drawing, and even then the time required to use it was too much for Dressmakers." McDowell's alternative, first patented in 1879, was an adjustable metal tool. By 1883 the prospective buyer could choose from a brass model that had "been submitted to a Gold Lacquer process that removes all brassy objectionable features" ($20.00) or a slightly more expensive "nickeled machine" ($22.50). Each piece or "bar" of the machine was inscribed with an inch scale. The user measured the wearer, then—in specified order—"set" each bar to the appropriate measurement.[53]

Mr. and Mrs. F. E. Buddington designed a similar, if not so popular, device. Their instructions for "setting the front" illustrate the way in which such a machine was meant to work (Figure 7):

  1.—Set Slide *1* (Shoulder Bar) to shoulder measure.
  2.—Set Slide *2* (Neck Bar) to Neck measure.
  3.—Set upper edge of Slide *3* (Neck Wire) to neck measure.
  4.—Set upper edge of Slide *4* (in Front Bar) to Arm's Eye measure.
  5.—Set Slide *5* (Arm's Eye Wire) to Arm's Eye measure.

When all of the adjustments had been made (the Buddington machine required fifteen steps), the dressmaker traced the pattern by drawing around the outlines of the device.[54]

Whether they employed squares or machines, direct-measure methods were undeniably superior to proportional and hybrid systems. But they were not foolproof, for their success depended on how skillfully the user wielded her inch tape. In fact, taking measurements, seemingly a straightforward matter, was a process governed by vague and often contradictory rules. "Neck Measure is taken around neck, inside collar tight," the user of the Buddington machine was instructed. The "bust measure," on the other hand, was not to be "taken too tight." Similarly, Gartland directed her readers to "take a close measure around the waist" but "a loose measure over the fullest part of the bust." Little wonder that a critic declared that "a good draughting system would be the cutting system par excellence . . . if it were possible to take exact measures. We claim that it is not."[55]

Figure 7. Mr. and Mrs. F. E. Buddington's "Improved Dress Cutting Machine" (1896) offered a relatively simple but less than accurate method of cutting dresses. The machine at left has been set in accordance with a series of measurements. The user would have traced around its outlines to draft the pattern. From *Instruction Book for Using the Buddington Dress Cutting Machine* (Chicago: n.p., 1896), cover. (Courtesy of the Library of Congress)

As this comment suggests, science rarely triumphed over art; systems rarely produced professional results. This drawback failed to discourage numerous purchasers lured by the promise of dressmaking made easy. No accurate sales statistics exist, but the sheer number of systems available provides some indication of their popularity. Who used them? Some inventors catered to amateurs, others to professionals, still others to both. *Every Lady Her Own Dressmaker* clearly intended itself for thrifty consumers. Taylor, on the other hand, offered his invention to "the practical dress maker that wishes to please her customers." Those who testified to the merits of the "Standard Garment-Cutter" included four dressmakers and seven home sewers; among the latter was twelve-year-old Hermene Crome, who announced that "since learning the System [I] can cut and fit my mamma's and my own clothes. I like to use it because it is so easy."[56]

By the 1890s, inventors who marketed their creations to amateurs and professionals alike probably made up the majority. This was a shrewd business tactic, because aiming for a dual market vastly increased the number of potential buyers. But by recommending their systems both "to dressmakers" and "to ladies in private life," the makers of systems increasingly blurred the boundaries between home and workshop.[57] Consciously or not, these mostly male inventors redefined both the nature and the meaning of women's work. By identifying dress cutting with middle-class domesticity—by classifying it as a variant of the housewifely labors that "all" women presumably performed—systematizers obscured the artisanal origins of the dressmaking trade. At a time when many middle-class women were moving self-consciously and decisively into public life, systematizers' pronouncements conveyed the message that woman's place was in the home.

What is more, these systems threatened to disrupt established traditions of female authority. For two centuries, novices had honed their skills at the workplace; Madame was the supreme arbiter of dressmaking knowledge. Advocates of scientific methods challenged her special expertise, for they argued not only that every lady could become her own dressmaker but also that with the aid of their systems every lady could become a professional dressmaker.

The recipient of "hundreds of letters from young girls and widows who have their living to make, and oftentimes from two to six children to support," Will C. Rood implored his readers to contribute to a fund that would supply poor women with his "Magic Scale." However charitable his motives, Rood preached a subversive doctrine. The lucky possessors of Magic Scales, he implied, were ready for business; they could set up shop without the benefit of apprenticeship. Certainly, this was the intention of Alice M. Avis of Blue Rapids, Kansas, a graduate of one of the "schools" sponsored by the Standard Garment Cutting Company. "In my future business as a dressmaker, I would not do without the System at any price."[58]

To be sure, in part the systems represented a response to the apprenticeship crisis that plagued the dressmaking trade. Mistress dressmakers—usually operating under considerable economic stress—were infamous for failing to impart promised knowledge. While complaints that apprentices learned nothing but plain sewing surfaced as early as the 1840s, the situation had clearly worsened by the closing decades of the nineteenth century. Madames particularly evinced reluctance to divulge the secrets of cutting. In 1885, one critic observed, "After thirty days" the novice "may know how to cut the inner side of a sleeve, instead of the whole dress which it was promised she should know how to fit"; ten years later another complained that "many a woman spends month after month in stitching fells till she has acquired a purely mechanical accuracy, and who could by no possibility either cut, fit, or make an entire garment."[59]

Nevertheless, scientific methods compounded the very problem they purported to solve. Much of dressmakers' ill will toward their apprentices could be attributed to the competitive nature of their trade; refusing to train novices was one way of limiting the number of future contenders. By providing a substitute for apprenticeship, systems only made matters worse, increasing the competition in an already overcrowded field. Moreover, given the technical limitations of systems, they hardly ensured commercial success for the inexperienced, a consequence that weighed especially heavily on women with slender resources who were unexpectedly obliged to support themselves. All too often, one suspects, systematizers' promises evaporated into cruel hoaxes.

Even when incorporated into long-standing trade practices, drafting systems had injurious effects. The dressmaker who informed the S. T. Taylor Company that "I have used your system of dresscutting about six years and . . . teach it to my girls" preserved the form if not the substance of apprenticeship. But she had exchanged a centuries-old female tradition for a "scientific" system made and marketed by men. In a sense, she had abdicated her own authority. Nothing prevented "her girls" from acquiring Taylor's methods on their own.[60]

Dressmakers' responses to cutting innovations are difficult to gauge because they lacked a forum in which to air their opinions. If testimonials can be believed (Taylor insisted that "every letter is, of course, genuine"), many wholeheartedly embraced scientific methods. "For fourteen years I have used your system, always giving perfect satisfaction to customers and myself," a New York tradeswoman wrote to Taylor in 1896. Hattie E. Gillespie of Cincinnati was equally enthusiastic: "I have used your system for the past eight years and don't think there is anything like it."[61]

In one respect, Gillespie's decision made a great deal of sense, for (most) scientific methods had a crucial advantage over older techniques: speed. Systems and sewing machines constituted a powerful combination: together they enabled dressmakers to fashion garments more quickly than ever before, simultaneously promising to satisfy the demands of impatient customers and to increase potential profits.[62]

Perhaps no prospect was more tantalizing than that systems did away with fittings. Never one to minimize the significance of his achievements, Taylor declared: "*By my system dresses can be cut to fit so perfectly, as to avoid any necessity of fitting!*"[63] Some tradeswomen agreed. "A waist cut, basted and prepared for the first fitting can be stitched without any alteration, thus requiring only two fittings, which saving of time only dressmakers can appreciate," a devotee of Taylor's system wrote. The New York dressmaker Annie O'Neill concurred: "A waist cut by your system is perfect at the first fitting, thereby doing away with so much standing and trying on, which is so wearisome to all ladies."[64]

At least one observer suggested that such claims should be taken with skepticism. No system, maintained Broughton, the author of *Suggestions for Dressmakers* and a staunch defender of traditional methods, could do away with the need for fittings; "'trying on' is bound to continue to be thought one of the bug-a-boos of dressmaking." "Dress fitting is not a mathematical problem that can be solved by learning a few rules," she warned. "Parisian dressmakers"—the model to which Broughton believed all American modistes should aspire—"are famous for their pooh-poohing of systems." These French apostles of perfection apparently showed little interest in time-saving techniques: "If the Parisian dressmaker requires your presence for ten fittings, she tells you so and gets them."[65]

Broughton's observations suggest that a quiet battle raged in the hearts and minds of dressmakers between quantity and quality, industry and art. Quite likely the dilemma resolved itself along class lines. "High-class fitters" disdained systems; "low-class" fitters evidently did not. Wealthy patrons could afford to pay "small fortunes" for carefully constructed garments, and the leisure to endure innumerable fittings was perhaps as much a symbol of conspicuous consumption as the dress itself.[66] More often than not, the customer with less time on her hands and less money to spend settled for "slovenly" work and—systematizers' claims to the contrary—a less than perfect fit.

Drafting systems appear to have been distributed by geography as well as class. A surprising number of inventors hailed from the small towns of the Midwest; Quincy, Illinois; Baraboo, Wisconsin; Steubenville, Ohio; and Webster City, Iowa, were places where apprenticeship traditions were likely to be weak. Perhaps not coincidentally, most of the North Dakota dressmakers interviewed for one study relied on charts.[67] Enthusiastic proponents of systems could be found in New York and Chicago as well as Beattie, Kansas, and Maryville, Missouri. But the pin-to-the-form technique probably survived longest in urban areas. Virtually every Cleveland dressmaking shop visited by the social investigator Edna Bryner in 1916 used a variant of this traditional method.[68]

While systems were not universally adopted, they gave rise to another even more troubling invention that benefited amateurs at female artisans' expense. "Graded"—that is, sized—patterns were the logical outgrowth of proportional methods. These fragile pieces of tissue paper offered significant advantages to home sewers—women who faced considerable pressure to dress fashionably *and* cheaply—but they had tragic consequences for the art of dressmaking. Patterns eliminated the need for drafting altogether; the modiste who relied on them was little more than a seamstress.[69]

Patterns were not new to Gilded Age Americans; unsized versions appeared in fashion periodicals as early as the 1850s. At best these provided only limited assistance. *Godey's* patterns, for example, were intended to fit "a lady of middle height and youthful proportion." Graded patterns were not invented until 1867, a distinction that Ebenezer Butterick, a former tailor, rightfully claimed. (Indeed, he parlayed his creative efforts into one of the longest-lived enterprises in corporate history; the Butterick Company still makes patterns today.) Butterick's creations followed the same principles as proportional drafting systems, that is, they were sized according to bust measurements. "Designed for the use of persons not very familiar with making garments," they were clearly intended to eliminate the need for skill (Figure 8). Butterick's arch rival, Madame Demorest, made much the same point; her patterns, she claimed, were "so accurately cut and notched that any novice can put them together."[70]

Figure 8. Illustration from *E. Butterick and Company*'s catalog, summer 1875. Perhaps because they recognized the deficiencies of the proportional techniques on which their products were based, pattern manufacturers' selections emphasized looser garments such as housedresses and wrappers. Note the low prices. (Courtesy of the American Antiquarian Society)

Like drafting systems, patterns were primarily a male invention. Herman and Schamu Moschcowitz, makers of "Bazar Cut Paper Patterns," presided over a New York establishment that employed ninety "man dressmakers." James McCall, a former tailor and the creator of the "Royal Chart," was responsible for another extraordinarily long-lived product, the McCall pattern. Ellen Curtis Demorest, who with her husband created a fashion empire that included *Demorest's Monthly Magazine,* the Demorest Sewing Machine Company, Demorest's patterns, and Madame Demorest's Excelsior System, constituted the sole exception; she evidently played some role (how significant is unclear) in designing the innovations that bore her name.[71]

Gender mattered little to consumers; patterns were a resounding commercial success. "Last year this firm sold over four millions of patterns," E. Butterick and Company declared in 1871. While exaggerated, this proclamation may have only slightly stretched the truth. And no wonder! Once possessed of graded patterns, home sewers and amateur craftswomen did not need to cut or draft to fit—only cut on the lines and sew.[72]

Patterns offered a substitute not only for the dressmaker's skill but also for her judgment. For unlike drafting systems, which required the user to exercise her imagination, they provided a finished template, a paper version of the actual garment. The pattern, in other words, *was* the fashion. Inexpensive and easy to use, patterns provided stylish apparel to women who could not afford the services of professionals. But the same development that heralded "democracy" for the consumer threatened penury for the dressmaker. Like sewing machines and drafting systems, patterns encouraged erstwhile patrons to make their own clothes. "I went a few days ago since to get a dress made, but the dressmaker could not make it at once, and I don't like to wait, so I came home, looked over the many patterns sent with the Demorest number, and with aid of those . . . have cut and fitted my dress," a satisfied subscriber informed *Demorest's* in 1879. One who dubbed herself "Country" was more blunt: "Until last year I employed a dressmaker, but I find I can, with a good pattern, suit myself better."[73]

Tradeswomen themselves might use patterns, but only the most inexperienced relied entirely on them. Like drafting systems, they met the needs of women unexpectedly thrown on their own resources; like systems, they were popular among hinterland dwellers who had few opportunities to "learn" their trades. "Mrs. Robt. C. H.," a "poor sewing woman" from Knox Point, Louisiana, found Demorest's patterns "quite a help." An Iowa dressmaker "with a large family to . . . provide for" agreed: "I do think your patterns . . . are the best and cheapest of any I have seen. They are a great help to me. I could not get along without them."[74] But the "fashionable" dressmaker who enthusiastically embraced patterns was likely to lose customers, for standardized styles failed to satisfy discriminating patrons. Manufacturers' protestations to the contrary, their "newest" designs copied last year's Paris fashions; despite the illusion of variety, their catalogs often betrayed a dull uniformity. "No woman wishes a gown made in a fashion already in common use when the pattern maker selects it," Broughton explained, noting that the typical pattern designer "gets his inspiration . . . at second or fifth hand." (Significantly, Broughton's reference to designers invoked the masculine pronoun.) By their very nature, patterns limited creativity; modistes who feared "'making two dresses alike[,]' . . . a fear for which . . . their customers are responsible," wisely avoided them.[75]

Skilled practitioners had even greater reason to eschew them, for patterns, based on the same theories of proportional drafting systems, exhibited all of those systems' weaknesses. However correct the principles upon which they were graduated, however "mathematically wrought," they seldom rendered a perfect fit. More often than not, the wearer faced two alternatives: an ill-fitting dress or a spate of alterations.[76]

* * *

The persistence of age-old practices and the not inconsiderable deficiencies of modern devices suggest that, by 1900, scientific methods had won an incomplete victory at best. We have no means of learning how much business dressmakers lost to newly emboldened home sewers; despite the availability of sewing machines, paper patterns, and drafting systems, the number of professionals continued to increase.[77] Some dressmakers clung to traditional methods; others embraced "scientific principles"; still others incorporated new techniques into long-standing practices. Some continued to learn their trades from Madame; others—with the help of patterns and systems—taught themselves. No doubt the ratio of one to the other will remain a mystery. One thing is certain: craftswomen who could not cut without the aid of patterns and systems, and who perhaps could not sew without the aid of machines, were far more prevalent in 1900 than in 1860. Indeed, one suspects that they accounted for many of the "incompetent" dressmakers of whom nineteenth-century Americans were so fond of complaining.

Perhaps more significant was that new technologies—eagerly proffered

to "ladies" and dressmakers alike—challenged tradeswomen's special expertise and eroded their unique authority. Certainly, the readers of "The Dressmaker in the House," a short story in the June 1909 issue of *Harper's Monthly
Magazine,* would have been hard-pressed to disagree. While Carolyn Wells's
authorial "monologue" was intended as a satirical sketch, it, like most sat-
ire, had a basis in fact. Her story concerns the interaction between two characters, Mrs. Lester, "a pretty, fussy little woman," and Miss Cotton, "a visiting dressmaker." Cotton had been commissioned to make a new pair of
sleeves, for the "elbow sleeves" that adorned Lester's gowns had passed from
fashion. (As Lester put it, "It isn't any fun to go to a luncheon and be the
only woman at the table with elbow sleeves!")[78]

Lester *was* "fussy"; indeed, she showed little respect for Cotton's skills.
"I'm going to superintend," she informed the dressmaker, "but I want you
to help, and to do the plain sewing." She had already purchased both fabric
and a "paper pattern"; "I trust a great deal to your judgment and experience,"
she explained, "though I always rely on my own taste." Lester relied on more
than her taste. As the dressmaker watched in horror, she insisted on cutting
out the sleeves herself. Predictably, her efforts ended in disaster: "A living
skeleton couldn't get into those." "What?" she asked the dressmaker. "I
should have allowed seams? Why didn't you tell me? Oh no, I didn't scorn
your advice! Why that's what I have you here for!"[79]

However unsuccessful her efforts, Lester had none too subtly questioned
Cotton's knowledge of her trade; significantly, she was abetted by a paper
pattern. As this story suggests, new technologies produced complicated and
sometimes contradictory results. Female clothiers increasingly competed
with male innovators to control the dissemination of craft knowledge, to
determine who could become a dressmaker. They also competed with amateur craftswomen and home sewers. Theoretically, aspiring modistes no longer needed to serve apprenticeships to mistress dressmakers, and the purchase
of patterns and systems meant home sewers could do without the services
of professionals, even if such devices yielded less than perfect results. But
innovations were not an unequivocal benefit—even for consumers. Less
work for the dressmaker, Ruth Schwartz Cowan reminds us, meant "more
work for mother."[80]

Viewed from the perspective of custom clothiers, new technologies had
far more ominous implications, for they paved the way for ready-to-wear
clothing. Constrained by fashion, they remained within the confines of custom production throughout the nineteenth century. But "sizes" based on

proportional theories, wholly inadequate for constructing Gilded Age vogues, were entirely appropriate for the more loosely fitting shirtwaists of the 1910s and—especially—the "flapper" dresses of the 1920s.[81] To be sure, mass production would replace a cumbersome and expensive system with one that offered immediately available ready-to-wear clothing at hitherto unheard of prices. But if the democratization of fashion represented an unmitigated blessing to consumers, it provided few advantages to the erstwhile producers of feminine apparel. Ready-made clothing did not simply relieve middle-class women from domestic drudgery, it also divested female artisans from relatively remunerative and satisfying employment. Scientific principles heralded a future without dressmakers, a future dominated by men.

Six

Commerce over Craft:
Wholesalers and Retailers
in the Millinery Trade,
1860–1930

*C*an we assist you?" asked *Hill's Milliners' Gazette,* a trade publication issued by a New York wholesaling firm, in 1887. "Ladies coming to New York for the first time and desiring to have some one meet them at the depot or wharf, have only to write us of their wishes, and we can arrange to accommodate them."[1] In many respects, the *Gazette's* offer reflected services that virtually all wholesale merchants—whether they sold drugs or dry goods, hardware or hosiery—provided to their out-of-town customers; they typically secured lodgings, suggested entertainments, and furnished "headquarters" where visiting retailers could store purchases and receive correspondence. Part paternalistic solicitude and part rational self-interest, these strategies comforted bewildered travelers—and encouraged them to patronize a single firm. Nevertheless, the sponsors of *Hill's Milliners' Gazette* recognized the peculiar circumstances of their trade: most of the retailers with whom they dealt were female. Indeed, the concern they expressed for "ladies coming to New York for the first time" acknowledged the special vulnerability that traveling women faced, especially when unaccompanied by men. Gender, the representatives of Hill Brothers believed, made a difference; gentlemanly consideration, not masculine solidarity, governed their conduct of business affairs.

The concept of gender rarely surfaces in business history, perhaps because the field has been slow to adopt the concerns of the "new" social and cultural histories, or perhaps because the notion—until recently applied almost exclusively to women—appears to be a superfluous one.[2] After all, is not the history of business—of self-made men, robber barons, and men in gray flannel suits—necessarily a chronicle of masculine activity? The existence of thousands of businesswomen suggests otherwise. While historians would do well to examine the ways in which issues of masculinity influenced relations between businessmen, the case of the millinery trade throws gendered concerns into particularly sharp relief. Like most businesspeople, millinery merchants looked out for their own economic interests. But cultural ideals about the nature of womanhood invariably influenced their supposedly rational economic decisions.

Indeed, an examination of relationships between male wholesalers and female retailers in the millinery trade reveals some of the ways in which gender structured the nineteenth- and early twentieth-century commercial world. Unlike their dressmaking sisters who usually crafted garments from materials furnished by their patrons, milliners typically "kept stock," a practice that entailed doing business with third parties. Wholesalers or "jobbers" supplied them with fabrics, feathers, flowers, ribbons, and lace—the stuff of which hats were made. Like their counterparts in other fields, wholesale milliners (merchants who resold imported and domestic goods) played no small part in determining the success or failure of their customers. They had the power to grant or withhold credit, to glorify or destroy reputations, even to determine the type of merchandise sold.[3] Millinery merchants confronted a novel situation, for they dealt primarily not with men but with women. More often than not, nineteenth-century wholesalers viewed their customers through Victorian glasses, valiantly assisting "helpless" females, symbolically transforming disreputable shopkeepers into "respectable" businesswomen, expecting and usually receiving the gratitude of those they served. Yet soon the tables turned; as the century drew to a close and as wholesalers adopted new, more "rational" methods of doing business, "respectable" proprietors became "unbusinesslike" businesswomen. At much the same time, wholesalers began to market different kinds of products; labor-saving devices, prefabricated "shapes," and, finally, ready-made hats, increasingly replaced the raw materials of an earlier day.

While they might appear relatively innocuous, these economic and cultural transformations had significant and less than happy consequences for female craftsmanship and enterprise. The ranks of the nation's milliners declined precipitously during the first three decades of the twentieth century, from nearly 128,000 in 1910 to just under 45,000 in 1930 (see Table A-1 in appendix). At the same time, the proportion of male retailers increased, altering substantially the composition of what once had been a resolutely female trade. In 1900 men made up only 2 percent of all milliners; thirty years later they accounted for more than a tenth.[4] This shift coincided with another, equally dramatic, change. In 1860, the typical milliner was a highly skilled craftsperson, an artisan-businesswoman who made the hats she sold, usually in accordance with the wishes of particular customers. Sixty or seventy years later she—or he—was a seller of prefabricated hats who was fighting a losing battle against department stores.

Readers who hope to find evidence of a male conspiracy will be disappointed. Nevertheless, by adopting more stringent credit policies, committing themselves to more "businesslike" behavior, aggressively marketing—and in some cases manufacturing—ready-made hats, wholesalers, however inadvertently, helped to transform the female economy of the nineteenth century into the fashion industry of the twentieth. By 1930 the manufacture and sale of feminine finery, once the province of women, was firmly in the hands of men.

Male Wholesalers, Female Retailers: Credit, Gender, and Paternalism

In 1850, a census enumerator visited Sarah Ayres's millinery shop, located on Boston's fashionable Washington Street. Ayres reported that she employed three workers, used 1,000 yards of silk and 1,500 yards of ribbon annually—and possessed a capital of $300. In this respect, she was representative of her trade. As late as 1900, the *Illustrated Milliner* estimated that 78 percent of all retail milliners in the United States were worth $1,000 or less.[5]

Wholesaling, on the other hand, was big business—and growing bigger all the time. In 1850, the same year Ayres was interviewed, the wholesale millinery firm of A. Partridge and Company estimated its worth at $8,000. Fifty years later, a trade publication lamented the lack of "millinery millionaires," but chances were that many jobbers fell only slightly short of that mark.[6] Wholesalers and retailers were separated by gender as well as capital. With few exceptions, the larger structure of the industry was neatly segmented by sex. "A strong, healthy man . . . in a millinery establishment," the labor reformer Virginia Penny declared in 1869, "is as out of place as a woman chopping wood, carrying coal, or sweeping the streets." Although such sanctions failed to deter a small contingent of male shopkeepers, Penny spoke the truth: retailers were predominantly female. Wholesaling, by contrast, was a man's world, as tales recounting the exploits of merchants, clerks, and traveling salesmen make clear. Headlines such as "Millinery Men in Bowling Battle" and "Chicago Milliners Go after Deer" frequently embellished the pages of trade journals, strident assertions of masculinity on the part of unjustly maligned "man milliners." They also conveyed an unmistakable message: men belonged in wholesaling, women in retailing.[7]

Thus, commercial dealings between wholesalers and retailers were also transactions between men and women, a form of exchange usually confined to prostitution and marriage. Gender was bound to affect the nature of these relationships, and indeed, a curious blend of paternalism and economic self-interest characterized wholesalers' attitudes toward their customers. To be sure, these two qualities did not always easily meld together; businessmen were often torn between compassion and profit. This tension was nowhere more evident than in the disposition of credit.

Many retail milliners avoided credit transactions entirely—and for good reason. Credit involved risk: there was always the chance that bills could not be paid when due. Moreover, women who bought goods on time often paid with their privacy. One prospective entrepreneur, a credit reporter announced, "has been divorced from her husband"; another's renegade spouse was "said to be in California."[8] While male proprietors suffered similar indignities, these sorts of semipublic revelations must have been particularly painful to women in a culture that celebrated female delicacy and modesty.

Those who sought credit were often refused, for most milliners had little collateral to offer: "Has no means outside her business" was the credit reporter's frequent lament.[9] Strapped for ready cash, female retailers were further hampered by the peculiarities of their trade. Milliners' livelihoods, as we have seen, depended on patrons who paid their bills late—or not at all. Even in the best circumstances, milliners found it difficult to meet their obligations. While "prompt" millinery customers settled every six months, wholesalers usually expected payment within thirty days. Caught between time-honored traditions of retailing and modern mercantile conventions, milliners could scarcely avoid—in wholesaler's terminology—being "slow."[10]

Whenever capital was the basis for credit, men won and women lost. But wholesalers' decisions were rarely governed by logic alone; indeed, in sharp contrast to portrayals that depict businessmen as "rational economic actors," they were far from immune to the cultural currents surrounding them. Millinery merchants, like most Americans, subscribed to popular notions about gender, a fact that was bound to influence their attitudes toward their customers. "Philo," a representative of a New York wholesaling firm, described retailers in a tone reminiscent of nineteenth-century women's magazines. "No one will contend," he wrote, "that the butcher or the blacksmith requires the delicate taste that enters into the construction of a becoming Hat; nor is he ever called upon to exercise the taste needed for the satisfactory arrangement of ribbons of various shades and colors."[11]

Condescending though it may have been, this kind of paternalistic sensibility—based on powerful if not entirely accurate notions of feminine behavior—could work to women's advantage; "gentlemanly" deportment might triumph over "rational" matters of assets and debits, credits and costs. Helpless females, forced by circumstance to earn their own livings, occasionally inspired sympathy in the hearts of potential creditors. As one commentator put it, "the financial status, on which women receive credit, would not warrant us in giving credit to men, whatever their business might be."[12] Indeed, a comparison of the credit histories of Boston milliners with those of their counterparts in the male-dominated tailoring trade lends support to this assertion. While milliners in search of credit were often turned down, they appear to have secured loans on less collateral than did their fellow clothiers.[13] But paternalistic leniency had its limits. Wholesalers seldom took any action that clashed too strongly with economic imperatives. Moreover, the assistance they rendered appears to have been contingent on "appropriate" female behavior. Tradeswomen who ventured beyond the stereotypes that wholesalers constructed for them did so at some risk.

The credit records of R. G. Dun & Co. provide tantalizing glimpses of interactions between jobbers and their customers, for the opinions of Dun & Co. correspondents and wholesale dealers, if not one and the same, were closely intertwined. The company's first historian made much of reporters' independence and objectivity. But if the Boston millinery trade is at all representative, his claim represented little more than wishful thinking.[14] Correspondents obtained information from a variety of sources: they questioned neighbors and landlords and occasionally interviewed the subjects of their investigations. But "the trade" provided their crucial source of information; most reporters paid a great deal of attention to what "those who sell [to] her" had to say. Some correspondents may even have been wholesalers themselves: one reporter referred to "our" trade.[15]

In other respects, Dun & Co. correspondents and the wholesalers they served were far from objective. As David A. Gerber has demonstrated, religious and ethnic prejudices clouded reporters' judgments, effectively reinforcing the economic dominance of white, Anglo-Saxon, Protestant—and male—elites.[16] Female proprietors occasionally faced similar forms of discrimination. Thomas Meagher, the author of a widely read exposé (1876) of Dun & Co. and its competitors, suggested that correspondents unjustly impugned businesswomen's reputations. As evidence, he revealed the alleged contents of one report: "Of . . . [a] lady in New-Jersey it is said, 'she has a neat millinery store, with a cozy room in the rear, and an inviting lounge.'" Meagher's outrage aside, unflattering intimations had a basis in fact; houses of ill repute occasionally lurked behind milliners' signs. But as he recognized, the symbolic meanings of malicious reports outdistanced their literal ones, for they implied that the respectability of any woman who entered the public, commercial world was open to question.[17]

If the Boston records of Dun & Co. are any indication, prurient speculation was the exception not the rule. Characters such as Mrs. A. Adell Shaw, who was "a hard case morally speaking," rarely appeared in its ledgers. At times, credit reporters appeared oblivious to gender. An overworked or preoccupied investigator might describe a female proprietor as "a good workman" or a former "salesman." One tradeswoman even earned the dubious distinction of being "a smart and capable man."[18] More often than not, correspondents viewed their subjects in gendered terms, although they painted more flattering portraits than Meagher's concerns suggested. Far more common than either indifference or innuendo was a sort of gentlemanly restraint; an aura of Victorian gentility hovers over the Dun & Co. ledgers. If the pronouncements of credit reporters may be believed, the milliners of Gilded Age Boston were overwhelmingly honorable, honest, upright, and industrious. No adjective recurred with greater frequency than "respectable." Men might be "upright and honorable" but with few exceptions only women were "respectable."[19]

Credit reporters' compliments should not be taken literally; they were neither accurate indexes to social status nor reliable representations of character. Rather, respectability provided wholesalers with a lens through which to view their clients, women whose entrepreneurial endeavors—even if confined to a "feminine" pursuit—were at odds with traditional notions of woman's place.

Two competing images of milliners, as we have seen, surface in nineteenth-century popular culture. The first, recalling the fears voiced by Meagher's exposé, portrays them as coarse, vulgar women—predatory purveyors of useless luxuries at best, barely disguised keepers of bordellos at worst. The second image depicts the proprietors of hat shops as "gentlewomen" down on their luck, hapless victims of circumstance who otherwise would not have ventured into the commercial world. Neither stereotype bears much resemblance to reality; the evidence indicates that the vast majority of tradeswomen hailed from working-class—not middle- or upper-class—backgrounds and that they ran legitimate businesses. Faced with two mutually exclusive alternatives, most credit investigators chose a variation on the second theme, constructing an image of the respectable businesswoman that preserved milliners' reputations and granted them honorary middle-class status. "Respectable," first and foremost, signified that the tradeswoman in question conducted a lawful enterprise, that Madame was not a madam. But the term also served as shorthand for an array of female traits—helplessness, timidity, and refinement—stereotypes that Dun & Co. reporters assumed their subjects would fit. While they felt free to describe a male proprietor as "worthless" or "rather boastful," or (as in the case of one corset seller) to note that he "gets tight sometimes on hardly anything," a woman's character was automatically above reproach, even if she failed to meet her obligations.[20]

Indeed, honesty and respectability carried little weight. Mrs. M. E. LaFontaine was "represented as honest and respectable—but of limited means." The verdict? "At present is not considered desirable for credit." Neither was Miss G. A. Nourse. Although "a respectable young woman," she had "failed once and paid [her creditors] little or nothing." Still, references to character were not always meaningless; respectability might rehabilitate an otherwise bad credit risk. Luckily for Mrs. Martha J. Davis, she was "trusted on her character rather than on any definite knowledge of her resources." Miss Mary McManus was "a lady of strict honesty and integrity." Without conscious irony, an admiring investigator concluded that "no drawback is known to exist except the want of more money."[21]

Wholesaler paternalism was not confined to Boston. Abigail Scott Duniway of Albany, Oregon, soon to emerge as a leading figure in the West Coast suffrage movement, became the family breadwinner when her husband met with a disabling accident in the late 1860s. After a brief stint as a teacher, she decided to try the millinery business. Truly desperate, Duniway journeyed to Portland to buy stock, with only thirty dollars in her pocket. When she arrived, she explained her predicament to Jacob Mayer, a sympathetic wholesaler. Much to her astonishment, he furnished her with $1,200 worth of goods and insisted that she keep her money. The author of a prize-winning essay on "How I Started in Business" told a similar tale. "I had no storeroom, no money, no friend to help or advise," she recalled. Nonetheless, she secured an interview with the four partners of a wholesale firm and left with millinery supplies worth eighty dollars. As she explained, "In the light of later knowledge, I marvel much that I ever gained a hearing."[22]

Wholesalers cultivated the image of the kindly millinery merchant, invariably portraying themselves not as profit-minded businessmen but as rescuers of damsels in distress. Philo, a spokesman for Hill Brothers, advised prospective businesswomen to patronize "an old, established house, that is widely and favorably known." The members of such a concern, "having had in their long experience hundreds of young Milliners come to them for advice in starting . . . are ready to give much valuable information to the beginner." Indeed, the representatives of Hill Brothers made much of their paternalistic solicitude. In answer to the *Illustrated Milliner*'s query, "Why are there no millinery millionaires?" a representative of the firm replied that wholesalers were "too gallant to get rich":

> These men, dealing for the major part with ladies, who do most of the retail business of the country, are too considerate to load their goods with a rate of profit which would put their accumulations into seven figures.
> If the great steel companies had to deal with the "gentler sex," instead of governments and corporations, their balance sheets would not show the annual profits which it makes us all dizzy to try to comprehend.[23]

Chivalric proclamations aside, capital remained the primary basis for credit; few wholesalers consistently ignored their own interests. Duniway's $1,200 loan betrays either uncommon generosity or her faulty memory. In any case, the millinery merchants of Boston were far more cautious; they trusted female retailers for amounts ranging from $10 to $2,000, but they seldom doled out more than $100–200 worth of goods at a time. Still, women held a modicum of power by virtue of their numbers; wholesalers' paternalistic proclamations had as much to do with economics as with chival-

ry. No doubt, jobbers eagerly competed for the business of larger, male-operated firms. But in retail millinery women constituted the majority, and creditors could expect little from them in the way of collateral. However they
justified their actions, wholesalers *had* to settle for less.[24]

Even so, paternalism was more than a sugarcoating for hard-boiled economic imperatives, for deeply embedded cultural assumptions influenced
supposedly rational business behavior. Like many of their contemporaries,
wholesalers and their representatives believed that women as a group were
endowed with special characteristics. P. R. Earling, who devoted a separate
section of his treatise on credit to "Women in Trade," argued that female
retailers were good credit risks because "they neither smoke, drink, play
billiards, [n]or do any of the countless things for which men spend."[25]

This is not to say that men never received assistance on the basis of their
"characters"; on the contrary, wholesalers in many lines of business expressed their willingness to aid deserving retailers. If "the character and
habits of the applicant for credit . . . are not good," Earling explained, "we
have not much use for him in any capacity, especially that of debtor." Or as
a Dun & Co. reporter noted of a Boston tailor: "Not thought to be making
any money—but considered an honest man [and] considered safe."[26] Definitions of character, however, varied according to gender. "Good character" connoted sobriety and integrity for both sexes; just as potential creditors bestowed their approval upon "respectable" women, they smiled on men
of "steady habits." But while commercial analysts spoke admiringly of men's
"indefatigable energy," they warned businesswomen not to "tax . . . their
strength beyond endurance." A man needed to be alert and aggressive to
succeed "in this age of competition and push" but "woman" was "not over-
ambitious, like man." Well into the twentieth century, trade journals that
catered to male merchants celebrated aspiring businessmen's pluck and initiative, chronicling their rise from rags to riches. In contrast, articles in millinery magazines depicted their subscribers as victims of sudden adversity.
For businesswomen—as for women generally—respectability implied not
ambition and assertiveness but helplessness and dependence.[27] This view,
implicit in the Dun & Co. records, found fuller expression in Earling's *Whom
to Trust:*

> When we find her in business at all, she is there for the sole purpose of
> making her living, and she engages in no hap-hazard operations whereby
> she might lose her foothold. Loss of her little capital would be an irretriev-
> able calamity, and she fully appreciates the hopelessness of her situation

in case of failure. She is not devoid of ambition, but she does not permit it to lead her into trying to out-do her neighbors or to eclipse the world.[28]

Earling's portrait of the typical businesswoman contains elements of truth. Few milliners entered the trade for frivolous reasons; ample evidence suggests that they rarely took extraordinary risks. But Earling presented an exaggerated view of feminine frailty. While he recognized that women were not "devoid of ambition," it is difficult to reconcile his pronouncements with the real-life facts of a trade that required ambition, skill, and confidence.

Ambition *is* visible in credit records, beneath the glowing rhetoric. More to the point, merchants who saw themselves as paternalistic benefactors expected women's gratitude. Deference to wholesalers was rewarded; irreverence and—in some instances—shrewd business behavior were not. Probably many a plucky milliner played the game; "honest" and "respectable" tradeswomen, the vast majority, followed the rules, at times perhaps manipulating popular notions of respectable womanhood to their own advantage. But apparently the behavior of some women was too much at odds with gender stereotypes. In a field crowded with "respectable" shopkeepers, they constituted a tiny but conspicuous contingent who merited the labels "unpopular," "disagreeable," "fussy," and "troublesome." Ann Rowe's credit report was anything but flattering: "Without improvement in credit or change in manners, parties would not sell her for cash, if busy at the time of [her] call," a correspondent declared emphatically. Rowe was not alone. Mehitabel Sampson was "disagreeable to deal with," while Maria and Catherine Roeth were "always finding fault and troublesome to collect from."[29]

Significantly, troublesome milliners did not represent the poorest or least successful of their trade. While the typical Boston milliner closed her shop after six years, Rowe and Sampson, each of whom enjoyed twenty-seven-year careers, evinced remarkable longevity. (With thirteen years to their credit, the Roeths were not far behind.) Indeed, Rowe owned a home valued at $5,000, Sampson an estate worth $8,000–10,000—assets that set them apart from many of their competitors.[30]

Wholesalers accustomed to dealing with retailers of limited means should have rushed to accommodate successful tradeswomen like Rowe, Sampson, and the Roeth sisters. Instead, they vociferously denounced their behavior, at times going so far as to refuse their custom. Why? Available evidence does not allow us to answer with certainty. Perhaps, as Dun & Co. reporters suggested, these women had unattractive personalities that rendered doing business with them less than a pleasure. Perhaps, too, their relative success gave them the confidence to resist the overtures of paternalistic wholesalers. And their credit entries suggest that they took their time in paying their bills, a failing that also marked most of their competitors. Equally important, correspondents' grumblings imply that their advantageous position within an impoverished trade allowed them to do what many milliners could not: demand good prices, superior merchandise, and favorable terms of credit and insist that millinery merchants—used to getting their way with relatively powerless retailers—live up to their "gentlemanly" reputations. Rowe, Sampson, and the Roeths emerge as shrewd operators, intent on getting the most for their money. If they proved to be tough customers, they also defied the comforting feminine stereotypes that wholesalers had constructed—and expected—of their clients.

Perhaps, then, it is not unreasonable to assume that in wholesalers' eyes "troublesome" retailers transgressed the boundaries of appropriate female behavior. Disagreeable women, we might surmise, were uniquely assertive. Milliners who were always finding fault or fussy insisted on carefully inspecting the goods they purchased, implicitly questioning the judgment and honesty of their benefactors. To be sure, women were not the only victims of unflattering descriptions. The "crank," as Earling described him, was the bane of wholesalers (although from the retailer's point of view he may simply have been someone who looked out for his own best interests). "He seems to live for and to have a special aptitude in the direction of finding fault with things," Earling explained. "Nor is he ever satisfied to accept your prices and terms without considerable haggling." Cranks, as the forgoing discussion demonstrates, could be of either sex. But their relative scarcity among milliners suggests that such women posed a potent challenge to prevailing standards of female behavior. Disagreeable women may have been particularly unsettling to businessmen accustomed to viewing their customers as helpless, dependent, and "feminine."[31]

Harriet Lowell's experience is particularly instructive. A former schoolteacher, she entered business in 1855 with questionable prospects. "Her means must be very limited," a correspondent noted. "Those who sell her rely more upon her good character and attentiveness to business than upon the amount she has to do with." Nevertheless, Lowell's business prospered. A decade later, with assets worth at least $15,000, she was buying goods in New York and Europe. In 1871, she astonished the trade by becoming a wholesaler herself. Crippled by an unsuccessful venture in New York and a series of unprofitable real estate investments, Lowell was unable to maintain her extraordinary commercial success throughout her twenty-eight years in business. From 1877–83, the date of her last mention in the Dun & Co. ledgers, she was continually "behind in her payments and not considered desirable for credit." Still, her career was one that few of her competitors could match.

Curiously, as Lowell's fortunes rose, her reputation declined. Credit reporters began to describe her as "too smart," "not very popular," and "disagreeable." We can only speculate about the reasons for this shift. Although Lowell's decision to buy and sell the superior products of Paris and New York was understandable, it was bound to alienate Boston wholesalers. ("Considered good for all she can be induced to buy in this market," one reporter commented.) She had dared to enter the jobbing trade, competing directly with her former benefactors. Perhaps they believed her insufficiently grateful for the assistance they had rendered in the days when character had been her only collateral. In sum, perhaps she had been too successful for her own good.[32]

It is difficult to assess the impact of such derogatory statements. Disagreeable as she was, Lowell prospered (although one wonders what role uncomplimentary references played in her downfall). But disparaging remarks—especially when read by an out-of-town wholesaler—could scarcely have worked to the retailer's benefit. If nothing else, Lowell's credit ledger betrays a certain uneasiness toward female success. To be sure, some successful retailers managed to remain "respectable," perhaps because they remained deferential. But scattered references to troublesome tradeswomen suggest that wholesalers sometimes found it difficult to reconcile their economic interests with their assumptions about "woman's place." Hardly rational economic actors, they remained imprisoned by widely shared cultural beliefs.

By the turn of the century, sympathetic assistance was on the wane. Wholesalers increasingly adopted "rational" (and seemingly gender-neutral) methods of doing business that adversely—if unintentionally—affected the fortunes of female entrepreneurs. Spurred by the increasing physical distance that separated them from retailers, the depression of the 1890s, and the "search for order" that infected much of American society, wholesalers struggled to do business according to "businesslike" principles.[33] This transformation reflected larger changes in the American economy as a whole. But the decline of wholesaler paternalism had significant and less than salutary consequences for those women who sought their livelihoods in the hatmaking trade.

The Rationalization of Wholesaling

Nineteenth-century paternalism had been bolstered by personal relationships. Occasionally, ties of family and friendship also connected retailers and
wholesalers. Catherine Bradley, a Boston milliner, had "a brother with Carpenter, Plimpton and Company and another with W. H. Horner and Company." When Mrs. E. T. Hanewacker of Brooklyn decided to try the millinery business, she "called on a salesman with whom I was acquainted, told
him just how I was situated, and through his kindness his house gave me
credit for $75 worth of millinery goods."[34]

In millinery, as elsewhere in the business world, late nineteenth-century
improvements in transportation began to transform wholesaler/retailer relations. Extensive railroad connections and cheaper freight rates brought
milliners across the nation in touch with the fabled markets of New York.
At the same time, newly established wholesaling centers in Chicago, St.
Louis, Dallas, and San Francisco vied with the eastern "establishment" for
the business of tradeswomen who set up shop in the hinterlands of the West
and Midwest. Milliners who had the time and money continued to make personal pilgrimages to urban markets; for those who wished to be sure that they
got what they paid for, this was a wise policy. Increasingly, however, retailers sacrificed certainty for convenience by ordering goods by mail from a
wholesaler they had never met or by dealing with his intermediary, the traveling salesman or "drummer." Simultaneously, the scale of wholesaling was
increasing; firms that employed hundreds of clerks could scarcely be expected
to maintain personal relationships with individual clients.[35]

The 1890s were as hard for wholesale milliners as for other businesspeople. Indeed, those who dealt in luxury items suffered disproportionately
during economic downturns. In November 1896, the *Millinery Trade Review*
acknowledged that "the jobbers have had a rough row to hoe for several
seasons . . . owing to the continued depression in all lines of business." Although the *Review* counseled lenience toward "the poor milliners [who] cannot pay the jobber," harsher attitudes soon prevailed.[36]

Perhaps more significant than either distance or economic depression was
the fact that wholesalers began to demonstrate a newfound awareness of their
common interests. "This is a period of co-operation in the business world,"
the *Millinery Herald* proclaimed in 1908, and wholesalers fulfilled the prophecy by banding together to impose order on a chaotic trade. Formed in 1901,
the Millinery Jobbers' Association represented firms in the West, Midwest,

and South. Twelve years later, eastern wholesalers followed suit. In this as in much else, millinery men were imitators not originators; they merely followed the lead established by dealers of men's hats, clothing, hardware, jewels, and furniture.[37]

Enthusiastic proponents claimed that cooperation benefited the retailer as well as the wholesaler. To some extent, they were correct. In 1908, for example, the Millinery Jobbers' Association warded off "a threatened change in the freight classification of feathers." But when the association asked, "Does every milliner in the great West and South realize what good fortune it is to have so powerful and successful an organization . . . in their midst?" many retailers might have disagreed, for such combinations only increased the unequal balance of power between millinery suppliers and their customers. Wholesalers and retailers needed each other, but their interests were not identical.[38]

The proliferation of trade journals also reflected wholesalers' newly awakened self-awareness. Founded in 1876, the *Millinery Trade Review* catered to jobbers and manufacturers, adding an occasional "Hints to Milliners." Around the turn of the century, the *Review* was joined by a series of periodicals published for the ostensible benefit of retailers. The *Milliner* appeared in 1898; the *Illustrated Milliner*, *Milliner's Designer*, and *Millinery Herald* followed in rapid succession.[39]

Trade journals were rarely guilty of objectivity. The *Millinery Herald*, published under the auspices of the Millinery Jobbers' Association, was not coincidentally the most strident advocate of wholesalers' interests. But the difference between the *Herald* and its competitors was more a matter of degree than kind; all such publications mirrored the opinions of their advertisers. To be sure, trade journals performed valuable services. They kept their readers posted on the latest millinery fashions by sending representatives to Paris every spring and fall. They offered an abundance of advice to retailers, ranging from the useful ("Do you figure profits rightly?") to the ridiculous ("The milliner has it in her power . . . to quiet the feeling of resentment against the hat pin"). But while they continually harped on "the mutuality of interests" between retailers and jobbers, they seldom advanced any proposition that conflicted with the interests of wholesalers.[40]

Both physical distance and cooperation, the pages of trade journals suggest, coincided with a new, businesslike attitude toward retailers. Paternalism did not disappear overnight, but by the early years of the twentieth century a new tone was evident. In 1915 the *Milliner* acknowledged that "your wholesaler is your friend and confidant" but argued that friendship could only be pushed so far. "It is appalling the presumption of some women in the matter of credits," its editors complained. "They think that the wholesaler will provide them with all the merchandise they need and that with them having little or practically no experience."[41]

Wholesalers were already experimenting with new, more "rational" methods of dispensing credit. Spurred by the depression of the 1890s and the new spirit of cooperation, jobbers began to question the relatively lenient standards that had previously governed lending. As the *Millinery Trade Review* complained in 1896, "Parties will be turned down in one house, and . . . will go to another, and secure what they want, especially from the houses from which they have not previously bought." The solution, the *Review* argued, lay in "a more cordial feeling . . . between competitors"; wholesalers should exchange "straightforward reports" about retailers "to obviate possible losses from contingencies above referred to." Credit bureaus, like the one organized by the Millinery Jobbers' Association in 1907, became the institutional manifestation of these sentiments. Each of the association's fifty-seven members was now privy to information about present and prospective customers, information that was more accurate and up-to-date than that provided by less specialized agencies such as R. G. Dun & Co.[42]

Although increased scrutiny did little to improve the prospects of marginal retailers, wholesalers' infatuation with uniform regulations was far more damaging. Organizations like the Millinery Jobbers' Association agreed to and enforced standard capital requirements, interest rates, and dates of payment. The new, no-nonsense approach was evident in the association's pronouncements. "Nothing is so destructive to the credit system as cheap credit, and nothing so conducive to cheap credit as haphazard credit methods," the association warned. "Special privileges are not just—they are dishonest."[43]

From the standpoint of wholesalers, tightening the loopholes made sense. The *Millinery Herald* went so far as to claim that uniform standards were a benefit to all retailers "who do their business properly," because they eliminated "that class of competition . . . having no capital at risk."[44] But the *Herald* failed to mention a crucial point. New credit policies, though not overtly sexist, were nonetheless vehicles of gender discrimination. Female retailers, disproportionately the proprietors of marginal concerns, had much to gain from "special privileges" and everything to lose from their abolition. Such seemingly gender-neutral measures had profoundly gendered consequences.[45]

If wholesalers did not consciously discriminate against women, they nevertheless made clear their growing irritation with "feminine" behavior. Certainly, twentieth-century trade publications often avoided gender-specific language, perhaps in deference to the growing numbers of man milliners, perhaps as part of their quest for rationality and efficiency, or perhaps because they borrowed the words of dealers in other pursuits. But discussions of retailers' deficiencies suggest oblique references to gender. Among other things, milliners exhibited "unbusinesslike customs," a "lack of business judgment," and an unfortunate tendency to forget "such little and prosaic things as prices and quantities." The editors of trade journals repeatedly castigated their subscribers for their unbusinesslike methods.[46]

If respectable was the code word for the Gilded Age, unbusinesslike was its twentieth-century counterpart. But if the latter term—with its implied avowal of "businesslike" behavior—suggested more "rational" standards of business conduct, it nevertheless revealed the continuing salience of gender to wholesaler/retailer relations. Indeed, the contrast between the two terms recalls the changing rationales employed by those who questioned women's fitness for clerical work. As Margery Davies has noted, arguments based on women's higher morality gave way to those that portrayed secretaries as "scatterbrained, unable to concentrate on the business at hand . . . too temperamental and emotional for the impersonal world of work." In a period when stereotypes of women as inherently unstable biological beings increasingly replaced references to female moral superiority, oblique discussions of "woman's nature" turned up in unlikely places—including the pages of millinery trade journals.[47] Respectability connoted dependence and frailty; unbusinesslike behavior conjured up a series of less savory female stereotypes: carelessness, irrationality, indecisiveness, and frivolity. If retailers failed to receive their merchandise on time, it was probably their own fault, the *Milliner* explained: "Most of these delays and troubles are caused by your own carelessness if you did but know it. . . . Let each and every one read *her* order over before making it out" (emphasis added).[48]

In the eyes of wholesalers, there was no better demonstration of unbusinesslike behavior than the "returned goods evil." During the first two decades of the twentieth century, this phenomenon—the propensity of retailers to return damaged or unsold merchandise to the supplier—was frequently the subject of trade editorials. "Avoid being a chronic returner of merchandise," the *Milliner's Designer* admonished its readers. "Don't Send Goods Back," the *Illustrated Milliner* warned. Not surprisingly, the *Millinery Herald* was particularly obsessed with the issue: "So much has been written and said on the subject that we feel an apology is due to our readers for dwelling upon this matter so persistently," its editors explained—before launching into another harangue.[49]

What was all the fuss about? As in many disagreements, money was involved. The *Herald* claimed that the members of the Millinery Jobbers' Association suffered yearly losses of $600,000–1,200,000—all because of returned merchandise. These calamities, the journal was careful to explain, hurt retailers as well as wholesalers: anything that "interfered with the profits of the jobber . . . interferes with his ability to render efficient service to the retailer."[50]

Whether or not efficient service was their primary concern, the returned goods evil was a matter of great significance to turn-of-the-century millinery merchants. No other single issue took more space in the pages of trade journals. Yet wholesalers' reasoned discussions revealed much that they themselves would have disputed. Repeated proclamations of their "mutuality of interests" notwithstanding, concerns of wholesalers and retailers were irreconcilable as far as returned goods were concerned. And retailers were hardly the scatterbrained incompetents that wholesalers labeled them. A careful reading of jobbers' complaints indicates that their customers had a very clear understanding of their own interests. Finally, despite their insistence that the milliners' welfare was their abiding concern, the returned goods controversy, like the standardization of credit requirements, signaled the end of wholesalers' paternalism. If wholesalers' changing attitudes suggest that henceforth they would give primacy to their own economic interests, their view of the evil was nevertheless colored by gendered assumptions.

Undoubtedly, jobbers had reason to complain; returned goods adversely affected their profits. With pecuniary concerns in mind, the *Illustrated Milliner* offered prizes to the authors of the best essays on "How I Work Off Old Stock," while the *Milliner* encouraged its subscribers to hold "summer clearance sales." But the ferocity with which jobbers condemned offending milliners suggests that something more than a simple business matter was involved: uppity retailers, trade editorials implied, were not to be tolerated.[51]

Wholesalers rarely missed an opportunity to vent their outrage. Not only did milliners return goods "promiscuously and unjustly," the *Millinery Herald* charged, they did so "on the slightest pretext." "In the first place such procedure is not business-like in any sense of the word," chided the *Milliner's Designer:* "It is a confession of weakness on the part of the milliner to buy a bill of merchandise and then return part of it. It shows lack of business judgment in that the purchaser does not know what can be sold and in the fact of her allowing herself to become overstocked. It is not fair to the person selling, as they never can tell what goods or how much will be returned to them."[52]

Adding insult to injury, wholesalers implicitly attributed the practice of returning goods to feminine caprice, a predictable by-product of women's unbusinesslike behavior. "Know exactly what you want and then buy it," the *Milliner's Designer* advised. Don't go around and have a lot of goods sent to you on approval, and then return three-quarters of it." Its vociferous competitor, the *Herald*, argued that milliners' tendency to "overbuy" was the root of the evil: overwhelmed by tantalizing displays of millinery materials, women were unable to restrain themselves. Indeed, while returned goods plagued wholesalers in a variety of pursuits, they assumed a unique—and perhaps disproportionate—significance in the millinery trade.[53] In general business discourse, the term "returned goods evil" referred not to the unfortunate propensities of errant retailers but to the buying practices of female consumers who took advantage of generous department store return policies. The ferocity with which millinery men condemned the phenomenon suggests that—consciously or not—they equated female retailers with supposedly irrational and unpredictable female consumers, "careless shoppers and inconsiderate customers." As one department store manager explained in 1916, "Men almost never return goods."[54]

These prejudices aside, returning goods was not intrinsically irrational or unbusinesslike. Millinery fashions were unpredictable at best, and it was difficult to determine at the beginning of a season what would subsequently sell. Here, too, wholesalers and their representatives were not free of blame, for they eagerly proffered their advice to buyers. Distance exacerbated the problem, and it was far cheaper to order goods in large lots than in small batches.

The laments of wholesalers, read carefully, reveal that retailers did not necessarily return goods "on the slightest pretext." When hundreds, or even thousands, of miles intervened between buyer and supplier, damage and delay were often the result. Both defects, wholesalers insisted, were the fault of the express company; milliners should not hold jobbers responsible for the carelessness of others.[55] Damaged goods aside, milliners had ample reason to return merchandise. "There is a charm in buying millinery goods of a house that makes it a point to fill orders exactly as a customer would have them filled," a jobber's advertisement claimed. Unfortunately, such "charm" was often lacking. Some suppliers habitually "stuffed orders," that is, they sent the retailer merchandise she had not requested. Predictably, the *Millinery Herald* claimed that "stuffing" was a rare occurrence. It very likely happened more often than wholesalers were willing to admit. There was also the problem of substitution; millinery merchants might send retailers *different* goods than those they had ordered. Once again, the editors of trade journals explained, wholesalers were right and retailers wrong. Milliners were expected to defer to the wisdom of their superiors; jobbers, who always had retailers' best interests at heart, judiciously made substitutions when the desired items were out of stock. A more cynical interpretation might view both stuffing and substituting as attempts on the part of unscrupulous wholesalers to fob off outdated, unfashionable, or poor quality goods on unsuspecting tradeswomen.[56] At the same time, the supposed foibles of unbusinesslike women—unschooled in the complexities of commerce and incapable of rational decision making—conveniently exempted less than principled businessmen from blame.

In any case, wholesalers held far greater power than retailers, especially when they presented a united front. In addition, they were willing to use their combined clout to punish errant milliners. "Read this," the *Millinery Herald* insisted, quoting a credit report: "Although the capital invested does not justify a high credit, we feel inclined to favor Mrs. _____, because, although a large portion of her last season's purchase was merchandise sent her on an open order, she did not take advantage of this fact to return any of the goods."[57] Nor were wholesalers above substituting the stick for the carrot. The Millinery Jobbers' Association announced that the "chronic returner of merchandise," whatever her financial circumstances, would be referred to its credit bureau.[58]

The returned goods controversy was never resolved; as late as the 1930s one analyst noted that "the unjust return of merchandise is . . . a pernicious evil in this industry." By then the terrain had changed considerably. In Boston, for example, the number of retail milliners fell by nearly a third between 1900 and 1930, even as the city's population increased by almost 40 percent. Ample evidence suggests that man milliners—owners of spacious shops—and department stores increasingly occupied the commercial niche once reserved for women.[59]

What role did wholesalers' businesslike proclivities play in this process? It is difficult to answer with any certainty. Many forces were at work. A new emphasis on display (requiring improvements that many businesswomen could ill afford), the growth of large retailing institutions, and, finally, the increasing popularity of factory-made hats also adversely affected the fortunes of female retailers. Credit bureaus, jobber's organizations, and the returned goods controversy were by no means unique to the millinery trade; rather, they reflected broader changes in the American business community as a whole. Trends toward rationalization and consolidation weighed heavily, if not always intentionally, on marginal operators in many lines of business, especially those who were members of racial and ethnic minorities.[60] In the economically significant field of feminine fashion, these innovations had gendered consequences, however unintended. Rigid credit requirements hurt women and favored men, for women's ventures were almost always perilous undertakings. It was probably no coincidence that the pages of trade journals abounded with glowing descriptions of millinery departments and elegantly appointed hat stores, businesses requiring amounts of capital that women rarely possessed. At the same time, jobbers and small retailers needed each other. "There is a chain as of the toughest steel, that binds the two together," the *Illustrated Milliner* declared in 1915. Its melodramatic language notwithstanding, the journal was right. For department stores, unlike most retail milliners, exhibited a disturbing tendency to buy directly from manufacturers, bypassing jobbers altogether.[61]

Imitating their counterparts in other lines of business, many millinery wholesalers solved the problem by taking up manufacturing. As early as 1885, Hill Brothers advertised themselves as "importers, jobbers and manufacturers of millinery goods." By 1926, the Millinery Jobbers' Association contemplated changing its name, since "practically every member . . . was a manufacturer as well as a jobber." But as long as milliners made most of the hats they sold, jobbers were still necessary; the numerous and ever-changing components of a hat could be produced under one roof only with difficulty. Jobbers, though increasingly under siege, did not pass from the scene until the 1930s.[62]

The same developments that threatened jobbers had a devastating impact on retailers. The decision to grant or withhold credit, whatever the rules regarding its disposition, affected milliners individually. But an ominous invention concerned the trade as a whole. Even as they aired their complaints about returned merchandise, wholesalers were offering their customers a strange new product. Ultimately, the ready-to-wear hat would put both jobbers (at least those who refused to become manufacturers) and craftswomen out of business.

Industrialization from Without:
The Separation of Production from Retailing

In the fall of 1864, the milliner Ida Nickerson visited Ordway Brothers, "importers and jobbers of ribbons, flowers, millinery and straw goods." She left with merchandise worth $85.92, including feathers, taffeta, trimming ribbons, turban frames, artificial flowers, and assorted millinery ornaments. Forty-seven years later the John M. Smyth Company, a manufacturer of women's headwear, advertised a "$25.00 outfit . . . made up entirely of ladies', misses' and children's hats that are ready to wear and ready to sell."[63] Smyth's advertisement signaled a momentous transformation in the making and selling of millinery. While Nickerson—probably assisted by a small number of employees—made most of the hats she sold, the purchaser of the "$25.00 outfit" merely sold hats produced in a distant factory. The contrast between the two exemplifies a process in which jobbers and manufacturers played a crucial role: the separation of production from retailing.

Retailers, by definition, are intermediaries who sell goods made elsewhere directly to consumers. Retailing in this sense, Stuart M. Blumin has observed, is a relatively recent development. In the eighteenth and early nineteenth centuries, shoemakers, jewelers, coopers, and silversmiths were both makers and sellers; more often than not, they "manufactured" their wares according to the specifications of particular customers. By the mid-nineteenth century, artisans had largely been replaced by shopkeepers, men who performed "head work" but not "hand work."[64]

In contrast to their masculine counterparts, milliners did not become retailers until the twentieth century. If for no other reason, the intricacies of feminine fashion kept the workroom in the millinery shop—and out of the factory. As early as the 1840s, enterprising manufacturers were turning out men's hats by the thousands. But women's hats, especially the "fluffy" styles of the Gilded Age, were ill-suited to mass production. While factories required uniformity, consumers expected diversity. Thus, customers who insisted on original creations helped to maintain what was, by nineteenth-century standards, an outmoded system. Fashion and consumer demand conspired to create a female repository of craft in a world where craftsmanship was becoming obsolete.[65] But the increasing tendency—evident by the early twentieth century—of factory-produced "outfits" to overtake individually created "works of art" placed both female craft and female entrepreneurship at risk.

A description of custom millinery, the art of "making something out of nothing," illustrates what was at stake. As in dressmaking, the trade offered creative labor and appealing future prospects, clearly exemplified in the structure and routines of the typical workroom. Ingredients and techniques might vary from year to year ("There is always something new to learn in millinery," a worker explained to the social investigator Lorinda Perry in 1915), but the mechanics of the craft changed little from the mid-nineteenth century to the advent of the ready-made hat.

First, millinery was teamwork, characterized by a division between makers (sometimes called milliners)—workers who fashioned the body or "shape" of a hat—and trimmers, the "artists" who adorned it with varying combinations of feathers, flowers, ribbons, and lace. To be sure, this principle might be violated. Self-employed milliners became both makers and trimmers, and "cheap" shops made less of a fuss over these distinctions than did fashionable establishments. But as a rule even the tiniest concern had its apprentice, maker, and trimmer.[66]

The organization of labor in the typical shop was at once cooperative and hierarchical, a scheme that reflected both time-honored divisions between different types of workers and the possibilities for advancement inherent in the trade. Each workroom contained a table whose "place settings" embodied the structure of authority. The trimmer—who supervised as well as trimmed—sat at the head; the apprentice at the foot. Gathered around the sides were four to six makers, busily engaged in preparing "shapes" for their superior. In smaller establishments, Madame did the trimming; larger concerns, more prevalent by the early twentieth century, boasted several tables, each presided over by a trimmer. At its best, the millinery shop functioned as both schoolroom and workplace. In 1917, one worker explained what must have been a long-standing tradition: "'The trimmer shows the maker, the maker shows the improver [a term occasionally used to designate an advanced apprentice], and the improver shows the apprentice.'" Sometimes this chain of command was disrupted; the apprentice might exchange her humble place for one beside the trimmer where she could "be instructed in various tricks of the trade" (Figure 9).[67]

Routine tasks occupied much of the beginner's time. She ventured outside the workroom to deliver hats to customers or to run errands for Madame; she rose frequently from her seat to fetch fabrics and adornments from the store's stock. In the best of circumstances, she also learned how to make hats. At first, her work consisted of making bandeaux (bands sewn into the crown

Figure 9. "Training an Apprentice." As milliners sit at their customary table, an experienced worker (possibly a trimmer) stands over an apprentice, instructing her in the tricks of the trade. From Mary Van Kleeck, *A Seasonal Industry: A Study of the Millinery Trade in New York* (New York: Russell Sage Foundation, 1917), following p. 152. (Courtesy of the Indiana University, Bloomington, Library)

of a hat so that it fits the wearer) and linings. She learned gradually to fashion frames and cover them with fabric or straw; when she was proficient at both, she became a maker.[68]

Contemporaries often identified making as the mechanical and trimming as the artistic side of millinery. In many respects, this was an accurate description, for makers normally played no part in designing the hat. Still, advancing from apprentice to maker was no minor accomplishment; as one early twentieth-century analyst explained, making "might seem comparatively simple if frames were always the same shape and always covered in the same way, but since they are made in almost every possible shape and size the skill required in hatmaking is considerable."[69]

The maker's first task was to construct the frame or foundation of a hat. Depending on prevailing vogues, this process varied from year to year, season to season. Frames were generally made with particular coverings in mind: buckram (a coarse cloth that resembles stiffened burlap) provided the foundation for heavier winter hats; wire for lighter spring and summer models. A host of other materials might be used in varying combinations; willow (a

mixture of wood and cotton fibers), crinoline, and net provided lighter and
more flexible alternatives to buckram (Figure 10).[70]

Fashioning the foundation represented the first and in many ways the most
important step toward translating a customer's instructions into material reality. The frame determined the hat's angle and shape; these were difficult or
impossible to alter once the covering was in place. Wires had to be bent so they
would not kink or curl; they had to be joined together firmly but carefully with
strong stitches, for any knots or bumps would show through light materials
such as silk or chiffon. Last but not least, a well-made frame indicated a hat of
superior quality; as one observer noted, "Many persons can tell you what part
of town a bonnet has been made in simply by the foundation."[71]

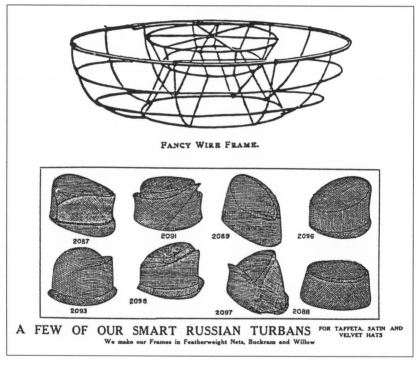

Figure 10. *Top:* Sketch of a wire hat frame. Frames like this, meant to be covered with light
fabrics such as silk or chiffon, provided the foundations for spring and summer hats. From
Kate J. Giblin, *Concerning Millinery* (Boston: Puritan Press, 1902), p. 41. *Bottom:* Ready-made
hat frames, available in net, buckram, or willow. While this advertisement conveys a sense
of the variety of available foundations, it also suggests the growing tendency of retail milliners to purchase frames from wholesalers instead of hiring makers to construct them. From
Milliner 25 (July 1914): 9. (Both courtesy of the Library of Congress)

Once the frame was complete, the next step involved its covering. This task required accuracy, neatness, and dispatch, qualities summarized in that universal requirement of employers: "nimble fingers." Millinery necessitated "the utmost delicacy in handling materials," one self-styled expert explained: "A piece of velvet may be ruined by the careless pressure of a finger." Another's advice was less lyrical but equally appropriate: a good milliner should have "above all, dry hands."[72] Equipped with these prerequisites, the maker faced a number of challenges. Some coverings were meant to lie smoothly atop the frame; in this case, she had to know the bias of the fabric in order to stretch it across curved areas without wrinkling. Other hats called for fabrics to be draped or gathered over the brim in uniform, carefully spaced folds, blurring the line between the maker and her superior. As one analyst put it, "shirring is in the nature of trimming."[73] Whatever the style, the skilled craftswoman attached the covering to the frame with strong but invisible stitches, a talent of particular importance when adornments were sparse or nonexistent (Figure 11).

Once the maker's task was complete, the trimmer added the "superstructure," adorning the hat with a pleasing combination of millinery ornaments, many of which (although available ready-made from wholesale dealers) she created herself. Feathers, flowers, ribbons, and bows had to withstand gale-force winds yet appear to be barely attached; "nailing the material to the hat"

Figure 11. Stylish winter hats, 1885. A maker fashioned these rather elaborate shapes; a trimmer added the ribbons, plumes, and flowers. From *Peterson's Magazine* 88 (Dec. 1885): 490. (Courtesy of the Indiana University, Bloomington, Library)

was a sure sign of amateur millinery.[74] Trimmers did more than handle the
needle; they "creat[ed] the style" as well as decorated the hat. "High-class"
shops separated the two functions, employing designers (who often commanded astronomical salaries) to design and trimmers merely to trim. But
most trimmers performed both mental and manual labor. For this reason,
they reportedly possessed a host of intangible faculties that their comparatively mundane coworkers lacked: "style," "taste," and "a nice discrimination of colors and shades."[75]

The psychological benefits of such labor—making as well as trimming—
were not lost on those who performed it. Motivated by "love of the work as
well as the need for earnings," milliners, like their dressmaking sisters, clearly
appreciated the creative features of their calling. Or, as one craftswoman put
it, millinery was "an interesting trade. It cultivates your mind, makes you
think, and gives you new ideas."[76]

By the early twentieth century, new ideas increasingly originated not in
the custom shop but in the factory, for growing numbers of female consumers
were buying ready-to-wear hats. Moreover, they increasingly patronized
retailers who played little part in producing the merchandise they sold. How
did this transformation occur? Just as dressmaking innovations originated
for the most part outside the custom shop, so too did the processes that turned
hatmakers into mere retailers. From the standpoint of retail millinery, these
changes involved not a full-scale transformation in the methods of production but the curtailment (for example, trimming ready-made shapes in lieu
of making the entire hat) or (in the case of the "pure" retailer who sold nothing but factory-made hats) the elimination of production itself. Milliners did
not turn their shops into hat factories. Rather, manufacturers—buoyed by
mechanical invention, national (or at least regional) markets, economies of
scale, and division of labor—began to produce goods more cheaply than
could tradeswomen. Fashion, once again, played a crucial role. The period
1900–1930 witnessed a growing trend toward simpler, "mannish" hats, styles
that adapted themselves nicely to machine production. Above all, the ready-
to-wear hat was cheap; the average consumer, finding prices at an all-time
low, was more than willing to sacrifice quality for quantity.[77]

These changes left the proprietors of custom millinery shops with little choice. If they wanted to stay in business, they bought and sold factory-made products. Tradeswomen who insisted on making hats the old way
found themselves undercut by competitors who heeded "the call of the
ready-to-wear."[78]

The transformation of milliners from makers into sellers had lasting consequences for both female craft and female entrepreneurship. The ready-to-wear hat put thousands of craftswomen out of work; one analyst estimated that retail shops operated with a sixth of the labor force employed by custom milliners. While the factory hat fulfilled the fondest hopes of the most exploitative employers, its ascendancy forced all milliners (apart from the most exclusive) to participate in the deskilling of their craft—a process that affected employers and employees alike. Skilled makers were superfluous when work consisted of "altering ready-made hats and . . . trimming pressed shapes." As the *Illustrated Milliner* curtly explained, it was "cheaper to buy hats ready made than to hire help to make them."[79]

With the advent of "trimmed hats" (inventions that dispensed with the services of trimmers as well as makers), the requirements of the millinery trade changed drastically. Success depended less on one's expertise as a craftswoman and more on one's skill as a buyer. Equally significant, the triumph of retailing challenged women's control over the trade. Factory-made hats better suited the needs of larger millinery shops and department stores, which were usually operated by men. Just as wholesalers' credit policies in effect favored men over women, so did wholesalers' products foster the growth of male enterprises at the expense of female entrepreneurship.

These changes first and foremost were the result of technological innovations pioneered not in millinery shops but in distant factories. But they also depended on a shift in attitudes. In the end, the triumph of retailing signaled a new propensity—on the part of wholesalers, consumers, and at least some tradeswomen—to exchange quality and craftsmanship for quantity and convenience.

The appearance of numerous time- and labor-saving devices—aggressively promoted in the pages of trade journals—suggests that by the turn of the century milliners had strayed far from their artisanal origins. "Snow-White Millinery Cement is helping milliners produce hats quicker, cheaper and neater," proclaimed a 1916 advertisement. For tradeswomen interested in saving time and money, this was truly a miraculous invention. The hallmark of a skilled milliner was her ability to craft hats using tiny, nearly invisible stitches, but "Snow-White Millinery Cement has made millinery without sewing most practical and profitable."[80] Products such as Jetum—a dye that turned hats of almost any color black—and Radium Dye served similar functions. "What are you going to do when a customer rushes in and demands a gobelin blue shaded plume and you have whites, champagnes and every color save the right one?" an advertisement asked in March 1914. A Radium Dye Outfit was the answer. With it, the producers explained, "you never miss sales; colors old and dingy are made new in a minute."[81]

Advertisements tell us much about the people who manufactured products but little about those who bought them. Clearly, though, some tradeswomen were interested in saving time and cutting labor costs. The very existence of Snow-White Millinery Cement, Jetum, and Radium Dye (which almost certainly were hazardous to employees' health) indicated a new emphasis on quantity over quality. Surely the "50,000 milliners" who allegedly used Jetum willingly dispensed with painstaking craftsmanship.

An ad for Pullastic Adjustable Hat Linings appearing in the *Milliner* in 1916 made the purpose of such devices painfully clear. "Which Method Is Yours?" it asked. "The Old Way—Wastes Time, Labor, Material and Money. The Pullastic Way—One Girl Does the Work of Six" (Figure 12). As the smiling milliner pictured in the advertisement explained,

> No matter what hat a woman picks out, the "PULLASTIC" lining makes it fit her head perfectly—and that is a wonderful help in boosting sales.
>
> Besides this, the "PULLASTIC" lining saves me time and money in my workroom. It is so easily and quickly placed in the hats. No cutting or fitting—just six stitches and the hat is lined—better looking and better lined than if we made the lining ourselves. One inexperienced girl can line as many hats as six experienced girls in the old way. That means a big saving in cost for me.[82]

"Inexperienced girls" may have saved their employers "time and money," but they enjoyed few of the psychological or pecuniary benefits that accrued to their sisters who labored in more traditional settings. Equally significant, the makers of the Pullastic lining assumed that milliners' shops stocked a wide variety of ready-to-wear hats. It could hardly have been otherwise, for a hat made to order would certainly fit the customer.

Indeed, as the social investigator Edna Bryner noted in 1915, "In the past few years the factory-made hat has become an important factor in millinery." This statement was something of an exaggeration; shortcuts had long been available to time-conscious milliners and impatient amateurs. Wire bonnet frames, produced by a partially mechanized process, were available as early as the 1850s. In the same period, wholesale manufacturers turned out straw bonnets by the thousands. In 1863, Penny reported that "'one million two hundred thousand are sold annually to the milliners of New York for their trade alone.'"[83]

"This Hat Will Fit Any Head Perfectly—

"So will every other hat in my stock.

"It wasn't always that way—but it is true now, and I am selling more hats and giving my customers greater satisfaction.

"When I woke up to the fact that, no matter how handsome and stylish a hat might be, a woman wouldn't buy it unless it fitted her head, I took the first step toward bigger and better business.

"I found the secret of the perfect-fitting hat in

ADJUSTABLE HAT LINING

"I now place a **'PULLASTIC'** lining in every hat, whether I make it in my work-room or buy it trimmed. No matter what hat a woman picks out, the **'PULLASTIC'** lining makes it fit her head perfectly—and that is a wonderful help in boosting sales.

"Besides this, the **'PULLASTIC'** lining saves me time and money in my work-room. It is so easily and quickly placed in the hats. No cutting or fitting—just six stitches and the hat is lined—better look-

ing and better lined than if we made the lining ourselves. One inexperienced girl can line as many hats as six experienced girls in the old way. That means a big saving in cost for me.

"I always carry a supply of **'PULLASTIC'** linings and display them on the counter, for all women who make their own hats are delighted with them. The national advertising makes many a sale for me, too."

THE PULLASTIC CO. OF AMERICA, Inc.

Exclusive Manufacturers of Fitted and Tailored Hat Linings—Capacity Three Million Annually

49-53 East 21st Street   **New York City**

Figure 12. According to this Pullastic Company ad, "One Girl Does the Work of Six." One of many millinery advertisements that promoted innovations as time and labor-saving devices, the text promises that tradeswomen who use Pullastic hat linings can employ fewer workers and substitute "inexperienced girls" for skilled craftswomen. From *Milliner* 27 (Sept. 1916): 10. (Courtesy of Oregon State University at Corvalis)

Early examples of factory production pale in comparison with the output of twentieth-century manufacturers. By 1900, milliners could purchase not only wire frames but also frames fashioned from buckram and net. In short, the foundations for nearly every conceivable type of hat could be obtained ready-made. "In a large city where frames are so reasonable and of such variety of shapes and sizes," the author of an instructional pamphlet noted in 1902, "it does not pay to make one, as the saving in money is overbalanced by the outlay of time." The tradeswoman interested in greater savings of time and labor could buy "pressed shapes" made of straw, felt, velvet, and silk and trim them herself. Even the prospective milliner who knew nothing of millinery need not despair: wholesale factories were making entire hats, "from frame to finish."[84] Fueled by economies of scale, division of labor, and mechanization in varying proportions, factories were making hats far more cheaply than could retail milliners.

By the turn of the century, contemporaries agreed that the factory-made hat had achieved a new prominence. In 1903 the *Illustrated Milliner* announced that "the millinery business . . . has greatly changed during the past few years, the new conditions having been gradually brought about by the steadily growing popularity of the 'ready to wear' and 'ready to trim' hat trade." To resist, its editors declared, was futile. Those who refused to "adapt themselves to the new order" had "been forced out."[85]

If some retailers resisted factory-made hats, others welcomed them. Moreover, jobbers and manufacturers did their best to speed the process by encouraging their customers to think of themselves as entrepreneurs and employers, not as craftswomen. A New York wholesaler's paean to ready-to-wear hats was notable for its frankness; it touted them not only as replacements for skilled workingwomen but as instruments of labor control (not insignificantly, the advertisement's text reserved particular hostility for trimmers, the most powerful workers in the custom shop). This was only one of a number of advertisements that aggressively conveyed the superiority of retailing over production.

What the
Millinery Workroom
Usually Means

—A monotonous uniformity of styles
—Too many traces of back number ideas
—Store space that must pay rent

—Overtime work when store is closed
—Costly materials wasted and spoiled
—Some hats that are hopeless failures
—Apprentices that are worse than useless
—Expert trimmers that are arbitrary and insolent
—Sick trimmers at home—with pay
—Holidays not suspended

With these drawbacks to contend with, no wonder storekeepers every-where are turning to Ready-to-Wear Hats for relief.[86]

The *Milliner*'s "Just among Ourselves" column was equally blunt: "I do not believe it possible for any milliner to make as becoming hats, or to make them as well as the hats she obtains from her wholesaler."[87]

These messages must have been especially comforting to "inexperienced persons" who were entering the trade in growing numbers. Many milliners *were* turning to ready-to-wear hats, though perhaps not with relief. Mary Van Kleeck's 1917 investigation of New York millinery documented several shops that were merely retail outlets. These establishments, she explained, "appear to the casual observer to demonstrate the continued survival of the indepen-dent hand worker. In reality they are merely adjuncts to the factory system."[88]

Custom hatmaking did not disappear overnight. Fashion, always fickle, often determined the method of production. As Van Kleeck shrewdly not-ed, "the machine-sewed straw or the pressed velvet or felt shape may be in the ascendancy one season, to the joy of the wholesale dealer, who turns these hats out in quantities, while a few months later fashion will demand hand-sewn hats of more varied design . . . and the retailer will be extraordinarily busy." "Is your work-room plentifully stocked with straw braids, dotted nets, chiffons, malines, silks and velvets?" the *Millinery Herald* asked its readers in the spring of 1908. "The hand-made hat is very popular this season." As late as 1926, the *Illustrated Milliner* could proclaim, "Demand for Hand Craft Keener than Ever."[89]

Even then most milliners probably employed a hodgepodge of methods. At one end of the spectrum were the high-class shops that made their hats entirely by hand. At the other were the retail outlets. The remainder, as Bryner observed, made do "with varying proportions of made-to-order and factory products."[90]

Nevertheless, the ready-to-wear hat was the wave of the future, for its popularity among consumers ensured its success. Although wealthy patrons continued to seek craftsmanship and "exclusive" styles, most customers were more than willing to exchange quantity and convenience for quality. Indeed, the factory hat was preferred "by the mass of indiscriminate buyers . . . because its low cost enables them to have several hats a year for what they formerly paid for two." The *Illustrated Milliner* observed that the ready-to-wear hat was a boon to "those who cater to a medium class trade."[91]

Milliners who cast their lot with factory-made hats sowed the seeds of their own demise. Ready-to-wear hats encouraged amateurs to enter the field, and more often than not these latecomers were men. Bryner's investigation of Cleveland milliners found male proprietors presiding over "the type of shop which deals largely in a factory-made product." One could conclude, with only slight exaggeration, that retailing's victory over production signaled the triumph of businessmen over businesswomen.[92]

While custom production admirably suited small-scale enterprise, retailing fostered larger concerns. The custom milliner could create an innumerable assortment of fashions from the stock she had on hand. But for the retailer who sold prefabricated hats, variety depended on the number of different styles purchased from the wholesaler. The small businesswoman had neither the space to display large numbers of ready-made hats nor the means to buy them: "It is impossible for her to offer the variety shown in the department stores," Bryner concluded. Wholesalers who routinely refused to "break lots" only made matters worse; like other rational methods of doing business, this practice exacerbated women's already precarious position within the trade. (A "lot" usually consisted of twelve identical hats.)[93]

The twentieth-century department store, in contrast, displayed ready-to-wear hats in bewildering profusion. Blessed with ample space and substantial capital, the millinery department offered a much wider selection than did most retail shops. Finally, department stores, dry goods firms, and other large male-operated establishments could afford to buy *and* sell more cheaply. A Chicago mail-order catalog declared emphatically, "We guarantee every price in this book to be from 35 to 60 per cent. lower than the same goods can be bought for from a retail milliner."[94]

* * *

The rise of the department store, the separation of production from retailing, the replacement of jobbers by manufacturers, the abandonment of competition for cooperation—these are familiar features of the business land-

scape of late nineteenth- and early twentieth-century America. In the economically significant field of fashion, they were gendered transformations.
Between 1860 and 1930 a system of production and retailing largely controlled by women was supplanted by one dominated by men.

These seemingly abstract changes would have very personal consequences, as a final example makes clear. In 1910, the *Illustrated Milliner* sponsored
a search for "the oldest milliner." It found likely candidates in Mr. and Mrs.
P. H. Welty of Pekin, Illinois. Assisted by a corps of loyal and almost equally
tenacious employees, the pair had managed to stay in business for forty-two
years. Mr. Welty spoke for the concern: "Great changes . . . have occurred
in millinery in these forty-two years, but we believe they have all been for
the better. We are sure the art has been on the upward tendency year by
year."[95]

Would all milliners have agreed? The Weltys spoke from the perspective
of success; like many husband-wife teams, they probably enjoyed greater
prosperity than competitors who depended on the meager resources that
women alone could muster. But many craftswomen, whatever their financial circumstances, might have disputed Welty's claims. For even as he waxed
poetic on his trade's "upward tendency," the ready-to-wear hat was destroy-
ing millinery as an "art." Welty made no mention of factory hats; custom
production, evinced by the presence of makers and trimmers, still prevailed
in his shop. Nevertheless, he had every reason to welcome the trade's most
influential innovation. An influx of factory-produced merchandise would
allow him to dispense with the relatively expensive services of head trimmer
Anna Heid, second trimmer Theresa Rust, and head maker Elizabeth
Carstens. Moreover, a shift into retailing might very well have altered the
balance of power within his marriage. A ready-made revolution would render his wife's skills unnecessary, skills that probably gave her a great deal of
influence if not authority.

Even our redoubtable (and perhaps unjustly maligned) Mr. Welty was
vulnerable to the onslaughts of mail-order houses and department stores,
enterprises that could easily undersell him. It is unlikely that the Weltys' heirs
enjoyed another forty-two years in the millinery business.

⟵⟶*⟵⟶ *Seven*

Engendering Change:
The Department Store and
the Factory, 1890–1930

𝒯he March 1914 *Milliner* published a glowing description of Miss Rosamond's "millinery shop de luxe" in Mexico, Missouri. "Artistic millinery parlors" such as this would have astonished the tradeswomen of an earlier day, who typically did business in sparsely furnished suites. Rosamond's model establishment had an elegant showroom decorated in "mahogany and green with a touch of gold and white," replete with green velvet rugs, "handsome mirrors," gold "counter trimmings," and even a "bust on the mantel" (Figure 13).[1]

Rosamond was a valiant soldier in a tenacious but losing battle that pitted dressmakers and milliners against the twin forces of industry and commerce. To some historians, the emergence of department stores and the manufacture of ready-to-wear clothing signaled a democratization of fashion; to others, it marked the beginning of a fundamentally antidemocratic culture of consumption. Relatively few historians have analyzed these developments from the perspective of the factory and department store workers, and virtually none has examined their implications for female artisans and entrepreneurs.[2] Given a scholarly literature that assumes a simple transition from homemade goods to factory products, this is not surprising; indeed, such an interpretation renders milliners and dressmakers invisible.

Yet viewed from the standpoint of custom clothiers—the missing links in a more complicated historical chain—the consequences of these changes were substantial. Beginning in the 1890s, ready-made dresses and mass-produced hats threatened the fortunes of custom clothiers; sumptuously furnished department stores forecast a grim future for tiny, female-operated concerns. Much was at stake. Hardly embodiments of entrepreneurial independence, department store dressmakers and milliners were subject to the whims of male management; consigned to monotonous, repetitive jobs that offered few opportunities for advancement, workers in garment factories and wholesale millineries enjoyed few of the benefits that accrued to their sisters in the custom shop. If mass production and large-scale retailing offered unprecedented advantages to consumers, they did so at the expense of producers.

As Rosamond's efforts demonstrate, dressmakers and milliners did not remain passive in the face of commercial innovation and technological change. Some adopted the tactics of their competitors, transforming their tiny shops into replicas of elegantly appointed millinery and dressmaking departments. Those who continued the traditions of custom production did not necessarily ignore the example presented by the hat or dress manufacturer. Many twentieth-century workshops resembled nothing so much as miniature factories, less refuges than prisons for those who toiled there. These "improvements" came at a cost that many tradeswomen could not afford. Nor in the end did they halt the changes that replaced female economies of fashion with male-controlled garment trades.

The Art of Selling: Dressmakers, Milliners, and Department Stores

In the waning years of the nineteenth century, L. S. Plaut and Company treated the readers of its catalog to a philosophical discussion of the nature of retailing:

> The needs and wants of the average man and woman are as numerous and varied as the stars that look down upon us so benignantly [*sic*] from their immeasurable distances in the stellar world. Time was—and not so many years ago—when trade and commerce were shackled by the bonds of old fogyism and dearth of capital. The people of to-day are witnesses of the great transformation brought about in all branches of trade, and are participators in the numerous benefits accruing therefrom.[3]

Figure 13. Miss Rosamond's Millinery Shop, Mexico, Missouri. Elegant shops such as this resembled miniature department stores. From *Milliner* 25 (Mar. 1914): 89. (Courtesy of Oregon State University at Corvalis)

Plaut and Company did indeed herald a "great transformation": the rise of the department store. Unlike its predecessors, this most recent product of mercantile evolution was "filled to repletion with supplies to readily gratify all the desires of the people at the minimum of expense." That claim was less hyperbolic than it seemed; consumers who once would have patronized a series of highly specialized shops could purchase everything from art embroidery to window shades, "banquet lamps" to "toilet requisites" at Plaut's Newark store.[4]

The department store achieved its greatest fame as a showcase for feminine finery. Fabrics, laces, shawls, petticoats, corsets, hats, and eventually dresses dominated its interior landscape. Any shopkeeper who specialized in a single line of merchandise had reason to fear the competition of this mercantile giant, but vendors of fashion had particular cause for alarm. Few if any merchants were more vulnerable to this commercial onslaught than custom dressmakers and milliners. "Shackled by . . . dearth of capital," they were singularly ill prepared to face the formidable, and ultimately successful, challenge posed by this retail giant. Indeed, with the advent of the department store, a world of relative scarcity—that had emphasized the purchase of one or two garments a year, the acquisition of a spring and fall bonnet, and a good deal of "making over"—confronted a world of luxury and abundance, where vast quantities of goods were displayed in bewildering profusion. Little wonder that many consumers found the "new kind of store" irresistible.[5]

Tradeswomen and their competitors coexisted for a remarkable length of time. The self-employed craftswoman who kept no shop, the medium-sized establishment that employed twenty workers, even arguably the department store were present in both 1860 and 1900. But by the turn of the century the balance had shifted in favor of larger concerns. By 1920, department stores had won a decisive victory.[6]

This transformation was not gender neutral; large-scale enterprise meant male enterprise. Women did not have vast amounts of capital at their disposal; rarely were they invited to join male partnerships. Indeed, Plaut and Company attributed its success to masculine vitality. "At every stage of its development it has been managed by young men, and to this fact may be ascribed the business life and enterprise it has so constantly shown." While its catalog noted that "Mrs. Emma Plaut, widow of the original founder" was one of the firm's four partners, she did not exercise "active control." This task was assumed by Louis and Moses Plaut and Oscar Michael, "the eldest of whom is but thirty-four years of age, thus bringing to the management of this vast business all those resources required of and typical of the successful young American business man of the present day." Despite the exaggerated nature of its statements, Plaut and Company implicitly recognized what subsequent scholars have not: that shifts from custom production to large-scale retailing were in part gendered transformations.[7]

These pronouncements notwithstanding, virility was an insufficient cause of prosperity. Money, combined with innovations in manufacturing and marketing, played as great a role as masculine vigor. Blessed with ample space and capital, department stores provided appropriate venues for the ready-to-wear dresses and factory-produced hats that flooded the market in the early twentieth century. Unlike made-to-order articles, prefabricated merchandise needed to be displayed, and in this the department store had a built-in advantage over smaller shops. The larger the square footage and the greater the sum invested, the greater the number and variety of goods that could be set before the consumer.

Ready-made clothing was not the sole source of the department store's triumph. In fact, large-scale retailing predated mass production.[8] Until the 1910s, much of the "fashion" displayed in department stores consisted of corsets, undergarments, capes, and cloaks. But institutions such as Jordan Marsh, Filene's, Macy's, and Gimbel's did not content themselves with "furnishings." Instead, they took up dressmaking and millinery themselves, a fact that suggests that they viewed women's concerns not as insignificant competitors but as serious threats. The millinery or dressmaking department offered several advantages over the custom shop. Bolstered by economies of scale, department stores consistently undersold their smaller competitors. For many consumers, convenience outweighed cost; they could shop for housewares as well as hats, dolls and dresses without leaving the store. Convenience of this sort must have had special appeal to dressmakers' patrons, for the dressmaking department housed under one roof not only the craftswoman but also the fabrics, trimmings, sewing silks, bustles, and buttons—items for which customers endured often exhausting searches in different shops. In contrast to the typical modiste, the department store "kept stock" on a grand scale.[9]

Money, of course, bought more than merchandise. As several scholars have noted, the department store derived its appeal as much from its elegant furnishings and elaborate displays as from "rational" matters of convenience and cost.[10] "The buyer must be fastidious, indeed," Plaut's catalog observed, "who cannot have his [*sic*] desires satisfied in these palatial, great stores, sumptuous in their fittings, resplendent with jewels and laces, silks, satins and velvets—everything imaginable for use or luxury; always alluring, fashionable, fascinating and irresistible."[11] Millinery and dressmaking departments proved no exception. In 1901, the New York firm of Abraham and Strauss introduced its "new salon of dress[,] . . . the finest room devoted to commercial purposes in the world. Such a chamber," its creators mused, "might, perhaps, be found as the most important in one of the old world palaces." Surroundings grew ever more elaborate with the passage of time. "Do people really know what's inside?" a spokeswoman for Jordan Marsh asked twenty-five years later: "The Dressmaking Salon, for instance . . . panelled in ivory, velvet floored, hung with mauve ceiling silk, softly lighted and silent, with a brilliant, parading model or two to bespeak Paris."[12]

Long after ready-to-wear clothing presented a practical option, custom dressmaking and millinery departments—endowed with "private recesses" and "French rooms" (special showrooms that admitted only the most elite clientele)—offered a refuge for wealthy customers repelled by the "democratic" tendencies of the department store. The society women of Newark, New Jersey, could adjourn to Plaut's "private . . . parlors wherein patrons may consult with the firm's designers and 'try on' exclusive model hats, entirely apart from the public congregated in the larger parlors." The R. H. White store of Boston offered women who patronized its dressmaking department "all the privacy that they would enjoy in their own chambers."[13]

While these amenities unabashedly appealed to class snobbery, they also represented conscious efforts to mediate between the public world of the mercantile establishment and the private world of the small female-operated shop. Thus, they were calculated attempts to gain the allegiance of customers who preferred "my little French milliner who makes hats just to suit me" to the relative anonymity of the department store. Department stores offered several advantages over their smaller competitors: luxury, convenience, and lower prices. But by appropriating the intimacy of the custom shop, they broke down the tradeswoman's last defense.

The department store was a workplace as well as a "palace of consumption." Salesclerks constituted its most visible inhabitants. One early twentieth-century study found that they made up more than half of the total workforce of Baltimore department stores. Milliners, by contrast, registered a mere 4 percent, dressmakers only a little over 1 percent. Nevertheless, "consumer palaces" engaged the services of a significant proportion of the millinery and dressmaking population. By 1916, almost 40 percent of the Boston milliners and over half of their Philadelphia counterparts toiled in department store workrooms.[14]

In many respects, the dressmaking or millinery department was a better employer than the retail shop. While wages were often lower, work was usually less seasonal, and conscientious employers made every effort to transfer idle craftswomen to the selling floor during dull times. Unlike their counterparts in custom shops, department store workers received their pay envelopes on a predictable weekly basis. Moreover, store employees often enjoyed better conditions than shop workers. In 1916, May Allinson noted that "department stores . . . usually have fairly good workrooms on one of the upper floors, where both light and air are secured."[15]

Perhaps even more than their retail counterparts, department stores provided role models for ambitious young women. Department managers, who sometimes also acted as buyers, were a force to be reckoned with; they commanded enviable salaries and exercised considerable authority over their preserves. They also reaped benefits that only the most exclusive tradeswomen enjoyed—annual trips to Europe and favorable (if condescending) mentions in trade journals.[16] Nonetheless, only the lucky few reached this lofty height. And if department stores offered relatively decent conditions—a fact that some observers disputed—and regular employment, their ability to provide job satisfaction was more ambiguous.[17] Both milliners and dressmakers found that consumer palaces transformed the nature of their work, more often than not diluting their skills and diminishing their authority.

How the mercantile milliner fared depended on whether she labored in an "exclusive department doing mostly order work" or in one "dealing entirely in . . . factory-made hats." Work in the first instance consisted of fashioning original creations for discriminating patrons; in the second, the tasks were pasting bands and bows on prefabricated shapes. As we have seen, twentieth-century retail shops were also guilty of "trimming . . . cheaper, ready-made hats, which do not require careful work." But in the transitional period of 1900–1930, when custom production had not yet been eclipsed, department stores were more likely than their smaller competitors to stock ready-to-wear and ready-to-trim models. This tendency had unhappy consequences for those who inhabited their workrooms; the denizen of the less exclusive millinery department found herself judged by her work's quantity, not quality. "Her speed," one observer explained, "is the gauge of her value." More often than not the department store workroom, which might employ forty, compared to the seven or eight who toiled in the typical retail shop, resembled nothing so much as a miniature factory—or sweatshop.[18]

Dressmakers confronted similar, if not identical, predicaments. If department store milliners found themselves affixing identical bows to prefabricated hats, their dressmaking sisters all too often applied their talents not to constructing new garments but to altering supposedly "ready-to-wear" clothing. To be sure, a modiste who fashioned a made-to-order gown for a department store patron differed little from her counterpart in a custom shop. In the more exclusive salons, craftsmanship was a source of pride. Abraham and Strauss advertised its "unusually competent corps of designers and fitters"; the Chicago firm of Mandel Brothers announced that "gowns made to measure are a lasting source of satisfaction, when the style, elegance of workmanship, and artistic selections of material and trimmings bear the imprint of our dressmaking and tailor department."[19] But by the 1910s, the privilege of donning custom attire was increasingly limited to members of the "carriage trade" who sequestered themselves in French rooms, far from the prying eyes of their social inferiors. Middle-class shoppers were more likely to purchase the less expensive (and often ill-fitting) ready-to-wear garments that decked department store racks. Thus, ready-made dresses created a need for a new type of worker: the alteration hand.

The advent of alteration departments provides an index to the growing popularity of factory-produced garments. By 1909, alteration hands outnumbered dressmakers ten to one in Baltimore department stores—and no wonder. In the early years of ready-to-wear, the alteration worker provided not a luxury but a necessity; only with her assistance could the factory have presented a viable alternative to the dressmaker. By offering alterations free of charge or at minimal cost, department stores hastened the triumph of ready-made clothing, for such garments were almost always cheaper than custom creations. "'We altered the prettiest little silk dress this afternoon,'" a dressmaker told Allinson. "'The customer bought it down town for $18. We couldn't have made one like it for less than $35 or $40.'"[20]

As this statement implies, independent modistes, too, did alteration work. Indeed, as the twentieth century progressed, such work constituted an increasing proportion of their business (today's dressmakers owe their livelihoods for the most part to alteration work). Unlike her counterpart in the custom shop, the department store alteration hand only lengthened or shortened hems and took in or let out seams.

This labor had its rewards. The typical alteration worker probably earned as much as the average custom finisher (a worker who sewed but did not cut). But her wages seldom approached those of cutters and fitters in fashionable shops. Alteration work was not necessarily unskilled work; as the social investigator Edna Bryner explained, "Making a chiffon evening dress made for a 38 size fit a woman of 34 size and preserving at the same time the line of the dress requires an amount of ingenuity which often taxes the ability of the . . . alteration worker to the utmost." Nevertheless, the alteration hand had reason to envy her dressmaking sister. "Alteration work," Allinson bluntly observed, "does not demand the highest creative and artistic ability."[21]

Alteration workers labored in a variety of circumstances. The most exclusive establishments imitated the traditions of custom production, employing "fitters" to plan the alterations and "hands" to execute them—a division of labor that roughly corresponded to the distinction between fitters and finishers in the custom shop. Much like mistress dressmakers, fitters had the "knack of getting along well with customers whom they fit, a very difficult task at times." But many department stores, particularly those specializing in clothing of the cheaper variety, hired no fitters, only hands. Larger firms instituted a minute subdivision of labor, in which some workers specialized in gowns, others in skirts, still others in coats—a differentiation that offered the alteration worker few chances for advancement.[22]

Terms of employment in the alteration department mimicked or even rivaled the worst features of the custom shop. While regular hands enjoyed a modicum of security—Bryner estimated that alteration workers in Cleveland worked for eleven months of the year—casual employees could be hired and fired at a moment's notice. The practice of employing "extra" hands "on Saturdays to finish garments . . . so that their customers may wear them Sunday morning" was particularly notorious. Those lucky enough to be hired often labored long into the night "to finish suits that have been ordered just as the store was about to close."[23]

Ranging from the haughty department head to the humble alteration hand, department store needlewomen were a heterogeneous lot. Most of them worked in environments that diverged sharply from the traditions of the custom shop, a fact evident not only in the ways in which their wares were produced but in how they were sold. As department stores instituted changes in the relations of consumption, craftswomen's prestige and authority declined; as bureaucratic layers multiplied, women found themselves increasingly subject to male managers.

The typical millinery or dressmaking shop drew little distinction between making and selling; indeed, the lowliest apprentice might venture out of the workroom to wait upon customers. As late as 1914, a milliner who installed an electric door buzzer that rang in the trimming room—thus signaling the presence of patrons in the waiting room—won praise for her ingenuity.[24] But those who toiled in department store workrooms might never see customers. Head dressmakers or milliners and certain alteration workers occasionally violated this decree; the extent of contact between producers and consumers depended in part on the degree to which the merchandise was truly "ready to wear." Nevertheless, most department store craftswomen did not sell the articles they made. This task fell to an army of saleswomen specially trained in the art of selling.

This stark separation between production and retailing signaled a decline in craftswomen's status. However bedeviled by imperious customers, nineteenth-century dressmakers and milliners exercised a modicum of power as arbiters of fashion. But in the department store their authority was usurped by "white-collar" saleswomen who believed themselves superior to "workers" who performed manual labor.[25] To be sure, milliners and dressmakers earned higher wages on average than their counterparts on the selling floor. But money came at the cost of respectability; unlike her sister in the custom shop, the department store needlewoman made clothing for "ladies" she would never meet.

Of course, the saleswoman played a very different role than her predecessor. While intimacy had been the hallmark of nineteenth-century producer/consumer relations, department stores developed a rationalized mode of selling with rules embodied in training courses and instructional pamphlets. Charlotte Rankin Aiken, author of *The Millinery Department*, expected her readers to memorize dozens of different types of straw braid and several kinds of trimmings. Students of a "salesmanship" course sponsored by the University of Pittsburgh were drilled on hat shapes, color combinations, beauty secrets, and customer relations. Courtesy was encouraged; intimacy was not: "You're here to sell hats, not to give advice to the lovelorn," a male floorwalker admonished a female salesclerk in the 1920s.[26]

The plight of the errant saleswoman illustrates another consequence of large-scale retailing: whether she was a head dressmaker, the manager of the millinery department, an alteration hand, or a salesclerk, the woman who worked in a department store labored in circumstances controlled by men.

The department head might rule her tiny fiefdom with an iron hand, but she was ultimately subject to the authority of male owners and managers. Even within the department, women might chafe under male authority. When buyer and manager were one, women usually held the upper hand, but as mercantile establishments grew larger and ever more bureaucratic, buying and overseeing often split into separate functions. In the latter case, the buyer became the superior of the workroom manager—and he was almost always a man. Virtually every twentieth-century social investigator referred to the buyer as "he."[27]

A final example suggests how a less personal mode of selling, male management, and ready-made apparel conspired to create a situation in which women exercised less control. Lilly Daché, a Parisian-trained milliner, recalled her experience in Macy's millinery department in the 1920s:

> My first customer was a very large lady with a very large, round face and several chins who was trying on a flirtatious little hat with daisies over each ear. It made her look something like a kittenish cow. As I approached her my hands were shaking, and I was remembering my lessons that "the customer is always right." This was an awful decision to make. I knew I should take her money and let her go, but I could not. It would be a sin against all good milliners to let that poor woman go out looking like a cow in mating season.

Daché showed the woman dozens of other hats but to no avail. Eventually the customer said, "'Guess I'll take the first one. The one with the daisies.'" Daché started to protest but saw the male floorwalker coming her way and quickly changed her mind. Customers may have appreciated Macy's dictum; few women wished to be informed—however politely—of their failings. As Daché's experience makes clear, saleswomen had to comply with rules not of their own making.[28]

The portly matron was not the end of Daché's troubles; the same supervisor later reprimanded her for trimming hats to suit individual customers instead of selling those already in stock. Her experience at Macy's reinforced her determination to start her own business, where *she* could exercise control. "In my own shop," she explained some years later, "when I have such a customer, I do not sell her again if she will not take the right advice when first she comes." By the 1920s, few could follow in Daché's footsteps; entrepreneurial opportunities for women in the millinery trade had drastically declined.[29]

The New Kind of Shop

The small shop did not vanish with the coming of the department store. As late as 1930, 503 dressmakers and 196 milliners advertised their services in Boston's city directory, their clientele increasingly limited to elites who disdained the masses thronging department stores. Transformations in retailing did not leave the custom shop unscathed. Confronted with wealthy patrons on the one hand and opulent dressmaking and millinery departments on the other, tradeswomen faced intense pressure to imitate the convenience, ambience, and sales techniques of department stores. These were improvements that many could ill afford.[30]

While these imperatives weighed heavily on milliners as well as modistes, they proved particularly burdensome to dressmakers, for they entailed fundamental changes in the nature of their business. Unlike dressmakers—whose customers ordinarily furnished materials—dressmaking departments "kept stock." Experts recognized that modistes might have to offer the same services as their larger competitors but failed to acknowledge the costs involved. "Exploit the fact that you have on exhibition the most complete assortment of everything that is new, popular and fashionable in late designs," the *American Dressmaker* admonished its subscribers in 1912. But the tradeswoman who kept fabrics, trimmings, and other "furnishings" on hand was one who possessed sizeable resources. As Allinson observed, "This system is possible only for the dressmaker who has a large reserve capital and extensive credit."[31]

Convenience was only one of the department store's many attractions, for the environment in which merchandise was displayed was as important as the stock itself. Some custom clothiers, who possessed substantial capital, were remarkably adept at aping their commercial rivals. By the second decade of the twentieth century, the typical "large" dressmaking establishment, as Allinson described it, bore a distinct resemblance to the dressmaking department of a department store: "The large quarters are emphasized and advertised by gilt signs on the door and on many windows overlooking the street." The "reception room," she noted, might contain "a wide selection of materials, laces, embroideries, and trimmings of all sorts [to] . . . tempt the eye of the visitor, or the room may present the luxurious appearance of a private parlor."[32]

Unlike their dressmaking sisters, milliners were accustomed to the financial burden of keeping stock. Nevertheless, they, too, faced new pressures.

Trade journal editors incessantly harped on the importance of display. "As the eyes are the window of the soul, the windows display the owner's ability," a contributor to the *Illustrated Milliner* explained in 1904. Five years later the *Milliner's Designer* offered a less poetic rendition of the same concept: "The show window is a great factor in gaining retail trade." Merely displaying hats was not enough; "progressive" milliners made use of lights, mirrors, and "electrical revolving machines."[33] The ideal hat shop was beautiful inside and out. In the eyes of the *Milliner,* Mr. S. Stahl's millinery store in Albany, New York, was an example to be emulated. Stahl's concern boasted woodwork of "white enamel and gold"—a scheme that imbued its interior with "a light, cheerful, dainty finish"—"burnished brass" chandeliers, and "three fine plate glass show cases . . . each fourteen feet long." The cases offered "a superb opportunity for the display of glittering ornaments, the finer flowers, ostrich plumes, fancy ribbons, aigrettes, etc."[34] That this venerable establishment belonged to *Mr.* Stahl was no coincidence. The new emphasis on display unleashed economic pressures that few female proprietors could meet. Moreover, the show window made sense only at the street level, where rents were exorbitant. While trade publications might insist that "attractive show rooms" could be secured "without any considerable expense," glass display cases, mahogany fixtures—even potted plants—cost money that many tradeswomen, bereft of capital and dependent on dilatory customers, did not have.[35]

Few tradeswomen had the means with which to turn their shops into showrooms, and most continued to depend on the loyalty of their patrons. By the early twentieth century, the most beguiling dressmaking and millinery establishments were those "with extensive capital, credit, prestige, and close connection with European centers of fashion," that is, those most closely resembling department stores. Best equipped to meet the challenge posed by these mercantile giants, such shops were more likely to be run by men. Customers were often none the wiser: "Of course, not all the shops which display a sign with the name 'Lillian' or 'Therese' really belong to Therese or Lillian," Mary Van Kleeck observed in 1917. "'Madam[e]' . . . may in reality be only the head trimmer or the manager."[36]

Many tradeswomen, shackled by limited capital, found that display cases, fabrics, and show windows constituted insurmountable expenses. They were equally unprepared to adopt a second convention of modern merchandising: advertising. Nineteenth-century businesswomen contented themselves with trade cards and occasional newspaper notices; most relied on word of mouth to attract customers. These outdated tactics, the *American Dressmaker* warned, were ill suited to the age of department stores and ready-to-wear products: "The time has long since gone by when business can be carried on in the slipshod manner of former years, when one customer would recommend another." Regular advertising "in your best local newspapers" provided the best substitute for "the old method of one customer asking another, 'Where can I find a good dressmaker?'" The *Milliner's Designer* agreed, its attitude toward advertising summarized in the motto: "PROMO-TION PUSH PUBLICITY."[37] These recommendations were not without merit. While ready-to-wear hats and dresses offered obvious advantages in matters of convenience and cost, their triumph was no means preordained; both benefited from aggressive marketing campaigns. Customers who associated ready-mades with "shoddy" apparel needed to be persuaded of their quality and respectability; the garments in question did not necessarily sell themselves. But virtually no modistes or milliners commanded the resources to compete with department stores who had hundreds of thousands of dollars to devote to advertising alone.[38]

These new imperatives of advertising and display extended even to tradeswomen's relations with customers. While dressmakers and milliners maintained their clientele by listening sympathetically to customers' woes, advocates of "progressive" business principles believed that appearance and personality took precedence over intimacy and friendship. The employees of "first-class" millinery establishments increasingly served not only as workers and salesclerks but as models; "frumpy" saleswomen, the *Milliner* explained, were bad for business. Not to be outdone, the *Milliner's Designer* urged its readers to cultivate "profitable business personalities" composed of qualities tradeswomen apparently lacked. Subtly commenting, perhaps, on milliners' working-class backgrounds, the journal warned, "There is an unrest and high pressure in the voice of the American woman which detracts from her charm. . . . Everyone, therefore, should take extreme care to cultivate the voice, as a well-modulated and sonorous voice is an important business asset."[39]

As these words suggest, trade journals wholeheartedly encouraged their subscribers to embrace the new emphasis on selling that was endemic in department stores. The properly trained saleswoman eschewed the "hard sell" in favor of subtle manipulation. Editors brazenly followed the lead of department stores. In 1900, the *Illustrated Milliner* presented a "shorter catechism for millinery salespeople" compiled by "a sagacious and successful

Millinery Manager, whose progressive methods and splendid discipline have made his department the most successful feature of a leading store in a great city." The "catechism," meant to be memorized by milliners and their employees, used the Socratic method to promote "efficient salesmanship."[40]

Progressive milliners embraced a mode of selling based less on personal relationships than on formal rules of salesmanship, an approach pioneered in department stores. The businesswoman who took seriously trade journal editorials acquired much the same knowledge as the salesclerk enrolled in a retail training course. Like her sister in the millinery department, she learned that "attractive," "chic," "smart," and "youthful" were appropriate designations for hats; "cheap," "classy," "Frenchy," and "nifty" were not.[41]

Much of the advice dispensed by trade journals assumed that readers employed a group of workers who sold but did not make hats. To be sure, the saleswoman's progress was a by-product of the ready-made hat; establishments that offered nothing but prefabricated items needed no makers or trimmers. But by the early twentieth century, larger custom shops had instituted a stark division between production and retailing, often embodied in the physical separation of workroom from showroom. Stahl's "small" millinery store employed fourteen trimmers and eighteen salesclerks. Even the larger dressmaking shops—on the whole less commercialized than their millinery counterparts—hired saleswomen specially trained to wait on customers.[42]

Like their sisters in the department store, dressmakers or milliners who worked in such an establishment might never see the clients for whom they labored. For craftswomen who once took pride in their interactions with "ladies," this must have been a bitter pill to swallow. Nor was this new scheme necessarily in the customer's best interest; salesclerks charged with conveying her instructions to the workroom staff might err in the translation. Nevertheless, experts warned, workers unschooled in the art of selling could not be trusted to serve the needs of patrons. "It is sometimes well to have the trimmer talk with the customer herself," a turn-of-the-century trade editorial acknowledged, but "the conference between customer and trimmer . . . should always be conducted by the saleslady."[43]

The ascendancy of salesmanship over production was a tendency and nothing more. Well into the twentieth century most dressmakers and milliners continued to serve as both workers and saleswomen. But without question the "new" kind of shop, commodious, elegantly furnished, and staffed with "professional" salespeople, had a hand in driving its smaller competitors out of business. Unable to compete with large dressmaking establishments, the proprietors of small- and medium-sized concerns were forced to abandon their businesses in favor of "going out by the day" or becoming employees in the workrooms of their former rivals. Confronted by better-equipped competitors, milliners, too, found self-employment—and independence—increasingly elusive.[44]

Larger shops, contemporaries agreed, more often than not were male-operated shops. While large-scale enterprises were not intrinsically masculine, men had access to greater financial resources. But if modern merchandising threatened the livelihoods of female proprietors, new methods of production would have equally dire consequences for the women employed.[45]

Millinery in the Wholesale Factory

Wholesale millinery* was not new to the twentieth century. Amateur milliners and impatient retailers had long been able to purchase ready-to-trim straw bonnets and factory-produced wire frames. But with the increasing popularity of the factory hat, available in greater numbers and variety than ever before, more and more craftswomen found themselves laboring in hat factories. Unlike their sisters in custom shops, wholesale millinery workers were judged not on the basis of originality and creativity but on their ability to duplicate speedily a given model. Also unlike those in custom shops, factory workers toiled not for women but for men.[46]

This is not to say that all labored in identical circumstances; diversity, not homogeneity, marked wholesale millinery. Some hat factories employed as few as forty workers, others as many as four hundred. Some manufactured superior products, others cheap merchandise. Some were models of corporate benevolence, others were ruthlessly exploitative. Wholesale establishments differed in function as well as form. Indeed, describing them was a task that confounded contemporaries. As one observer explained in 1919, "the wholesale millinery trade presents the most complex division of the industry." Some firms specialized in "making hand-made and trimmed hats," oth-

---

*Contemporaries used "wholesale millinery" to refer both to wholesale *merchants*, the subject of the preceding chapter, and to the large-scale *manufacture* of ready-made hats. By the 1930s, as jobbers (merchants who sold goods others made to retailers) vanished from the scene, the two definitions had become basically interchangeable. This chapter embraces the second meaning of "wholesale millinery," that is, the production of factory-made hats.

ers in producing "wire and buckram frames." (Such frames might be sold to wholesale merchants, directly to retailers, or even to factories that did not make their own frames.) The manufacture of straw, velvet, and felt "shapes"—a process usually undertaken with the aid of machines—was likely to be carried on in separate establishments, but some factories added this specialty to their traditional repertoire. By the 1930s, with the near elimination of the jobber and the dominion of the "mannish" felt hat, consolidation was the rule rather than the exception.[47]

Like their retail counterparts, wholesale factories ranged from the high-class to the humble, a variable that directly affected life in the workroom. The social investigator Elizabeth Beardsley Butler found that the "freshly painted walls" of wholesale workshops in Pittsburgh, specializers in "medium-grade" hats, presented a sharp contrast to the factories of New York, "where women are paying for the cheapness by life itself." Two hundred and fifty miles away in Philadelphia, a city known for manufacturing hats of "the cheaper, ready-made variety," Lorinda Perry encountered a "dark, dirty wholesale workroom."[48]

The "dainty" workrooms of Pittsburgh and the "dirty" factories of Philadelphia suggest that the wholesale worker's lot varied from city to city, shop to shop. Nonetheless, some generalizations can be hazarded. Hat factories tended to offer higher wages to makers, but lower wages to trimmers, than did their retail counterparts, a phenomenon that reflected the overall tendency of profit-minded factory managers to homogenize workers' tasks and wages (Table 19). Hat factories also offered longer seasons; wholesale employees on average had work for eight to ten months of the year compared to the custom milliners' six to eight. But in general, wholesale millinery workers endured all of the abuses suffered by their sisters in the custom shop: overtime, biannual—unpaid—"vacations," and less than ideal working conditions.[49]

Hat factory workers had additional complaints. Time clocks and disciplinary fines, relatively rare in the custom workshop, were familiar features of their workplace. Whenever the demand for speed prevailed over concern for craftsmanship, a common occurrence in wholesale shops, piecework resulted. More often than not wholesale milliners labored at an exhausting pace, ever vulnerable to speedups. Many, especially those who made cheaper hats, took additional work home with them; employees who ostensibly labored from 8 A.M. to 6 P.M. might in reality toil long into the night.[50]

In the final analysis, it was not wages, seasons, or conditions that distin-

Table 19. Women Earning $8.00 or More per
Week in Wholesale and Retail Millinery Shops,
1913–19

	Percentage of Total	Total Surveyed
Boston, 1913		
Retail		
Makers	33.3	27
Trimmers	100.0	31
Wholesale		
Makers	8.6	35
Trimmers	60.0	10
Cleveland, 1913–14		
Retail		
Makers	59.0	n.a.
Trimmers	100.0	n.a.
Wholesale		
All workers	63.0	n.a.
New York, 1914		
Retail (all workers)	66.5	215
Wholesale (all workers)	79.9	693
Massachusetts, 1919		
Retail		
Makers	66.8	202
Trimmers	100.0	61
All workers	61.0	351
Wholesale		
Makers	28.6	112
Trimmers	100.0	6
All workers	53.2	393
Straw machine operators	87.7	618

Note: These figures exclude pieceworkers.

Sources: Perry, *Millinery Trade,* 77, 84; Bryner, *Dressmaking and Millinery,* 63, 65–66; Van Kleeck, *Wages,* 28; MMWC, *Report on the Wages of Women,* 31, 33–34.

guished wholesale workrooms from their retail counterparts but the nature of work itself. To be sure, wholesale nomenclature mimicked the custom shop: almost every hat factory had its trimmers, makers, and even occasionally apprentices. "The best of the wholesale milliners," Van Kleeck noted in 1917, "create models as distinctive and unique as those to be found in retail shops." Designers in these establishments commanded impressive salaries—perhaps $40–50 a week. Busily engaged in turning out high quality models for retailers to sell or "pattern hats" for them to copy, makers and trimmers in the "best" shops performed much the same labor as their namesakes in custom millineries.[51]

Unfortunately for milliners, most factories, dedicated to supplying consumers of limited means, did not fall into the high quality category. Traditional occupational labels masked tedious labor and diluted skills. Makers in "cheap" shops were likely to be engaged in adorning hundreds of identical frames with identical coverings; trimmers added identical bands or bows. Van Kleeck encountered a manufacturer of "slightly trimmed" hats who "declared that the trimmers in his shop were not even milliners. 'Anybody who can handle a needle can do our work,' he said. . . . 'In a retail shop they would spend half a day trimming a hat that we trim in five minutes.'"[52]

Wholesalers' penchant for manufacturing hats "by the dozen or the gross" gave rise to a new type of milliner, the copyist, "who can make a hat from frame to trimming, copying exactly the model before . . . [her]." Copyists, who made up half of the wholesale millinery workers in New York, were more likely to work in establishments where quantity took precedence over originality. As Van Kleeck explained, "The more uniform the style, the less is the need for the corps of apprentices, improvers, preparers, makers, trimmers, and designers" (Figure 14).[53]

More often than not, the predominance of quantity over quality, of sameness over originality, culminated in mindless, repetitive labor. As Van Kleeck's description of the making of "tailored hats" (ready-to-wear affairs that boasted few adornments) makes clear, the "typical wholesale shop" where "workers are divided into distinct groups according to processes" was a far cry from the custom workroom. One contingent cut the materials for a particular style of hat, compiling "sets" that could be distributed to an army of copyists who assembled the same model over and over again. Other groups did nothing but "make linings by machine, or tuck or hem materials like chiffon or silk for trimming."[54]

This scheme, Van Kleeck was careful to emphasize, was "radically dif-

MAKING A DOZEN ALIKE

Figure 14. A wholesale millinery worker, most likely a copyist, engaged in "making a dozen alike." Unlike custom milliners, workers in wholesale factories fashioned identical products. From Mary Van Kleeck, *A Seasonal Industry: A Study of the Millinery Trade in New York* (New York: Russell Sage Foundation, 1917), frontispiece; photograph by Lewis Hine. (Courtesy of Widener Library, Harvard University)

ferent from the division of work in a retail shop or in a wholesale establishment where high grade hats are made." Workers in the custom millinery, we should recall, sat around a table presided over by a trimmer who also did most of the designing. Each hat was a collaborative effort; the apprentice stitched the lining or perhaps made the frame, the maker covered this foundation with fabric, and the trimmer added the adornments. As Van Kleeck explained, "each worker in the group has the advantage of watching every other part of the hat trimming, and increase in experience leads to more and more responsibility."[55]

The apprentice in the custom shop could hope one day to become a trimmer, but the wholesale maker who specialized in "covering crowns, covering brims," or "sewing crowns and brims together" never learned to fashion an entire foundation, let alone to trim it. Similarly, the worker who did nothing but hem fabrics or attach price tags could expect little in the way of upward mobility. Indeed, advancement was inimical to the purposes of the wholesale shop. Concerned with producing hats at the fastest possible speed, employers encouraged workers to perfect one tiny part of the process, not to acquire a general knowledge of hatmaking.[56]

Van Kleeck's description illustrates another distinctive characteristic of wholesale millinery: mechanization. Although much of the work performed in twentieth-century hat factories was still done by hand, in some wholesale shops up to 50 percent of the workers had exchanged the needle for the machine.[57]

While it represented a far cry from custom millinery, machine operating was neither uniformly unskilled nor consistently ill-paid work. Lining makers—who stitched away at ordinary sewing machines—performed an unenviable task, for which they received scant reward. But straw sewers, who used a machine specially adapted to the purpose, garnered impressive earnings; according to one survey, about 80 percent merited at least nine dollars a week, compared to 40 percent of their coworkers in the wholesale factory. In this case, wages reflected skill. Stitching together a length of straw or horsehair braid into a series of concentric circles to form the crown or brim of a hat was by no means easy; it was a craft that took years to acquire. Little wonder that straw sewers were among the oldest workers in the millinery trade; nearly half of the straw machine operators in post–World War I Massachusetts were over age forty.[58]

Whatever its benefits, the monotonous repetition that characterized much wholesale work exacted its toll. This fact was nowhere more evident than in the poignant recollections of Mary Asia (later Hilf), a Russian Jewish milliner trained in Warsaw, "the Paris of Poland." Much to her dismay, the Milwaukee hat factory in which she secured her first American job bore little resemblance to an old world millinery shop:

> Soon I discovered that both by temperament and by training, I was unsuited to working in the wholesale branch of millinery. Making the same hat over and over, with no change of detail, for days on end, first bored and then annoyed me, and ended by bringing on a constant nervous headache, caused by monotony and frustration. I had been trained to design hats, no two alike. In the wholesale business where I worked, a completed model was given to me, and my task was to copy it, over and over.
>
> One day, in sheer desperation, I made a few changes which I thought would improve the style of the hats I was making. When the forewoman discovered what I was doing, she angrily fired me, though I was turning out more finished hats than any other girl in the workroom.

Asia left the shop with mixed emotions: "I . . . had no more nervous headaches, but neither did I have a job."[59]

As her experience suggests, ethnic barriers often separated wholesale workers from their retail counterparts. While "American girls" dominated the custom workplace, wholesale shops provided a refuge for immigrants, especially Russian Jews. Four-fifths of the custom milliners in early twentieth-century New York were native-born women who fulfilled proprietors' and patrons' preferences for "genteel" employees. By contrast, well over half of the city's wholesale workers, who never saw the consumers for whom they labored, were of foreign birth.[60]

To be sure, native-born women were not strangers to wholesale millinery, but neither were they randomly distributed throughout the industry. They congregated in the "better" shops and monopolized the most prestigious positions in wholesale workrooms. This state of affairs cannot be blamed on unskilled immigrants—Asia's millinery credentials were impeccable—but on a system of discrimination that reserved the more creative tasks for native-born women, consigning immigrants to routine, monotonous labor.[61]

A custom milliner who visited a wholesale factory may have been struck less by the ethnic composition of the labor force than by the near universality of male ownership and management. Few women could amass the capital necessary to fund even the smallest hat factory: start-up money for the average wholesale concern was $26,000 in 1914. Thus, even the most celebrated designers labored for male employers. By the early twentieth century, a small number of men had trespassed onto female terrain. "In a very few instances," Van Kleeck observed, "men are engaged in the task of designing."[62]

By the 1930s, designers—male and female—had gone the way of the fluffy hat. Dedicated to producing simple felt models, most wholesale houses followed the lead of a small number of firms. Fittingly enough it was the mannish hat that opened the doors of the workroom to men, for blockers—workers who shaped straw, velvet, and felt "bodies" with the aid of hydraulic presses—were uniformly males who likely had gained experience in factories that produced men's hats. This development, contemporary advertisements suggest, reflected more than superior expertise; just as nineteenth-century commentators equated "feminine" hats with "feminine" capabilities, twentieth-century observers evidently believed that "mannish hats" should be made by "man hatters." As the gendered connotations of women's headwear shifted, sexual divisions of labor no longer worked to women's advantage (Figure 15).

Figure 15. An advertisement promoting hats "tailored in the man's-hatter manner" illustrates the gendered associations of production and consumption. Male hatters, not female milliners, the text implies, were the appropriate makers of the simpler women's hats of the 1920s and 1930s, themselves modeled after men's hats. From *Harper's Bazaar* 70 (Jan. 1936): 117. (Courtesy of Widener Library, Harvard University)

These changes, it should be emphasized, occurred gradually. In the early years of the twentieth century, the making of "pressed shapes" was usually an industry unto itself, a situation that physically segregated male blockers from the bulk of female milliners. By 1930, the wholesale millinery merchant, who might purchase shapes, flowers, feathers, and frames from a variety of producers, had been replaced by a manufacturer who sold directly to the retailer. A multitude of specialized firms had been succeeded by the hat factory, which concentrated all facets of production under one roof. Consequently, the wholesale shop of the 1930s was a "mixed" workplace where women labored beside men.

While not inherently problematic, the actual circumstances of mixed workrooms penalized women and rewarded men. Male and female coworkers were not equals. On the contrary, the modern millinery manufacturer instituted a division of labor that recalled the distinction between (male) finishers and (female) trimmers in the men's hatting industry, a distinction that carried weighty if nonsensical connotations about masculine and feminine capabilities.[63] Blockers claimed the exclusive right to perform "the heavy machine processes" and thus "earned" the designation as the most skilled of millinery workers, relegating trimmers—once the aristocracy of the trade—to second-class citizenship. Blockers were amply rewarded. In 1937, they earned an average of sixty dollars a week, two and a half times the salary of the typical maker or trimmer. The triumph of the mannish hat and the demise of the single-sex workshop ushered in an all too familiar scenario: a "mixed" but segregated workforce divided into highly "skilled," highly paid men's jobs and "unskilled," ill-paid women's jobs.[64]

The Efficient Millinery

At the same time, changes were sweeping through the custom shop. First, its scale was increasing: in 1850 the average Boston firm employed six craftswomen, by 1916 this figure had jumped to nine. These statistics tell only part of the story. At mid-century the city's largest retail millinery employed twenty workers. More than sixty years later, Perry found one custom workshop with a force of seventy, a sight that would have astonished tradeswomen of an earlier day.[65] The large millinery, with its larger labor force, was a byproduct of the battle between custom shops and department stores. Elegantly appointed, commodious establishments—funded with substantial capital and dependent on substantial profits—required more workers than a tiny, sparsely furnished concern. But for those who inhabited the workroom, bigger was not always better.

More often than not, growth had less than salutary implications for craftsmanship. Scholars have rarely applied the concept of deskilling to women workers, because they have assumed that the women labored at unskilled or at best semiskilled jobs. But female craftworkers, no less than male artisans, experienced this process, and, as Asia's story suggests, they found it no less painful.[66] As elsewhere in the garment industry, changes proceeded unevenly and work arrangements varied considerably. Some larger millinery establishments merely duplicated the small shop several times over; these might contain five to seven tables, presided over by trimmers. Others implemented a rudimentary subdivision of labor that mimicked the organization of the wholesale factory. One New York workroom, with ninety-seven milliners, included the requisite makers, trimmers, and apprentices but also employed feather hands, stock girls, errand girls, and shoppers, workers who remained outside traditional channels of advancement. By the 1910s, some makers confined themselves to certain parts of the foundation or to particular types of hats; trimmers, too, might "specialize on children's hats, evening hats, bonnets, or toques."[67]

Schemes of this sort undoubtedly captured the imagination of employers hard-pressed to equal the convenience of the ready-to-wear hat. But as retailers promoted quantity at the expense of quality, the interests of proprietors and employees increasingly diverged. However sensible or efficient, the division of labor stymied advancement; the milliner who "knew" nothing but children's hats could scarcely expect to run her own shop one day.

Reflecting prevailing trends in managerial philosophy, a newfound preoccupation with efficiency followed on the heels of specialization. "Trimmers," one Madame complained, "work so much from the artistic side of their nature that they ofttimes lose sight of the fact that their work is not a real success unless it yields beneficial results to their employer in a financial way." Her solution substituted "system in the smallest detail" for "art." A second "graduate of the trimming room" offered a discourse on "rational work room methods": "No millinery show room will be a huge success if there is any lack of discipline in the work room," she declared. "The first work room requisite is a complete and perfect order." We have no way of learning how obediently such dictates were followed. Period photographs suggest anything but order, and few milliners possessed the resources, inclination, or rationale to implement fully what was becoming known as "scientific management," a set of principles devised with the interests of the captains of heavy industry in mind (Figure 16). Nevertheless, the style if not the substance of Taylorism had penetrated even the tiniest work sites; by the first decades of the twentieth century, some custom shops had adopted the organization, regimentation, and ethos of the factory.[68]

Like their wholesale counterparts, retail shops were increasingly places where "man" and "woman" milliners mingled. Men had previously confined themselves almost entirely to management. By the early twentieth century, a tiny contingent of male designers had invaded the custom workroom, albeit against the vigorous protests of women workers. Women were willing to go to great lengths to protect their terrain; a Fifth Avenue milliner who hired a "smooth-faced boy" was forced to erect a barricade between the "genius" and his female coworkers. In truth, the "girls" had reason to complain; man milliners—never found among apprentices or makers—almost always occupied the most prestigious and lucrative positions.[69]

Figure 16. Busy season in a New York millinery shop. This photograph evokes both the hectic pace of custom production during rush times and the custom shop's resistance to standardization, efficiency, and order. From Mary Van Kleeck, *A Seasonal Industry: A Study of the Millinery Trade in New York* (New York: Russell Sage Foundation, 1917), between pp. 126–27. Photograph by Lewis Hine. (Courtesy of the Indiana University, Bloomington, Library)

In the long run, men trimmers and male designers were of minor importance compared to the devastation wrought by the ready-to-wear hat. Fifth Avenue milliners survived the initial onslaught; they continued to practice their art, fashioning original creations for individual customers well into the twentieth century. Their humbler competitors were not so lucky. Retailers who sold nothing but factory products had little need for craftswomen; custom trimmers who did nothing but paste bows on prefabricated shapes differed little from their counterparts in the wholesale workroom. Both might have sympathized with their dressmaking sisters. Just as the ready-made hat drove many a milliner out of the workshop and into the factory, so did the ready-to-wear dress replace the haughty modiste with the lowly garment worker.

From Dressmaker to Garment Worker

"Garment making," Butler observed in 1909, "has reached out and gathered one garment after another beneath the metal guides of its power machines." By 1900, a substantial proportion of the feminine wardrobe had met this fate. By 1920, the factory claimed an undisputed victory over the custom shop.[70]

The women's ready-to-wear industry, hampered by intricate and tightly fitting vogues, evolved slowly. Looser garments succumbed to the factory first: cloaks and mantillas in the 1860s, "wrappers" (loosely fitting housedresses), petticoats, and chemises in the 1870s. Factory production began in earnest in the late 1890s, when shirtwaists (blouses) and separate skirts came into vogue. The ready-made dress was a relative latecomer; apart from a few largely unsuccessful experiments, it did not get its start until the 1910s. Once again fashion played a role: loosely fitting "tea gowns" and "lingerie dresses" were more easily adapted to the exigencies of mass production (Figures 17–19). But as late as 1910 only 39 percent of garment workers in the United States manufactured women's clothing.[71]

A brief discussion cannot begin to capture the complexity of the ladies' garment trade, which rivals even the considerably complicated nature of the wholesale millinery industry. Glove, coat, dress, shirtwaist, and skirt making were separate endeavors. More often than not, the organization of labor differed from industry to industry. Conditions varied enormously, stretching from the well-lit factory to the dimly lit, airless tenement sweatshop. Some garment makers labored in establishments that sapped the energies of

Figure 17. Shirtwaists were the first women's garments to be successfully mass produced. From *Harper's Bazar* 41 (Oct. 1907): 955. (Courtesy of the Indiana University, Bloomington, Library)

hundreds of workers, others in concerns that employed five or six. Both "inside" shops—where all processes were performed under the same roof—and "outside" shops—where precut garments were sewn in separate establishments—were common. In the worst circumstances, outside work degenerated into homework, an abuse that a flurry of Progressive Era labor legislation often failed to curb.[72]

Because theirs was a newer industry, workers who made women's clothing tended to labor in larger establishments, and sometimes in better circumstances, than did those who manufactured male garb. But "ladies'" garment workers endured some of the most exploitative conditions in the industrial workplace. In contrast to custom dressmaking where native-born women constituted a majority as late as 1910, garment factories preyed upon the most vulnerable segments of the population: new immigrants from Southern and Eastern Europe, who themselves provided a profitable market for the cheaper varieties of factory-made finery.[73] Much as it reinforced the distinctions between wholesale and retail millinery, ethnicity bolstered the boundaries between factory dressmaking and the custom branches of the trade.

Wages, like conditions, varied. In 1911, a forewoman in one of the better Boston dress factories took home $20 a week; the employees of New York's girl. The jumper dress, banished from women's fashions this year, will still form part of the girl's. It is too pretty and, above all, too utilitarian to be given up before absolutely necessary, for it "helps out" wonderfully in providing fresh settings for the face, according to the waist worn under it. A house gown somewhat of this order, designed for a college girl's dress, will be seen on this page. It is of tan panama and may be worn over a lingerie bodice. A novel feature, and one which will be seen in connection with wool dresses for girls throughout the winter, is the little embroidered linen collars and bands.

Wide shoulder effects with mandarin

MORNING GOWN of pale tan pan-
ama; embroidered in colors.

sleeves and bre-
telles, any of
which drape
girls' figures
most advanta-
geously, are to
be features of all
girls' house
and party dress-
es. The form
followed in the

SIMPLE HOUSE GOWN of any preferred color light-weight material, tucked, and trimmed with bands of filet lace; filet lace yoke to match

Figure 18. House and morning gowns. The relatively loose fit of garments such as these made them amenable to factory production. From *Harper's Bazar* 41 (Oct. 1907): 949. (Courtesy of the Indiana University, Bloomington, Library)

Figure 19. Ready-made dresses, 1924. Note the loose fit and low price. From *Household Magazine* 25 (Mar. 1925): 27. (Courtesy of Widener Library, Harvard University)

infamous Triangle Shirtwaist Company were lucky to make $6. Few garment workers, even those who labored in the best establishments, made as much as their counterparts in dressmaking shops. Allinson found that nearly 50 percent of custom dressmakers but only 36 percent of factory clothiers earned weekly wages of $9 or more; 36 percent of custom but only 22 percent of factory workers earned $10 or more; 18 percent of the former but only 7 percent of the latter took home more than $11. "Much greater standardization of wages . . . appears in the factory trade," she concluded.[74]

Wages were only part of the story. As in millinery, the most striking difference between the factory and the custom shop lay in the nature of work. Skilled work and creative labor, we have seen, were the twin virtues of the dressmaking trade. Craftswomen took pride in mastering delicate fabrics, fashioning original creations, and cutting garments that fit. But garment workers were hired for very different purposes. As Susan A. Glenn has argued, factory investigators—imbued with preconceived notions about men's and women's work—attempted "to find a gendered order in a messy and chaotic industry." Considerable fluidity not rigid distinctions characterized the sexual division of labor in the garment trades, and the jobs that women held were not necessarily unskilled.[75] But in the final analysis, those who toiled in garment factories encountered arrangements that assigned the most monotonous and repetitive work to women and the most highly skilled and creative tasks to men. In the typical custom shop, Madame planned and cut the dress from the cloth; in the typical garment factory, cutting and designing became separate functions, both largely controlled by men. Indeed, men were more likely to work in factories that manufactured women's clothing than in factories that produced male attire. In early twentieth-century Cleveland, men constituted 40 percent of the labor force of the latter but only about 33 percent of the former.[76]

The sexual division of labor instituted by the garment factory was by no means inevitable. Rather, it suggests how flexible such seemingly "natural" arrangements really are. Two possible models presented themselves to a prospective owner or manager. The first, exemplified by the dressmaking shop, entrusted all tasks to women. The second, typified by the establishment that produced men's clothing, apportioned jobs between the sexes, a practice that almost always worked to women's disadvantage. Perhaps it is not surprising that the second model prevailed. Many manufacturers of feminine attire undoubtedly had prior experience in the men's apparel trade.

Nonetheless, woman's place in the ladies' garment factory was neither natural nor preordained. Nor did it encompass the most desirable positions. As in the wholesale millinery trade, employers (and, one suspects, male workers) used gendered arguments to justify less than equitable divisions of labor. "The designer," Bryner observed, "is the autocrat of the garment industry." In a smaller firm, he might be an owner or partner; in larger establishments, he was subject to the whims of management. In either case, he was the factory's best-paid employee—and he was almost always a man. There were exceptions; managers occasionally recruited female designers for "their superior ability in designing dainty garments," especially shirtwaists, dresses, and underwear. These supposedly gender-specific faculties were not always utilized. While they may have been more plentiful elsewhere, women accounted for only 7 percent of the designers in early twentieth-century Cleveland. The near absence of women from the ranks of designers had little to do with aptitude. As Bryner herself remarked, "There is no valid reason why women should not become competent . . . designers, provided they have the necessary trade and technical training."[77]

Female garment workers were even more likely to be excluded from the task that was the dressmaker's pride and joy: cutting. As we have seen, cutting had already become a mechanical process by the turn of the twentieth century. But whether she used a system, a pattern, or the traditional pin-to-the-form technique, the modiste cut the garments she sewed. Garment manufacturing was a very different matter. Less than 1 percent of the cutters in Cleveland garment factories were women, and this appears to have been a national trend. To be sure, cutting in the garment factory bore little resemblance to cutting in the dressmaking shop. The custom clothier cut one-of-a-kind garments to fit individual patrons; the factory worker cut hundreds of identical garments according to patterns graded in standard sizes. Unlike the dressmaker, he did not use shears but a specialized tool, the electric cutting machine. This instrument admirably suited the purposes of mass production; depending on the weight of the fabric, it could cut through as many as two hundred layers with one stroke. Contemporaries were quick to recognize its time-saving features. "These machines," Bryner commented, "can do the work of cutting in one-eighth the time consumed by hand."[78]

Employers and employees alike claimed that women lacked the physical strength to use the cutting machine; nor apparently did women possess "knowledge of materials" or "judgment in the lay-out of the cloth." Such strictures in all probability had less to do with women's alleged incapacities than with male workers' determination to preserve cutting—which, except for designing, was "the best paid of any occupation in the trade"—for themselves. And no wonder! A cutter might earn five times as much as the average female employee.[79]

Barred from cutting and designing, women were relegated to sewing, the least desirable and least remunerative aspect of the industry. Power machine operating engaged the largest number of employees, almost all of them women. As Butler's vivid description of a garment factory emphasizes, operators enjoyed few of the benefits that accrued to their male coworkers:

> As you enter the workroom, in addition to the roar of wheels and the quivering of the wooden framework, you hear the unmistakable sound of many needles being driven through cloth. Breaking upon the light, steady, determined whirr of the steel, come the clamp of a button stamper and half a dozen other abrupt utterances of the power, momentarily released in some new machine. The long high-ceilinged room is keyed to quick production. The power carries with it its own tenseness. The operators feel the spur and never relax. Near the door are long tables stacked high with piles of cloth just sent from the cutting room below. They are arranged in bundles so that a lot can be easily carried away by each girl to replenish the pile she has finished.[80]

Thus, the garment factory offered for women not creative labor but relentless, monotonous work. Custom dressmakers might stitch away at a dizzying speed during rush seasons, but their labor more closely paralleled the irregular rhythms of artisanal production than the incessant pace of the factory.

Garment workers owed their speed in part to mechanization but also to employers' conscious efforts to hasten the pace of production. Power machines and electric cutters vastly increased output. In 1916, Bryner observed that "a factory-made garment is produced in less than one-sixteenth of the time required by hand methods." The speed with which garments were produced depended on nimble fingers as well as machines or, as Bryner put it, the "ability to do ordinary plain sewing at considerable speed." The finisher, who attached fastenings of various sorts, wielded her needle efficiently, accurately, and above all rapidly, "without bungling her sewing by knotting her thread or doing uneven work," a task that she performed again and again. Little wonder that Bryner concluded that "hand sewing is more fatiguing than machine operating because of the greater expenditure of effort and the eye strain."[81]

The factory finisher did bear a superficial resemblance to her counterpart in the custom shop. But as late as the 1920s, the custom finisher performed varied and highly skilled work. She sewed curved seams, attached trimmings, stitched delicate fabrics, and even added decorative embroidery. She also en-joyed opportunities for advancement unavailable to her garment-making sis-ter. At best, the factory finisher could become forewoman of the sewing di-vision. Exceptional circumstances aside, she was forever shut out of the cutting room.

Some operators and finishers were better off than others, and it is impor-tant to remember that seemingly insignificant differences mattered a great deal to workers themselves. How factory seamstresses fared depended in part on whether they labored according to the "piece" or the "section" system. In the piece system, for instance, "each operator sews up all the seams on one 'piece' or garment, and each finisher does the hand sewing on one garment." The section system, "based on the subdivision of processes" contained far greater potential for exploitation: "The workers are divided into groups, each group making a certain part or section of the garment." Some stitched the seams of the bodice, others worked on sleeves, and still others devoted them-selves to collars, cuffs, or buttonholes. Finally, the finisher added hooks and eyes, button, and clasps.[82]

Whenever craftsmanship counted, the piece system prevailed; dresses and skirts, especially the high-grade models, tended to be made according to the "entire garment" method. Whenever quantity triumphed over quality, the section system was adopted, for it produced garments at a speedier pace. The phenomenally inexpensive shirtwaist was almost always manufactured in this manner, but its low price—as little as fifty cents—was purchased at consid-erable human cost.[83]

The Specialized Dressmaking Shop

In many respects, the typical twentieth-century dressmaking establishment was a far cry from the garment factory. The small shop continued to pre-vail; as late as 1911 more than half of the dressmaking shops in urban Mas-sachusetts employed fewer than nine workers. But the smaller establishments, always tenuous enterprises at best, were losing their footholds. Besieged by department stores on the one hand and ready-made clothing on the other, many businesswomen abandoned their shops in favor of "going out by the day." Larger firms that kept stock, rented elaborate quarters, and advertised regularly were better able to withstand the onslaughts of mass production. The early years of the twentieth century witnessed a decided shift in that direction, a transition that had significant consequences for those who inhab-ited the workroom.[84] As competition from ready-to-wear clothiers mounted, the proprietors of dressmaking concerns increasingly adopted practices pioneered nearly a century before by merchant capitalists in trades such as tailoring, shoe making, and furniture making. Employees who entered twentieth-century custom shops encountered intricate subdivisions of labor that enhanced productivity but diluted their skills, occupational ladders that thwarted their ambitions, and even an altered sexual division of labor that rarely worked to women's advantage.[85]

"The general tendency," Bryner noted in 1916, "is toward specialization." To be sure, dressmakers had long made distinctions between fitters and finishers, between those who cut and those who merely sewed. But few nineteenth-century establishments evinced the degree of elaboration Bryner found in an early twentieth-century Cleveland shop. This particular concern, characterized by an organization of labor "that resembles a miniature feudal system," employed thirty-four workers, some of whom specialized in waists or bodices, others in skirts, others in sleeves, and still others in coats. The workers included:

    1 waist draper
    1 helper to waist draper
    5 waist finishers
    6 helpers to waist finishers
    1 head sleeve girl
    1 skirt draper
    2 helpers to skirt draper
    2 skirt finishers
    2 helpers to skirt finishers
    2 coat makers
    2 helpers to coat makers
    1 lining maker
    1 apprentice
    1 embroiderer and collar maker
    1 helper to embroiderer
    1 hemstitcher (power machine)
    1 guimpe maker
    1 shopper
    1 stock girl
    1 errand girl[86]

In this establishment, Bryner explained, the employer "plans the gown, sometimes cuts the lining, and does most of the fitting." But she delegated much of her authority to the waist draper, "a specialist who does nothing but cut the outside material and pin or baste it in shape on the fitted lining." This division of labor was unknown to mid-nineteenth-century shops, where cutting and draping were one.[87]

Boston evidently surpassed Cleveland in both size and specialization. Allinson visited one Boston dressmaking establishment that employed sixty-five workers, rigidly segregated into waist, lining, sleeve, skirt, and tailoring divisions. Schemes of this sort were not necessarily confined to larger concerns. Only 7 of the 23 Cleveland dressmaking shops visited by Bryner "were not openly specialized." Allinson paid a visit to "Shop N" in Boston, which employed seven workers, including one head waist girl, one waist finisher, one coat girl, three skirt girls, and one plain sewer.[88]

The dressmakers' answer to the ready-to-wear dress was an accelerated division of labor, an attempt to duplicate the efficiency and dispatch of mass production. Although custom production could never match the speed of the garment factory, specialization produced one-of-a-kind garments much more quickly, ameliorating the demands of newly impatient consumers. Ironically, the specialized shop bore no small resemblance to the notorious section system that produced hundreds of shirtwaists at lightning speed. If the new order boosted the profits of proprietors and reduced the cost of garments, it had less salutary effects on the prospects of workers.

On the one hand, even a humble lining maker had reason to count her blessings. Unlike her sister in the garment factory, the custom worker enjoyed endless variety instead of dull monotony. Because craftsmanship still counted, she seldom adopted the relentless pace of the shirtwaist maker. And larger dressmaking shops tended to pay higher wages than their smaller, less specialized competitors.

On the other hand, specialization offered dim prospects for the worker who hoped one day to become a "mistress dressmaker." Rather, it encouraged her to become an expert at making part of a dress, never learning how to fashion it in its entirety. Only with difficulty could the collar maker advance to skirt finisher, the skirt finisher to waist draper. Different sorts of workers were often physically segregated from each other; larger establishments contained "a separate workroom for each division of production." "'I make sleeves all day long,'" one worker told Allinson, "'and never see the waists to which they belong. The waists are made in another room.'"[89]

Theoretically at least, the custom shop—unlike the garment factory—continued to preserve all of the rungs on the occupational ladder for women, even if they became more difficult to climb. But the tendency toward larger and ever more elaborate establishments exhausted the financial capacities of many businesswomen. In these circumstances, men, who on balance had access to greater resources, were almost a necessity. "Sometimes a husband or brother has charge of the financial department and sometimes a man appears as sole head of . . . an establishment," Allinson explained.[90]

By the early twentieth century, dressmakers encountered men not only as employers but also as coworkers. Partly as a concession to the popularity of tailored suits and partly in an attempt to imitate the convenience of department stores, larger establishments began to employ "man tailors" to fashion the more "mannish" elements of the feminine wardrobe.[91] With the addition of tailors, dressmakers—previously inhabitants of a largely female world—experienced discrimination firsthand. As early as 1900, male employees constituted 10 percent of the labor force of American dressmaking shops—and earned 20 percent of the total wages. Eleven years later, Allinson discerned a similar pattern in Boston: "While almost two-thirds of the women employed in custom dressmaking earned less than $10 a week, practically the same proportion of the men earned $20 or more." The head tailor of one particularly prestigious establishment commanded a weekly salary of $45, fifteen dollars more than the reigning female employee. This inherently unequal division of labor was a relatively permanent one in the eyes of contemporaries. The line between male tailors and female dressmakers was a boundary that could not be crossed; women could be "tailors' helpers" but never tailors.[92]

In the end, dressmakers hired tailors to no avail. In dressmaking as well as millinery, the various tactics deployed against factories and department stores bore little fruit. The number of "milliners and millinery dealers" in the United States declined by more than 40 percent between 1910 and 1920; the number of dressmakers decreased by nearly half during the same period. These figures signaled a decrease in the ranks of proprietors as well as workers. By 1930, Boston had only slightly more than half of the dressmaking and millinery shops that had graced the city twenty years before (see Table A-2 in appendix).[93]

Two kinds of shops remained. The first, exemplified by the high-class custom establishment, catered to a dwindling group of wealthy customers. The second, typified by the retail milliner who stocked little except ready-made hats or the dressmaker who did little except alterations, served the needs of a local, often ethnic or working-class, clientele, providing a valuable resource for women who felt less than welcome in department stores. While the existence of these hardy survivors attests to the continuing attractions of custom production and small-scale retailing, the scales had clearly tipped in favor of the factory and the department store.[94]

* * *

In August 1922, Franklin Simon, president of the American Garment Retailers' Association, reviewed with pride the achievements of the previous twenty-five years. Ready-made clothing, he reported, had accounted for only 10 percent of the garments produced in the United States in 1897; by 1922, this figure had risen to an astonishing 90 percent. Twelve years after Simon's pronouncement, a dressmaker employed in a Fifth Avenue shop voiced her deepest fears: "Our trade is breaking down slowly. . . . Customers who used to order twelve dresses at an order now only take six at a time. Those who ordered only one or two, do not order now at all."[95]

The contrast between the gleeful Simon and the melancholy modiste vividly illustrates the ever-widening gulf that separated producers from consumers in twentieth-century America. If Simon's figures—no doubt inflated—can be believed, American women had eagerly embraced the products of the factory, seldom pondering the circumstances of those who made them, for ready-made dresses and mass-produced hats promised unprecedented convenience and at lower prices than ever before. By the 1920s, looser, simpler styles had solved the once vexing problem of fit. Fashion, so long the dressmaker's ally, now boosted the fortunes of garment manufacturers. Even as the triumph of ready-made apparel offered untold advantages to consumers, it also posed a grim future for fashion's erstwhile makers.

Although the dresses and hats of the 1920s and 1930s displayed few of the ruffles, ribbons, laces, and bows that had bedecked Gilded Age apparel, they were every bit as "feminine" by the standards of their day. Nonetheless, the flapper dress and the felt hat ushered in a world that bore little resemblance to its nineteenth-century predecessor. The intimacy of the custom shop had given way to the impersonal elegance of the department store. In Madame's place stood a saleswoman who made none of the wares she sold. Male-operated factories, where male cutters and blockers held sway, had triumphed over women's concerns; the monotony of "machine operating" had finally eclipsed a centuries-old female craft tradition. While women were as visible as ever in the twentieth-century economy of fashion—as operators and finishers in garment factories, as salesclerks in department stores, as makers and trimmers in wholesale millineries, and—above all—as consumers, they bought and sold, produced and consumed in a world that was largely controlled by men.

Conclusion

The demise of the female economy paralleled larger changes in the early twentieth-century social landscape—the breakdown of separate spheres, the refashioning of working-class leisure from "homosocial" to "heterosocial" pursuits, and the transformation of the new woman (a figure defined in large part by her rejection of marriage and her allegiance to a female community) into the "mannish lesbian."[1] These diverse developments shared a common theme: the replacement of female worlds with arenas in which men and women mingled (or, many believed, *should* mingle). Similarly, while the custom fashion trades had primarily confined themselves to relations between women, garment factories and department stores employed workers of both sexes. Unlike clerical work, but certainly like midwifery, the making of women's clothing had become not "feminized" but "masculinized."

As several historians have shown, these changes brought both new possibilities and new disappointments. While women gained new political rights and social freedoms, they often found their collective power diluted by the disintegration of single-sex institutions and their agendas compromised by adaptations to male political structures.[2] Just as the transformations that marked women's history in the first decades of the twentieth century are complicated ones, the rise of mass production and large-scale retailing fail to lend themselves to simple judgments of progress or regression.

Certainly, the ladies' garment trades—concentrated in readily identifiable districts in the nation's largest cities—provided the setting for one of the nation's most militant labor movements. Events such as the "uprising of the twenty thousand" in the shirtwaist industry as well as kindred strikes sprang not only from what the union activist Clara Lemlich justly termed "intolerable working conditions" but also from the individual aspirations and communal values of thousands of young Jewish women. Bolstered by a radical Jewish subculture, which was literally "foreign" to the native-born and Irish

American women who dominated the custom fashion trades, garment workers forged a movement that far outpaced the activism of other groups of women wage earners. Nor did mixed workrooms necessarily result in gender antagonism; as Susan A. Glenn has shown, male cutters and inside contractors often supported their female coworkers' efforts to secure higher wages, better conditions, and "humane treatment."[3]

Similar arguments might be made for the liberating features of department stores. As Susan Porter Benson has so skillfully demonstrated, consumer palaces inadvertently fostered a lively female work culture that allowed saleswomen to collectively resist the demands of both female customers and male managers. The larger, less personal arena of the selling floor and near ubiquity of male management created a psychological space in which salesclerks could act; in contrast, Madame's small shop and "maternal" demeanor helped to dampen craftswomen's enthusiasm for collective resistance.[4]

Nevertheless, department stores and garment factories created new hierarchies. The addition of men—as owners, supervisors, or coworkers—invariably placed women in inferior positions; unlike most dressmakers and milliners, saleswomen and garment workers were subject to male authority. They also labored in settings where men's work merited the highest value and reaped the highest rewards. The benefits that clerking or factory sewing offered notwithstanding, neither entailed the skill and creativity that had long distinguished dressmaking and millinery from other female employments—and as the nineteenth century drew to a close, from many male employments as well.[5] Finally, apart from the most exceptional circumstances, both garment manufacturing and large-scale retailing foreclosed the possibility of female entrepreneurship and the attendant prospect of female economic independence. Milliners and dressmakers may not have consciously embraced "separatism as strategy,"[6] but the world that they inhabited offered white working-class women a degree of economic authority and psychological satisfaction unknown to their successors.

Perhaps the issues were least ambiguous for consumers. After all, factory-produced dresses and hats could be had for a fraction of the cost of custom creations, and ready-made garments put an end to the often exasperating process of "trying on." Equally important, the demise of custom production freed producers and consumers alike from often troubling personal relationships. Yet patronizing dressmakers and milliners had imbued middle-class and upper-class customers with a sense of superiority; by embracing mass production, consumers lost a modicum of power—however contemptible or corrupt. With the triumph of the new order, they also lost a good deal of control over their clothing: the ability to specify the dimensions of a dress or hat, its fabrics, colors, and trimmings. Nor did the rise of simpler—and presumably more liberating—modes of dress necessarily represent an improvement. Valerie Steele has argued persuasively that Victorian clothing, by concealing much, enabled the average woman to adhere more easily to contemporary standards of beauty than subsequent more revealing styles. Moreover, Joan Jacobs Brumberg has shown that ready-made clothing and standardized sizes "gave legitimacy to the idea of a normative size range" that many women achieved only through ruthless self-denial. New styles and methods of production—not to mention the emergence of new types of advertising—served only to increase consumers' anxieties about personal appearances.[7]

But to romanticize the female economy is to ignore the exploitation—by proprietors of workers, by consumers of both—that it engendered. Such a perspective also overlooks the essential inequalities that sustained its worst features. If the nineteenth-century fashion trades offered considerable opportunities to those who pursued them, they also reflected all women's unequal access to economic resources. Moreover, to view the chain of relations that bound worker to proprietor and producer to consumer as a variant of a larger women's culture neglects the fact that the female economy was never entirely a separatist enterprise; nosy credit investigators, paternalistic wholesalers, and parsimonious husbands all played a part in orchestrating an ostensibly female preserve. Millinery and dressmaking may have been unique among female employments, but they existed within both a larger sex-segregated labor market and a larger system of gender relations that rewarded men at women's expense.

Today, in an era of declining unions and increasing global assembly lines, female garment workers—in both the United States and overseas—toil under conditions that resemble or even rival the worst nineteenth-century custom shops and early twentieth-century shirtwaist factories.[8] Nonetheless, vestiges of the female economy survive and perhaps even prosper. Largely confined to alterations and bridesmaids' gowns, dressmakers still keep shop today, although milliners by and large have gone the way of women's hats. New types of female-controlled enterprises have taken their place. The daily dramas enacted in even the lowliest of beauty parlors replicate the intimate but contentious interactions that marked the heyday of the millinery and dressmaking trades. As in the past, women still operate small groceries and variety stores—on their own and as part of family enterprises; commentators speak casually of "mom and pop" stores but rarely investigate the role that "moms" play in these businesses.[9] The challenge for future scholars will be to render these women visible, to see them neither as exceptional path breakers nor pathetic victims but as part of the gendered fabric of social and economic life.

Appendix

Table A-1. Dressmakers and Milliners in the United
States, 1860–1930

Year	Dressmakers	Milliners	Total
1860	35,165	25,722	60,887
1870[a]	—	—	92,084
1880[b]	—	—	285,401
1890[c]	290,308	60,653	350,961
1900	347,076	87,881	434,957
1910[d]	449,342	127,936	577,278
1920[d]	235,855	73,255	309,110
1930[d]	158,380	44,948	203,328

Note: Includes proprietors as well as employees.

   a. Milliners, dress, and mantua makers.

   b. Milliners, dressmakers, and seamstresses.

   c. Women only.

   d. Dressmakers and seamstresses (not in factory); milliners and
millinery dealers.

Sources: USBC, *Population of the United States in 1860,* 668–69;
Statistics of the Population . . . Ninth Census, 682, 692; *Statistics of
the Population . . . Tenth Census,* 759; *Twelfth Census . . . 1900,* 507;
Statistics of Women at Work, 39; *Fifteenth Census . . . 1930,* 5:41.

Table A-2. Self-Employed Dressmakers and Milliners in Boston, 1846–1930

Year	Dressmakers	Milliners	Total
1846	133	69	202
1850	88	71	159
1855	38	87	125
1860	118	104	222
1865	134	125	259
1870	300	134	434
1875	296	156	449
1880	454	167	621
1885	470	147	617
1890	325	152	477
1895	462	217	679
1900	625	280	905
1905	681	305	986
1910	845	357	1,202
1915	1,186	348	1,534
1920	930	313	1,243
1925	666	283	949
1930	503	196	699

Sources: Adams's New Directory; Boston Directory (1850, 1855, 1860, 1865, 1870, 1875, 1880, 1885, 1890, 1895, 1900, 1905, 1910, 1915, 1920, 1925, 1930).

Essay on Primary Sources

Sources for dressmakers and milliners are plentiful but fragmentary; recounting their experiences necessitates a good deal of patient reconstruction. Such an effort also demands recognition of both the biases of particular sorts of sources and the paucity of testimony from craftswomen themselves. When surviving evidence allows us to hear their voices, we must listen carefully to what they say.

Three sources—the 1860 and 1870 federal manuscript census schedules (I chose not to analyze the 1880 census because it does not include real and personal property, key variables for assessing proprietors' success), the business section of city directories, and the records of R. G. Dun & Co.—are indispensable for reconstructing the careers of Boston's female proprietors. Business directories allow us to distinguish proprietors from employees and to measure the longevity of particular enterprises. The two censuses reveal much about both groups: age, ethnicity, marital status, wealth, and household structure.[1] The reports of Dun & Co., the predecessor to Dun & Bradstreet, furnish information of a different sort. Before the firm developed standardized credit ratings in the 1890s, its ledgers were filled with observations that yield a wealth of evidence. In evaluating a businesswoman's prospects, a Dun & Co. correspondent considered—in addition to her net worth—her personal character, past experience, familial relationships, and even the "quality" of her customers. The reporter unwittingly left behind much more than simple assessments of creditworthiness. To be sure, the Dun & Co. records illuminate the careers of more substantial businesswomen—those who were considered potential recipients of credit. For example, 26 percent (42 of 162 for whom Dun & Co. records provided some estimate of "means") of the millinery and dressmaking proprietors evaluated by Dun & Co. correspondents possessed either "some means"—rather than "no means" or "small means"—*or* capital valued at five hundred dollars or more; only 11 percent (14 of 125) of their counterparts in the 1860 census sample and only 6 percent (7 of 111) in 1870 held equivalent amounts of real or personal estate. While "means"—that is, capital—and property are not strictly comparable, this suggests that Dun & Co. wisely confined its investigators to firms whose assets suggested that their proprietors might be good credit risks. Because they were more likely to keep stock—and thus to need to buy goods on time—milliners endured the firm's scrutiny much more frequently than did their dressmaking sisters. (Dun & Co. ledgers contained evaluations of 58 percent of the milliners but only 3 percent of the dressmakers listed in the 1880 *Boston Directory*.) These limitations notwithstanding, the company's reports provide unsurpassed descriptions of the inner workings of women's businesses.

Several sources illuminate interactions between producers and consumers. Craftswomen rarely left behind diaries and letters, but those of their customers—precisely because the latter represented middle- and upper-class women—have survived in abundance. Although they tell only one side of the story, patrons' diaries and correspondence detail the frequency of their visits to dressmakers and milliners, their attitudes toward those who served them, and the satisfactions and frustrations they encountered. The records of the Protective Committee of the Boston Women's Educational and Industrial Union, an organization that directly intervened in producer/consumer relations, also prove useful in this respect. Caroline H. Woods's fictionalized memoir of her experience as the proprietor of a Boston millinery shop does much to redress the interpretive imbalance. Her *Diary of a Milliner* (1867) offers a perceptive, often comic, account of her dealings with her customers. The anonymously authored "As a Dressmaker Sees Women," published in the August 1908 issue of the *Ladies' Home Journal,* also depicts producer/consumer relations from the tradeswoman's perspective.

Instructional pamphlets produced by the inventors of "scientific" dress-cutting techniques furnish the best means of measuring the gendered implications of innovations such as drafting systems and proportional patterns. An analysis of the methods reveals their distance from craft traditions. Equally important, inventors' pronouncements, which clearly denigrate dressmakers' skills, indicate the extent to which they relied on flexible definitions of women's work to challenge female authority and promote their own technological agendas.

Millinery trade journals, most of which began publication around 1900, shed light on several issues: commercial transactions between wholesalers and retailers, consumer relations, and the impact of technological and commercial change on the trade as a whole. Although the journals reflect the viewpoint of their sponsors—(male) wholesale milliners—their comments and complaints about *their* customers (predominantly female retailers) inadvertently reveal much about the attitudes of businesswomen themselves. Milliners' voices surface more directly in the advice columns that appeared in trade publications, although such statements should be interpreted with caution. Although wholesalers set the agenda and edited contributors' words, they could not entirely control their content.

Sources that illuminate the experiences of millinery and dressmaking workers are difficult to find, especially for the earlier period, when most accounts were penned by reformers who saw all workingwomen as pathetic victims. Virginia Penny's *Employments of Women* (1863) provides the most useful—and most open-minded—discussion of wages, conditions, and opportunities in the nineteenth-century fashion trades. Finally, early twentieth-century studies of both the custom and ready-made branches of the trades, most undertaken by female labor economists, are essential for understanding workers' attitudes and shop floor life, as well as the consequences of economic change. Although marred by middle-class assumptions and the Progressive Era preoccupation with—even celebration of—efficiency, these monographs are unparalleled in their detailed discussions of work and conditions, their sympathy and concern for wage-earning women, and their sophisticated analyses of the relative benefits and disadvantages of custom and mass production. This book would have been far poorer without the insights of Mary Van Kleeck, May Allinson, Edna Bryner, Lorinda Perry, and Elizabeth Beardsley Butler; explaining their absence from the canon of labor history would require a book in itself.

Notes

Abbreviations

AAS	American Antiquarian Society, Worcester, Massachusetts
AD	*American Dressmaker*
D	*Demorest's Monthly Magazine*
EI	Essex Institute, Salem, Massachusetts
FD	*French Dressmaker*
FMMC	Federal Manuscript Manufacturing Census, National Archives Microfilm Publications
FMPC	Federal Manuscript Population Census, National Archives Microfilm Publications
FTR	*Fincher's Trades' Review*
GTEL	Girls' Trade Education League
IM	*Illustrated Milliner*
M	*Milliner*
MD	*Milliner's Designer, Illustrated*
MH	*Millinery Herald*
MBSL	Massachusetts Bureau of Statistics of Labor
MHS	Massachusetts Historical Society, Boston
MMWC	Massachusetts Minimum Wage Commission
MTR	*Millinery Trade Review*
RGD	R. G. Dun & Co. Collection, Baker Library, Harvard University Graduate School of Administration, Boston, Massachusetts (MA = Massachusetts volumes; NY = New York volumes)
SL	Arthur and Elizabeth Schlesinger Library on the History of Women, Radcliffe College, Cambridge, Massachusetts
USBC	U.S. Bureau of the Census
WC	Warshaw Collection of Business Americana, Archives Center, National Museum of American History, Smithsonian Institution, Washington, D.C.
WEIU	Women's Educational and Industrial Union Papers, Arthur and Elizabeth Schlesinger Library on the History of Women, Radcliffe College, Cambridge, Massachusetts
WWPU	Working-Women's Protective Union

Introduction

1. Hunt, *Glances and Glimpses*, 49–52; James et al., *Notable American Women*, 2:235–36.

2. Hunt, *Glances and Glimpses*, 50–51, 365–66, 412–13.

3. Sumner, *History of Women*, 117, 145, 156; Carey, "Essays on the Public Charities," 194.

4. See Scott's now-classic discussion "Gender: A Useful Category."

5. *IM* 1 (Aug. 1900): 79.

6. Wilentz, *Chants Democratic*, 111–34.

7. Stansell, *City of Women*. For an exploration of female economies in early America, see Ulrich, *Midwife's Tale*, esp. 75–90. The relationships Ulrich describes were based on reciprocity and exchange of labor. The nineteenth-century female economy of fashion was based on market relations and exchange of cash.

8. The work of Alfred D. Chandler has dominated the "new" business history until relatively recently. See his *Visible Hand* and *Scale and Scope*. For scholarship that examines the history of smaller businesses, see Blackford, "Small Business"; Scranton, "Diversity in Diversity"; Nenadic et al., "Record Linkage."

9. Lerner, "Placing Women in History," 5. For examples of the celebratory approach, see Dexter, *Colonial Women* and *Career Women;* Bird, *Enterprising Women;* Clark, "Carrie Taylor"; Jerde, "Mary Molloy"; Daily, "Woman's Concern." Exceptions include Murphy, "Her Own Boss" and "Business Ladies"; Cleary, "'She Merchants'"; Goldin, "Economic Status of Women"; Formanek-Brunell, *Made to Play House*, esp. 61–89.

10. Gerber, "Cutting Out Shylock," esp. 617, 624–35; Kessler-Harris, *Out to Work*, esp. 68–70, 116–17, 128–41.

11. Benson, *Counter Cultures;* Abelson, *When Ladies Go A-Thieving;* Peiss, *Cheap Amusements.*

12. Thompson, *Making of the English Working Class*, 9–11, quotation from p. 11.

13. Rorabaugh, *Craft Apprentice*, 11, 102–4. Laurie, in *Artisans into Workers*, also assumes that artisans were men.

14. Faler, *Mechanics and Manufacturers*, esp. 30–57, 126–33; Laurie, *Working People*, esp. 53–83, and *Artisans into Workers*, esp. 35–38, 63–73, 79–86; Wilentz, *Chants Democratic*, esp. 65–97.

15. Turbin, "Beyond Conventional Wisdom," 57.

16. For the best review of this literature and for a perceptive discussion of the dangers of the "ghettoization" of women's labor history, see Baron, "Gender and Labor History." For examples, see Benson, *Counter Cultures;* Dublin, *Women at Work;* Turbin, *Working Women;* Blewett, *Men, Women, and Work;* Cooper, *Once a Cigar Maker*, esp. 218–40; Cobble, *Dishing It Out;* Cameron, *Radicals of the Worst Sort.*

17. Baron, "Gender and Labor History."

18. Welter, "Cult of True Womanhood"; Lerner, "Lady and the Mill Girl"; Cott,

Bonds of Womanhood; Ryan, *Cradle of the Middle Class,* esp. 187–225. For interpretations of the family wage, see May, "Bread before Roses"; Kessler-Harris, *Woman's Wage,* esp. 8–12, 19–20.

19. Marshall and Paulin, "Employments and Earnings," 10; Perry, *Millinery Trade,* 5; Allinson, *Dressmaking,* 5.

20. MMWC, *Report on the Wages of Women,* 9.

21. Ingham, "Patterns of African-American Female Self-Employment and Entrepreneurship," esp. 5–6.

Chapter 1: Fashion and Independence

1. *Boston Common* (2d ed., Boston: E. O. Libby, 1858), 181, has been attributed to both Mrs. R. G. Varnham and Mrs. Farren (Wright, *American Fiction,* 344).

2. *Boston Directory* (1805); *Adams's New Directory;* Blumin, "Hypothesis of Middle-Class Formation," 330.

3. Kidwell, *Cutting a Fashionable Fit,* esp. 98; Kidwell and Christman, *Suiting Everyone,* 135–38.

4. Clark, *Working Life of Women,* 195, 234; Kidwell, *Cutting a Fashionable Fit,* 3–4, 11–13; Clark, *Hats,* 77–78; Coffin, "Woman's Place," 28–43.

5. *Essex Gazette,* Aug. 14–21, 1770, quoted in Allinson, *Dressmaking,* 14; *Boston Directory* (1805 and 1830). The 1830 directory listed 222 dressmakers and milliners.

6. Simon, "'She Is So Neat,'" 64, 70; 1850 FMPC, Piscataquis County, Maine, M432, reel 267, p. 477, line 31; Esther Bodwell to Sarah Carter, Mar. 24, 1846, Holmes Family Papers, MHS; Dublin, *Women at Work,* 32–35.

7. Simon, "'She Is So Neat,'" 73; 1850 FMMC, T1204, reel 6; *Boston Directory* (1850). The manufacturing census listed only 14 of the 159 dressmakers and milliners who did business in the city. There is good reason to suspect that these represented the more substantial proprietors. It is impossible to ascertain whether the economic circumstances of millinery and dressmaking proprietors changed significantly between the 1820s and 1850s.

8. Louisa Chapman diary, June 24, 1847, EI; Sumner, *History of Women,* 134. In 1844, Boston seamstresses earned between $1 and $1.25 a week. In 1846 in New York they earned average weekly wages of $1.50–2.00.

9. Eliza Dodds, account book, May 1821, quoted in Simon, "'She Is So Neat,'" 76.

10. Simon, "'She Is So Neat,'" 60–61, 74–76; Rorabaugh, *Craft Apprentice,* 11, 102–4.

11. Simon, "'She Is So Neat,'" 117; Esther Bodwell to Sarah Carter, Mar. 24, 1846; Rorabaugh, *Craft Apprentice,* 72–75; Johnson, *Shopkeeper's Millennium,* 43–48; Wilentz, *Chants Democratic,* 48.

12. *New York Tribune,* quoted in Sumner, *History of Women,* 117, 156.

13. Halttunen, *Confidence Men and Painted Women,* 59–67. See also Hazen, *Panorama of Professions and Trades,* 62.

14. Beecher, *Treatise on Domestic Economy*, 115–16. For historians' views on tight-lacing and nineteenth-century fashion, see Banner, *American Beauty*, esp. 14–15, 48–49, 149–50; Roberts, "Exquisite Slave"; Kunzle, "Dress Reform" and *Fashion and Fetishism;* Steele, *Fashion and Eroticism*, 4–5, 99–100, 165–91; Hunt, *Glances and Glimpses*, 412–13.

15. Hunt, *Glances and Glimpses*, 134, 383, 402–3, 412–13.

16. Farrar, *Young Lady's Friend*, 103.

17. Arthur, "Blessings in Disguise," *Godey's Lady's Book* 21 (July 1840): 16.

18. Leslie, *Leonilla Lynmore, and Mr. and Mrs. Woodbridge*, 71–79, 82–83, 94, 96–102, 106–7.

19. Leslie, *Miss Leslie's Lady's House-Book;* Blumin, *Emergence of the Middle Class*, 185–86.

20. Alice B. Neal, "The Milliner's Dream; or, The Wedding-Bonnet," *Godey's Lady's Book* 52 (July 1855): 30; Burdett, *Chances and Changes*, 7–8.

21. Ingraham, "The Milliner's Apprentice; or, The False Teeth: A Story that Hath More Truth than Fiction in It," *Godey's Lady's Book* 22 (Jan. 1841): 194–95, 201 (later republished as *Caroline Archer; or, The Miliner's* [*sic*] *Apprentice: A Story that Hath More Truth than Fiction in It* [Boston: Edward P. Williams, 1844]); Weathersby, *J. H. Ingraham*, 90, 154.

22. *Caroline Tracy*, 18.

23. Gilbert and Gubar, *Madwoman in the Attic*, 16–44. See Reynolds, *Beneath the American Renaissance*, 363–65, for a discussion of the "feminist criminal," a stereotype to which Randall partially conforms.

24. Jones, *Tom, Dick, and Harry*, 45; Hicks, *Milliner and the Millionaire*, 8–9.

25. Foster, *New York by Gas-Light*, 66; *New York Dispatch*, reprinted in *Caroline Tracy*, 15; quotation from *New York Tribune*, reprinted in *Caroline Tracy*, 6.

26. Ryan, *Women in Public*, esp. 3–4, 143–46.

27. *Caroline Tracy*, 12, 18, 21; Gilbert and Gubar, *Madwoman in the Attic*, 28.

28. Ingraham, *Grace Weldon*, 3, 21–24, 53–55, 60, 64, 68–76, 81–84.

29. Emeret H. Sedge, "Grace Ellerslie," *Peterson's Magazine* 34 (Sept. 1858): 167, 172.

30. Ingraham, "Milliner's Apprentice," 194, 201–2, 205–6; Neal, "Milliner's Dream," 30–31.

31. Gilman, "'Cogs to the Wheels,'" esp. 185. See also Buhle, "Needlewomen," esp. 147–53.

32. Abelson, *When Ladies Go A-Thieving*, 13–41.

33. See Turbin, *Working Women*, 10–13, for a perceptive discussion of the pitfalls of relying on dichotomous categories to describe women's experiences.

Chapter 2: A Precarious Independence

1. Howells, *Woman's Reason*, 365–68, 378–91, 446–48.

2. Buhle, *Women and American Socialism*, 54–55; Penny, *Employments of Wom-*

en, v–xiii, and *Think and Act*, esp. 19–22, 25–26; Dall, *College, the Market, and the Court*, 178–79, 185–86; "Money-Making for Ladies," *Harper's New Monthly Magazine* 65 (June 1882): 112–16; Jennie June [pseud.], "What to Do with a Thousand Dollars," *D*, Sept. 1880, 489–91, and "What Can I Do?," *D*, Jan. 1870, 24–25; Mme. Demorest, "Business Education for Girls," *D*, Jan. 1870, 23. See also "Thousand Dollars," *D*, Aug. 1880, 474; H.P.R., "What She Did," *D*, Aug. 1885, 651.

3. Stimson, "Small Business," 337–40; Kessler-Harris, "Independence and Virtue."

4. See, for example, MA 83:140 (Eliza Brewster); MA 76:360 (Annie Fell), RGD.

5. Matthaei, *Economic History of Women*, 187–97; Kessler-Harris, *Out to Work*, esp. 53–70, 138–41. Whether or not female proprietors' propensity to cluster in businesses that catered to other women was a distinctly nineteenth-century phenomenon is a subject of debate. See Goldin, "Economic Status of Women," esp. 401–2.

6. Ten of 222 (4.5 percent) of the millinery and dressmaking proprietors listed in the 1860 directory could be identified as men; for 1890, these figures are 18 of 325 (5.5 percent). A substantial proportion of fancy goods dealers in Boston were women (about 28 percent in 1876), but male retailers still comprised the majority. No doubt this figure underestimates the number of female purveyors of fancy goods because some women listed only their initials, forsaking the titles "Miss" and "Mrs." Needless to say, there is no easy way to distinguish them from their male counterparts (*Boston Directory* 1860, 1876, 1890).

7. Blumin, *Emergence of the Middle Class*, 83–92.

8. L. M. Babcock, "Employments for Women.—No. 6: Millinery," *Delineator*, Oct. 1894, 516. Babcock's description was equally applicable to dressmaking.

9. *Boston Directory* (1860 and 1890).

10. *M* 24 (Dec. 1913): 50.

11. Boston business directories listed 159 milliners and dressmakers in 1850, 222 in 1860, 434 in 1870, and 621 in 1880. That number dropped to 477 in 1890 (I have no explanation for the decline) and rose to 905 in 1900. See table A-2 in the appendix.

12. In 1860, 15 percent of all dressmakers and milliners were proprietors; in 1870, this figure was 25 percent. To arrive at these figures, I divided the number of proprietors listed in the city directory by the total number of dressmakers and milliners listed in the federal manuscript population census for that year (see Essay on Primary Sources). Since neither source is perfect, these results should be considered rough estimates. Business directories may have excluded private milliners, women who served a small group of regular customers, as well as dressmakers who went out by the day.

13. MA 77:33, RGD; *Boston Evening Transcript*, May 11, 1878, 1.

14. In 1880, 65.8 percent (50 of 76) kept shops separate from their residences, while 34.2 percent (26 of 76) worked at home. Dressmakers adhered to a different pattern. Only 19 percent (16 of 84) kept shops, while 81 percent (68 of 84) worked at home. To arrive at these figures, I compared business and residential addresses for about half the milliners listed in the 1880 business directory and about a fifth of the dressmakers. Howells, *Woman's Reason*, 185, 376; King, *King's How-to-See Bos-*

ton, 99; Blumin, *Emergence of the Middle Class*, 86; Perry, *Millinery Trade*, 27–28; Van Kleeck, *Seasonal Industry*, 35–37, 108–9.

15. Married businesswomen, like married female wage earners, were almost certainly underreported in the census. For example, both James J. Grace and his wife, Margaret Costello Grace, were milliners. But the census of 1870 lists James as a milliner and Margaret as "keeping house." MA 78:439, RGD; 1870 FMPC, Boston, M593, reel 647, ward 11, p. 58, line 4. The R. G. Dun & Co. figures on marital status (table 3) may also reflect the preponderance of milliners, who also seem somewhat more likely than dressmakers to have been married. Since married women had access to greater amounts of capital than their single counterparts, it is not surprising that the Dun & Co. records would boast a larger proportion of married women than the census samples (see Essay on Primary Sources). For discussions of the uses of the Dun & Co. records, see Norris, *R. G. Dun & Co.*; Madison, "Evolution of Commercial Credit Reporting Agencies" and "Credit Reports."

16. MA 85:283; 87:261; 81:271, RGD. See also MA 78:82, 310, 333; 79:342; 91:331.

17. 1860 FMPC, Boston, M653, reel 523, ward 10, p. 476, line 39. Unfortunately, few of the women whose careers were detailed by Dun & Co. reporters turned up in earlier censuses. Thus, their social origins are difficult to determine. We can learn something about their backgrounds by considering the circumstances of prospective entrepreneurs—that is, of millinery and dressmaking workers. More than 80 percent of those who lived with their fathers were the daughters of either skilled or unskilled workingmen (see chap. 3, table 15). It should be noted that these statistics describe only those women who lived in two-parent families; half of all dressmaking and millinery workers were boarders who lived away from home. See chapter 3 for a more detailed discussion of these issues.

18. USBC, *Statistics of the Population . . . Ninth Census*, 778. Only one woman in either census sample had been born in France; 1870 FMPC, Boston, M593, reel 648, ward 14, p. 97, line 27.

19. MA 67:216 a/9; 86:225; 84:491; 78:183; 74:416; 86:49, RGD; Dublin, *Transforming Women's Work*, esp. 154–170.

20. Consider, for example, the very different resources of Sarah Weiscoff and Julia Butler, both of whom kept shop in Boston's fashionable downtown, catering to an "aristocratic trade"; Weiscoff owned property worth $6,200, Butler possessed "no means." MA 89:333; 85:283, RGD; *Boston Directory* (1884).

21. MA 82:169, 277; 81:470, RGD.

22. This conclusion is based on an analysis for the 195 proprietors for whom correspondents recorded an estimate of "means." Some reporters listed numerical estimates; others made do with such notations as "no means," "small means," "some means," or "means unknown." I assumed that amounts of $500 or less fell in the "no means" and "small means" categories.

	N	Percentage
No means, small means, or up to $500	120	61.5
Some means or $501+	42	21.5
Unknown	33	16.9
	195	99.9

23. To reach this conclusion, I traced the careers of the proprietors in the 1860 census sample. Not surprisingly, the women who fell under the scrutiny of Dun & Co. fared better; on average their businesses lasted nine years.

24. Griffen and Griffen, *Natives and Newcomers,* 103–17; Katz, *People of Hamilton,* 176–208.

25. Griffen and Griffen, *Natives and Newcomers,* table 6.2, p. 124. See also note 22, this chapter.

26. One study of business mortality from 1844–1927 found that 64 percent of retail, 66 percent of craft, and 67 percent of service businesses persisted for five years or less; this figure was 60 percent for Boston tradeswomen. See Hutchinson et al., "Study in Business Mortality," 509.

27. This conclusion is based on an examination of Dun & Co. records.

28. These figures, drawn from the 1860 census sample, compare male retail milliners to female retail milliners. The average property holdings of female dressmakers were $79 in 1860, $150 for female dressmakers and milliners combined. On average, men's businesses lasted for fifteen years. MA 74:378, RGD.

29. Howells, *Woman's Reason,* 43.

30. Blewett, *Men, Women, and Work,* esp. 117–41, 167–82, 197–218, 274–319; Turbin, *Working Women,* 107–28, 155–68, 172–90; Cameron, *Radicals of the Worst Sort.*

31. *Boston Directory* (1869), 238–40; Lucy Stone to Maria Hollander, Dec. 31, 1884, folder 1, and Deborah North Baldwin to Hollander, May 22, 1853, folder 2, Maria Theresa Baldwin Hollander Papers, no. AH734, SL. Of course, during the early nineteenth century the links between economic independence and political participation broke down under the pressure of a market revolution that increasingly eroded the prospect of independence for many white men. But ideological associations between independence and political rights persisted even in the wake of "universal" suffrage laws. See Watson, *Liberty and Power,* 42–53, 231–45.

32. New England Women's Club, *Report of the Committee on Needlewomen, April 12, 1869* (Boston: John Wilson and Son, 1869), p. 4, box 6, folder 12, New England Women's Club Records, SL.

33. 1860 FMPC, Boston, M653, reel 525, ward 12, p. 102, line 16; MA 86:226; 75:174; 78:310, RGD.

34. On this point, see Blewett, *Men, Women, and Work*, xvii–xxii.

35. Dublin, *Transforming Women's Work*, 187–90.

36. MA 88:335; 86:226; 91:331, RGD; 1860 FMPC, Boston, M653, reel 525, ward 12, p. 102, line 16.

37. Proprietors were more likely than nonproprietors to possess real or personal property. About 31 percent (35 of 112) of the former but only about 7 percent (49 of 663) of the latter owned property in 1860; the corresponding figures for 1870 are 10 percent (11 of 108) and 3 percent (12 of 398). Millinery and dressmaking workers who lived with their parents or adult brothers were excluded from this analysis; such women were unlikely to have held property in their own names. 1870 FMPC, Boston, M593, reel 648, ward 13, p. 137, line 25.

38. *D*, Feb. 1877, 109.

39. Chambers-Schiller, *Liberty, a Better Husband*. On working-class women, see Lasser, "'World's Dread Laugh,'" 77–79.

40. The social and economic experiences of the women in Chambers-Schiller's sample and those of native-born milliners and dressmakers overlapped to a certain extent; a very large proportion of the former worked as teachers and at least two as seamstresses. See her *Liberty, a Better Husband*, 277–80.

41. *D*, Jan. 1870, 24; Woods, *Diary*, 1, 3, 5. Woods's novel is autobiographical, though no doubt embellished. See Mainiero and Faust, *American Women Writers*, 4:456–57.

42. 1860 FMPC, Piscataquis County, Maine, M652, roll 433, p. 802, line 31; Bodwell to Carter, Mar. 24, 1846; anonymous to Carter, Nov. 5, 1847; Mary Carter to Carter, June 1, 1848; James R. Holmes to Carter, Dec. 31, 1854; Sarah Evans Holmes Clark to Carter, May 25, 1860, all in Holmes Family Papers, MHS.

43. Clark to Carter, Sept. 17, 1855; see also Clark to Carter, n.d. [185?]; Aug. 1854; Oct. 29, 1854; n.d, 1857, all in Holmes Family Papers, MHS.

44. 1860 FMPC, Piscataquis County, Maine, M652, roll 433, p. 802, line 31; Clark to Carter, Apr. 12, 1860; May 25, 1860, Holmes Family Papers, MHS.

45. 1870 FMPC, Piscataquis County, Maine, M593, roll 556, p. 762, line 21; Clark to Carter, Oct. 29, 1854, Holmes Family Papers, MHS.

46. Surviving correspondence does not include Carter's responses.

47. Chambers-Schiller, *Liberty, a Better Husband*, 18.

48. MA 91:136, 331, RGD. Thernstrom, *Poverty and Progress*, 20, estimated that unskilled laborers in the mid-nineteenth century earned $.75–1.50 a day (about $4.50–9.00 a week); dressmakers averaged $7.50 a week during the same period. See chap. 3 for a more detailed discussion of wages.

49. MA 84:491; 78:156; 89:327, RGD. I used business directories to calculate the length of Adams's and Capen's entrepreneurial careers.

50. MA 75:202; 76:327, RGD. Thirty-nine percent of the widows investigated by Dun & Co. were refused credit at some point during the course of their careers. This figure was 22 percent for never-married women and 27 percent for married women.

51. MA 71:200 a/24; 84:288; 89:33, RGD.

52. MA 86:231; 76:367, RGD.

53. MA 79:39; 87:223, RGD.

54. For example, 54.5 percent (18 of 33) of married proprietors, 36.4 percent (20 of 55) of widowed proprietors, and 35.8 percent (24 of 67) of never married proprietors had assets worth $500 or more. These figures, based on Dun & Co. records, include only those milliners and dressmakers for whom we have a numerical estimate of means. An analysis of business longevity by marital status, based on the 1860 census sample, reveals that married proprietors were in business, on average, for fifteen years, never married proprietors for six years, and widows for seven years.

55. *IM* 1 (June 1900): 30–31. See Chambers-Schiller, *Liberty, a Better Husband*, 190–204.

56. MA 81:112, 119, RGD. A census taker confirmed the Dun & Co. reporter's statement; he listed no occupation beside John Forgeot's name. 1870 FMPC, Boston, M593, reel 645, ward 8, p. 10, line 15.

57. *IM* 1 (June 1900): 30.

58. Dressmakers and milliners were not the only occupational group that experienced tensions between work and marriage. See Drachman, "'My "Partner,"'" 231–42.

59. MA 75:91, 195; 71:96, 200 a/3, 200d; 75:44; 78:179–80, RGD.

60. MA 71:616, RGD.

61. These statements should be interpreted with caution. Property held in Margaret's name could not be seized by James's creditors.

62. MA 78:82, 105–6, 111, 439, 442, RGD; 1870 FMPC, Boston, M593, reel 647, ward 11, p. 58, line 4.

63. MA 73:390, RGD; King, *King's How-to-See Boston*, 99.

64. MA 73:390, RGD; Ernst, *Law of Married Women*, 128.

65. Ernst, *Law of Married Women*, esp. 140–42.

66. Basch, *In the Eyes of the Law*, esp. 208–11; Griffen and Griffen, *Natives and Newcomers*, 114–17; Lebsock, *Free Women*, 56–86; Hoff, *Law, Gender and Injustice*, 121–32, 187–90.

67. For a demonstration of the complexity of these statutes, see Ernst, *Law of Married Women*, a treatise designed to "explain" property laws for married women.

68. *IM* 1 (June 1900): 30.

69. MA 85:32, 33; 80:448, RGD.

70. Blumin, *Emergence of the Middle Class*, 121–33.

71. MA 70:612; 82:2, RGD.

72. Earling, *Whom to Trust*, 83–84; Deutsch, "Business of Women," 18.

73. Gerber, "Cutting Out Shylock," 626–27; MA 85:355; 73:114; 80:186, RGD.

74. Berthoff, "Independence and Enterprise," 41–44; Robertson, "Small Business Ethic"; Hutchinson et al., "Study in Business Mortality," 497–514; Stimson, "Small Business," 337–40.

75. Blair, *Clubwoman as Feminist;* Smith-Rosenberg, *Disorderly Conduct,* 245–96.

76. *IM* 1 (June 1900): 30.

77. On this point, see Taylor, "Work that Women Do," 1, 9.

Chapter 3: The Female Aristocracy of Labor

1. Laughton diary, Aug. 27, 1837, EI. The classic statement of this view is Tentler, *Wage-Earning Women,* esp. 3–10, 27–57, 180–81. For a variation on this theme, see Eisenstein, *Give Us Bread,* 19–22, 32–33.

2. Benson, *Counter Cultures,* 227–58; Turbin, *Working Women,* esp. 46–62, 71–102; Blewett, *Men, Women, and Work,* esp. 106–10, 122–23, 155–63, 321–23. See also Cobble, *Dishing It Out,* esp. 34–58.

3. Allinson, *Dressmaking,* 162.

4. Ibid.; Allinson, *Industrial Experience;* Perry, *Millinery Trade;* Bryner, *Dressmaking and Millinery;* Van Kleeck, *Wages* and *Seasonal Industry.*

5. Allinson, *Dressmaking,* 6.

6. 1870 FMPC, M593, reel 640, ward 1, p. 43, line 28. See also note 1 (this chapter) above.

7. Unless otherwise noted, all information concerning Boston milliners and dressmakers in 1860 and 1870 is based on two samples drawn from the federal manuscript population schedules; these are described in greater detail in the essay on sources. Bryner, *Dressmaking and Millinery,* 23.

8. Kessler-Harris, *Woman's Wage,* 13; Matthaei, *Economic History of Women,* 141–43.

9. Baron and Klepp, "'If I Didn't Have My Sewing Machine,'" esp. 22–25; Turbin, *Working Women,* esp. 49–52, 208–14; Blewett, *Men, Women, and Work,* xvi, 104–10, 138–39, 324–25; Benson, *Counter Cultures,* 201–3.

10. Mary Kyle Dallas, "Martha Mead; or, Money's Worth and Money's Weight," *New York Ledger,* Nov. 7, 1868, 1; Van Kleeck, *Seasonal Industry,* 114; Allinson, *Dressmaking,* 137–38; Perry, *Millinery Trade,* 95–96; MMWC, *Report on the Wages of Women,* 28.

11. About 31 percent (255 of 827) of Boston dressmaking workers and 13.8 percent (72 of 521) of the city's millinery workers in 1860 were age thirty or older. In 1870, these figures (based on a 45 percent sample) were 33.8 percent (197 of 582) and 18.6 percent (26 of 140). 1860 FMPC, Boston, M653, reels 520–25; 1870 FMPC, Boston, M593, reels 640–49. For ages of milliners in Boston and Philadelphia, see Perry, *Millinery Trade,* 97. In 1914, 11 percent of New York milliners were at least thirty years old. See Van Kleeck, *Wages,* 64.

12. Sumner, *History of Women,* 137.

13. Kessler-Harris, *Out to Work,* esp. 68–70, 116–17, 128–41; Kemp, *Women's Work,* esp. 209–51; Bradley, *Men's Work, Women's Work;* Reskin and Hartmann, *Women's Work, Men's Work; IM* 1 (Aug. 1900): 79; 1 (June 1900): 30–31.

14. Of the dressmaking and millinery workers who appeared in the 1860 Boston

manuscript census, 28.2 percent (381 of 1,351) had a least one foreign-born parent; 83.5 percent (318) of these women were second-generation Irish. These figures include only women who lived with at least one parent. In 1905, 71.8 percent of Boston dressmakers had foreign-born parents, according to Allinson, *Dressmaking*, 75. On the presence of new immigrants, especially Russian Jews, in *wholesale* (that is, factory) millinery, see Van Kleeck, *Seasonal Industry*, 67; Perry, *Millinery Trade*, 92, 95.

15. Van Kleeck, *Seasonal Industry*, 68; Des Moulins, "Dressmaker's Life Story," 943.

16. Des Moulins, "Dressmaker's Life Story," 946.

17. Dressmaking offered greater opportunities to African American women than did many other pursuits (Table 12). It is difficult to determine the proportion of black women within the trades before 1900. In Boston in 1860 they accounted for 6 of 1,348 dressmakers, but no milliners. Published census material for 1870, which includes occupational portraits of several cities, provides information on ethnicity but not race.

18. 1860 FMPC, Boston, M653, reel 521, ward 6, p. 898, line 21; reel 525, ward 12, p. 102, line 16.

19. Turbin, *Working Women*, 76–91.

20. 1860 FMPC, Boston, M653, reel 524, ward 11, p. 910, line 11; reel 521, ward 6, p. 801, line 3; 1870 FMPC, Boston, M593, reel 642, ward 4, p. 134, line 4; 1860 FMPC, Boston, M653, reel 525, ward 12, p. 549, line 16; reel 521, ward 3, p. 777, line 16; reel 522, ward 9, p. 895, line 5.

21. Van Kleeck, *Seasonal Industry*, 59–60.

22. Ibid.; Allinson, *Dressmaking*, 69.

23. For the occupational distribution of Boston's male labor force in 1880, see Thernstrom, *Other Bostonians*, 50, table 4.1. Allinson, *Dressmaking*, 74–75; Bryner, *Dressmaking and Millinery*, 55; Perry, *Millinery Trade*, 98–99.

24. *D*, July 1885, 611.

25. Blewett, *We Will Rise*, 16; see also Turbin, "Beyond Conventional Wisdom," esp. 48–54.

26. About fifteen percent (198 of 1,348) of all nonproprietors in Boston in 1860 had been born in Maine, 7.0 percent (95) in New Hampshire, and 2.2 percent (29) in Vermont. It is impossible to ascertain how many Massachusetts natives (39.3 percent or 530 of 1,348) had been born in Boston and how many came from elsewhere in the state. In most cases, the census taker recorded state of birth only. 1860 FMPC, M653, reels 520–25.

27. The classic interpretation of migration as desperation is Thernstrom, *Other Bostonians*, esp. 38–42. For a summary of dissenting views and an alternative hypothesis, see Dublin, "Rural-Urban Migrants," esp. 628–32. See also Dublin, *Women at Work*, 23–57; Preston, "Learning a Trade"; 1860 FMPC, Boston, M653, reel 532, ward 10, p. 399, line 22.

28. In 1860, the average age of boarders was 28, compared to 23 for workers who lived with their parents.

29. 1870 FMPC, Boston, reel 647, ward 11, p. 10, line 14. In 1860, 93.3 percent of boarding dressmakers and milliners held no real or personal property.

30. The average age of *all* boarders in 1860 was 27.6, of boarders who lived with proprietors, 27. Penny, *Employments of Women*, 319, 325; Lewis, "Female Entrepreneurs," 4; Johnson, *Shopkeeper's Millennium*, 48–55; Wilentz, *Chants Democratic*, 48.

31. Dublin, *Transforming Women's Work*, 201–4; USBC, *Statistics of Women at Work*, 73, 80.

32. Perry, *Millinery Trade*, 14; Bryner, *Dressmaking and Millinery*, 84.

33. DeVault, *Sons and Daughters*, 58–60, 102–3; Allinson, *Dressmaking*, 68–69.

34. Allinson, *Dressmaking*, 69; Van Kleeck, *Seasonal Industry*, 61.

35. DeVault, *Sons and Daughters*, 97–104; Turbin, "Beyond Conventional Wisdom," 53–54.

36. Allinson, *Dressmaking*, 77; Perry, *Millinery Trade*, 14.

37. Matthaei, *Economic History of Women*, 147–49; DeVault, *Sons and Daughters*, 97–104.

38. These figures probably underestimate the extent of generational continuity. Census takers often failed to record married women's occupations. Moreover, we have no means of learning how many mothers were dressmakers, milliners, or tailoresses before marriage.

39. 1870 FMPC, Boston, reel 645, ward 8, p. 241, line 12; *Boston Directory* (1865–1880).

40. See Blewett, *Men, Women, and Work*, xx–xxi, and *We Will Rise*, 15–19.

41. Van Kleeck, *Seasonal Industry*, 61.

42. Allinson, *Dressmaking*, 72–73; de Aguirre, *Women in the Business World*, 202–6.

43. Porter, *Operative's Friend*, 17; Campbell, *Prisoners of Poverty*, 61; Perry, *Millinery Trade*, 16–18; Allinson, *Dressmaking*, 41. For a discussion of similar attitudes among collar sewers, see Turbin, *Working Women*, 57–58.

44. Steele, *Fashion and Eroticism*, 3.

45. Penny, *Employments of Women*, 315, and *Think and Act*, 366; Wright, *Working Girls*, 118–121, 125; Sanger, *History of Prostitution*, 524.

46. Baron, "Gender and Labor History," 27; Blewett, *Men, Women, and Work*, 222–25; Perry, *Millinery Trade*, 17–18; Allinson, *Dressmaking*, 79–80.

47. Allinson, *Dressmaking*, 79.

48. Benson, "'Customers Ain't God,'" 191.

49. Steedman, *Landscape for a Good Woman*, 6–9.

50. Lerner, "Lady and the Mill Girl"; see also Abelson et al., "Interview with Joan Scott," 51–52.

51. Carey, "Essays on the Public Charities," 194; Martineau, *Society in America*, 3:149; Penny, *Employments of Women*, 315; Sumner, *History of Women*, 145–46.

52. Wright, *Working Girls*, 76–81.

53. Allinson, *Dressmaking*, 130–31. The proportion of milliners earning weekly

wages of nine dollars or more (57.2 percent) was calculated using information presented in Van Kleeck's table 5 (*Wages*, 28). Only retail milliners were included in this analysis.

54. In the mid-nineteenth century, the average dressmaker earned about as much as an unskilled male laborer, between $.75 and $1.50 per day. In 1913, more than half of the makers in the Boston and Philadelphia millinery trades earned less than $8 a week. This was true of only 18 percent of male textile operatives in New England in 1900. Thernstrom, *Poverty and Progress*, 20; Perry, *Millinery Trade*, 73; USBC, *Special Reports*, 1145.

55. Kessler-Harris, *Woman's Wage*, 13.

56. The relative proportion of skilled to unskilled workers is difficult to determine, especially for the nineteenth century. Bryner estimated that one out of every eight Cleveland dressmakers became a draper, the twentieth-century equivalent of fitter. Allinson, on the other hand, classified a third of Boston modistes as "professional workers"; these included forewomen, cutters, fitters, and drapers (by the early twentieth century, work in the larger dressmaking shops had become considerably more specialized; see chap. 7). Perry and Van Kleeck agreed that trimmers accounted for about 12 percent of all milliners. In doing so, they may have painted an overly dreary picture. Twentieth-century trade studies tended to focus on larger shops simply because larger concerns were more likely to furnish payroll data that could be analyzed. Therefore, they may have underestimated the number of workers who occupied the most privileged positions. The "true" ratio of trimmers to other workers may have been closer to one in four than their figure of one in eight. Certainly, smaller shops were more typical of the nineteenth century and were the norm in rural areas and small towns as late as the 1910s. See Bryner, *Dressmaking and Millinery*, 35, 53; Allinson, *Dressmaking*, 129, 134, 138; Perry, *Millinery Trade*, 80, 90–91; Van Kleeck, *Wages*, 16, and *Seasonal Industry*, 110; Richardson, *Long Day*, 51, 83, 216, 232.

57. Allinson, *Dressmaking*, 138; Perry, *Millinery Trade*, 90.

58. Kessler-Harris, *Woman's Wage*, 7–22; McDowell *Standard System*, n.p.

59. Van Kleeck, *Seasonal Industry*, 25; Allinson, *Dressmaking*, 83.

60. Penny, *Employments of Women*, 319; MBSL, *Report*, 217; Allinson, *Dressmaking*, 83, 85; Perry, *Millinery Trade*, 44–45; *MTR* 22 (Feb. 1897): 31–32.

61. Wright, *Working Girls*, 98–102; Van Kleeck, *Seasonal Industry*, 79–80, 122; Allinson, *Dressmaking*, 83–94; Bryner, *Dressmaking and Millinery*, 42; Perry, *Millinery Trade*, 14.

62. Keyssar, *Out of Work*, 96–109.

63. Perry, *Millinery Trade*, 14.

64. Wright, *Working Girls*, 100–101; Allinson, *Dressmaking*, 15; Van Kleeck, *Seasonal Industry*, 95–96.

65. Bryner, *Dressmaking and Millinery*, 69; Allinson, *Industrial Experience*, 95.

66. Penny, *Employments of Women*, 320; Allinson, *Dressmaking*, 106.

67. Perry, *Millinery Trade*, 91.

68. Penny, *Employments of Women*, 315; WWPU, *Fifth Annual Report*, 21–22.

69. Woods, *Diary*, 66–68, 72–74, 89–92, esp. 84–88; MBSL, *Report*, 216.

70. Penny, *Employments of Women*, 315, 325, and *Think and Act*, 58; *IM* 1 (July 1900): 53; Bryner, *Dressmaking and Millinery*, 55–56; Van Kleeck, *Wages*, 73.

71. Woods, *Diary*, 85, 165; Penny, *Employments of Women*, 325–26; MBSL, *Report*, 217.

72. Protective legislation varied from state to state. See Dye, *As Equals and as Sisters*, 145–46, 154; Bryner, *Dressmaking and Millinery*, 74–75; Allinson, *Dressmaking*, 113–23; Van Kleeck, *Seasonal Industry*, 139–42; Perry, *Millinery Trade*, 45, 62–65; Edgar Fawcett, "The Woes of the New York Working-Girl," *Arena* 5 (Dec. 1891): 29.

73. Van Kleeck, *Wages*, 73; Perry, *Millinery Trade*, 63; Campbell, *Prisoners of Poverty*, 62.

74. *Report of the Women's Educational and Industrial Union . . . 1885* (Boston: n.p., 1885), pp. 35–36, in carton 1, vol. 1, and Minutes, Protective Committee, Dec. 19, 1892, carton 6, vol. 106, WEIU (unprocessed); Willett, *Employment of Women*, 82; Allinson, *Dressmaking*, 41, 45, 147–50.

75. Bradlee diary, esp. Nov. 9–27, 1875, MHS; Deutsch, "Learning to Talk," 381, 388–94; Blair, *Clubwoman as Feminist*, 73–91; *Women's Educational and Industrial Union* (Cambridge, Mass.: Co-Operative Press, 1899), p. 51, in carton 1, vol. 2, WEIU (unprocessed).

76. Wirt Sikes, "Among the Poor Girls," *Putnam's Magazine*, Apr. 1868, excerpted in Stein, *Out of the Sweatshop*, 12–15; WWPU, *Fifth Annual Report*, 16–25; Campbell, *Prisoners of Poverty*, 46–47, 58–60; *Report of the Women's Educational and Industrial Union . . . 1881* (Boston: n.p., 1881), p. 41, and *Report . . . 1880* (Boston: n.p., 1880), p. 38, both in carton 1, vol. 1, WEIU (unprocessed); MA 79:284, RGD.

77. Formanek-Brunell, *Made to Play House*, 77–81; Murphy, "Her Own Boss," 174–75; Daily, "Woman's Concern," 31; Campbell, *Prisoners of Poverty*, 46, 57–59.

78. Penny, *Employments of Women*, 317, and *Think and Act*, 26, 70; de Aguirre, *Women in the Business World*, 37–38.

79. Stansell, *City of Women*, 118; Wilentz, *Chants Democratic*, 33, 123, 127–30.

80. Penny, *Employments of Women*, 315.

81. Wilentz, *Chants Democratic*, 107–21.

82. Campbell, *Prisoners of Poverty*, 60; Allinson, *Dressmaking*, 54–58.

83. Stansell, *City of Women*, 145; Andrews and Bliss, *History of Women*, 39–40, 81, 119, 125, 129–31; *FTR*, Nov. 11, 1863, 98.

84. Turbin, *Working Women*, 111; Andrews and Bliss, *History of Women*, 119, 125, 129–31.

85. Turbin, *Working Women;* Blewett, *Men, Women, and Work;* Van Kleeck, *Seasonal Industry*, 69.

86. Turbin, *Working Women*, 94–99; Blewett, *Men, Women, and Work*, 168, 225.

87. Andrews and Bliss, *History of Women*, 18; Tentler, *Wage-Earning Women*, 78–80.

88. *FTR*, Apr. 2, 1864, 70.

89. *Report of Manufacturing Industries*, pt. 2, 70–76; Dublin, *Women at Work;* Blewett, *Men, Women, and Work;* Turbin, *Working Women;* Cameron, *Radicals of the Worst Sort;* Van Kleeck, *Seasonal Industry*, 69, 135, quotation from 135.

90. De Aguirre, *Women in the Business World*, 202–3; Benson, *Counter Cultures*, esp. 240–65.

91. On the relationship between upward mobility and labor protest, see Dublin, "Women Workers."

92. MA 87:261; 78:333; 79:342, RGD; *IM* 5 (Oct. 1904): 24; Bryner, *Dressmaking and Millinery*, 39–41, 54; Perry, *Millinery Trade*, 80; MA 89:333; 76:327; 79:342, RGD.

93. Woods, *Diary*, 77–78, 99, 105, 114–16.

94. Allinson, *Dressmaking*, 61; Perry, *Millinery Trade*, 63.

95. Brody, "Labor and Small-Scale Enterprise," esp. 273–76; Des Moulins, "Dressmaker's Life Story," 946; Campbell, *Prisoners of Poverty*, 62.

96. On the concept of work culture, see Melosh, *"Physician's Hand,"* esp. 5–6, 175–77, 207–19; Benson, *Counter Cultures*, 227–30; Leonardo, "Women's Work"; Costello, "'WEA're Worth It!'"; Lamphere, "Bringing the Family to Work"; Zavella, "'Abnormal Intimacy'"; Cooper, *Once a Cigar Maker*, esp. 2–7, 123–35, 218–40.

97. Van Kleeck, *Wages*, 62, and *Seasonal Industry*, 93; Allinson, *Dressmaking*, 66, 108; Des Moulins, "Dressmaker's Life Story," 945.

98. Penny, *Employments of Women*, 317; Allinson, *Dressmaking*, 64–65; Bryner, *Dressmaking and Millinery*, 43; *MH*, Spring 1908, 22; *M* 24 (July 1913): 71.

99. *IM* 1 (July 1900): 53; Montgomery, *Workers' Control*, 11–15; Cooper, *Once a Cigar Maker*, 41–42.

100. MA 88:335, RGD.

Chapter 4: The Social Relations of Consumption

1. Eliot, diary, June 9, 1864, Sophia Smith Collection, Smith College, Northampton, Mass.

2. Boorstin, *Americans*, 91–100; Kidwell and Christman, *Suiting Everyone*, esp. 14–17, 53–64, 135–39; Daves, *Ready-Made Miracle*, esp. 9–15.

3. George Fish, "An Essay on Millinery," *M* 22 (Apr. 1912): 48.

4. Cott, *Bonds of Womanhood*, 1. For an excellent discussion of difference, see Hewitt, "Beyond the Search for Sisterhood."

5. Boorstin, *Americans*, 91–164; Ewen, *Captains of Consciousness*, esp. 3–19; Fox and Lears, *Culture of Consumption*, 3–38; Benson, *Counter Cultures;* Blumin, *Emergence of the Middle Class*, 138–91; Lears, "Beyond Veblen."

6. Lears, "From Salvation to Self-Realization," 18.

7. Ryan, *Cradle of the Middle Class*, 199–203; Halttunen, *Confidence Men and Painted Women*, 61–63; Blumin, "Hypothesis of Middle-Class Formation," 330–34, and *Emergence of the Middle Class*, 184–88.

8. Boydston, *Home and Work*, 76–85.

9. Horowitz, *Morality of Spending*, xxvi; Fernandez, "'If a Woman Had Taste,'" esp. 1–15, 103–9.

10. Kidwell, *Cutting a Fashionable Fit*, esp. 94–98.

11. Cott, *Bonds of Womanhood*, 66–74; Ryan, *Cradle of the Middle Class*, esp. 146–85, 198–229.

12. Allinson, *Dressmaking*, 29–52; Perry, *Millinery Trade*, 27–43; MA 75:190; 83:336; 84:345; 89:327, RGD.

13. Blumin, "Hypothesis of Middle-Class Formation," 313–14, 319–29, and *Emergence of the Middle Class*, 83–107.

14. NY 130:210; 141:274; 258:3423, RGD; MA 69:599 a/120; 76:318; 80:141, RGD; Woods, *Diary*.

15. Charlotte F. Paddock, "Miss Esther's Millinery Album," *IM* 1 (Dec. 1900): 32; Perry, *Millinery Trade*, 30. Similar arrangements persisted into the 1940s and 1950s. See Eva Moseley (Curator of Manuscripts, Schlesinger Library, Radcliffe College, Cambridge, Mass.), interview, June 21, 1989, 27, SL.

16. Perry, *Millinery Trade*, 31; *M* 22 (Apr. 1912): 43.

17. The Boston city directory for 1930 listed 503 self-employed dressmakers and 196 millinery shops, a sharp decline (42 percent) from twenty years earlier (845 dressmakers and 357 milliners) but still a considerable number. *Boston Directory* (1910 and 1930).

18. Browne to her mother, n.d. [June 1857?], folder 2, Browne Family Papers, #MC 232, SL.

19. Allinson, *Dressmaking*, 11; Perry, *Millinery Trade*, 39.

20. *IM* 16 (Feb. 1915): 79.

21. Van Kleeck, *Seasonal Industry*, 64.

22. Banner, *American Beauty*, 28–29.

23. Broughton, *Suggestions for Dressmakers*, 36–37; Keckley, *Behind the Scenes;* Moseley, interview, 8; Woods, *Diary*, esp. 144–45, 150–58, 172–75, 195–200; *IM* 1 (May 1900): 45.

24. Smith-Rosenberg, *Disorderly Conduct*, 53–76. See also Cott, *Bonds of Womanhood;* DuBois et al., "Politics and Culture." Daily, "Woman's Concern," and Murphy, "Her Own Boss," suggest that intimacy and friendship characterized relationships between tradeswomen and their clients. Their conclusions are not surprising given their focus on small towns; still they probably overemphasize the degree of harmony that prevailed.

25. Hochschild, *Managed Heart*, esp. 3–23, 162–84; "As a Dressmaker Sees Women," 8. See also Moseley, interview, 15. Present-day hairdressing requires men's as well as women's emotional labor, although many of the male hairdressers interviewed for one study spoke of the "control" that they had gained over their clients. See Schroder, *Engagement*, 4–6, 75, 139.

26. *D*, July 1879, 398.

27. Dudden, *Serving Women*, 5–8, 12–43; Mary Huntting to Bessie Huntting, Feb.

23, 1855, box 1, folder 10; Bessie Huntting to Philema Slate Huntting, n.d., box 1, folder 1, Huntting-Rudd Family Papers, #MC 284, SL; *IM* 1 (June, 1900): 30.

28. MA 74:440; NY 243:1959; 312:463, RGD; MA 81:241; 89:330, RGD.

29. Van Kleeck, *Seasonal Industry*, 35.

30. Kidwell, *Cutting a Fashionable Fit*, 13–16; Blumin, "Hypothesis of Middle-Class Formation," 312–16, 318, 330–32; Stansell, *City of Women*, 164; MA 78:82, 183, RGD; Perry, *Millinery Trade*, 34; *IM* 1 (Sept. 1900): 65. I have taken the liberty of translating the journal's clumsy attempt at African American dialect.

31. Beecher and Stowe, *American Woman's Home*, 325.

32. Hale diary, July 11, 1859, Hale Family Papers, Sophia Smith Collection, Smith College, Northampton, Mass.; "As a Dressmaker Sees Women," 8; Marion Harland, "The Incapacity of Business Women," *North American Review* 149 (1889): 711.

33. Almy to Mary Almy, [June 3, 1908], box 2, folder 24, Almy Family Papers, #MC 235, SL; see the various obituaries in box 2, folder 49; "Report of Investigations Regarding the Opportunities for Skilled Labor in New Bedford," typescript, n.d., p. 4, box 7, folder 59, WEIU#B-8, ; Keckley, *Behind the Scenes*, esp. 152, 208–20, quotation from 152.

34. Smith-Rosenberg, *Disorderly Conduct*, 53–76; Moseley, interview, 8. See also Rollins, *Between Women*, 166–67.

35. Keckley, *Behind the Scenes*, 152; "As a Dressmaker Sees Women," 8.

36. Boydston, *Home and Work*, esp. 75–98; Cowan, *More Work for Mother*, esp. 40–68.

37. Katzman, *Seven Days a Week*, 146–50; Dudden, *Serving Women*, 108–26; Stansell, *City of Women*, 159–61; Moseley, interview, 14–15.

38. Quotation from Alice B. Neal, "The Milliner's Dream; or, The Wedding-Bonnet," *Godey's Lady's Book* 52 (July 1855): 30.

39. *Stranger's Guide*, n.p.; Bessie Huntting to Philema Slate Huntting, Nov. 9, 1850, box 1, folder 1, Huntting-Rudd Family Papers, #MC 284, SL.

40. See Deutsch's discussion of Boston's Fragment Society in "Learning to Talk," 402.

41. Benson, *Counter Cultures*, 128–34, 139–46.

42. Duniway, *Path Breaking*, 16–27.

43. Parton, *Autobiography of Mother Jones*, 11–13.

44. Wilson, *Adorned in Dreams*, 3; Steele, *Fashion and Eroticism*, 8–9.

45. Sarah Elizabeth Appleton Lawrence diary, June 15, 1853, box 7, vol. 7, A. A. Lawrence Diaries, MHS; Steele, *Fashion and Eroticism*, 51–71.

46. Steele, *Fashion and Eroticism*, 145–50; Banner, *American Beauty*, 86–105; Lauer and Lauer, "Battle of the Sexes"; Leach, *True Love*, 243–260.

47. Woods, *Diary*, 2; Walker, *Woman's Thoughts*, 66.

48. Lawrence diary, Mar. 15, 1858, A. A. Lawrence Diaries, MHS. My discussion of dress reform relies heavily on Steele's analysis of the phenomenon in *Fashion and Eroticism*, 145–50, 161–72. The art historian David Kunzle also emphasizes the antifeminist aspects of dress reform, although his convictions regarding the plea-

sures of tight-lacing are less than convincing. See his "Dress Reform" and *Fashion and Fetishism*.

49. Tobey, "Educated Woman," 118.

50. Broughton, *Suggestions for Dressmakers*, 37–38; MA 76:282; 80:262, RGD.

51. Woods, *Diary*, 69; Woolson, *Woman in American Society*, 232–33.

52. Browne to her mother, n.d.; n.d. [June 1857?], folder 2, Browne Family Papers, #MC 232, SL.

53. Lincoln to Harris, Dec. 28, [1864], reprinted in Turner and Turner, *Mary Todd Lincoln*, 196; Baker, *Mary Todd Lincoln*, 165–66, 192–96; Lawrence diary, Nov. 2, 1852, A. A. Lawrence Diaries, MHS.

54. *Women's Educational and Industrial Union . . . 1897* (Cambridge, Mass.: Co-Operative Press, [1897]), p. 50, in carton A, vol. 2, WEIU (unprocessed).

55. Schroder, *Engagement*, 132–35; Lears, "From Salvation to Self-Realization," 17–27; Mary Carter to Sarah Carter, June 1, 1848, 1841–49 folder, Holmes Family Papers, MHS; Des Moulins, "Dressmaker's Life Story," 946.

56. *Guide to Dressmaking*, 10–14; Fox and Lears, *Culture of Consumption*, vii–xvii.

57. Woods, *Diary*, 84–88, 99–103, 165–66; "As a Dressmaker Sees Women," 8.

58. Almy diary, Dec. 16–18, 1880, box 1, vol. 23, Almy Family Papers, #MC 235, SL.

59. Hartley, *Ladies' Book*, 25, 27–32.

60. Amelia Burnett diary, Sept. 26, 1847; Martha Fisher Anderson diary, Nov. 26, 1847, Sept. 23, 1869, and July 19, 1878, MHS. For evidence on the size of women's wardrobes and the place of fashion in women's lives, see especially the diaries of Persis Sibley Andrews, 1842–57, Dabney Papers; Mary Elizabeth Bradlee, 1871–76; Charlotte F. Foster, 1851, 1858, 1878, 1880–83; and Sarah Goell Putnam, 1868–85; and the papers of the Crosby and Holmes families (all at MHS).

61. *D*, Feb. 1870, 55; Thernstrom, *Poverty and Progress*, 20.

62. Sewall to Abby Sewall, May 8, 1862; Mar. 8, 1863, folder 9, Sewall Family Papers, #MC 385, SL; Woods, *Diary*, 39.

63. Business card, Mrs. J. J. Grace, "Hats," box 2, WC; Almy diary, Sept. 20, 1880, box 1, vol. 23, Almy Family Papers, #MC 235, SL.

64. S. R. Hodges to Katharine Craddoc Hodges, May 11, 1860, folder 1, Hodges Family Papers, #A H688, SL; Beecher and Stowe, *American Woman's Home*, 355; Keckley, *Behind the Scenes*, 220–25. See, for example, Lucy Parker diary, Feb. 3, June 7, Oct. 10, and Nov. 17, 1842; Jan. 3, 1843; Susan C. Clarke diary, Oct. 15, 1846, 1830–50 box, folder 1846, Warren-Clarke Papers; Elizabeth Clapp diary, May 20, May 29, June 7, 1852, David Clapp Papers, all at MHS.

65. Woods, *Diary*, 116; Browne to her mother, [June 1857?], folder 2, Browne Family Papers, #MC 232, SL.

66. Lincoln to Harris, Nov. 21, 1861, reprinted in Turner and Turner, *Mary Todd Lincoln*, 115.

67. Des Moulins, "Dressmaker's Life Story," 944; see also Moseley, interview, 6.

68. Gardner, "'Paradise of Fashion,'" 62; Perry, *Millinery Trade*, 32; Allinson, *Dressmaking*, 55–57; "As a Dressmaker Sees Women," 38; *MH*, Winter 1910–11, 24; Des Moulins, "Dressmaker's Life Story," 946.

69. *MH*, Winter 1910–11, 24; Wilbur, *Every-day Business*, 101.

70. Wilbur, *Every-day Business*, 101. I recorded the name of every tenth tailor (N = 38) listed in the Boston business directory for 1880 and then searched for these individuals in the Dun & Co. records, finding entries for 22 of them. Credit reporters offered numerical estimates of worth for 18 of these concerns. Using the *lowest* estimate given for each, their assets averaged $10,750. While 51.8 percent of the dressmakers and milliners who appeared in the Dun & Co. ledgers possessed "no means," "small means," or up to $500 (see chap. 2, note 22), this was true of only 2 (9 percent) of the tailors in the sample.

71. *Report of the Women's Educational and Industrial Union . . . 1880* (Boston: n.p., 1880), p. 38, in carton 1, vol. 1, WEIU (unprocessed); Blair, *Clubwoman as Feminist*, 73–91, esp. 82.

72. *Report of the WEIU . . . 1891* (Boston: George E. Crosby, 1891), pp. 42–43, in carton 1, vol. 1; *Women's Educational and Industrial Union . . . 1896* (Cambridge, Mass.: Press of the Cambridge Co-Operative Society, [1896]), p. 43, in carton 1, vol. 2, WEIU (unprocessed). The more analytical approach was adopted in two twentieth-century studies, conducted under the auspices of the WEIU. See Allinson, *Dressmaking*, 54–58; Perry, *Millinery Trade*, 32. On changes that affected the WEIU, see Deutsch, "Learning to Talk," 392–97.

73. Minutes, Protective Committee, Mar. 8, 1880, carton 6, vol. 106, WEIU (unprocessed); *Report of the WEIU . . . 1882* (Boston: n.p., 1882), p. 47, in carton 1, vol. 1, WEIU (unprocessed).

74. MA 78:156, RGD; 1870 FMPC, Boston, M593, reel 642, ward 4, p. 13, line 239; *Report of the WEIU . . . 1880*, 38; *Report of the WEIU . . . 1888* (Boston: ["Washington Press"] George E. Crosby, 1888), p. 35; *Report of the WEIU . . . 1885* (Boston: n.p., 1885), p. 35, in carton 1, vol. 1, WEIU (unprocessed).

75. Allinson, *Dressmaking*, 55–56.

76. Cott, *Bonds of Womanhood*, 45; Ryan, *Cradle of the Middle Class*, 199–201; Blumin, *Emergence of the Middle Class*, 184–88; Abelson, *When Ladies Go A-Thieving*, 166–67; Boydston, *Home and Work*, esp. 87–88, 142–63.

77. Fish, "Essay on Millinery," 48.

78. Howells, *Woman's Reason*, 185, and *Habits of Good Society*, 178.

79. Veblen, *Theory of the Leisure Class*, 126–27.

80. Penny, *Think and Act*, 193.

81. S. E. Hodges to Katherine Craddoc Hodges, n.d. [1860], folder 1, Hodges Family Papers, #A H688, SL; Keckley, *Behind the Scenes*, 146–51; Turner and Turner, *Mary Todd Lincoln*, 163–64; Baker, *Mary Todd Lincoln*, 234–35.

82. MA 79:284, RGD.

83. Minutes, Protective Committee, Nov. 19, 1883, carton 6, vol. 106, WEIU (unprocessed). See also *Report of the WEIU . . . 1882*, and *Report of the WEIU . . .*

1889 (Boston: George E. Crosby, 1889), p. 39, in carton 1, vol. 1, WEIU (unprocessed); Dudden, *Serving Women,* 183.

84. Woods, *Diary,* 111–12; *IM* 1 (Aug. 1900): 59.

85. The exact amount of Mary Lincoln's bill is a subject of dispute; for varying estimates, see Keckley, *Behind the Scenes,* 146–51; Turner and Turner, *Mary Todd Lincoln,* 163–64; Baker, *Mary Todd Lincoln,* 234–35. It is clear that her debt amounted to tens of thousands of dollars. For a discussion of A. T. Stewart's concern, see Gardner, "'Paradise of Fashion,'" 62–68; Kerber, "Separate Spheres."

86. *IM* 1 (Aug. 1900): 81.

87. Bryner, *Dressmaking and Millinery,* 47.

88. Abelson, *When Ladies Go A-Thieving,* esp. 166–67, 173–96; Leach, *Land of Desire,* 128–30. While it documents the marital tensions wrought by consumerism, Leach's analysis fails to consider the unequal distribution of economic and legal power between husbands and wives, preferring instead to heap all of the blame on the "new commercial economy."

Part 2 Introduction

1. Catalog, J. R. Libby, n.d., p. 17, "Dry Goods," box 2, Maine folder, WC.

2. Daves, *Ready-Made Miracle,* esp. 9–38.

Chapter 5: A Feminine Skill

1. Penny, *Employments of Women,* 324. See Roscoe Conkling's comments on reformers, quoted in Keller, *Affairs of State,* 248.

2. There were 92,084 "milliners, dress and mantua makers" in the United States in 1870; 90,480 were female, 1,604 were male. In 1900, women accounted for 98 percent of dressmakers and 94 percent of milliners. USBC, *Compendium of the Ninth Census,* 612, and *Statistics of Women at Work,* 70, 75.

3. See Matthaei, *Economic History of Women;* Baron, "Contested Terrain Revisited," and the essays in Baron, *Work Engendered.*

4. Walsh, "Democratization of Fashion." For general discussions of this approach, see Daves, *Ready-Made Miracle,* 9–14; Boorstin, *Americans,* 91–100 (Boorstin limits his analysis to men's clothing); Kidwell and Christman, *Suiting Everyone,* esp. 14–17. For criticisms of this approach, see Ewen and Ewen, *Channels of Desire,* esp. 75–187; Benson, *Counter Cultures,* esp. 78–116; Strasser, *Satisfaction Guaranteed,* esp. 288–91; Leach, *Land of Desire,* esp. 3–12, 71–93.

5. Of course, male carpenters, contractors, plumbers, and kindred workers would encounter a similar process as the do-it-yourself craze gained currency in the post–World War II years. This is a subject that awaits its historian and is one that no doubt has important implications for changing definitions of masculinity.

6. Research Department, WEIU, "Industrial Opportunities for Women in Somerville," typescript, 1910–11, p. 46, box 7, folder 16, WEIU, #B-8, SL; Benson,

Counter Cultures, 229; McGaw, "No Passive Victims"; Phillips and Taylor, "Sex and Skill"; Scott, *Gender and the Politics of History,* 93–112.

7. Broughton, *Suggestions for Dressmakers,* 4; Kidwell, *Cutting a Fashionable Fit,* 16–18.

8. *D,* Aug. 1879, 460; Broughton, *Suggestions for Dressmakers,* 13, 15, 17; Kidwell, *Cutting a Fashionable Fit,* 18.

9. Broughton, *Suggestions for Dressmakers,* 13; Kidwell, *Cutting a Fashionable Fit,* 18; *D,* July 1885, 600–601; Des Moulins, "Dressmaker's Life Story," 945.

10. Penny, *Employments of Women,* 325; Preston, "'To Learn Me the Whole of the Trade'"; Broughton, *Suggestions for Dressmakers,* 21; Kidwell, *Cutting a Fashionable Fit,* 11–13. Tailors might employ women—to sew—but they rarely taught them to cut.

11. Kidwell, *Cutting a Fashionable Fit,* 20; Penny, *Employments of Women,* 326.

12. Broughton, *Suggestions for Dressmakers,* 29; Rayne, *What Can a Woman Do?,* 213.

13. Penny, *Employments of Women,* 324; Broughton, *Suggestions for Dressmakers,* 29; Bryner, *Dressmaking and Millinery,* 79; Allinson, *Dressmaking,* 33.

14. Broughton, *Suggestions for Dressmakers,* 1–3; Drysdale, *Helps for Ambitious Girls,* 428–429.

15. Emma M. Hooper, "What It Means to Be Dressmaker," *Ladies' Home Journal,* July 1899, 24; Allinson, *Dressmaking,* 42.

16. Rodgers, *Work Ethic,* esp. 22–29, 65–93; Eisenstein, *Give Us Bread,* 21, 125, 139.

17. Perry, *Millinery Trade,* 99. Certainly this comment applies to dressmakers as well.

18. Montgomery, *Worker's Control,* esp. 113–19, and *Fall of the House of Labor,* 28–29, 41–46, 214–65; Braverman, *Labor and Monopoly Capital,* esp. 47–58, 72–93, 124–37.

19. *D,* Aug. 1880, 473; Penny, *Employments of Women,* 325.

20. Greeley et al., *Great Industries,* 587; Hale diary, Mar. 22, 1859, Hale Family Papers, Sophia Smith Collection, Smith College, Northhampton, Mass.; see Boydston, *Home and Work,* esp. 75–98; Matthews, *"Just a Housewife,"* esp. 11–17, 98–106; Strasser, *Never Done,* esp. 11–144, for histories of housework.

21. Laughton diary, Feb.–Aug. 1837, EI; Persis Sibley Andrews diary, Jan. 14, 1842, Dabney Papers, MHS. For a critique of the home/work dichotomy, see Boydston, *Home and Work,* esp. xiv–xvii, 142–63.

22. Fernandez, "'If a Woman Had Taste,'" 103–5, and "Women, Work, and Wages," 8–10.

23. *Ladies' Hand-Book of Millinery and Dressmaking;* Pullan, *Beadle's Dime Guide.* For do-it-yourself advice in fashion magazines, see *Godey's Lady's Book* 53 (Oct. 1856): 307–8; 53 (Nov. 1856): 433–35; 53 (Dec. 1856): 527–29; 56 (May 1858): 413–14; 56 (June 1858): 523–24; *D,* Jan. 1870, 18; Apr. 1880, 231; July 1885, 600–601.

24. Walsh, "Democratization of Fashion," 299–313; Daves, *Ready-Made Mira-*

cle, 9–14; Boorstin, *Americans,* 91–100; Kidwell and Christman, *Suiting Everyone,* 15–16; *D,* Feb. 1877, 107; Sept. 1879, 518.

25. When the moralist T. S. Arthur suggested that all "young ladies" learn dressmaking and millinery just in case they were someday forced to support themselves, he did not provide instructions; he recommended a term as an apprentice in a dressmaker's or milliner's shop. See his *Advice to Young Ladies,* 28–35.

26. Pullan, *Beadle's Dime Guide,* 8; Carens, *Dressmaking Self Taught,* 3, 120–27.

27. *D,* Feb. 1887, 256.

28. Rorabaugh, *Craft Apprentice,* 33–36, 220nn. 2–3. The do-it-yourself home improvement market, aimed primarily at male consumers, provides a contemporary exception.

29. Pullan, *Beadle's Dime Guide,* 10. Ninety-five percent (41 of 43) of the dressmaking establishments listed in the 1870 Boston manuscript manufacturing census possessed at least one sewing machine compared to none (0 of 3) ten years earlier. These figures should be considered suggestive, not definitive, for census takers overlooked the vast majority of the city's dressmaking businesses, enumerating less than 3 percent (3 of 118) in 1860 and only 14 percent (43 of 300) in 1870. 1860 FMMC, Boston, T1204, reel 15, reel 24 (1870); *Boston Directory* (1860 and 1870).

30. *D* (June 1885): 539; Baron and Klepp, "'If I Didn't Have My Sewing Machine,'" esp. 38–52; Kessler-Harris, *Out to Work,* 77–79.

31. Fernandez, "'If a Woman Had Taste,'" 233–35; Gartland, *Original American Lady Tailor System,* 36; Boston Public Schools Trade School for Girls, *Bulletin* 20 (Nov. 1927): n.p.; Waters, "Comparison and Contrast of Two Atlanta Historical Society Gowns," 47. The custom-made gowns that Waters examined hailed from Paris, but American sources indicate that custom dressmakers in the United States continued to employ a great deal of hand sewing well into the twentieth century. Broughton, *Suggestions for Dressmakers,* 25.

32. Allinson, *Dressmaking,* 39, 68; Gartland, *Original American Lady Tailor System,* 35–36.

33. This sampling was taken from Trautman, *Clothing America,* 32, 41, 54.

34. Hecklinger, *Dress and Cloak Cutter,* preface; Buddington, *Instruction Book;* Trautman, *Clothing America,* 64–65. Eighty-four (27.4 percent) of the 307 systems for drafting women's garments listed in Trautman's bibliography were invented or coinvented by women.

35. Hecklinger, *Dress and Cloak Cutter,* preface.

36. *S. T. Taylor's System,* 21, 23.

37. Trautman, *Clothing America,* 82–84; Taylor, *System for Cutting Ladies' Garments,* 1–3, 18; *S. T. Taylor's System,* 42–43; *Instruction Book.* See, for example, *FD* 10 (Jan. 5, 1894): n.p.; *AD* 1 (June 1910): n.p.; 1 (Dec. 1910): 5.

38. *McDowell Standard System,* 2; *S. T. Taylor's System,* 27. All systems cited (that is, instruction booklets for drafting systems) are in the collection of Patricia Trautman, School of Family Studies, University of Connecticut, Storrs, Conn.

39. Hecklinger, *Dress and Cloak Cutter,* n.p. (preface); Griffen and Knox, *Science*

and Art of Cutting, 6. For a discussion of historical and contemporary linkages between masculinity and science, see Keller, *Reflections on Gender and Science,* esp. 7–13, 33–65, 75–94. Drafting systems appear to be less than scientific from the vantage point of the late twentieth century. But as several scholars have shown, the line that separated science from pseudoscience in the nineteenth century was often a thin one. See especially Wrobel, "Introduction," 1–20; Greenway, "'Nervous Disease'"; Shuttleworth, "Female Circulation." Women, too, might appropriate the language of science, as did Madame Mallison, the author of *Dressmaking Reduced to a Science: The Eclectic Lady-Tailor System of Dress Cutting* (mentioned in Kidwell, *Cutting a Fashionable Fit,* 50).

40. Taylor, *Dress Cutting Simplified;* Kidwell, *Cutting a Fashionable Fit,* 2, 35, 99–100, 127–50. During this period, 363 systems for drafting women's garments received patents; of course, not all of them actually reached the marketplace. Much of the following discussion relies on Kidwell's pioneering study.

41. Hooper, "What It Means to Be a Dressmaker," 24.

42. Kidwell, *Cutting a Fashionable Fit,* 25–30; Tentler, *New System,* 6.

43. Kidwell, *Cutting a Fashionable Fit,* 24–26.

44. Ibid.

45. Ibid., 28–30.

46. Ibid., 31–35; Gartland, *Original American Lady Tailor System,* 5.

47. Kidwell, *Cutting a Fashionable Fit,* 28–30; Taylor, *System for Cutting Ladies' Dresses,* 3.

48. *S. T. Taylor's System,* 16.

49. Coleman, *Science of Gynametry,* 10; Kidwell, *Cutting a Fashionable Fit,* 31–45.

50. Taylor, *System for Cutting Ladies' Garments,* 5–10.

51. Kidwell, *Cutting a Fashionable Fit,* 45–50.

52. Gartland, *Original American Lady Tailor System,* 11–17.

53. Kidwell, *Cutting a Fashionable Fit,* 53–55; *McDowell Standard System,* n.p.

54. Kidwell, *Cutting a Fashionable Fit,* 55, 65–68; Buddington, *Instruction Book,* 6.

55. Buddington, *Instruction Book,* 3; Gartland, *Original American Lady Tailor System,* 12, 33; Broughton, *Suggestions for Dressmakers,* 8.

56. Trautman, *Clothing America,* 53–54, 85; Taylor, *Dress Cutting Simplified,* 2; Standard Garment Cutting Company, *Standard Square Inch Tailoring System,* 38–39.

57. Kidwell has suggested that amateurs and home sewers were more likely to use proportional and hybrid methods whereas professional dressmakers more often used direct-measure systems. But the inventors of systems were far more ecumenical in their marketing. See her *Cutting a Fashionable Fit,* 80–81, 90–93; Gartland, *Original American Lady Tailor System,* 8.

58. Rood, *Supplement No. 2,* 16; Standard Garment Cutting Company, *Standard Square Inch Tailoring System,* 39.

59. Sumner, *History of Women*, 117; *Report of the WEIU . . . 1885* (Boston: n.p., 1885), p. 36, in carton 1, vol. 1, WEIU (unprocessed); Campbell, "Darkness and Daylight," 260. Stitching fells meant to finish seams by turning under the raw edges.

60. *S. T. Taylor's System*, 57.

61. Ibid., 44, 47, 49.

62. Buddington, *Instruction Book*, n.p.

63. Taylor, *System for Cutting Ladies' Dresses*, 4.

64. *S. T. Taylor's System*, 46.

65. Broughton, *Suggestions for Dressmakers*, 8, 11. While Broughton defended the pin-to-the-form technique, she should not necessarily be considered an advocate of traditional methods of training, for her book represents part of a larger trend that substituted book learning for craft traditions.

66. Hooper, "What It Means to Be a Dressmaker," 24; *S. T. Taylor's System*, 7–11; Veblen, *Theory of the Leisure Class*, esp. 68–72, 118–31.

67. Trautman, *Clothing America*, 17, 63–64, 85–87; Jonason, "Dressmaking in North Dakota," 19, 23.

68. *S. T. Taylor's System*, 44–45; Standard Garment Cutting Company, *Standard Square Inch Tailoring System*, 38–39; Bryner, *Dressmaking and Millinery*, 29.

69. The best discussion of the evolution of patterns is Kidwell, *Cutting a Fashionable Fit*, 81–90.

70. *Godey's Lady's Book* 52 (July 1855), quoted in Fernandez, "'If a Woman Had Taste,'" 174; Kidwell, *Cutting a Fashionable Fit*, 83–85; *Ladies' Report of New York Fashions* (1867), quoted in Kidwell, 83; *Mirror of the Beautiful; or, Catalogue of Mme. Demorest's New and Reliable Patterns of Ladies' and Children's Dress, Fall and Winter Fashion, 1872–1873*, inside front cover, Trade Catalog Collection, AAS. Most historians credit Butterick with inventing graded patterns, but Autumn Stanley attributes them to Demorest. See Stanley, *Mothers and Daughters of Invention*, 464.

71. Kidwell, *Cutting a Fashionable Fit*, 85–86.

72. *Catalogue of E. Butterick and Company's Patterns for Winter 1870–71*, 1, Trade Catalog Collection, AAS.

73. *D*, Feb. 1879, 112; July 1883, 591.

74. *D*, Oct. 1885, 818; Mar. 1885, 340; Jonason, "Dressmaking in North Dakota," 20.

75. Broughton, *Suggestions for Dressmakers*, 9.

76. Kidwell, *Cutting a Fashionable Fit*, 86–90; *Catalogue of E. Butterick and Company's Patterns for Summer 1870*, inside front cover, Trade Catalog Collection, AAS. Walsh's "Democratization of Fashion," 313, overstates the extent to which patterns solved the problem of fit.

77. Boston's dressmaking history is a case in point. Three hundred tradeswomen graced the pages of the city directory of 1870; 454 in 1880; 325 in 1890 (the reason for the decline is unclear); 625 in 1900; and 845 in 1910. See tables A-1 and A-2 in the appendix. These figures include both proprietors of establishments and dress-

makers who went out by the day, but not employees. Hence the total number of dressmakers in the city was actually quite a bit higher.

78. Wells, "The Dressmaker in the House: A Monologue," *Harper's Monthly Magazine* 119 (June 1909): 155–56.

79. Ibid., 156–57.

80. Cowan, *More Work for Mother,* esp. 64–65.

81. Kidwell, *Cutting a Fashionable Fit,* 1, 94–98.

Chapter 6: Commerce over Craft

1. *Hill's Milliners' Gazette* 4 (Feb. 1887): 14, in "Hats," box 2, WC.

2. Two excellent exceptions are Benson, *Counter Cultures,* and Kwolek-Folland, *Engendering Business.* See also Ditz, "Shipwrecked."

3. For general histories of wholesaling, see Porter and Livesay, *Merchants and Manufacturers;* Moeckel, *Development of the Wholesaler.*

4. USBC, *Twelfth Census . . . 1900: Population,* 507; *Statistics of Women at Work,* 39, 75; *Fifteenth Census . . . 1930,* 5:41. Because these figures include workers as well as proprietors, the increase in the proportion of male retailers was in all likelihood far more dramatic, for men rarely appeared in millinery shops as employees.

5. 1850 FMMC, Boston, T1204, reel 6, ward 7, p. 203, line 3; *Boston Directory* (1850); *IM* 1 (Jan. 1900): 71.

6. 1850 FMMC, Boston, T1204, reel 6, ward 7, p. 225, line 12; *IM* 1 (Apr. 1900): 53.

7. Penny, *Think and Act,* 25; *M* 26 (Feb. 1915): 81; 25 (Dec. 1914): 42.

8. MA 75:118; 87:1, RGD.

9. At some point in their careers, 55 percent (85 of 155) of the milliners listed in the Boston records of Dun & Co. were considered "undesirable for credit."

10. Thirty days appears to have been the usual payment period in the nineteenth century; the milliner who paid her bills within the month, like the one who paid with cash on the spot, was entitled to a 5 percent discount. Other terms (e.g., sixty days, four months) surface in the Dun & Co. records, though not as frequently. Bill of sale, Carpenter, Plimpton and Company, Nov. 5, 1864, "Hats," box 1, WC; MA 77:48; 78:410; 88:335; NY 395:54, RGD. For a discussion of overall trends, see Moeckel, *Development of the Wholesaler,* 147.

11. Philo, *Twelve Letters to a Young Milliner,* 6.

12. Earling, *Whom to Trust,* 151.

13. I base these conclusions on an examination of a small sample of tailors (see chap. 4, note 71). Although credit reporters estimated Harry Harris's means at $2,000–5,000 (a sum that most milliners would have envied) they concluded that "few . . . want to sell" to him. Nor were the Simon Brothers—estimated worth of $3,000–8,000—considered "desirable" for credit. These decisions in part reflected the fact that wholesalers could impose higher standards on tailors because they generally possessed greater assets than did milliners; the assets of the tailors in the sam-

264 * *Notes to Pages 161–69*

ple averaged $10,750. As in the millinery trade, correspondents' evaluations depended on assessments of character as well as material assets. Henry A. Cann, a "man of character," was recommended for small credits despite his relatively small assets of about $3,000. MA 69:599 a/109, 405; 81:341, RGD.

14. Vose, *Seventy-five Years of the Mercantile Agency,* 106–7.

15. MA 91:81; 68:444; 76:321; 88:335; 78:156, RGD.

16. Gerber, "Cutting Out Shylock."

17. Foster, *New York by Gas-Light,* 66; *Frank Leslie's Illustrated Newspaper* 7 (Feb. 12, 1859): 160; Lewis, "Female Entrepreneurs," 16.

18. MA 76:286; 69:599 a/99; 88:87, RGD.

19. I have examined all Dun & Co. reports for male milliners in Boston as well as those for a small sample of tailors (see chap. 4, note 71, and note 13 above). In sharp contrast to the regularity with which this adjective was applied to female proprietors, the partners of only one firm were described as respectable. Interestingly, the term served a similar purpose, rendering members of a "suspect" group (in this case not "public women" but German tailors) respectable. MA 70:815, RGD.

20. MA 75:91; 73:78; 75:411; 67:216 a/4, RGD. After the Civil War, Dun & Co. reporters increasingly favored economic considerations over those based on moral character. But character remained an important basis for credit. See Norris, *R. G. Dun & Co.,* xvii, 93–94, 130.

21. MA 72:456; 75:256; 84:197; 78:318, 156, RGD.

22. Duniway, *Path Breaking,* 17–19; *IM* 4 (May 1903): 46.

23. Philo, *Twelve Letters to a Young Milliner,* 14–15. See also *IM* 4 (Apr. 1900): 70.

24. Earling, *Whom to Trust,* 151.

25. Ibid., 150–51.

26. Ibid., 58, 64, 149–50; MA 70:898.

27. Earling, *Whom to Trust,* 58, 64; Philo, *Twelve Letters to a Young Milliner,* 5–6; *Dry Goods Merchants Trade Journal* 22 (Nov. 1921): 60; 23 (Dec. 1921): 17; Stimson, "Small Business," 337–40; *IM* 4 (May 1903): 46; 4 (July 1903): 43. See also Kessler-Harris, "Independence and Virtue," esp. 3–5.

28. Earling, *Whom to Trust,* 150.

29. MA 70:699, 857; 75:131; 67:216a/9, RGD.

30. MA 70:857; 75:131, RGD.

31. Earling, *Whom to Trust,* 163–65. Lewis, "Female Entrepreneurs," 9, notes that those Albany, New York, milliners described as respectable by Dun & Co. reporters tended to be those with little capital.

32. MA 68:444; 75:283, 287, RGD.

33. Wiebe, *Search for Order,* esp. 17–27.

34. MA 74:416, RGD; *IM* 4 (July 1903): 43.

35. Earling, *Whom to Trust,* 241; Moeckel, *Development of the Wholesaler,* 59, 117–22.

36. *MTR* 21 (Nov. 1896): 57.

37. *MH*, Autumn 1908, 23; *IM* 27 (Jan. 1926): 127; *M* 24 (Nov. 1913): 19; Earling, *Whom to Trust*, 233; *MTR* 21 (May 1896): 8.

38. *MH*, Spring 1908, 35; Spring 1910, 25.

39. Mott, *History of American Magazines*, 3:577, 4:188.

40. *M* 22 (Mar. 1912): 39; *MH*, Winter 1910–11, 25.

41. *M* 26 (Feb. 1915): 76.

42. *MTR* 21 (Aug. 1896): 25; *MH*, Spring 1907, 23.

43. *MH*, Spring 1907, 22; Summer 1907, 23.

44. *MH*, Summer 1907, 23.

45. Faue makes a similar point in "Paths of Unionization," 297–301.

46. *MH*, Autumn 1907, 22; Spring 1907, 23; Autumn 1908, 23; *MD* 4 (Sept. 1908): 6.

47. Davies, *Woman's Place*, 84; Smith-Rosenberg, *Disorderly Conduct*, 258–62, 265–80.

48. *M* 24 (Apr. 1913): 50.

49. *MD* 5 (Mar. 1909): 7; *IM* 1 (May 1900): 45; *MH*, Autumn 1910, 24.

50. *MH*, Autumn 1907, 22.

51. *IM* 4 (Sept. 1903): 41; 4 (Oct. 1903): 45; *M* 22 (June 1912): 27–28.

52. *MH*, Winter 1907–8, 22; Summer 1910, 25; *MD* 4 (Sept. 1908): 6.

53. *MD* 5 (Mar. 1909): 7; *MH*, Summer 1907, 23. For discussions of returned goods from wholesalers' perspectives, see *Merchants Trade Journal* 19 (June 1918): 32; *History of the National Wholesale Druggists' Association*, 55. General business journals such as *System* and *Bradstreet's Weekly* paid little attention to returned goods.

54. H. M. Maxwell, "What Can Be Done about Trade Abuses?" *System*, June 1925, 734–37; *Merchants Trade Journal* 19 (June 1918): 13; Clara Savage, "Buying that Isn't Buying," *Good Housekeeping* 63 (July 1916): 29–30; "Fewer Returns," *System*, Dec. 1915, 650–51; "The Problem of Returned Goods," *Monthly Labor Review* 25 (Oct. 1927): 917–18.

55. *MH*, Summer 1907, 23; *MD* 5 (Mar. 1909): 7.

56. *MTR* 21 (May 1896): 25; *M* 22 (June 1912): 31–21; *MH*, Winter 1907–8, 23.

57. *MH*, Winter 1907–8, 23.

58. *MH*, Spring 1910, 25; Winter 1907–8, 12.

59. James C. Worthy, quoted in *Rebuilding an Industry*, 23. Boston business directories listed 280 retail milliners in 1900, 196 in 1930. During that period, the population increased from 560,892 to 781,188. *Boston Directory* (1900 and 1930). Population figures are from Thernstrom, *Other Bostonians*, 11.

60. Peter R. Earling, "Credits and Collections," *System*, July 1904, 44–54; Griffen and Griffen, *Natives and Newcomers*, 257; Gerber, "Cutting Out Shylock"; Norris, *R. G. Dun & Co.*, 92.

61. Moeckel, *Development of the Wholesaler*, 145–49, 222–26; *IM* 1 (May 1900): 40; 1 (Feb. 1900): 31, 33; 1 (Mar. 1900): 47–48, 65; 16 (Feb. 1915): 79; *MTR* 21 (Nov. 1896): 57–58; 22 (Jan. 1897): 59.

62. *IM* 27 (Jan. 1926): 77, 90; catalog, Hill Brothers, "Hats," box 2, WC; U.S. Federal Trade Commission, *Report*, Nov. 21, 1939, 11, 47. For general discussions of the decline of jobbers and their continued importance in some lines, see Porter and Livesay, *Merchants and Manufacturers*, 154–65, 197–227; Moeckel, *Development of the Wholesaler*, 210–33.

63. Bill of sale, Ordway Brothers, Oct. 8, 1864, "Hats," box 6; bill of sale, Carpenter, Plimpton, and Company, Nov. 5, 1864, box 1; catalog, John M. Smyth Company, spring and summer 1911, p. 40, box 4, WC.

64. Blumin, "Hypothesis of Middle-Class Formation," 312–18, "Black Coats to White Collars," and *Emergence of the Middle Class*, 8–91.

65. Greeley et al., *Great Industries*, 779–80; Bryner, *Dressmaking and Millinery*, 48–49; Perry, *Millinery Trade*, 16; Griffen and Griffen, "Small Business and Occupational Mobility" and *Natives and Newcomers*, 139–43.

66. Bryner, *Dressmaking and Millinery*, 45–46; Perry, *Millinery Trade*, 16, 18–19. The earliest reference I have found to the distinction between makers and trimmers appeared in the *New York Daily Tribune* in 1845. See Sumner, *History of Women*, 156.

67. Bryner, *Dressmaking and Millinery*, 54–55; Van Kleeck, *Wages*, 22, and *Seasonal Industry*, 146. I have no reason to believe that the "table" was not a longstanding institution.

68. Mary Kyle Dallas, "Martha Mead; or, Money's Worth and Money's Weight," *New York Ledger*, Nov. 7, 1868, 1; GTEL, *Vocations*, 3; Perry, *Millinery Trade*, 19–20, 108.

69. Dallas, "Martha Mead," 1; Babcock, "Employments for Women," 516; GTEL, *Vocations*, 8–9. See also Perry, *Millinery Trade*, 18–19.

70. I have relied on a variety of works to develop my description of the art of millinery: Hazen, *Panorama of Professions and Trades*, 61–62; *Ladies' Hand-Book of Millinery and Dressmaking*, 9–27; *Ladies' Self-Instructor in Millinery*, 27–33; Pullan, *Beadle's Dime Guide*, 56–58; Penny, *Employments of Women*, 314–19; Philo, *Twelve Letters to a Young Milliner*, 21–24; Babcock, "Employments for Women"; GTEL, *Vocations*, 3–5; Bryner, *Dressmaking and Millinery*, 52–55; Perry, *Millinery Trade*, 18–26; Van Kleeck, *Wages*, 20–26, and *Seasonal Industry*, 40–51; Bertyne R. Smith, "Training Notebook for Bonnets," guidebook, 1986–87, Old Sturbridge Village; Dreher, *From the Neck Up*.

71. *Godey's Lady's Book* 53 (Nov. 1856): 433.

72. Penny, *Employments of Women*, 318; Babcock, "Employments for Women," 517; GTEL, *Vocations*, 8.

73. GTEL, *Vocations*, 3–4; Bryner, *Dressmaking and Millinery*, 47.

74. Bryner, *Dressmaking and Millinery*, 104; Pullan, *Beadle's Dime Guide*, 57–58.

75. Perry, *Millinery Trade*, 22; Penny, *Employments of Women*, 315; Babcock, "Employments for Women," 516.

76. Van Kleeck, *Seasonal Industry*, 61–62; Perry, *Millinery Trade*, 99.

77. Bryner, *Dressmaking and Millinery*, 48–49.

78. *IM* 11 (Jan. 1910): 38.

79. Bryner, *Dressmaking and Millinery*, 49, 53; Perry, *Millinery Trade*, 16, 34; Van Kleeck, *Wages*, 21–22; *IM* 4 (Mar. 1903): 47.

80. *M* 27 (Sept. 1916): n.p. (inside cover).

81. *M* 22 (Mar. 1912): 84; 25 (Mar. 1914): 30.

82. *M* 27 (Sept. 1916): 10.

83. Bryner, *Dressmaking and Millinery*, 47–48; Penny, *Employments of Women*, 315–16.

84. *M* 24 (Dec. 1913): 27; Van Kleeck, *Wages*, 19; catalog, Ridley and Sons Wholesale Millinery and Straw Goods, spring 1902, p. 15; catalog, John Miles, Inc., Wholesale Millinery Goods, Apr. and May 1905, p. 8, both in "Hats," box 3, WC; Giblin, *Concerning Millinery*, 33; *MH*, Spring 1907, 12; Autumn 1907, 30.

85. *IM* 4 (Mar. 1903): 47.

86. *IM* 1 (Jan. 1900): 22.

87. *M* 24 (Feb. 1915): 74.

88. Van Kleeck, *Seasonal Industry*, 38.

89. Ibid., 30; *MH*, Spring 1908, 10; Spring 1907, 12; *IM* 27 (Mar. 1926): 61. See also *IM* 1 (Mar. 1900): 37.

90. Bryner, *Dressmaking and Millinery*, 53.

91. Ibid., 47; *IM* 4 (Mar. 1903): 47; U.S. Federal Trade Commission, *Report*, 14.

92. Bryner, *Dressmaking and Millinery*, 53.

93. Ibid., 49–50, 57; catalog, New York Millinery and Supply Company, spring 1908, "Hats," box 3, WC.

94. *IM* 4 (Mar. 1903): 47; catalog, John M. Smyth Company, spring and summer 1911, n.p.

95. *IM* 11 (Jan. 1910): 150.

Chapter 7: Engendering Change: The Department Store and the Factory, 1890–1930

1. *M* 25 (Mar. 1914): 87, 89.

2. For examples of the first approach, see Boorstin, *Americans*, 91–100; Daves, *Ready-Made Miracle*, esp. 9–14. For the second, see Ewen and Ewen, *Channels of Desire*, esp. 45–46, 123–35, 142–44; Leach, *Land of Desire*, esp. 3–12, 71–93. Both Leach and Ewen and Ewen discuss the conditions under which garment workers and department store employees labored, as does Gardner in "'Paradise of Fashion.'" See Leach, *Land of Desire*, 95–98, 117–22; Ewen and Ewen, *Channels of Desire*, 134–39; Gardner, "'Paradise of Fashion,'" 69–74. The best discussion of department store salesclerks is Benson's *Counter Cultures*, esp. 124–271.

3. Catalog, L. S. Plaut and Company, [1895?], n.p., "Ladies' Clothing," box 2, WC.

4. Ibid.

5. Leach, *Land of Desire*, 39–93. As scholars have recently pointed out, the contrast between the consumer culture of the early to mid-nineteenth century and the

culture of consumption that appeared in the late nineteenth and early twentieth centuries should not be overemphasized. See Blumin, *Emergence of the Middle Class*, 78–107; Lears, "Beyond Veblen."

6. Gardner, "'Paradise of Fashion,'" 61–64; Boorstin, *Americans*, 101–9.

7. Catalog, Plaut and Company.

8. Department stores sponsored some of the earliest attempts at fashioning women's ready-to-wear. But these efforts met with less than resounding success. See Kidwell and Christman, *Suiting Everyone*, 63–64, 108–9, 135–48.

9. Catalog, Plaut and Company; Woolson, *Woman in American Society*, 232–33.

10. Leach, *Land of Desire*, esp. 39–90, 104–11; Abelson, *When Ladies Go A-Thieving*, 42–48, 66–78, 86–90; Benson, *Counter Cultures*, 18–20; Boorstin, *Americans*, 101–9; Duncan, *Culture and Democracy*, 123–31.

11. Catalog, Plaut and Company.

12. *Town and Country*, Oct. 19, 1901, 33, in "Dry Goods," box 16; Julia Houston Railey, *Retail and Romance, Diamond Jubilee Edition* (Boston: n.p., 1926), 25, in "Dry Goods," box 10, both in WC.

13. Catalog, Plaut and Company; catalog, Herpolsheimer's, pp. 12, 31; Charlotte Rankin Aiken, *The Millinery Department* (New York: Ronald Press, 1918), 6–7; *R. H. White and Company's Illustrated Catalogue*, spring and summer 1883 (Boston: Press of Deland and Barth, 1883), 7, all in "Dry Goods," box 10, WC.

14. Boorstin, *Americans*, 101; Butler, *Saleswomen*, 59; Perry, *Millinery Trade*, 40.

15. Van Kleeck's study of New York milliners found that retail milliners made more than their counterparts in department stores (*Seasonal Industry*, 251). Bryner, who investigated the milliners and dressmakers of Cleveland, claimed that department stores offered higher wages than retail shops (*Dressmaking and Millinery*, 62, 75). See also Benson, *Counter Cultures*, 182–84. For discussions of seasonal unemployment in department stores, see Bryner, *Dressmaking and Millinery*, 42, 74; Butler, *Saleswomen*, 95; Van Kleeck, *Seasonal Industry*, 95; Allinson, *Dressmaking*, 48; Benson, *Counter Cultures*, 184–87.

16. *MTR* 21 (July 1896): 112; 21 (Aug. 1896): 57; 22 (Jan. 1897): 103; *IM* 16 (Aug. 1915): 107.

17. For general discussions of working conditions in department stores, see Benson, *Counter Cultures*, esp. 177–200; Leach, *Land of Desire*, 95–98, 117–22. See also Bryner, *Dressmaking and Millinery*, 56.

18. Bryner, *Dressmaking and Millinery*, 56; Perry, *Millinery Trade*, 37–38.

19. *Town and Country*, Oct. 19, 1901, 33; *Mandel's Shopping Guide, Fall and Winter*, n.d., p. 2, "Dry Goods," box 6, Mandel Brothers folder, WC.

20. Butler, *Saleswomen*, 59. According to Butler's analysis of thirty-four Baltimore department stores, dressmakers constituted 1.4 percent of the labor force and alteration hands 9.6 percent. See also Bryner, *Dressmaking and Millinery*, 35; Allinson, *Dressmaking*, 62.

21. Bryner, *Dressmaking and Millinery*, 35–36, 41, quotation from 35–36; Allinson, *Dressmaking*, 47.

22. Allinson, *Dressmaking*, 47–48; Bryner, *Dressmaking and Millinery*, 35–36, quotation from 36.

23. Bryner, *Dressmaking and Millinery*, 42; Butler, *Saleswomen*, 92–94.

24. *M* 25 (Mar. 1914): 89.

25. "Making Money Out of Making Women Look Lovely," *American Magazine* 83 (May 1917): 49.

26. Aiken, *Millinery Department*, 8–31, 70–99; Research Bureau for Retail Training, *Manual for a Millinery Department;* Daché, *Talking through My Hats*, 73. See also Benson, *Counter Cultures*, 147–53.

27. Perry, *Millinery Trade*, 38; Bryner, *Dressmaking and Millinery*, 56. Only Butler avoided gender-specific pronouns (*Saleswomen*, 49–50).

28. Daché, *Talking through My Hats*, 70–72. To be sure, Benson's study of department store saleswomen demonstrates that they exerted considerable control over the selling process (*Counter Cultures*, 227–71). But Madame was the ultimate authority in the dressmaking shop; the saleswoman, however recalcitrant, was beholden to the (usually) male floorwalker.

29. Daché, *Talking through My Hats*, 73. Daché's shop grew into a huge establishment that sold hats both wholesale and retail and employed 150 milliners by the 1940s. Hill, *Women in Gainful Occupations*, esp. 28, 35, 90, 96.

30. This predicament was not unique to dressmakers and milliners. Wholesalers and manufacturers encouraged many sorts of retailers to imitate their larger competitors. See Strasser, *Satisfaction Guaranteed*, 246–51.

31. *AD* 3 (Jan. 1912): 45; Allinson, *Dressmaking*, 42.

32. Allinson, *Dressmaking*, 37. See also Perry, *Millinery Trade*, 33–36.

33. *IM* 4 (Sept. 1903): 39; *MD* 4 (Aug. 1908): 15; *M* 22 (June 1912): 56; *IM* 27 (Mar. 1926): 33.

34. *M* 22 (June 1912): 56; *IM* 1 (May 1900): 40.

35. Allinson, *Dressmaking*, 20–21, 25, 37–38; *IM* 5 (Apr. 1904): 44.

36. Allinson, *Dressmaking*, 27, 37–38; *IM* 1 (May 1900): 40; Van Kleeck, *Seasonal Industry*, 64.

37. *AD* 3 (Jan. 1912): 45. Many tradeswomen ignored this advice. As late as the 1950s the dressmaker Isabella Zetlin Steiner relied solely on trade cards and personal recommendations. See Moseley, interview, 4–5; *MD* 5 (Mar. 1910): 18; 5 (Feb. 1909): 5.

38. Schorman, "Truth about Good Goods," 30.

39. *IM* 1 (June 1900): 27, 43; *MD* 5 (Feb. 1909): 5; Susman, "'Personality.'"

40. *IM* 1 (Jan. 1900): 63.

41. *IM* 27 (Feb. 1926): 45, 54. The *Illustrated Milliner* borrowed "the words that make the sale" from the Research Bureau for Retail Training (at the University of Pittsburgh), *Manual for a Millinery Department*, 82, 91. See 80–91 for full text.

42. Perry, *Millinery Trade*, 26; *IM* 1 (May 1900): 40; Allinson, *Dressmaking*, 44.

43. *IM* 1 (Feb. 1900): 59.

44. Allinson, *Dressmaking*, 24–25; Levine, *Women's Garment Workers*, 383.

45. Allinson, *Dressmaking*, 38, 43, 63; Van Kleeck, *Seasonal Industry*, 64.

46. Anonymous salary account (Ladies' Bonnets), AAS; MMWC, *Report on the Wages of Women*, 5–8.

47. Van Kleeck, *Wages*, 73; MMWC, *Report on the Wages of Women*, 8, 13; Van Kleeck, *Seasonal Industry*, 41; Perry, *Millinery Trade*, 9–10; Butler, *Women and the Trades*, 143; von der Nienburg, *Conditions in the Millinery Industry*, 37.

48. Butler, *Women and the Trades*, 141–43; Perry, *Millinery Trade*, 17–18.

49. Van Kleeck, *Wages*, 28–29; Perry, *Millinery Trade*, 45, 76, 78, 85; Bryner, *Dressmaking and Millinery*, 62; MMWC, *Report on the Wages of Women*, 12–13; Dublin, *Women at Work*, esp. 159–62.

50. Butler, *Women in the Trades*, 145; Perry, *Millinery Trade*, 69; Van Kleeck, *Wages*, 14, 72, and *Seasonal Industry*, 108, 119, 142.

51. Van Kleeck, *Seasonal Industry*, 46, 59, 220, 228; Bryner, *Dressmaking and Millinery*, 58, 65. According to Van Kleeck's table 42 (p. 220), 20 of 99 designers (out of a total of 3,203 millinery workers) earned weekly salaries of at least fifty dollars. Here she did not distinguish between wholesale and retail shops. Table 48 (p. 228) shows that 8 of 2,233 wholesale workers earned forty dollars a week or more; these employees were undoubtedly designers.

52. Perry, *Millinery Trade*, 21; MMWC, *Report on the Wages of Women*, 15; Van Kleeck, *Seasonal Industry*, 50–51.

53. Van Kleeck, *Seasonal Industry*, 46, 49; Bryner, *Dressmaking and Millinery*, 57–58. Some retail shops might employ copyists, to copy French models or "pattern hats" obtained from high-class wholesale factories. But these workers were far more likely to be found—and in far greater numbers—in wholesale factories. See Perry, *Millinery Trade*, 21.

54. Van Kleeck, *Seasonal Industry*, 46.

55. Ibid., 48–49.

56. MMWC, *Report on the Wages of Women*, 15, 17.

57. According to Van Kleeck, 82 (5.8 percent) of the 1,405 workers in the wholesale establishments investigated operated machines (this figure includes straw sewers, machine operators, lining makers, and frame makers; *Wages*, 25). Investigators for the Massachusetts Minimum Wage Commission visited ten wholesale houses that employed a total of 393 workers, 216 (55 percent) of whom were machine operators of some sort. The proportion of machine operators in straw hat factories—618 (65.9 percent) of 938 workers—was higher (*Report on the Wages of Women*, 31, 33). Whether the contrast between New York in 1914 and Massachusetts in 1919 reflects regional differences, changes over time, or the idiosyncrasies of the two samples is unclear.

58. MMWC, *Report on the Wages of Women*, 20–22, 31, 33. Excluding straw machine operators, 38.9 percent of wholesale millinery workers earned weekly salaries of nine dollars or more.

59. Hilf, *No Time for Tears*, 94–102, quotation from 126. See also Glenn, *Daughters of the Shtetl*, 102–3.

60. Van Kleeck, *Seasonal Industry,* 67.

61. Ibid., 77.

62. Ibid., 64; Van Kleeck, *Wages,* 12. In 1914, there were 2,079 wholesale millinery firms in the United States, funded by a total of $53,101,000 in capital (MMWC, *Report on the Wages of Women,* 67). Wholesale hat manufacturers were small concerns by American industrial standards; as late as 1939 a study undertaken by the Women's Bureau of the U.S. Department of Labor noted that only 8 percent of millinery manufacturers boasted annual sales of more than $300,000. Nevertheless, in capital, labor, and volume of product, the typical wholesale establishment dwarfed the typical retail shop. See von der Nienburg, *Conditions in the Millinery Industry,* 18.

63. Bensman, *Practice of Solidarity,* 131–33.

64. MMWC, *Report on the Wages of Women,* 14; von der Nienburg, *Conditions in the Millinery Industry,* 51.

65. 1850 FMMC, Boston, T1204, reel 6; Perry, *Millinery Trade,* 24, 36.

66. Montgomery, *Worker's Control,* esp. 26–27, 32–44, 113–18; Braverman, *Labor and Monopoly Capital,* 72–83. On this point, see Glenn, *Daughters of the Shtetl,* 102.

67. Van Kleeck, *Wages,* 23, and *Seasonal Industry,* 44–45; Perry, *Millinery Trade,* 19.

68. Mrs. Z. B. Dexter, "Born Trimmers: Why Only a Few Women Succeed in the Millinery Work Room," *IM* 1 (Dec. 1900): 52; *IM* 1 (Feb. 1900): 59. The best discussion of scientific management is Braverman, *Labor and Monopoly Capital,* 85–123.

69. *IM* 1 (Aug. 1900): 79; 1 (Jan. 1900): 37.

70. Butler, *Women and the Trades,* 101; Everett, *Dress Industry,* 24–27.

71. Kidwell and Christman, *Suiting Everyone,* 63–64, 135–51; Wertheimer, *We Were There,* 297; Bryner, *Garment Trades,* 13, 17.

72. For detailed descriptions of the garment industry, see Butler, *Women and the Trades,* 101–40, 148–50; Bryner, *Garment Trades,* esp. 17–46. Both discussions, especially Butler's, consider the making of men's as well as women's garments. See also Wertheimer, *We Were There,* 293–335; Research Department, WEIU, "Industrial Opportunities for Women in Somerville," 1910–11 [typescript], p. 46, box 7, folder 100, WEIU, #B-8, SL.

73. Levine, *Women's Garment Workers,* 9–17, 382–417; ILGWU Educational Department, *Story of the I.L.G.W.U.,* 20–24. Exploitative conditions in garment making were not new to the twentieth century, but the vast majority of nineteenth-century garment workers labored on men's clothing. Baron and Klepp, "'If I Didn't Have My Sewing Machine,'" 25–30, 38–45; Kessler-Harris, *Out to Work,* 65–66; Stansell, *City of Women,* 106–19; Peiss, *Cheap Amusements,* 62–68.

74. Allinson, *Dressmaking,* 129, 131, 133–35; Wertheimer, *We Were There,* 294–95.

75. Glenn, *Daughters of the Shtetl,* 106–17, quotation from p. 115.

76. Bryner, *Garment Trades,* 19.

77. Ibid., 48, 51; Glenn, *Daughters of the Shtetl,* 110–11.

78. Bryner, *Garment Trades,* 32–33, 48, 50. Bryner's investigation encompassed 8,337 garment workers, 619 of whom were cutters. Three of the latter were women. See also Butler, *Women and the Trades,* 110; Allinson, *Dressmaking,* 128; Wertheimer, *We Were There,* 296; Levine, *Women's Garment Workers,* 522; Everett, *Dress Industry,* 30.

79. Butler, *Women and the Trades;* Bryner, *Garment Trades,* 66. According to Bryner's study, the lowest wage for female machine operators in ladies' garment factories in early twentieth-century Cleveland was six dollars per week; the highest wage for cutters was thirty dollars per week.

80. Butler, *Women and the Trades,* 102–3. Butler may have been describing a factory that produced men's garments (see this chap., note 72). But the conditions of work and the organization of labor in a dress or shirtwaist factory would have been similar.

81. Levine, *Women's Garment Workers,* ix, 523; Bryner, *Garment Trades,* 16, 43.

82. Bryner, *Garment Trades,* 24; Butler, *Women and the Trades,* 110, 112–13. The subdivision of labor reached its greatest extreme in the men's clothing trade. See Kidwell and Christman, *Suiting Everyone,* 94–95.

83. Bryner, *Garment Trades,* 41; Everett, *Dress Industry,* 31; Kidwell and Christman, *Suiting Everyone,* 145.

84. Levine, *Women's Garment Workers,* 383. Allinson and her associates visited 152 custom shops in Boston, Cambridge, Somerville, Lowell, and Worcester. Seventy-nine (52 percent) employed eight or fewer workers (*Dressmaking,* 32, 35, 38, 45). Allinson's figures did not include self-employed dressmakers. In rural areas and small towns, the number of workers per shop was undoubtedly smaller. In 1900, the last year that the U.S. manufacturing census included custom dressmaking, there were 14,479 such establishments employing 45,595 workers, an average of three per shop.

85. Wilentz, *Chants Democratic,* 119–29; Faler, *Mechanics and Manufacturers,* 22–27; Laurie, *Working People,* 20–24, and *Artisans into Workers,* 38–43; Blewett, *Men, Women, and Work,* 14–19, 97–108.

86. Bryner, *Dressmaking and Millinery,* 30–31. A guimpe is a piece of lacy, transparent fabric that forms the collar and upper part of a bodice.

87. Ibid., 31.

88. Allinson, *Dressmaking,* 38–39; Bryner, *Dressmaking and Millinery,* 34–35.

89. Allinson, *Dressmaking,* 37, 41.

90. Ibid., 38.

91. Bryner, *Dressmaking and Millinery,* 34; Allinson, *Dressmaking,* 38. Occasionally, the order was reversed; "ladies' tailors" might add dressmaking—and dressmakers—to their repertoire.

92. Allinson, *Dressmaking,* 38–39, 127, 129.

93. The number of "milliners and millinery dealers" declined from 121,446 in

1910 to 69,598 in 1920, a decrease of 42.7 percent. In the same period, the number of dressmakers decreased from 446,555 to 235,519, a 47.3 percent decline (Hill, *Women in Gainful Occupations*, 33). Hill's figures are slightly different from those reported by the 1910 and 1920 censuses (see Table A-1 in appendix).

94. Perry, *Millinery Trade*, 34; Van Kleeck, *Seasonal Industry*, 37–38; Bryner, *Dressmaking and Millinery*, 52–53.

95. *Retail Dry Goods* 23 (Aug. 1922): 3. See also Mayfield, *Department Store Story*, 42; "Fifth Avenue Dressmaking Shop," in Hourwich and Palmer, *I Am a Woman Worker*, 7–8. The exact date of the dressmaker's remarks, recorded at the Bryn Mawr Summer School for Workers, is unclear. *I Am a Woman Worker* is a compilation of the writings of several classes of students.

Conclusion

1. Cott, *Grounding of Modern Feminism*, 3–10; Peiss, *Cheap Amusements*, esp. 6–8, 61–62, 104–8; Smith-Rosenberg, *Disorderly Conduct*, 271–83. See also Chambers-Schiller, *Liberty, a Better Husband*, 198–203.

2. Freedman, "Separatism as Strategy"; Cott, *Grounding of Modern Feminism*, esp. 93–97; Deutsch, "Learning to Talk."

3. Glenn, *Daughters of the Shtetl*, 167–206, esp. 168, 173–75, 187–88. See 191, for a discussion of American women's negative attitudes toward unions. I do not mean to suggest that labor militancy was an "ethnic" trait; both Yankee and Irish American women had activist traditions. But given the geographic dispersal of dressmaking and millinery, the opportunities for advancement and respectability that they offered, and the unique environment of the custom shop, dressmakers and milliners failed to demonstrate the sorts of militancy associated with the garment trades. See Dublin, *Women at Work*, 86–131; Turbin, *Working Women*, 155–90; Blewett, *Men, Women, and Work*, 33–43, 115–31, 167–89, 230–36, 274–85; Cameron, *Radicals of the Worst Sort*, 47–72. Factory milliners also formed unions, though their efforts were less successful than those of garment workers. See Foner, *Women and the American Labor Movement*, 182–85.

4. Benson, *Counter Cultures*, esp. 227–71.

5. Rodgers, *Work Ethic*, esp. 30–93; Braverman, *Labor and Monopoly Capital*.

6. Freedman, "Separatism as Strategy."

7. Steele, *Fashion and Eroticism*, 122; Brumberg, *Fasting Girls*, 240; Barthel, *Putting on Appearances*, esp. 59–70.

8. Fuentes and Ehrenreich, *Women in the Global Factory*, 20–22, 31–32, 35–39, 48–53.

9. Schroder, *Engagement*, esp. 132. Men account for many of the owners of beauty salons, especially the more prestigious operations. Blewett has noted the tendency of working-class historians to view women merely as "appendages of their families"; much the same can be said of the way in which "mom and pop" stores are interpreted. See Blewett, *We Will Rise*, 16–19.

Essay on Primary Sources

1. I recorded information for all dressmakers and milliners (N = 1,477) listed in the federal manuscript census for Boston in 1860 and for a systematic sample (N = 790) in 1870. For the sample, I recorded information for every third dressmaker or milliner, but 790 represents about 45 percent of all dressmakers and milliners reported by the census (this suggests that published census reports left some craftswomen out) and about 25 percent of the proprietors listed in the 1870 city directory. I found 125 proprietors (about 60 percent of those listed in the Boston business directory) in the 1860 census and 111 in 1870. While the records of R. G. Dun & Co. disproportionately represent wealthier businesswomen, the census samples may be skewed in the opposite direction. Credit reports indicate that some prosperous entrepreneurs lived in the suburbs; they would, of course, be omitted from the census data, which is limited to the city of Boston (1860 FMPC, Boston, M653, reels 520–25; 1870 FMPC, Boston, M593, reels 640–49).

Bibliography

Abelson, Elaine S. *When Ladies Go A-Thieving: Middle-Class Shoplifters in the Victorian Department Store.* New York: Oxford University Press, 1989.

Abelson, Elaine S., David Abraham, and Marjorie Murphy. "Interview with Joan Scott." *Radical History Review* 45 (1989): 41–59.

Adams's New Directory of the City of Boston. Boston: George Adams, 1846.

Allinson, May. *Dressmaking as a Trade for Women in Massachusetts.* Boston: Women's Educational and Industrial Union, 1916.

———. *Industrial Experience of Trade School Girls.* Boston: Women's Educational and Industrial Union, 1917.

Andrews, John B., and W. D. Bliss. *History of Women in Trade Unions.* 1911. New York: Arno Press, 1974.

Arthur, Timothy Shay. *Advice to Young Ladies on Their Duties and Conduct in Life.* Boston: Abel Tompkins, 1849.

"As a Dressmaker Sees Women: In Their Homes, and Now in a Shop of Her Own." *Ladies' Home Journal,* Aug. 1908, 8.

Baker, Jean H. *Mary Todd Lincoln: A Biography.* New York: W. W. Norton, 1987.

Banner, Lois. *American Beauty.* New York: Alfred A. Knopf, 1983.

Baron, Ava. "Contested Terrain Revisited: Technology and Gender Definitions of Work in the Printing Industry, 1850–1920." In *Women, Work, and Technology: Transformations,* ed. Barbara Drygulski Wright, Myra Marx Ferree, Gail O. Mellow, Linda H. Lewis, Maria-Luz Daza Samper, Robert Asher, and Kathleen Claspell. Ann Arbor: University of Michigan Press, 1987. Pp. 58–83.

———. "Gender and Labor History: Learning from the Past, Looking to the Future." In *Work Engendered,* ed. Baron. Pp. 1–46.

———, ed. *Work Engendered: Toward a New History of American Labor.* Ithaca, N.Y.: Cornell University Press, 1991.

Baron, Ava, and Susan E. Klepp. "'If I Didn't Have My Sewing Machine . . .': Women and Sewing Machine Technology." In *A Needle, a Bobbin, a Strike: Women Needleworkers in America,* ed. Joan M. Jensen and Sue Davidson. Philadelphia: Temple University Press, 1984. Pp. 20–59.

Barthel, Diane. *Putting on Appearances: Gender and Advertising.* Philadelphia: Temple University Press, 1988.

Beecher, Catharine E. *A Treatise on Domestic Economy, for the Use of Young Ladies at Home, and at School.* 2d ed. Boston: Thomas H. Webb, 1842.

Beecher, Catharine E., and Harriet Beecher Stowe. *The American Woman's Home; or, Principles of Domestic Science, Being a Guide to the Formation and Maintenance of Economical, Healthful, Beautiful and Christian Homes.* 1869. Watkins Glen, N.Y.: Library of Victorian Culture, 1979.

Bensman, David. *The Practice of Solidarity: American Hat Finishers in the Nineteenth Century.* Urbana: University of Illinois Press, 1985.

Benson, Susan Porter. *Counter Cultures: Saleswomen, Managers, and Customers in American Department Stores, 1890–1940.* Urbana: University of Illinois Press, 1986.

———. "'The Customers Ain't God': The Work Culture of Department-Store Saleswomen, 1890–1940." In *Working-Class America: Essays on Labor, Community, and American Society,* ed. Michael H. Frisch and Daniel J. Walkowitz. Urbana: University of Illinois Press, 1983. Pp. 185–211.

Berthoff, Roland. "Independence and Enterprise: Small Business in the American Dream." In *Small Business in American Life,* ed. Bruchey. Pp. 28–48.

Bird, Caroline. *Enterprising Women.* New York: W. W. Norton, 1976.

Blackford, Mansel G. "Small Business in America: A Historiographic Survey." *Business History Review* 65 (1991): 1–26.

Blair, Karen J. *The Clubwoman as Feminist: True Womanhood Redefined, 1868–1914.* New York: Holmes and Meier, 1980.

Blewett, Mary H. *Men, Women, and Work: Class, Gender, and Protest in the New England Shoe Industry, 1780–1910.* Urbana: University of Illinois Press, 1988.

———. *We Will Rise in Our Might: Workingwomen's Voices from Nineteenth-Century New England.* Ithaca, N.Y.: Cornell University Press, 1991.

Blumin, Stuart M. "Black Coats to White Collars: Economic Change, Nonmanual Work, and the Social Structure of Industrializing America." In *Small Business in American Life,* ed. Bruchey. Pp. 100–121.

———. *The Emergence of the Middle Class: Social Experience in the American City, 1760–1900.* Cambridge: Cambridge University Press, 1989.

———. "The Hypothesis of Middle-Class Formation in Nineteenth-Century America: A Critique and Some Proposals." *American Historical Review* 90 (1985): 330–32.

Boorstin, Daniel J. *The Americans: The Democratic Experience.* New York: Random House, 1966.

Boston Directory. Boston: Edward Cotton, 1805; Boston: Charles Stimpson Jr., 1830; Boston: George Adams, 1850; Boston: Adams, Sampson, 1860; Boston: Sampson, Davenport, 1867–84; Boston: Sampson, Murdock, 1885–1900, 1910, 1915, 1920, 1925, 1930.

Boydston, Jeanne. *Home and Work: Housework, Wages, and the Ideology of Labor in the Early Republic.* New York: Oxford University Press, 1990.

Bradley, Harriet. *Men's Work, Women's Work: A Sociological History of the Sexual Division of Labor in Employment.* Minneapolis: University of Minnesota Press, 1989.

Braverman, Harry. *Labor and Monopoly Capital: The Degradation of Work in the Twentieth Century.* New York: Monthly Review Press, 1974.

Brody, David. "Labor and Small-Scale Enterprise during Industrialization." In *Small Business in American Life,* ed. Bruchey. Pp. 263–79.

[Broughton, Catherine]. *Suggestions for Dressmakers.* New York: Morse-Broughton, [1896].

Bruchey, Stuart W., ed. *Small Business in American Life.* New York: Columbia University Press, 1980.

Brumberg, Joan Jacobs. *Fasting Girls: The Emergence of Anoxeria Nervosa as a Modern Disease.* Cambridge, Mass.: Harvard University Press, 1988.

Bryner, Edna. *Dressmaking and Millinery.* Cleveland: Survey Committee of the Cleveland Foundation, 1916.

———. *The Garment Trades.* Cleveland: Survey Committee of the Cleveland Foundation, 1916.

Buddington, Mr. and Mrs. F. E. *Instruction Book for Using the Buddington Improved Dress Cutting Machine.* Chicago: n.p., 1896.

Buhle, Mari Jo. "Needlewomen and the Vicissitudes of Modern Life: A Study of Middle-Class Construction in the Antebellum Northeast." In *Visible Women: New Essays on American Activism,* ed. Nancy A. Hewitt and Suzanne Lebsock. Urbana: University of Illinois Press, 1993. Pp. 145–65.

———. *Women and American Socialism, 1870–1920.* Urbana: University of Illinois Press, 1981.

Burdett, Charles. *Chances and Changes; or, Life as It Is: Illustrated in the History of a Straw Hat.* New York: D. Appleton, 1846.

Butler, Elizabeth Beardsley. *Saleswomen in Mercantile Stores: Baltimore, 1909.* New York: Russell Sage Foundation, 1912.

———. *Women and the Trades: Pittsburgh, 1907–1908.* 1909. Pittsburgh: University of Pittsburgh Press, 1984.

Cameron, Ardis. *Radicals of the Worst Sort: Laboring Women in Lawrence, Massachusetts, 1860–1912.* Urbana: University of Illinois Press, 1993.

Campbell, Helen. "Darkness and Daylight in New York: Life in the Great Metropolis by Day and Night as Seen by a Woman." In *Darkness and Daylight; or, Light and Shadows of New York Life,* by Helen Campbell, Thomas W. Knox, and Thomas Byrnes. 1895. Detroit: Singing Tree Press, 1969.

———. *Prisoners of Poverty: Women Wage-Workers, Their Trades and Their Lives.* Boston: Little, Brown, 1900.

Carens, Madam Edith Marie. *Dressmaking Self Taught in Twenty Complete Lessons.* Toledo, Ohio: B. F. Wade and Sons, 1911.

Carey, Mathew. "Essays on the Public Charities of Philadelphia . . ." In *Miscellaneous Essays.* Philadelphia: Carey and Hart, 1830. Pp. 153–203.

Caroline Tracy: The Spring Street Milliner's Apprentice; or, Life in New York in 1847–48. New York: Stearns, 1849.

Chambers-Schiller, Lee Virginia. *Liberty, a Better Husband: Single Women in Amer-*

ica—*The Generations of 1780–1840*. New Haven, Conn.: Yale University Press, 1984.

Chandler, Alfred D. *Scale and Scope: The Dynamics of Industrial Capitalism*. Cambridge, Mass.: Harvard University Press, 1990.

———. *The Visible Hand: The Managerial Revolution in American Business*. Cambridge, Mass.: Harvard University Press, 1977.

Clark, Alice. *Working Life of Women in the Seventeenth Century*. 1919. New York: Augustus M. Kelly, 1968.

Clark, Fiona. *Hats*. London: Anchor Press, 1982.

Clark, Sallye. "Carrie Taylor: Kentucky Dressmaker." *Dress* 6 (1980): 13–23.

Cleary, Patricia. "'She Merchants' of Colonial America: Women and Commerce on the Eve of the Revolution." Ph.D. dissertation. Northwestern University, 1989.

Cobble, Dorothy Sue. *Dishing It Out: Waitresses and Their Unions in the Twentieth Century*. Urbana: University of Illinois Press, 1991.

Coffin, Judith G. "Woman's Place and Women's Work in the Paris Clothing Trades, 1830–1914." Ph.D. dissertation. Yale University, 1985.

Coleman, Mrs. M. V. *The Science of Gynametry*. Atlanta: Byrd and Patillo, 1887.

Cooper, Patricia A. *Once a Cigar Maker: Men, Women, and Work Culture in American Cigar Factories, 1900–1919*. Urbana: University of Illinois Press, 1987.

Costello, Cynthia B. "'WEA're Worth It!': Work Culture and Conflict at the Wisconsin Educational Association Insurance Trust." *Feminist Studies* 11 (1985): 496–518.

Cott, Nancy F. *The Bonds of Womanhood: "Woman's Sphere" in New England, 1780–1835*. New Haven, Conn.: Yale University Press, 1977.

———. *The Grounding of Modern Feminism*. New Haven, Conn.: Yale University Press, 1987.

Cowan, Ruth Schwartz. *More Work for Mother: The Ironies of Household Technology from the Open Hearth to the Microwave*. New York: Basic Books, 1983.

Daché, Lilly. *Talking through My Hats*. Ed. Dorothy Roe Lewis. New York: Coward-McCann, 1946.

Daily, Christie. "A Woman's Concern: Millinery in Central Iowa, 1870–1880." *Journal of the West* 21 (1982): 26–32.

Dall, Caroline H. *The College, the Market, and the Court; or, Woman's Relation to Education, Labor, and Law*. 2d ed. Boston: Lee and Shepard, 1868.

Daves, Jessica. *Ready-Made Miracle: The American Story of Fashion for the Millions*. New York: G. P. Putnam's Sons, 1967.

Davies, Margery. *Woman's Place Is at the Typewriter: Office Work and Office Workers, 1870–1930*. Philadelphia: Temple University Press, 1982.

de Aguirre, Gertrude G. *Women in the Business World; or, Hints and Helps to Prosperity by One of Them*. Boston: Arena Publishing, 1894.

Des Moulins, Amelia. "The Dressmaker's Life Story." *Independent* 56 (Apr. 28, 1904): 939–46.

Deutsch, Sarah. "The Business of Women: Female Petty Entrepreneurship in Boston, 1870–1950." Paper presented at the Shelby Cullom Davis Center, Princeton University, Feb. 3, 1995.

———. "Learning to Talk More Like a Man: Boston Women's Class-Bridging Organizations, 1870–1940." *American Historical Review* 97 (1992): 379–404.

DeVault, Ileen A. *Sons and Daughters of Labor: Class and Clerical Work in Turn-of-the-Century Pittsburgh.* Ithaca, N.Y.: Cornell University Press, 1990.

Dexter, Elisabeth A. *Career Women of America, 1776–1840.* Francestown, N.H.: Marshall Jones, 1950.

———. *Colonial Women of Affairs: A Study of Women in Business and the Professions in America before 1776.* Boston: Houghton Mifflin, 1924.

Ditz, Toby L. "Shipwrecked; or, Masculinity Imperiled: Mercantile Representations of Failure and the Gendered Self in Eighteenth-Century Philadelphia." *Journal of American History* 81 (1994): 51–80.

Drachman, Virginia G. "'My "Partner" in Law and Life': Marriage in the Lives of Women Lawyers in Late 19th- and Early 20th-Century America." *Law and Social Inquiry* 14 (Spring 1989): 221–50.

Dreher, Denise. *From the Neck Up: An Illustrated Guide to Hatmaking.* Minneapolis, Minn.: Madhatter Press, 1981.

Drysdale, William. *Helps for Ambitious Girls.* New York: Thomas Y. Crowell, 1900.

Dublin, Thomas. "Rural-Urban Migrants in Industrial New England: The Case of Lynn, Massachusetts, in the Mid-Nineteenth Century." *Journal of American History* 73 (1986): 623–44.

———. *Transforming Women's Work: New England Lives in the Industrial Revolution.* Ithaca, N.Y.: Cornell University Press, 1994.

———. *Women at Work: The Transformation of Work and Community in Lowell, Massachusetts, 1826–1860.* New York: Columbia University Press, 1979.

———. "Women Workers and the Study of Social Mobility." *Journal of Interdisciplinary History* 9 (1979): 647–65.

DuBois, Ellen, Mari Jo Buhle, Temma Kaplan, Gerda Lerner, and Carroll Smith-Rosenberg. "Politics and Culture in Women's History: A Symposium." *Feminist Studies* 6 (1980): 26–64.

Dudden, Faye E. *Serving Women: Household Service in Nineteenth-Century America.* Middletown, Conn.: Wesleyan University Press, 1983.

Duncan, Hugh Dalziel. *Culture and Democracy: The Struggle for Form in Society and Architecture in Chicago and the Middle West during the Life and Times of Louis H. Sullivan.* Totowa, N.J.: Bedminster Press, 1965.

Duniway, Abigail Scott. *Path Breaking: An Autobiographical History of the Equal Suffrage Movement in Pacific Coast States.* 2d ed. New York: Schocken Books, 1971.

Dye, Nancy Schrom. *As Equals and as Sisters: Feminism, Unionism, and the Women's Trade Union League of New York.* Columbia: University of Missouri Press, 1980.

Earling, P. R. *Whom to Trust: A Practical Treatise on Mercantile Credits.* Chicago: Rand McNally, 1890.

Eisenstein, Sarah. *Give Us Bread, but Give Us Roses: Working Women's Consciousness in the United States, 1890 to the First World War.* London: Routledge and Kegan Paul, 1983.

Ernst, George A. O. *The Law of Married Women in Massachusetts.* 2d ed. Boston: Little, Brown, 1897.

Everett, Helen. "The Dress Industry: A Study of the Impact of Fashion on the Ways of Business." Report no. 19, U.S. Department of Labor, Consumers' Project, Mar. 15, 1937.

Ewen, Stuart. *Captains of Consciousness: Advertising and the Social Roots of the Consumer Culture.* New York: McGraw-Hill, 1976.

Ewen, Stuart, and Elizabeth Ewen. *Channels of Desire: Mass Images and the Shaping of American Consciousness.* New York: McGraw-Hill, 1982.

Faler, Paul. *Mechanics and Manufacturers in the Early Industrial Revolution: Lynn, Massachusetts, 1780–1860.* Albany: State University of New York Press, 1981.

[Farrar, Eliza Ware]. *The Young Lady's Friend.* Boston: American Stationers, 1837.

Faue, Elizabeth. "Paths of Unionization: Community, Bureaucracy, and Gender in the Minneapolis Labor Movement of the 1930s." In *Work Engendered,* ed. Baron. Pp. 296–319.

Fernandez, Nancy Page. "'If a Woman Had Taste . . .': Home Sewing and the Making of Fashion, 1850–1910." Ph.D. dissertation. University of California, Irvine, 1987.

———. "Women, Work, and Wages in the Industrialization of American Dressmaking, 1860–1910." Paper presented at the Ninth Berkshire Conference on the History of Women, June 1993.

Foner, Philip S. *Women and the American Labor Movement: From World War I to the Present.* New York: Free Press, 1980.

Formanek-Brunell, Miriam. *Made to Play House: Dolls and the Commercialization of American Girlhood, 1830–1930.* New Haven, Conn.: Yale University Press, 1993.

Foster, George C. *New York by Gas-Light: With Here and There a Streak of Sunshine.* New York: Dewitt and Davenport, 1850.

Fox, Richard Wightman, and T. J. Jackson Lears, eds. *The Culture of Consumption: Critical Essays in American History, 1880–1980.* New York: Pantheon, 1983.

Freedman, Estelle. "Separatism as Strategy: Female Institution Building and American Feminism, 1870–1930." *Feminist Studies* 5 (1979): 512–29.

Fuentes, Annette, and Barbara Ehrenreich. *Women in the Global Factory.* Boston: South End Press, 1983.

Gardner, Deborah S. "'A Paradise of Fashion': A. T. Stewart's Department Store, 1862–1875." In *A Needle, a Bobbin, a Strike: Women Needleworkers in America,* ed. Joan M. Jensen and Sue Davidson. Philadelphia: Temple University Press, 1984. Pp. 60–80.

Gartland, Elizabeth. *The Original American Lady Tailor System.* Philadelphia: n.p., 1884.

Gerber, David. "Cutting Out Shylock: Elite Anti-Semitism and the Quest for Moral

Order in the Mid-Nineteenth-Century American Marketplace." *Journal of American History* 69 (1982): 615–37.

Giblin, Kate J. *Concerning Millinery.* Boston: Puritan Press, 1902.

Gilbert, Sandra M., and Susan Gubar. *The Madwoman in the Attic: The Woman Writer and the Nineteenth-Century Literary Imagination.* New Haven, Conn.: Yale University Press, 1979.

Gilman, Amy. "'Cogs to the Wheels': The Ideology of Women's Work in Mid-Nineteenth-Century Fiction." *Science and Society* 47 (1983): 178–204.

Girls Trade Education League (GTEL). *Vocations for Boston Girls, No. 6: Millinery.* Boston: GTEL, 1911.

Glenn, Susan A. *Daughters of the Shtetl: Life and Labor in the Immigrant Generation.* Ithaca, N.Y.: Cornell University Press, 1990.

Goldin, Claudia. "The Economic Status of Women in the Early Republic: Quantitative Evidence." *Journal of Interdisciplinary History* 16 (1986): 375–404.

Greeley, Horace, et al. *The Great Industries of the United States: Being an Historical Summary of the Origin, Growth, and Perfection of the Chief Industrial Arts of This Country.* Hartford, Conn.: J. B. Burr and Hyde, 1872.

Greenway, John L. "'Nervous Disease' and Electric Medicine." In *Pseudo-Science and Society in Nineteenth-Century America,* ed. Arthur Wrobel. Lexington: University Press of Kentucky, 1987. Pp. 46–73.

Griffen, Caleb H., and David Knox. *The Science and Art of Cutting and Making Ladies' Garments, as Demonstrated by Griffen and Knox's Great American Drafting Machine.* Lynn, Mass.: Charles F. Bessom, 1873.

Griffen, Clyde, and Sally Griffen. *Natives and Newcomers: The Ordering of Opportunity in Mid-Nineteenth-Century Poughkeepsie.* Cambridge, Mass.: Harvard University Press, 1978.

———. "Small Business and Occupational Mobility in Mid-Nineteenth-Century Poughkeepsie." In *Small Business in American Life,* ed. Bruchey. Pp. 122–41.

Guide to Dressmaking. Boston: J. Henry Symonds, 1876.

Halttunen, Karen. *Confidence Men and Painted Women: A Study of Middle-Class Culture in America, 1830–1870.* New Haven, Conn.: Yale University Press, 1982.

Hartley, Florence. *The Ladies' Book of Etiquette and Manual of Politeness.* Boston: DeWolfe, Fiske, 1837.

Hazen, Edward. *The Panorama of Professions and Trades; or, Every Man's Book.* Philadelphia: Uriah Hunt, 1839.

Hecklinger, Charles. *The Dress and Cloak Cutter, in Two Parts.* New York: Root and Tinker, 1883.

Hershberg, Theodore, Michael Katz, Stuart Blumin, Laurence Glasco, and Clyde Griffen. "Occupation and Ethnicity in Five Nineteenth-Century Cities: A Collaborative Inquiry." *Historical Methods Newsletter* 7 (1974): 174–216.

Hewitt, Nancy A. "Beyond the Search for Sisterhood: American Women's History in the 1980s." In *Unequal Sisters: A Multicultural Reader in U.S. Women's History,* ed. Ellen Carol Dubois and Vicki L. Ruiz. New York: Routledge, 1990. Pp. 1–14.

Hicks, Rebecca. *The Milliner and the Millionaire*. Philadelphia: Lippincott, Grambo, 1852.

Hilf, Mary Asia. *No Time for Tears*. As told to Barbara Bourns. New York: Thomas Yoseloff, 1964.

Hill, Joseph A. *Women in Gainful Occupations, 1870 to 1920: A Study of the Trend of Recent Changes in the Numbers, Occupational Distribution, and Family Relationships of Women Reported in the Census as Following a Gainful Occupation*. Census Monographs 9. Washington, D.C.: Government Printing Office, 1929.

A History of the National Wholesale Druggists' Association. New York: National Wholesale Druggists' Association, 1924.

Hochschild, Arlie Russell. *The Managed Heart: Commercialization of Human Feeling*. Berkeley: University of California Press, 1983.

Hoff, Joan. *Law, Gender and Injustice: A Legal History of U.S. Women*. New York: New York University Press, 1991.

Horowitz, Daniel. *The Morality of Spending: Attitudes toward the Consumer Society in America, 1875–1940*. Baltimore: Johns Hopkins University Press, 1985.

Hourwich, Andria Taylor, and Gladys L. Palmer, eds. *I Am a Woman Worker*. 1936. New York: Arno Press, 1974.

Howells, William Dean. *The Habits of Good Society: A Handbook for Ladies and Gentlemen*. New York: Carleton, 1865.

———. *A Woman's Reason*. Boston: James R. Osgood, 1883.

Hunt, Harriot K. *Glances and Glimpses; or, Fifty Years Social, including Twenty Years Professional Life*. Boston: John P. Jewett, 1856.

Hutchinson, Ruth Gillette, Arthur R. Hutchinson, and Mabel Newcomer. "A Study in Business Mortality: Length of Life of Business Enterprises in Poughkeepsie, New York, 1843–1936." *American Economic Review* 28 (1938): 497–514.

Ingham, John N. "Patterns of African-American Female Self-Employment and Entrepreneurship in Ten Southern Cities, 1880–1933." Paper presented at the Tenth Berkshire Conference on the History of Women, June 1996.

Ingraham, Joseph Holt. *Grace Weldon; or, Frederica, the Bonnet-Girl: A Tale of Boston and Its Bay*. Boston: H. L. Williams, 1845.

Instruction Book with Diagrams for S. T. Taylor's System of Cutting Ladies' Garments. New York: S. T. Taylor, 1915.

International Ladies' Garment Workers' Union (ILGWU) Educational Department. *The Story of the I.L.G.W.U.* N.p.: ABCO Press, 1935.

James, Edward T., Janet Wilson James, and Paul S. Boyer, eds. *Notable American Women, 1607–1950*. Vol. 2. Cambridge, Mass.: Harvard University Press, 1971.

Jerde, Judith. "Mary Molloy: St. Paul's Extraordinary Dressmaker." *Dress* 7 (1981): 82–89.

Johnson, Paul E. *A Shopkeeper's Millennium: Society and Revivals in Rochester, New York, 1815–1837*. New York: Hill and Wang, 1978.

Jonason, Linda Novak. "Dressmaking in North Dakota between 1890 and 1920:

Equipment, Supplies, and Methods." Master's thesis. North Dakota State University, 1977.

Jones, Justin. *Tom, Dick, and Harry; or, The Boys and Girls of Boston.* Boston: Star Spangled Banner Office, 1849.

Katz, Michael B. *The People of Hamilton, Canada West: Family and Class in a Mid-Nineteenth-Century City.* Cambridge, Mass.: Harvard University Press, 1975.

Katzman, David M. *Seven Days a Week: Women and Domestic Service in Industrializing America.* New York: Oxford University Press, 1978.

Keckley, Elizabeth. *Behind the Scenes; or, Thirty Years a Slave, and Four Years in the White House.* New York: G. W. Carleton, 1868.

Keller, Evelyn Fox. *Reflections on Gender and Science.* New Haven, Conn.: Yale University Press, 1985.

Keller, Morton. *Affairs of State: Public Life in Late Nineteenth Century America.* Cambridge, Mass.: Harvard University Press, 1977.

Kemp, Alice Abel. *Women's Work: Degraded and Devalued.* Englewood Cliffs, N.J.: Prentice-Hall, 1994.

Kerber, Linda K. "Separate Spheres, Female Worlds, Woman's Place: The Rhetoric of Women's History." *Journal of American History* 75 (1988): 9–39.

Kessler-Harris, Alice. "Independence and Virtue in the Lives of Wage-Earning Women: The United States, 1870–1930." In *Women in Culture and Politics: A Century of Change,* ed. Judith Friedlander, Blanche Wiesen Cook, Alice Kessler-Harris, and Carroll Smith-Rosenberg. Bloomington: Indiana University Press, 1986. Pp. 3–17.

———. *Out to Work: A History of Wage-Earning Women in the United States.* New York: Oxford University Press, 1982.

———. *A Woman's Wage: Historical Meanings and Social Consequences.* Lexington: University Press of Kentucky, 1990.

Keyssar, Alexander. *Out of Work: The First Century of Unemployment in Massachusetts.* Cambridge: Cambridge University Press, 1986.

Kidwell, Claudia B. *Cutting a Fashionable Fit: Dressmakers' Drafting Systems in the United States.* Washington, D.C.: Smithsonian Institution Press, 1979.

Kidwell, Claudia B., and Margaret C. Christman. *Suiting Everyone: The Democratization of Clothing in America.* Washington, D.C.: Smithsonian Institution Press, 1974.

King, Moses. *King's How-to-See Boston.* Boston: Moses King, 1895.

Kunzle, David. "Dress Reform as Antifeminism: A Response to Helene E. Roberts's 'The Exquisite Slave: The Role of Clothes in the Making of the Victorian Woman.'" *Signs* 2 (1977): 570–79.

———. *Fashion and Fetishism: A Social History of the Corset, Tight-Lacing and Other Forms of Body-Sculpture in the West.* Totowa, N.J.: Rowman and Littlefield, 1982.

Kwolek-Folland, Angel. *Engendering Business: Men and Women in the Corporate Office, 1870–1930.* Baltimore: Johns Hopkins University Press, 1994.

The Ladies' Hand-Book of Millinery and Dressmaking, with Plain Instructions for Making the Most Useful Articles of Dress and Attire. New York: J. S. Redfield, 1844.

The Ladies' Self-Instructor in Millinery, Mantua Making, and All Branches of Plain Sewing, with Particular Directions for Cutting Out Dresses, etc. Philadelphia: G. B. Zieber, 1845.

Lamphere, Louise. "Bringing the Family to Work: Women's Culture on the Shop Floor." *Feminist Studies* 11 (1985): 520–40.

Lasser, Carol. "'The World's Dread Laugh': Singlehood and Service in Nineteenth-Century Boston." In *The New England Working Class and the New Labor History,* ed Herbert G. Gutman and Donald H. Bell. Urbana: University of Illinois Press, 1987. Pp. 72–88.

Lauer, Jeanette, and Robert H. Lauer. "The Battle of the Sexes: Fashion in 19th Century America." *Journal of Popular Culture* 8 (Spring 1980): 581–89.

Laurie, Bruce. *Artisans into Workers: Labor in Nineteenth-Century America.* New York: Hill and Wang, 1989.

———. *Working People of Philadelphia, 1800–1850.* Philadelphia: Temple University Press, 1980.

Leach, William R. *Land of Desire: Merchants, Power, and the Rise of a New American Culture.* New York: Pantheon, 1993.

———. *True Love and Perfect Union: The Feminist Reform of Sex and Society.* New York: Basic Books, 1980.

Lears, T. J. Jackson. "Beyond Veblen: Rethinking Consumer Culture in America." In *Consuming Visions: Accumulation and Display of Goods in America, 1880–1920,* ed. Simon J. Bronner. New York: W. W. Norton, 1989. Pp. 73–97.

———. "From Salvation to Self-Realization: Advertising and the Therapeutic Roots of the Consumer Culture, 1880–1930." In *Culture of Consumption,* ed. Fox and Lears. Pp. 17–27.

Lebsock, Suzanne. *The Free Women of Petersburg: Status and Culture in a Southern Town, 1784–1860.* New York: W. W. Norton, 1984.

Leonardo, Michaela di. "Women's Work, Work Culture, and Consciousness." *Feminist Studies* 11 (1985): 490–519.

Lerner, Gerda. "The Lady and the Mill Girl: Changes in the Status of Women in the Age of Jackson, 1800–1840." In *A Heritage of Her Own: Toward a New Social History of American Women,* ed. Nancy F. Cott and Elizabeth H. Pleck. New York: Simon and Schuster, 1979. Pp. 182–96.

———. "Placing Women in History: Definitions and Challenges." *Feminist Studies* 3 (1975): 5–14.

Leslie, Eliza. *Leonilla Lynmore, and Mr. and Mrs. Woodbridge; or, A Lesson for Young Wives.* Philadelphia: Carey and Hart, 1847.

———. *Miss Leslie's Lady's House-Book: A Manual of Domestic Economy.* 11th ed. Philadelphia: A. Hart, 1850.

Levine, Louis. *The Women's Garment Workers: A History of the International Ladies' Garment Workers' Union.* New York: B. W. Huebson, 1924.

Lewis, Susan Ingalls. "Female Entrepreneurs, Artisans, and Workers: Milliners in Albany, 1840–1885." Paper presented at the North American Labor History Conference, Oct. 1990.

Madison, James H. "The Credit Reports of R. G. Dun & Co. as Historical Sources." *Historical Methods Newsletter* 8 (1975): 128–31.

———. "The Evolution of Commercial Credit Reporting Agencies in Nineteenth-Century America." *Business History Review* 48 (1974): 164–86.

Mainiero, Lina, and Langdon Lynne Faust, eds. *American Women Writers: A Critical Reference Guide from Colonial Times to the Present.* Vol. 4. New York: Frederick Ungar, 1982.

Marshall, Ray, and Beth Paulin. "Employments and Earnings of Women: Historical Perspective." In *Working Women: Past, Present, Future,* ed. Karen Shallcross Koziara, Michael H. Moskow, and Lucretia Dewey Tanner. Washington, D.C.: Bureau of National Affairs, 1987. Pp. 1–36.

Martineau, Harriet. *Society in America.* Vol. 3. 1837. New York: AMS Press, 1966.

Massachusetts Bureau of Statistics of Labor (MBSL). *Report of the Bureau of Statistics of Labor, Embracing the Account of Its Operations and Inquiries from March 1, 1870, to March 1, 1871.* Boston: Wright and Potter, 1871.

Massachusetts Minimum Wage Commission (MMWC). *Report on the Wages of Women in the Millinery Industry in Massachusetts.* Boston: Wright and Potter, 1919.

Matthaei, Julie A. *An Economic History of Women in America: Women's Work, the Sexual Division of Labor, and the Development of Capitalism.* New York: Schocken Books, 1985.

Matthews, Glenna. *"Just a Housewife": The Rise and Fall of Domesticity in America.* New York: Oxford University Press, 1987.

May, Martha. "Bread before Roses: American Workingmen, Labor Unions, and the Family Wage." In *Women, Work, and Protest: A Century of U.S. Women's Labor History,* ed. Ruth Milkman. Boston: Routledge and Kegan Paul, 1985. Pp. 1–21.

Mayfield, Frank M. *The Department Store Story.* New York: Fairchild Publications, 1949.

The McDowell Standard System of Garment Cutting. New York: McDowell Garment Drafting Machine, [1886].

McGaw, Judith A. "No Passive Victims, No Separate Spheres: A Feminist Perspective on Technology's History." In *In Context: History and the History of Technology,* ed. Stephen H. Cutcliffe and Robert C. Post. Bethlehem, Pa.: Lehigh University Press, 1989. Pp. 178–84.

Melosh, Barbara. *"The Physician's Hand": Work Culture and Conflict in American Nursing.* Philadelphia: Temple University Press, 1982.

Moeckel, Bill Reid. *The Development of the Wholesaler in the United States, 1860–1900.* New York: Garland Publishing, 1986.

Montgomery, David. *The Fall of the House of Labor: The Workplace, the State, and American Labor Activism, 1865–1925.* Cambridge: Cambridge University Press, 1987.

———. *Workers' Control in America: Studies in the History of Work, Technology, and Labor Struggle*. Cambridge: Cambridge University Press, 1979.

Mott, Frank Luther. *A History of American Magazines*. 4 vols. Cambridge, Mass.: Harvard University Press, 1939, 1957.

Murphy, Lucy Eldersveld. "Business Ladies: Midwestern Women and Enterprise, 1850–1880." *Journal of Women's History* 3 (1991): 65–89.

———. "Her Own Boss: Businesswomen and Separate Spheres in the Midwest, 1850–1880." *Illinois Historical Journal* 80 (Autumn 1987): 155–76.

Nenadic, Stana, R. J. Morris, James Smyth, and Chris Rainger. "Record Linkage and the Small Family Firm: Edinburgh, 1861–1891." *Bulletin of the John Rylands University Library of Manchester* 74 (Autumn 1992): 169–95.

Norris, James D. *R. G. Dun & Co., 1841–1900: The Development of Credit-Reporting in the Nineteenth Century*. Westport, Conn.: Greenwood Press, 1978.

Parton, Mary Field, ed. *The Autobiography of Mother Jones*. 3d. ed. Chicago: Charles H. Kerr, 1976.

Peiss, Kathy. *Cheap Amusements: Working Women and Leisure in Turn-of-the-Century New York*. Philadelphia: Temple University Press, 1986.

Penny, Virginia. *The Employments of Women: A Cyclopedia of Woman's Work*. Boston: Walker, Wise, 1863.

———. *Think and Act: A Series of Articles Pertaining to Men and Women, Work and Wages*. 1869. New York: Arno Press, 1971.

Perry, Lorinda. *The Millinery Trade in Boston and Philadelphia: A Study of Women in Industry*. Binghamton, N.Y.: Vail-Ballou, 1916.

Phillips, Anne, and Barbara Taylor. "Sex and Skill: Notes towards a Feminist Economics." *Feminist Review* 6 (1981): 79–88.

Philo [pseud.]. *Twelve Letters to a Young Milliner*. New York: Hill Brothers, 1883.

Porter, Glenn, and Harold C. Livesay. *Merchants and Manufacturers: Studies in the Changing Structure of Nineteenth-Century Marketing*. Baltimore: Johns Hopkins University Press, 1971.

Porter, Rev. James. *The Operative's Friend and Defence; or, Hints to Young Ladies, Who Are Dependent on Their Own Exertions*. 3d ed. Boston: Charles H. Peirce, 1850.

Preston, Jo Anne. "Learning a Trade in Industrializing New England: The Expedition of Hannah and Mary Adams to Nashua, New Hampshire, 1833–1834." *Historical New Hampshire* 39 (Spring/Summer 1984): 24–44.

———. "'To Learn Me the Whole of the Trade': Conflict between a Female Apprentice and a Merchant Tailor in Ante-Bellum New England." *Labor History* 24 (1983): 259–73.

Pullan, Marion M. *Beadle's Dime Guide to Dress-Making and Millinery, with a Complete French and English Dictionary of Terms Employed in Those Arts*. New York: Beadle, 1860.

Rayne, Martha Louise. *What Can a Woman Do?* 1893. New York: Arno Press, 1974.

Rebuilding an Industry: The History of the Eastern Women's Headwear Association. New York: Eastern Women's Headwear Association, Inc., [1951].

Research Bureau for Retail Training. *Manual for a Millinery Department.* Pittsburgh: Carnegie Institute of Technology, 1923.

Reskin, Barbara F., and Heidi I. Hartmann, eds. *Women's Work, Men's Work: Sex Segregation on the Job.* Washington, D.C.: National Academy Press, 1986.

Reynolds, David S. *Beneath the American Renaissance: The Subversive Imagination in the Age of Emerson and Melville.* New York: Alfred A. Knopf, 1988.

Richardson, Dorothy. *The Long Day: The Story of a New York Working Girl.* In *Women at Work,* ed. William O'Neill. New York: Quadrangle/New York Times, 1972.

Roberts, Helene E. "The Exquisite Slave: The Role of Clothes in the Making of the Victorian Woman." *Signs* 2 (1977): 554–69.

Rodgers, Daniel. *The Work Ethic in Industrial America, 1850–1920.* Chicago: University of Chicago Press, 1978.

Rollins, Judith. *Between Women: Domestics and Their Employers.* Philadelphia: Temple University Press, 1985.

Rood, Will C. *Supplement No. 2: Advanced Studies for Those Using Dressmakers' Magic Scale.* Quincy, Ill.: Rood Magic Scale, 1889.

Rorabaugh, W. J. *The Craft Apprentice: From Franklin to the Machine Age in America.* New York: Oxford University Press, 1986.

Ryan, Mary P. *Cradle of the Middle Class: The Family in Oneida County, New York, 1790–1865.* Cambridge: Cambridge University Press, 1981.

———. *Women in Public: Between Banners and Ballots, 1825–1880.* Baltimore: Johns Hopkins University Press, 1990.

Sanger, William W. *The History of Prostitution: Its Extent, Causes, and Effects.* 1939. New York: AMS Press, 1974.

Schorman, Rob. "The Truth about Good Goods: Clothing, Advertising, and the Representation of Cultural Values at the End of the Nineteenth Century." *American Studies* 37 (Spring 1996): 23–49.

Schroder, David. *Engagement in the Mirror: Hairdressers and Their Work.* San Francisco: R. and E. Research Associates, 1978.

Scott, Joan. *Gender and the Politics of History.* New York: Columbia University Press, 1988.

———. "Gender: A Useful Category of Historical Analysis." *American Historical Review* 91 (1986): 1053–75.

Scranton, Philip. "Diversity in Diversity: Flexible Production and American Industrialization, 1880–1930." *Business History Review* 65 (1991): 27–90.

Shuttleworth, Sally. "Female Circulation: Medical Discourse and Popular Advertising in the Mid-Victorian Era." In *Body/Politics: Women and the Discourses of Science,* ed. Mary Jacobus, Evelyn Fox Keller, and Sally Shuttleworth. New York: Routledge, 1990. Pp. 47–68.

Simon, Amy. "'She Is So Neat and Fits So Well': Garment Construction and the Millinery Business of Eliza Oliver Dodds, 1821–1833." Master's thesis. University of Delaware, 1993.

Smith-Rosenberg, Carroll. *Disorderly Conduct: Visions of Gender in Victorian America*. New York: Oxford University Press, 1985.

Standard Garment Cutting Company. *Standard Square Inch Tailoring System*. Chicago: n.p., 1896.

Stanley, Autumn. *Mothers and Daughters of Invention: Notes for a Revised History of Technology*. Metuchen, N.J.: Scarecrow Press, 1993.

Stansell, Christine. *City of Women: Class and Sex in New York*. New York: Alfred A. Knopf, 1986.

Steedman, Carolyn. *Landscape for a Good Woman: A Story of Two Lives*. New Brunswick, N.J.: Rutgers University Press, 1987.

Steele, Valerie. *Fashion and Eroticism: Ideals of Feminine Beauty from the Victorian Era to the Jazz Age*. New York: Oxford University Press, 1985.

Stein, Leon. *Out of the Sweatshop: The Struggle for Industrial Democracy*. New York: Quadrangle Books, 1977.

Stimson, H. A. "The Small Business as a School of Manhood." *Atlantic Monthly* 93 (1904): 337–340.

The Stranger's Guide in the City of Boston. Vol. 1, no. 2. Boston: Andrews, 1849.

Strasser, Susan. *Never Done: A History of American Housework*. New York: Pantheon, 1982.

———. *Satisfaction Guaranteed: The Making of the American Mass Market*. New York: Pantheon, 1989.

Sumner, Helen L., *History of Women in Industry in the United States*. Vol. 9 of *Report on Condition of Woman and Child Wage-Earners in the United States*. 61st Cong., 2d Sess., Senate document no. 645. Washington, D.C.: Government Printing Office, 1910.

Susman, Warren I. "'Personality' and the Making of Twentieth-Century Culture." In *New Directions in American Intellectual History*, ed. John Higham and Paul K. Conkin. Baltimore: Johns Hopkins University Press, 1979. Pp. 212–26.

Taylor, Nancy J. "The Work that Women Do: Continuity and Change in Women's Paid Employments in Industrializing Cincinnati, Ohio, 1840–1860." Paper presented at the Ninth Berkshire Conference on the History of Women, June 1993.

Taylor, Samuel T. *Dress Cutting Simplified and Reduced to Science*. Baltimore: John W. Woods, 1850.

———. *S. T. Taylor's System of Dress Cutting*. New York: S. T. Taylor, 1896.

———. *A System for Cutting Ladies' Dresses*. New York: T. Holman, [1875].

———. *A System for Cutting Ladies' Garments*. New York: T. Holman, 1871.

Tentler, Aaron A. *A New System for Measuring and Cutting Ladies' Dresses, Cloaks, Collars, Capes, Yokes, etc.* Philadelphia: J. Sharp, 1842.

Tentler, Leslie Woodcock. *Wage-Earning Women: Industrial Work and Family Life in the United States, 1900–1930*. Oxford: Oxford University Press, 1979.

Thernstrom, Stephan. *The Other Bostonians: Poverty and Progress in the American Metropolis, 1880–1970*. Cambridge, Mass.: Harvard University Press, 1973.

————. *Poverty and Progress: Social Mobility in a Nineteenth Century City.* Cambridge, Mass.: Harvard University Press, 1980.

Thompson, E. P. *The Making of the English Working Class.* New York: Vintage, 1966.

Tobey, Evelyn Smith. "The Educated Woman in Millinery." In *Vocations for the Trained Woman: Opportunities Other Than Teaching, Introductory Papers,* ed. Agnes F. Perkins. Boston: Women's Educational and Industrial Union, 1910. Pp. 116–18.

Trautman, Patricia A. *Clothing America: A Bibliography and Location Index of Nineteenth-Century American Pattern Drafting Systems.* N.p.: Costume Society of America, Region 2, 1987.

Turbin, Carole. "Beyond Conventional Wisdom: Women's Wage Work, Household Economic Contribution, and Labor Activism in a Mid-Nineteenth-Century Working-Class Community." In *"To Toil the Livelong Day": America's Women at Work, 1780–1980,* ed. Carol Groneman and Mary Beth Norton. Ithaca, N.Y.: Cornell University Press, 1987. Pp. 47–67.

————. *Working Women of Collar City: Gender, Class, and Community in Troy, 1864–86.* Urbana: University of Illinois Press, 1992.

Turner, Justin G., and Linda Levitt Turner. *Mary Todd Lincoln: Her Life and Letters.* New York: Alfred A. Knopf, 1972.

Ulrich, Laurel Thatcher. *A Midwife's Tale: The Life of Martha Ballard, Based on Her Diary, 1785–1812.* New York: Vintage, 1991.

U.S. Bureau of the Census (USBC). *A Compendium of the Ninth Census (June 1, 1870).* Washington, D.C.: Government Printing Office, 1872.

————. *Fifteenth Census of the United States: 1930, Population.* Vol. 5: *General Report on Occupations.* Washington, D.C.: Government Printing Office, 1933.

————. *Population of the United States in 1860 . . . Eighth Census.* Washington, D.C.: Government Printing Office, 1864.

————. *Report on Manufacturing Industries in the United States at the Eleventh Census: 1890.* Pt. 2: *Statistics of Cities.* Washington, D.C.: Government Printing Office, 1895.

————. *Special Reports: Employees and Wages.* Washington, D.C.: U.S. Census Office, 1903.

————. *The Statistics of the Population of the United States . . . Ninth Census.* Washington, D.C.: Government Printing Office, 1872.

————. *Statistics of the Population of the United States . . . Tenth Census.* Washington, D.C.: Government Printing Office, 1883.

————. *Statistics of Women at Work.* Washington, D.C.: Government Printing Office, 1907.

————. *Twelfth Census of the United States, Taken in the Year 1900:* Pt. 2: *Population.* Washington, D.C.: Government Printing Office, 1902.

U.S. Federal Trade Commission. "Report to the President of the United States on Distribution Methods in the Millinery Industry." Nov. 21, 1939.

Van Kleeck, Mary. *A Seasonal Industry: A Study of the Millinery Trade in New York.* New York: Russell Sage Foundation, 1917.

—————. *Wages in the Millinery Trade.* New York: J. B. Lyon, 1914.

Veblen, Thorstein. *The Theory of the Leisure Class.* Boston: Houghton Mifflin, 1973.

von der Nienburg, Bertha Marie. *Conditions in the Millinery Industry in the United States.* Washington, D.C.: Government Printing Office, 1939.

Vose, Edward Neville. *Seventy-five Years of the Mercantile Agency: R. G. Dun & Co., 1841–1916.* New York: R. G. Dun, 1916.

Walker, Mary Edwards. *A Woman's Thoughts about Love and Marriage, Divorce, etc.* New York: Miller, 1871.

Walsh, Margaret. "The Democratization of Fashion: The Emergence of the Women's Dress Pattern Industry." *Journal of American History* 66 (1979): 299–313.

Waters, Deane Gayle. "Comparison and Contrast of Two Atlanta Historical Society Gowns." Master's thesis. University of Georgia, 1980.

Watson, Harry L. *Liberty and Power: The Politics of Jacksonian America.* New York: Noonday Press, 1990.

Weathersby, Robert W. II. *J. H. Ingraham.* Boston: Twayne Publishers, 1980.

Welter, Barbara. "The Cult of True Womanhood, 1820–1860." *American Quarterly* 18 (1966): 151–74.

Wertheimer, Barbara Mayer. *We Were There: The Story of Working Women in America.* New York: Pantheon, 1977.

Wiebe, Robert H. *The Search for Order, 1877–1920.* New York: Hill and Wang, 1967.

Wilbur, Mary Aronetta. *Every-day Business for Women: A Manual for the Uninitiated.* Boston: Houghton Mifflin, 1910.

Wilentz, Sean. *Chants Democratic: New York City and the Rise of the American Working-Class, 1788–1850.* New York: Oxford University Press, 1984.

Willett, Mabel Hurd. *The Employment of Women in the Clothing Trade.* Studies in History, Economics, and Public Law. Vol. 26, no. 2. New York: Columbia University Press, 1902.

Wilson, Elizabeth. *Adorned in Dreams: Fashion and Modernity.* Berkeley: University of California Press, 1985.

Woolson, Abba Goold. *Woman in American Society.* Boston: Roberts Brothers, 1873.

Woods, Caroline H. [Belle Otis]. *The Diary of a Milliner.* New York: Hurd and Houghton, 1867.

Working-Women's Protective Union (WWPU). *Fifth Annual Report.* New York: John A. Gary and Green, 1868.

Wright, Carroll D. *The Working Girls of Boston.* 1884. New York: Arno Press and the New York Times, 1969.

Wright, Lyle H. *American Fiction, 1851–1875: A Contribution toward a Bibliography.* San Marino, Calif.: Huntington Library, 1957.

Wrobel, Arthur. "Introduction." In *Pseudo-Science and Society in Nineteenth-Century America,* ed. Arthur Wrobel. Lexington: University Press of Kentucky, 1987. Pp. 1–20.

444

Zavella, Patricia. "'Abnormal Intimacy': The Varying Networks of Chicana Cannery Workers." *Feminist Studies* 11 (1985): 540–57.

Index

for men, 10, 98, 177; "democratic" features claimed for, 97, 128, 156, 190; customers and, 101, 124, 182, 187–88; growth of, 124, 227; new technologies as basis for, 124, 126, 137, 155–56, 183; impact of, on custom clothiers, 156, 177, 183, 186–89, 190, 191, 204, 216; and department stores, 194, 197

Reed, Julietta, 42

reformers, 5, 26, 57, 73–74, 86, 87, 109–11

Remick, Mrs. H. B., 46

rents, 202

respectability, 162–63, 199

retailing, 4, 183. *See also* custom shops (dressmaking and millinery): changes in, under new pressures; department stores; dry goods houses

returned goods, 172–73, 174, 175

R. G. Dun & Co. *See* Dun & Co.

Roeth, Maria and Catherine, 34, 166

Rogers, Mrs. M. M., 48

Rogers, W. Hosken, 48

Rood, Will C., 148–49

Rowe, Ann, 166

saleswomen: in department stores, 108, 195, 199–200, 227, 230; in large custom shops, 203, 204

Sampson, Mehitabel, 166

Santin, Madame, 31

scientific management, 214–15

scientific methods, 128, 154. *See also* drafting systems; patterns

seamstresses, 59, 87, 88, 137, 223; distinguished from custom clothiers, 5, 12, 77, 87, 129

seasonal unemployment, 60, 80, 81–83, 85, 90, 196

section system, 223, 225

selling: new emphasis on, 126, 203–4. *See also* retailing

Sewall, Augusta, 115, 116

sewing machines, 137–38, 150

sexual divisions of labor, 1, 51, 56; continual redefinition of, 2–3, 127, 220; contradictory effects of, on custom clothiers, 2–3, 56, 61, 95, 127–28, 212, 220–21

shirtwaists (blouses), 216, 217, 223

shoe workers, 74, 88

Simon, Franklin, 227

single women, 1, 2, 40, 58, 71; as proprietors of custom shops, 11, 27, 40–45, 47, 54

skills: "male," 4, 221–22; of custom dressmakers, 12, 129–34; of custom milliners, 12, 178–79, 181–82, 183. *See also* deskilling

skirts, 131, 216

Smith, Mrs. C. P., 45

Smyth Company (John M. Smyth Company), 177

spinsters. *See* single women

Stahl, Mr. S., 202, 204

Standard Garment Cutting Company, 149

Steedman, Carolyn, 75

Steele, Valerie, 73, 109, 231

Steiner, Isabella Zetlin, 102

stereotypes of women workers, 57, 59, 60; in clothing trades, 6, 163. *See also* literary images; popular culture

Stevens, Jonathan, 37

Stone, Lucy, 38

Stowe, Harriet Beecher, 105, 115–16

straw sewers, 210

Strittmatter, Mary A., 47

S. T. Taylor Company, 141, 149

styles. *See* fashion

subcontracting, 87

Sumner, Helen, 1, 13–14

"sweating," 87

tailoresses, 87, 88, 129

tailors, 10, 71, 117, 130–31, 138, 226

Taylor, Samuel T., 138–39, 141–44, 148, 150

Taylor Company (S. T. Taylor Company), 141, 149

Taylorism, 215

technologies, new: and ready-made clothing, 124, 126, 137, 155–56, 183; gender implications of, 125–26, 128, 134, 136–37, 138–39, 148–49, 154–56. *See also* drafting systems; patterns

Tentler, Aaron, 140

textiles: factory production of, 99

WENDY GAMBER is an assistant professor of history at Indiana University, Bloomington. She has published articles in a number of journals, including the *Journal of Women's History* and *Technology and Culture,* and is working on a book about boardinghouses in antebellum cities from the perspectives of women's work, domestic ideology, and popular culture.

Books in the Series Women in American History

Women Doctors in Gilded-Age Washington: Race, Gender, and Professionalization   *Gloria Moldow*

Friends and Sisters: Letters between Lucy Stone and Antoinette Brown Blackwell, 1846–93   *Edited by Carol Lasser and Marlene Deahl Merrill*

Reform, Labor, and Feminism: Margaret Dreier Robins and the Women's Trade Union League   *Elizabeth Anne Payne*

Private Matters: American Attitudes toward Childbearing and Infant Nurture in the Urban North, 1800–1860   *Sylvia D. Hoffert*

Civil Wars: Women and the Crisis of Southern Nationalism   *George C. Rable*

I Came a Stranger: The Story of a Hull-House Girl   *Hilda Satt Polacheck; edited by Dena J. Polacheck Epstein*

Labor's Flaming Youth: Telephone Operators and Worker Militancy, 1878–1923   *Stephen H. Norwood*

Winter Friends: Women Growing Old in the New Republic, 1785–1835   *Terri L. Premo*

Better Than Second Best: Love and Work in the Life of Helen Magill   *Glenn C. Altschuler*

Dishing It Out: Waitresses and Their Unions in the Twentieth Century   *Dorothy Sue Cobble*

Natural Allies: Women's Associations in American History   *Anne Firor Scott*

Beyond the Typewriter: Gender, Class, and the Origins of Modern American Office Work, 1900–1930   *Sharon Hartman Strom*

The Challenge of Feminist Biography: Writing the Lives of Modern American Women   *Edited by Sara Alpern, Joyce Antler, Elisabeth Israels Perry, and Ingrid Winther Scobie*

Working Women of Collar City: Gender, Class, and Community in Troy, New York, 1864–86   *Carole Turbin*

Radicals of the Worst Sort: Laboring Women in Lawrence, Massachusetts, 1860–1912   *Ardis Cameron*

Visible Women: New Essays on American Activism   *Edited by Nancy A. Hewitt and Suzanne Lebsock*

Mother-Work: Women, Child Welfare, and the State, 1890–1930   *Molly Ladd-Taylor*

Babe: The Life and Legend of Babe Didrikson Zaharias   *Susan E. Cayleff*

Writing Out My Heart: Selections from the Journal of Frances E. Willard, 1855–96   *Carolyn De Swarte Gifford*

U.S. Women in Struggle: A *Feminist Studies* Anthology   *Edited by Claire Goldberg Moses and Heidi Hartmann*

In a Generous Spirit: A First-Person
Biography of Myra Page
Christina Looper Baker

Mining Cultures: Men, Women, and
Leisure in Butte, 1914–41
Mary Murphy

Gendered Strife and Confusion: The
Political Culture of Reconstruction
Laura F. Edwards

The Female Economy: The Millinery
and Dressmaking Trades, 1860–1930
Wendy Gamber

Books in the Series *The Working Class in American History*